'Many authors have attempted to overcome the well-known methodological shortcomings of traditional mainstream economics: methodological individualism, externalisation of society, abstract rational agents. Romagnoli creates a forceful attempt to overcome these by taking a unique approach, that of systems theory!'

Zoltan Pogatsa *University of West Hungary*

The Structure and Operation of Modern Economies

This book is about the economy rather than economics. It explores the structures, inner workings and problems of modern economies, showing how the organisations and networks that shape the structure of the economy are arranged to provide society with goods and services.

At the centre of the analysis there is the economic system, characterised by organisational components carrying out economic functions (production, consumption, distribution, and establishment and control of the economic activities as well as provision of public goods and services) and by a co-evolving dynamic with the state. The economic system is thus a 'machine' that modern states have organised through their laws and international agreements. The book incorporates a historical approach which reveals the varieties, structure and evolution of capitalism as the defining economic system of the modern age. Ultimately, the book demonstrates that the economic sphere and the political sphere are the two powers ruling people's lives: the economy is the result of their interactions.

This book will be of great interest to readers in political economy, economics, sociology and political science.

Alessandro Romagnoli is Alma Mater Professor of the University of Bologna (Italy), where he taught economics of the firm, economic development in the Middle East and North Africa and economic system analysis. His research interests encompass productive processes and firm structural evolution in agricultural and industrial sectors, the development process of the Middle East and North Africa and the structure of economic systems.

Routledge Frontiers of Political Economy

The Meaning of Shared Value
New Perspective on Creating Shared Value
Paolo Ricci, Patrick O'Sullivan and Floriana Fusco

Declining Profitability and the Evolution of the US Economy
A Classical Perspective
Ascension Mejorado and Manuel Ramon

Value, Money and Capital
The Critique of Political Economy and Contemporary Capitalism
Guido Starosta, Gastón Caligaris and Alejandro Fitzsimons

Transformations of Contemporary Capitalism
The Second Industrial Divide and Flexible Specialization
David J. Evans

The Financial Foundations of Production and Uncertainty
Andres Cantillo

Cooperative Firms and the Sustainable Development Goals
Pursuing Decent Work and Reducing Inequality
Jae Myong KOH

Economic Theory for the Real World
Victor A. Beker

The Structure and Operation of Modern Economies
Alessandro Romagnoli

For more information about this series, please visit: www.routledge.com/Routledge-Frontiers-of-Political-Economy/book-series/SE0345

The Structure and Operation of Modern Economies

Alessandro Romagnoli

Routledge
Taylor & Francis Group
LONDON AND NEW YORK

First published 2024
by Routledge
4 Park Square, Milton Park, Abingdon, Oxon OX14 4RN

and by Routledge
605 Third Avenue, New York, NY 10158

Routledge is an imprint of the Taylor & Francis Group, an informa business

British Library Cataloguing-in-Publication Data
A catalogue record for this book is available from the British Library

ISBN: 978-1-138-93152-7 (hbk)
ISBN: 978-1-032-61229-4 (pbk)
ISBN: 978-1-315-67973-0 (ebk)

DOI: 10.4324/9781315679730

Typeset in Times New Roman
by Apex CoVantage, LLC

To Vania, Manuel and Jessica

Contents

Figures

Tables

Acknowledgements

The idea to write a book on the economic system dates back to nearly 20 years ago, when I was tasked to teach a module of economic systems in a degree course on development and international cooperation at the University of Bologna. Later I integrated those contents in my introductory course of economics at the Faculty of Engineering. Thus, the people who must be thanked first for having tested some results of my investigation on the matter, now presented in the book, and having kept alive my interest for the subject are certainly the students that attended my courses thenceforth. I have discussed the contents and the approach adopted with colleagues but mainly with my son Manuel who, belonging to another generation of economic scholars, frankly challenged some unconventional arguments I propose. I appreciate the help that Giuliana Campanelli, since the year dot a peer reviewer of my works, offered me; her scrupulous reading of all the chapters and the suggestions always fitting have been useful for my work. Thanks also go to Maria Pia Capozzoli, who, acting as well-read person, helped me through her advice to avoid a for experts' jargon. My daughter Jessica contributed to my work by translating some lecture notes that have become a chapter, that were originally in Italian, and thus she deserves a thanks too. Of course, I am responsible for the ideas and the contents of the book. For a long time, I gave up the time to stay with my wife, family and friends; thus, I thank all for their patience. Finally, thanks go to the CEPII – Recherche et expertise sur l'économie mondiale/Research and expertise on the world economy arnaud.richet@cepii.fr for allowing the reproduction of 'Figure 21 – Cumulative share of bilateral trade flows, by trade route', published in Michel Fouquin and Jules Hugot, 'Two Centuries of Bilateral Trade and Gravity Data: 1827–2014, Working Paper,' no. 2016–14, May, page 24.

Introduction

This volume isn't a book of economics but a book about the economy. Inside it there aren't dissertations on economic subjects behaving according to some economic principles but detailed studies on functional organisations that shape the structure of the economy and put it into operation. No explanation of how the economic subjects cope with scarcity to satisfy their productive and consumption needs is presented throughout the chapters, but just the description of how economic organisations and networks are arranged to provide society with goods and services. Therefore, this is a book aiming to acquaint the reader with the nature and the structure of the economies that historically emerged in the time of capitalism.

Taking into consideration these aspects, the volume is a book about capitalism too. Such a topic is among the most discussed not only in economics but also in history, sociology and political sciences. A lot of debates on the different aspects of capitalism have enlivened the academy and politics and even now continue to do so. The definition, the origin and the nature of such a socioeconomic phenomenon are the main arguments disputed, but insufficient attention has been paid to a joined-up study of the structure and operation of its organisational components inside modern economies. The book tries to fix this shortage by pinpointing and putting together these organisational components in the highest and a more complete unit of analysis: the economic system.

The economic system is a 'stone guest' in the textbooks of economics. It stands behind the economic activities carried out by the subjects and by the economic organisations (consumers, firms, markets and states), but only as an abstract entity resulting from the behavioural principles and the efficiency criteria they apply. In fact, in books on microeconomics it is the reference point justifying the application of behavioural principles and efficiency criteria, while in macroeconomics it is a set of equilibrium values resulting from the right choices made by the economic subjects. The concentration of the economic analysis only on the operational rules implemented by the economic subjects in doing the economic activities not only makes the economic system disappear but also provides a partial image of the object of the economic study; in fact, the material processes (production, consumption, exchange) on which the behavioural rules are applied don't have room in the analysis. Such a lack even avoids the comprehension both of the features distinguishing the capitalist economies from the preceding economic systems and of the conditions

DOI: 10.4324/9781315679730-1

that the traditional economies presented when capitalism has been introduced. To bridge all these gaps this book, bringing back to light the concept of the economic system, proposes it as an introductory knowledge to the study of economics.

The reasons why, in the author's opinion, such a pre-theoretical learning is necessary are first of educational nature. The textbooks on economics, especially introductory courses, set up the economic activities in a framework (like that summarised previously) that, tracing them back to an exchange mechanism favouring the efficient assignment of resources, neglects the processes of goods and service creation and use. In this way the actual components of the production and the consumption in modern economies are vanishing, and the constitutive elements of such organised activities like technology, human skills, financial resources and purchasing power are disregarded at once. In so doing students cannot gain knowledge on the structure of current economies; neither can they be aware that their emergence and evolution are time processes. They cannot realise that some specific traits of capitalism have been modulated in different ways during the introduction of the new socioeconomic system in national backgrounds and thus that there are different models of capitalism. These deficiencies not only prevent the students from deeply understanding the subject matter of economics but also risk making transient the contents issued in minor courses and unproductive the training of the majors in economics.

A pre-analytic knowledge of the structure and workings of modern economies doesn't emerge only as a need to improve the students' learning of economics but also to promote the economic culture. The abstraction of the economic tale and the divide between the economic explanation offered by disciplinary analysis and economic facts end up characterising economics in students' and people's eyes as an irrelevant and boring discipline or as something made by specialists for specialists. This prevents people from having a believable image of the economic events and the economists from creating a society-friendly economic culture.

The pivotal role given in the book to the study of the neglected aspects of the modern economies is among the reasons for its originality, but another one can be found in the methodology used to deal with the arguments. As a first instrument of the explanatory procedure, a historical overview is proposed to present both the whole dissertation and the single topics of the chapters. Such introductions stand for a further in-depth analysis of the capitalist originality and for the presentation of stylised facts emerging from the capitalist evolution. It is just this inquiry that, by revealing the importance of the complexity and the connections for the comprehension of the structure and the evolution of capitalism and of its components, puts forward the second instrument of our explanatory procedure: systems analysis.

Systems analysis is an appropriate investigative instrument for our enquiry because it puts in evidence that the economic system isn't either the sum of all the economic activities carried out by the single economic subjects or a holistic entity, but an evolving 'hyper-structure' (that is a system of sub-systems vertically structured) constituted by networks of systemic subjects. If all the components and organisations of the economy are systems, systems analysis allows for their study consistently with that of the whole economy. Moreover, as such an analytical instrument entails an evolutionary perspective, it enables the examination of economic facts as processes. The possibility of representing the economy and its components by the same methodological framework isn't a sort of micro-foundation of the economic system. Contrary to what happens in the neoclassical synthesis (where macroeconomic entities represent the sum of micro ones), in a systemic perspective the economic system is a system of a higher level whose outcome is more than the sum of its components and whose behaviour is different. Thus, systemic analysis provides only a descriptive characterisation of economic facts that is useful to consider the nature of the process they are part of.

The third explanatory instrument is represented by the institutions. Since the institutions are co-ordinated sets of operative rules, economic analysis can put in evidence many kinds among them. The behavioural principles pushing the subject to carry out economic activities are the only ones considered by economics. The analysis of the economic system that is the object of this book is instead more interested, for example, in the laws structuring economic organisations, in the procedures elaborated to make machines, firms and markets work, and in the guidelines that implement the international agreements signed by states on trade or financial circulation. Such an instrument is consistent with the previous one because representing a finalistic organisation can be considered a system.

In line with this premise, the volume first portrays modern economies and all the subject matter related to them by gathering the pertinent stylised facts put forward by the capitalist evolution over the last two and a half centuries. Then it uses systems analysis to go beyond the basic organisational forms of a modern economy (the economic system, the firm, the household, the market and the state) to assess them both as systemic objects and as components of higher systems. In so doing, any modern economy appears as a complex, closely knit hyper-structure entity whose image is, in a nutshell, exactly the economic system. Moreover, its structure emerges as based on networks of components and connections, and its dynamics on a process of co-evolution whose participants also belong to other social realms (private life, political field, etc.).

In this perspective any capitalist economic system (likewise any other form of social organisation) subsumes elements of reality by revealing the background in which it operates: therefore, it can be regarded as a specific modulation of capitalism. In fact, each economy is characterised on one side by the organisational structures that came to light in a capitalist environment and by the economic principles whose implementation is encouraged in the new socioeconomic context; on the other side it is distinguished by endless transformations in time and space in response to social needs. In addition, because of this responsiveness, the modern economy can be conceived also as an organised system providing welfare that is a purposeful set of economic organisations processing material and immaterial resources according to economic behavioural principles (self-interest, aptitude for exchange, cooperation, rent seeking) and to social relations (cultural, technical, legal and organisational rules).

The first part of the book focuses on the advent and evolution of capitalism, on the methodological approach needed to inspect the capitalist economies in accordance with the stylised facts emerging in an historical frame of reference, and on a congruent representation of their configuration and outcome. In Chapter One the analysis of the emergence of the new socioeconomic arrangement aims to deepen the transition from traditional societies to capitalism through the productive, social, and technological transformations that characterised this move, and to highlight the structural novelties of such an organisational pattern. Thus, the appearance of economic and social changes, of technological advances and of new institutions in the pre-capitalist environment will be explored to present the shattering consequences that they had on ancient equilibria in all facets of human life. The chapter examines some historical changes triggering the move from traditional society towards capitalism, starting from agricultural restructuring, demographic transition and social transformations, passing through the technological process (inventions and new techniques alongside new forms of division of labour) which made possible new productive subjects and new commodity sectors (such as the steel industry, electricity, transportation and communication). It also puts in evidence the importance of institutions – that is, the new rules for organising economic and social life. Moreover, this historical review highlights the features of the new economic arrangement, opening for discussion the originality of capitalism with respect to all other socioeconomic systems organised by mankind before.

The transition towards capitalism first began in Great Britain and then moved to Western Europe and to the United States, spreading gradually in some other countries all over the world, staggered over time. This expansion has been characterised by a pace neither continuous nor regular due to the succession of 'industrial revolutions'. It was, in fact, an evolutionary process starting from 1820 and moving forward through booms and crises whose main results were the structural transformation of both mankind's social and material conditions and of the economic organisation. The capitalist advent and strengthening were supported and shaped by factors such as the dynamics and the structure of the population (influencing the human capital quantity and quality), the presence of capitals (physical, human, and financial) and by the building of institutions enabling the capitalist dynamics (techno-organisational procedures, legal norms and economic behavioural principles). Chapter Two, aiming at highlighting the dynamic features of capitalist economies, thus reviews these 'long-run dynamic forces' enabling the capitalist advent and strengthening.

Chapter Three presents the methodological approach enabling the portrayal of modern economic systems starting from the capitalist stylised facts and the trends highlighted in the first two chapters. Since the interdependence and fast-growing links among economic subjects, the creation of new organisations and goods, and the competition and adaptation in economic activities are the features of capitalist economy, a systems analysis is required to picture and study its configuration and operation. Thus, the basic concepts of this analytical instrument will be presented by focusing particularly on the consequences that result from its adoption for picturing both the economic subjects and the system dynamics. Regarding the first aspect, the methodology portrays the economic subject as a social subject (*Homo hetero-economicus*) characterised by connections, competition and adaptation instead of as an isolated subject following natural preferences and economic behavioural principles (*Homo economicus*). With respect to the capitalist dynamics, the workings of the system result as a process of co-evolution (to which political and private social domains also contribute) creating a temporary consistency instead of as a mechanism producing a mathematical equilibrium. The producers of this circumstance are institutions that enable the evolution of the system through their changes; to understand this effect a dynamic representation of institutions is necessary, and a systemic analysis can provide it, as will be shown in the chapter. Thus, in light of systems analysis the economies are complex, adaptive systems evolving thanks to the contribution of all social domains, whose structure, speed of growth and outcomes can be organised to provide welfare for their citizens.

Chapter Four discusses the systemic representation and the appraisal of modern economies starting from the 'circular flow of income'. Consistent with the methodological framework of the book, this concise picture of the structure and mechanics of a national capitalist economy highlights the functional distinction of organisations operating in an economic system in the four categories of the arrangement and support of its workings, the production of goods and services, their uses, their organisation and distribution and their exchange; the first three organisations are components of the economic system (production, consumption and state), and the fourth represents the repeated connections among the components (markets) enabling the operation of the economy (real and monetary flows). After the definition of the 'economic units' and of the legal categories of 'economic activities', an evaluation of the performance of the economic system is discussed through the concepts of 'aggregate demand' and 'sectors account'.

The second part of the book analyses the economic system's structure and workings through an in-depth inspection of both the functions that characterise it and the organisations that carry these functions out. In view of the central role that the state has in the capitalist economy, the analysis of its function opens the part. In Chapter Five the ways by which the state behaves, both as the counterpart of the economy and the principal supporter of its evolutionary path, are historically reviewed as moments of a co-evolving process. These multifaceted historical dialectics show the state as an economic institutions builder, a supporter and rescuer of the economy, a designer of the social protection and a promoter of the civil and economic upgrading. Such functions are carried out by sharing with the private sector production and consumption activities and by managing its own economic prerogatives through public works and taxation. The exclusive economic role of the state displays in the public budget a tool enabling it to fulfil economic and extra-economic purposes within the law and in accordance with the political commitments assumed by governments.

In Chapter Six the production will be inspected with respect to the technical nature of the transformation and to the industrial systems' configuration (business organisation and market structure). The continuous advance of technological development, the increasing number of goods and services and the rising complexity of productive methods in the capitalist era have revealed the nature of production: an increasingly complex and protracted process, partitioned by intermediate markets, managed by the principle of agents' idleness removal and by the 'just in time', 'total quality control', and 'total productive maintenance' operating methods. Setting system methodology at work to analyse this phenomenon, three dimensions will be explored shedding lights on three units of economic analysis: the production operating unit, the economic unit and the operating environment of the firm. The evolution of the factory (that is, the production operating unit) came along with the technological progress of machineries requiring a consistent division of labour, the creation of new capabilities through the training and development of human capital and the creation of routines. The firm, being the economic unit of production, discloses an evolutionary path affected not only by the entrepreneurial role but also by its organisation, its governance, and its strategies. The interplay of the firms gives rise to aggregations that represent structural sub-units of the production system or systems of higher level in respect to the firm, that is the operating environment of the firm.

Chapter Seven analyses the consumption as an essential complement to the production in the economic system, which enables the fulfilment of the capitalist process. Historically developed as the process of needs satisfaction in a framework drawn by the production conditions, the long-distance trade to stock up unproduced goods and the control of authorities, the consumption in the capitalist society results from the coevolution of production with social phenomena like urbanisation and lifestyles. The role of the production in favouring access to markets has been relevant not only in informing potential consumers by advertising but also by enhancing consumption through the increase of consumer purchasing power, a chance offered by the financial support of the consumer credit industry.

The market is the co-ordinating mechanism allowing capitalism to manage its complexity. It originates from the increasing impossibility of self-sufficiency for the individual living in a capitalist reality, who is forced to exchange to survive. Thus, the market, as a social tool allowing the capitalist economy to function, is a complex institutional structure. Starting from this point, Chapter Eight reviews the historical process of the creation of markets for exchanging goods, financial services and labour to show both the different meanings of the term exchange and organised exchange mechanism (market) and the role of the state in building the institutions that enforce it. The taxonomy of the market as organisations promoting safe economic exchanges leads to the consideration of the multiplicity of market types and of the conditions characterising transactions (nature of the process, agents' behaviour, etc.). The analysis of the structure and operation of the market which follows aims to deepen the distribution channel, the different market processes and pricing in retailing and wholesale, the financial markets, and the labour institutions. In this respect, specific markets (such as the stock exchange, primary resource markets and price discrimination) are analysed.

After the presentation of the structure of modern economic systems and the study of their organisations and workings, the book moves in Part Three to an analysis of the coordination of the economic relations among states that takes place in the world economy. Such a step is necessary to understand what changes have been produced inside the networks of national economies by the evolution of national capitalisms and their spread beyond the state borders. Chapter Nine starts with the definition of the world economy like the structure of the configurations of the economic relations established by the states to manage international economic relations – that is, the exchanges of goods, labour and financial services. The analysis of the evolution of capitalist countries and of their contribution to the world economy and to international trade will provide a picture of the evolution of the international exchanges of goods and services and of the economic power relationships among capitalist economies. Such configurations, which have been mirrored in the international agreements on trade and the international systems of payments, will be reviewed up to the end of the Second World War to show the diligence spent by the economic powers to co-ordinate internationally their economic developments.

Chapter Ten continues the analysis of the evolution of the 'world economy' to put in evidence its structural features in the period after the Second World War. First examined will be the configuration of the world economy in the time of well-established capitalism (the so-called 'Golden Age') from the point of view of the international economic order and of the developing economies. Then the new institutional and technological driving forces that have pushed the capitalist advances in the last four decades (the third industrial revolution, the new economics of the powers, and the globalisation) will be presented as foundations of the new international economic order that configures the world economy as a 'self-ruled mechanism'.

The writing of the book has been driven fully from my research interests and my long experience in teaching economics, mainly in curricula whose majors are devoted to technical, applied and social expertise (agriculture, industrial engineering and political sciences). In attuning my teaching methods and the disciplinary contents to the major aims and to the background of the classes, I experienced the need for introductory programs and textbooks concerning the structure of the economy it's working on. I also noticed how much the contents of the handbooks of economics are poor in 'economic culture' that is capable of providing the instruments to understand the problems of everyday life and to take advantage of the learnt economic contents in the professional fields. To offer an instrument bridging this gap the arguments of the book trace an introductory textbook of economics; however, the choice of the layout of the contents, of the development of the dissertation and of the arguments to be treated has been made consistently with the main object of the analysis (the capitalist economic system) and the methodology adopted. So, as to the first item, the treatise of the structure and workings of modern economies has been preceded by a historical and methodological background to show the originalities of the capitalist economic system and the most suitable methodology to study it. As to the second item, the economic role of the state deserved to be treated after the chapter showing the representation of an economic system and before the study of the other economic aggregates shaped by its legislative and executive functions. As to the third item, the analysis of modern economic systems cannot overlook their expansion outside national borders to support their growth; for this reason, the third part of the book deepens the configurations of trade relations and of the international systems of payments to understand the international trade of goods and services and to highlight the complexity and the difficulties of the current 'world economy'.

The choices made in writing the book about the arguments that must be treated have been a hard challenge overall because the matters must be non-disciplinary – that is, they couldn't represent an object of economic theorising, as it is the case of the 'long waves' in the capitalist evolution, the 'market demand', the 'varieties of capitalism' and so on. To maintain the general framework and aims of the book some problems of the actual economic systems have been omitted too. Certainly the problem of economic development, the challenges that the lack of natural resources and climate change address regarding the models of economy spreading in the world and the future of 21st century capitalism are all arguments that would have deserved supplementary chapters, but they couldn't find room in this introductory book on economics because their analysis would shift the focus of the work towards the actual problems of capitalism.

As the book is addressed both to students and to people keen on understanding the economic environment of their everyday life, it presents instruments to facilitate reading. At the end of each chapter there are references that can help one find important sources elaborating the discussed arguments and a glossary to acquaint oneself with the terms and concepts presented in the text. Nevertheless, some parts of the exposition could appear too specialised or technical, but their insertion has been necessary to validate some stylised facts, to present some basic economic concept or to rebut some misconceptions.

Part I

Emergence, evolution and representation of modern economies

1 The historical pathways to the emergence of modern economies

There are plenty of historic documentaries and literary works providing evidence on the everyday life, working conditions, and economic wellbeing of human beings in pre-industrial societies (see Mosley and Wallerstein 1978). The comparison of the socioeconomic pre-industrial situation with the current one underlines the gap between the recent past (just two and a half centuries in the case of the first countries approaching industrialisation and much less for the latecomers) and the present. The divergences between the two scenarios are the result of the transformations experienced by traditional societies in all the fields of social life. The list includes social engineering (the rise of new social classes and the fall of old ones) and new human conditions (the breaking of natural bonds and people taking possession of their own lives); new techniques, products, and forms of production organisation (the firm), the modern labour market conditions, and a total separation between production and consumption; the spatial aggregation of social life and economic activities (towns, production clusters, etc.); and the spatial diffusion of their coordination thanks to communication systems. Moreover, the complexity, networking and speed of change characterising modern economies are stylised environmental conditions that were unknown to pre-industrial societies.

Retracing the transitional path bringing human beings to such a new lifestyle condition is important not only in order to gain awareness of the overall and irreversible process carried out but also to highlight both the main events of this change and the distinctive features of the new socioeconomic structure compared to the previous one. For such a fact-finding survey, a multi-step analysis is required. Of course, the first step of this path is to review the features of the pre-industrial economy – i.e. of the agricultural activities carried out in an 'ecosystem' framework by self-sufficient communities following natural rhythms. Then it is necessary to focus on the productive and socioeconomic transformations in the countryside because they broke, step-by-step, the stabilising mechanisms of the old economic arrangement by implementing agricultural transformation, population growth and the emergence of new social classes. After that, we must turn our attention to the creation of mechanical energy through fossil fuels, the exploitation of technological progress, and the spread of transport and communication systems as events that promoted the rise and strengthening of industry. Also, the institutional change and the transformations in social mores and lifestyles are

DOI: 10.4324/9781315679730-3

interesting matters for understanding how much modern socioeconomic life differs from the previous one.

The pre-industrial society: A setup at one with nature

Before the advent of industrialisation, the economy created by human beings to provide for their everyday life needs was characterised by production and consumption activities carried out for the most part inside the agricultural sector. Production, which was mostly aimed at providing food for the peasant family (self-consumption) and paying in kind the lord and master, was effectively and efficiently organised over time through 'agricultural production systems' that took account of seasons and soil conditions. This dependence on nature turned the agricultural systems into 'ecosystems . . . which were modified and administrated by people to produce the goods that were useful to them' (Grigg 1982: 79). The aforementioned socioeconomic conditions, common worldwide to all human beings at that time, were so different from the current ones (in both developed and emerging countries) that only a mention of the concept of ecosystem can aid in understanding them.

The 'human ecosystem' as a foundation for pre-industrial economies

An 'ecosystem' is a set of living organisms and material interacting in a specific environment or area so that they constitute a balanced, self-sufficient system. In every 'ecosystem', some chemical transformations, fuelled through energy flows, originate 'food chains.' In these food chains, vegetable organisms (called 'elementary producers') obtain their own nourishment through the process of photosynthesis, which is promoted by sunlight and at the same time provide food for herbivores ('elementary consumers'). The latter, in turn, feed 'carnivores' ('secondary consumers'). Finally, the chain is closed by 'decomposers', organisms that reduce vegetation, dead animals and wastes into simple compounds ('humus'), which are then put back into the ecosystem to replenish 'natural capitals' on a regular basis, according to appropriate timeframes (see all the dashed, continuous and dotted straight lines in Figure 1.1). In the 'human ecosystem' human beings stand at the top of the chain, for they are organisms which reproduce and produce at the same time: in addition to nourishing themselves like all the other organisms on Earth by eating lower-level organisms, human beings also create material goods (see curved lines in Figure 1.1).

The living process taking place within the aggregate of ecosystems on Earth (i.e. within the 'biosphere') is a closed cycle, except for the solar energy flow. In the biosphere every single process is revocable, meaning that the organisms of each species can reproduce only because they are kept alive by the beings preceding them in the chain and because they in turn feed those that follow. The waste produced in all living processes directly nourishes the 'decomposers'; in the presence of normal conditions and within a period acceptable for nature itself, these decomposers reconstitute the natural order. Living processes are irreversible, and all living beings withdraw orderly resources (inferior organisms) and release disorderly

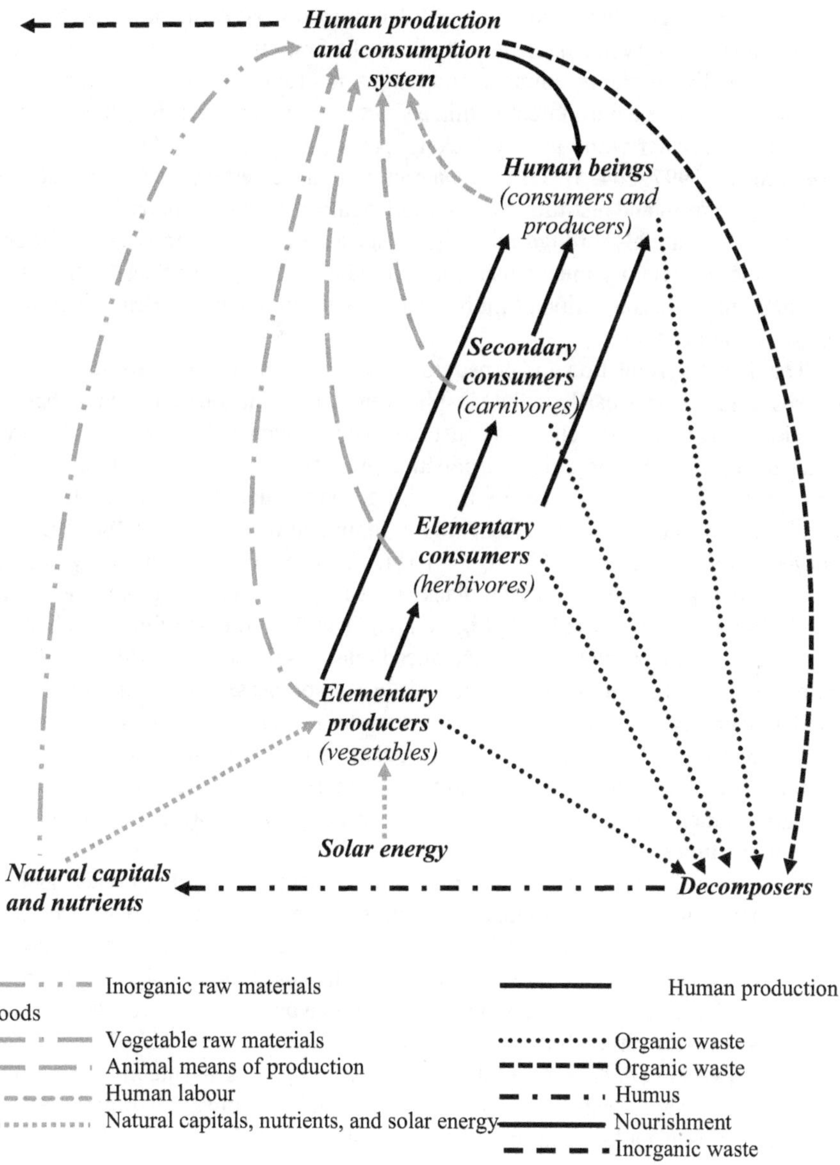

Figure 1.1 Representation of the biosphere with human productive system

Source: Author's elaboration

resources (refuses); therefore, each ecosystem maintains its own living order at the expense of the natural environment. This is because the new equilibrium created by decomposers is never the same as the one that existed at the beginning: it differs by a certain 'disorder', an entity whose amount is measured by an indicator named 'entropy'.

The dynamics of these ecosystems is determined by specific bio-geo-chemical cycles and regulatory mechanisms. Thanks to the first, 'the chemical elements constituting the living plants, animals, and natural matter of ecosystems return to the physical inanimate environment within a shorter or longer time; from this environment, they are later withdrawn to become part of a living ecosystem once again.' (De Agostini 1997: 264–5). These dynamics maintain a certain proportion between withdrawals from and restitutions to the soil, a ratio that makes it possible to reconstruct natural capitals through the waste disposed of by decomposers and after a given time. Regulatory mechanisms, on the other hand, ensure that the life cycle works through the adaptation of Individuals to the natural environment and through the selection of species.

The 'human production and consumption system' that no other species on Earth possesses takes place partly in the biosphere and partly outside of it. Human beings, by taking part in the food chain as consumers and, as such, using plants, herbivores, and carnivores in the 'organic' reproduction process, carry out artificial production processes also. In these processes they use growing quantities of natural capitals as well as vegetable raw materials, animal input and human labour. (See the grey curved arrow on the left in Figure 1.1.) Thus, their waste can be not only organic but also inorganic. (See the dotted black curved arrows on the right and the dotted black straight arrow on the left in Figure 1.1.) Over the increase of industrialisation this fact poses the problem of an unbalanced relationship between withdrawals and restitutions because the wastes of such production processes may present a limited biodegradability in the short run. Such a disorder increases the degree of 'entropy' in the ecosystem. Thus the 'ecological problem' concerning the relations between human production, other species, and nature itself is rooted in existence when the human production and consumption system progressively leaves the human ecosystem dynamics.

In the presence of economies that are predominantly agricultural ones, such as traditional systems, this ecological problem is raised only marginally or occasionally. In fact, plant cultivation and animal breeding are activities mainly integrated into the corresponding ecosystems. In addition, they use tools which originate from the processing of plant and animal raw materials (wood, textile fibres, leather, fur, etc.), just like foodstuff. Since these economies entail a reasonably low level of use of the raw materials obtained through extraction processes (metals, rocks, etc.) by craftsmen, their wastes are mainly organic: the withdrawal/restitution mechanism thus presents a low entropy[1] (Georgescu-Roegen 1971). The implementation of industrial activities requiring increasing quantities of natural capitals created the ecological problem; thus, this is a typical problem connected with industrial societies.

Structure and operation of pre-industrial economies

In the most part of world pre-industrial societies agriculture was the core of the economic system, providing nearly 80 per cent of the goods produced. Agriculture was aimed at the survival of the communities at large, thus the output obtained by each farm was partly transferred to non-producer classes trough the tributes paid, generally in kind, by peasants. The leftovers constituted both the foodstuff for the peasant family and the input for the next production cycle: thus, this production system was devoted to 'self-consumption'. Moreover, each farm was organised in accordance with the availability of work within the family itself (Chayanov 1966: 51 and 71). Therefore, arable lands and soil/weather conditions being equal, the amount of goods produced by an economic system so strongly centred on agricultural enterprises was affected by the structure of the peasant family (the number, ages and 'productivity' of its members). As for the social distribution of lands, there were different organisational patterns, but the most prevalent ones were the 'estate' (a single and very extensive property owned by upper classes) or 'small-scale-farming' (a small size communal or private property made up of separated fields). The working conditions of countryfolk were heavy and unstable:

> In England 'most of these agricultural workers were tenants who paid rent in cash or produce, or day laborers who were hired by landlords and tenant farmers. Day laborers might find work by going door to door or by presenting themselves at 'mops', or regional hiring fairs. Domestic servants, especially in smaller households helped out with harvesting and dairying, and urban workers might migrate to the countryside during the harvest to make extra income. In some cases, craftsmen combine a trade, like weaving, with farming. Farm life was especially arduous before many tasks were mechanized. . . . Harvest time was jubilant, with cheers and the rumbling of laden wagons saluting the stubbled fields, and harvest was followed by feasting, revelry, and courtship. But if the harvest was poor, or if the rain came too soon and ruined the standing grain, there might be little joy. In any case, harvest was a prelude of more hard work. The poorest members of the community came through the fields to 'glean', or search for stray grain dropped from the stalks during the harvest.
>
> (Olsen 1999: 122–3).

From the standpoint of the territorial arrangement, in Europe activities were usually organised throughout the territory according to a specific order: dwellings were located at the centre of the settlement; the area surrounding them was dedicated to the vegetable gardens owned by families; outside this area there were fields, which were divided by types of crops; finally, outwards there were woods. Since countryside people ate mostly a vegetarian diet, the 'ecological support' (i.e. the space necessary to provide food) was generally limited to the territories outside the village. Because of this and because of self-consumption, the quantity of goods sold at the nearest town markets was low, and the local economic units were seldom in contact with one another (except for seasonal fairs). However, the commercial exchanges between villages and urban centres around which they gravitated increased as soon as the introduction of new techniques in agricultural production made it possible for people to enhance the quantity of goods produced per unit of land or work (i.e. when the 'productivity of the resources' used in farming production increased).

The pre-capitalistic economic system described previously functioned in conditions almost perfect equilibrium due to three mechanisms acting together. These mechanisms were the following:

i. a biological production system
ii. a process of self-regulated demographic development
iii. a political system centred around communities divided into social classes with limited mobility

Traditional agriculture was an ecologically balanced system because it worked according to a real biological production scheme: on the one hand the waste from production and consumption activities decayed and became fertilizers (brushwood, organic waste, macerating products), while on the other hand renewable forms of energy were used. In this respect the system took advantage of the labour of animals (used for the traction and transport of materials and to perform agricultural work such as tillage), but it also gained power from human labour (when performing operations such as sowing, pruning and harvesting). Even workshop activities such as the transformation of agricultural products (for example flour milling) and manufacture of products (for example, spinning and weaving plant fibres such as flax, hemp and cotton as well as animal fibres such as silk and wool) used renewable energies as they made use of natural power sources such as water and wind. But there were indeed growing manufacturing activities (such as brick, glassware and steel productions) that impoverished natural capitals as they required thermal energy; they increasingly pushed for deforestation and threw the ecosystem off balance by withdrawing more than they returned.

As for the demographic balance, the complex mechanism for population growth of the pre-capitalist societies was based on the availability of foodstuff. Considering both the quantity of goods needed for the survival of one person and the tax regime (the portion of harvest owed to nobles and clergy) organised according to the bargaining power of classes, every level of output in the primary sector made it possible to feed a certain amount of the rural population,[2] together with the operators of non-agricultural productions and people belonging to non-working classes. Every time the productivity of the land increased, a larger amount of agricultural goods was generated, and the population grew, while an insufficient harvest led to a population decline. The mechanism restoring the balance between resources and population worked as follows. Whenever agricultural products exceeded the needs, the number of marriages increased and the infant mortality decreased, causing population growth. Conversely, when the harvest was scarce, famine, poor nutrition, impoverishment of the lowest classes and poor hygiene conditions caused epidemic outbreaks (generally plagues), thus causing the death rate to rise. Another push toward an increased mortality rate come from the sociopolitical consequences of bad economic conditions: in fact, the dissatisfaction of the populace frequently gave rise to uprisings, the suppression of which (or sometimes wars waged in pursuit of a solution to a long period of deprivations) increased the death rate. This way the system returned[3] to the proper balance between population and foodstuff.[4]

With respect to the role played by the political system in the equilibrium of traditional societies, it must be noted that the monopoly of the power belonged to the nobility, which exercised it by means of administration and the army. This guaranteed that the rulers would receive a compulsory funding ('tribute') from the farmers, artisans and merchants in exchange for maintaining internal security and protection from possible outside invasions. Thus, sociopolitical rules formed the basis for the 'income distribution' among the classes. Moreover, the political and institutional structure of society, together with the production traits of agriculture, were the key elements that determined the reproduction of the traditional economy. However, there were also some constraints limiting the achievement of a greater balance between the population size and its welfare.

The change of the reproduction mechanism in the traditional economy was very slow, so much so that new production procedures or goods needed a long time to be accepted (consider that nearly 200 years were necessary to cultivate unknown products coming from the Americas, such as tomatoes or potatoes). This was because the human mind shaped itself on social habits and customs which didn't consider 'equality', or 'private interest' and 'profit' positive values (Hirschman 1977).

The departure from the pre-industrial economy

Within the framework described previously, the pre-industrial economy's expansion was bound to develop agriculture, when the population was growing. However, the increase of sectoral production, being that the technology was unchanged, was limited by the number of cultivable lands and the energy available for farming and stock-breeding activities. Deforestation was the method applied so long as it provided a solution to the first problem and until the traditional farming system proved to be ineffective in achieving its aim despite the increased land use. Just then a process of technological change began to re-establish the balance between the agricultural output and the population size. Since technological changes can provide solutions for both technological and socioeconomic problems, their appearance led to a restructuring of 'agricultural techniques' and social rules governing agricultural activities. These changes, however, went beyond the countryside; in fact, they made possible the birth of town industries, a restructuring of the entire society and a rearrangement of human life.

Challenging famine through production transformations in agriculture

From a historical perspective, humans attempted to improve agricultural output to meet the feeding requirements of a growing population many times before the 18th century. With respect to this aim, for example, the 'medieval agricultural revolution' that had spread across the plains of Central-Europe between the 9th and 13th centuries had already made great strides forward. In fact, to counter the shortage of lands, it organised a production process based on the 'three-year crop rotation' system and introduced ploughs with iron ploughshares, while to deal with the scarcity of peasants' muscle power it used horses for farming operations. As for the alternation of crops, it had been long known that cultivations reduced soil fertility year after year and that, to restore it, half of the plots of tillable land had to either be left uncultivated for a year or be used for pasture ('fallow'). But in medieval times it was discovered that, if the plots of land were left uncultivated for one year and then, in the following two, they were consecutively cultivated with cereals first and legumes next,[5] the fertility of the soil would not decrease. The introduction of such a 'three fields' organisation in the farm production meant that every year two-thirds of the lands could be cultivated (with cereals and legumes) instead of just one-half, as had previously been the case. Moreover, the use of the iron plough made it possible to dig and overturn deeper layers of soil, bringing to the surface the clumps that were the richest in nutrients. While the first organisational innovation increased the size of the land area that was cultivated every year, the second improved the productivity of each plot. Meanwhile, the replacement of oxen with horses enabled farmers to speed up their heavy work (especially ploughing), meaning that each peasant could cultivate a larger area. These changes in the agriculture processes resulted in a greater availability of foodstuff and especially of cereals and vegetables, whose yield in terms of flour production benefited from the introduction and upgrading of wind and water mills that increased foodstuff amounts and quality.

The production transformations that brought about the aforementioned improvements in agricultural output and food availability consisted mainly of the introduction of both new agricultural 'production techniques' and the mill grinder. By and large the 'production technique' is the set of organisational and operational arrangements that must be implemented to produce a good or service unit. In such a process, not only the specific number of materials is involved but also the land (if necessary), tools and workers who offer their services in accordance with a technically efficient procedure and a mutual codependent relationship determined by the functional role they play within the transformation process.[6] Thus, thanks to the changes in the features, quality and abilities of the capitals (land, tools, peasants and animals) used in the production process, the medieval agricultural revolution was able to deal with the challenge of a growing population.

The introduction of these new techniques enabled the feeding of a larger number of people, but with the passing of time the imbalance between foodstuff and population once again became the main economic problem. A new increase in agricultural produce through the introduction of other innovations was, however, hindered by the sociopolitical rules governing the organisation of agricultural production. Up to that time the access to cultivable lands had been guaranteed to all villagers; this had led to the subdivision of such lands into numerous strips, which were assigned by rotation to the community's families according to a principle of long-term compensation for the quality of the land. This allocation system was inefficient due to both the territorial scattering of each family's fields, which reduced the labour productivity, and the short stay on the bestowed lands, which discouraged investments because the return on which couldn't be guaranteed for the investor. After all, while farmers frequently didn't have enough money to pursue such an activity, the landowners who were able to invest were not interested in land improvements or in the introduction of better techniques and cultivations.

The way out from this predicament came from the availability of financial capitals, generated by international trade activities between the 16th and 18th centuries and by an important sociopolitical change: the privatisation of the communal lands. The latter process, labelled 'enclosures', began in Great Britain in the late 16th century. It resulted in the abolition of the right to free pasture and estovers on common lands, the assignment of these assets to country squires and the promotion of an entrepreneurial kind of farming designed for the market, not for self-consumption. The sectoral consequence of the accumulation of financial capitals coupled with enclosures gave rise to the 'British agricultural revolution' characterised, alongside the restructuring of the land tenure and agricultural estates, by the adoption of new farming techniques. The new methods of production were based on the 'Norfolk rotation' system, an arrangement of crops introducing fodder cultivations (clover, alfalfa, etc.) on the plots that the traditional three-year rotation scheme required to be left uncultivated ('fallow'). This innovation extended the production to all the cultivable lands on standby, made it possible to feed animals at pasture with the new crops and led to an increase in livestock, animal power available for farmers and natural fertilizers. Thus, the output of each plot increased thanks to the adoption of this intensive cropping system.[7] Moreover, the introduction of the high-powered seeding machine – which dropped seeds into the furrows and covered them – reduced the quantity of seeds necessary per plot because it prevented their scattering and loss due to birds.

Little by little, the increasing production and the gradual 'market-oriented agriculture' shifted the nature of farming activities from a peasant family activity for the socioeconomic survival of human beings towards a farm – i.e. towards a new organised entity of the economic system endowed with a specific structure, behaviour and goals. Farming became more and more sensitive to the demands of the market, leading farms to increase the production of textile fibres required by the industries that were emerging in towns. In addition, they reduced production costs by reorganising the production process and increased the productivity of resources through investments aimed at improving lands, introducing new machines and providing more energy. These trends gained a foothold in the late 19th century, when they were further boosted by the 'green revolution', which updated the agricultural production techniques to consider the new scientific discoveries in the agronomic, genetic and engineering fields. The discovery made by von Liebig,[8] on the chemical nature of the production processes carried out in agriculture, made it possible to develop some technically efficient production programs for every type of cultivation and led to the use of effective chemical products such as fertilizers, herbicides and pesticides. Genetics contributed to selecting the varieties of cultivations that were particularly fit for the climatic conditions of each region, while the use of machines reduced the time required for agricultural operations, thus increasing farmers' productivity. All these innovations raised the output of cultivations to an average of two to three times the previous amount and resulted in land and/or labour savings for each product unit; in fact, agronomic and genetic technical changes were 'land-saving' innovations, while the mechanical ones were 'labour-saving' ones.

The historical evidence of Britain and the experience of the 'first-comers' show the importance of agricultural restructuring for the transition of traditional societies towards industrialisation. In fact, the sociotechnological change in this sector of economic activities made it possible to solve the following problems:

i. Feed a growing population, especially in industrialising towns
ii. Encourage the emergence of profit seeking entrepreneurs, and that resulted in an accumulation of capital in that sector
iii. Create wage labour in cities also by displacing surplus farm workers from the countryside. Both 'freed' resources (capitals and workforce) are crucial for the development of the industrial sector, which was mainly present in cities.[9]
iv. Generate a demand for agricultural raw materials by industrial firms: this was the way the cultivation of plants such as flax, cotton, hemp, etc. increased, as did the percentage of means of production on the sectoral output.

Thus, agricultural revolutions not only made it possible to deal with the challenge of feeding the increasing population but also implemented and supported the industrial revolution.

New conditions for human beings and demographic transition

In the 18th century the agricultural revolution in the English countryside triggered a number of socioeconomic transformations that were so overwhelming that human existence itself was forced to change. The emergence of new social and economic players was one of these transformations. In fact, the privatisation of the lands and enclosures separated the capitals of farms (land, tools and livestock) from other means of production (working abilities of farmers), turning them over to a new individual: the 'entrepreneur'. Entrepreneurs enjoyed full availability of the material and financial capitals necessary for production. They were also the coordinators and managers of all the farming activities, deciding the type and quantity of products to be cultivated, based on the demand of markets in both the countryside and the growing towns. Thus, the only thing peasants could do was to offer their labour and work experience to the entrepreneurs in exchange for a salary. This restructuring led to the creation of two new groups of economic players, 'paid workers' and 'entrepreneurs', and their corresponding social classes. Soon, since the number of potential workers in the countryside was higher than that needed to farm the land (due to the new production techniques), another new individual appeared as well: the 'unemployed'. The unemployed person, an unknown social player up until then, became henceforth an individual forced to hunt for a job if necessary, even by migrating within and outside the country.

It must be stressed that the 'social engineering' described just now had been encouraged by an important institutional process: the creation of 'land, labour, and financial markets' – i.e. of a set of rules governing the exchange of these resources by specific contracts. It was actually due to this commodification that the work changed its nature. While earlier it had been an activity focused merely on obtaining goods and services for survival, afterwards it became a flux of work and skills lent for a salary, according to the specific needs of a factory process or of the farm. The income paid to workers represented their 'purchasing power' – i.e. the amount of money they had to buy the goods they needed. Thus, people were forced to receive an income by taking part in the first market as sellers of 'workforce' and to use that income in the second market as buyers of goods to fulfil their needs. In a socioeconomic perspective, the emergence of labour markets separated the creation of goods from their enjoyment (i.e. the process of production from that of consumption), thus bringing to light the socioeconomic subject called the 'consumer'. The total value of the goods and services obtained by people with their salary would no longer be based on their needs but on the value attributed to their labour in the production process.

Labour market transformations changed people's living conditions because they generated processes of internal migration from the countryside towards towns (urbanisation), household reorganisation (mononuclear families) and role redistribution for each member of the family: women and even children entered the wage labour market. These transformations, however, also shaped everyday human life and people's procreative behaviour: the birth rate decreased due to family planning, the progresses made by medical science reduced the mortality rate, and together with better economic conditions these phenomena led to an extension of the average life expectancy and to a change in the population's age structure.

The combined effect of the improved economic conditions and the already mentioned social changes gave rise to the implementation of the population dynamics. This process, blocked earlier by the food availability, was freed by the increase in the foodstuff that pushed ahead the food restriction even overshadowing the recurring challenge that the sustainability of a growing population represented for the economy.[10] The path of the process was governed by the changes in two social variables: the birth rate and the death rate. The resulting population dynamics, called 'demographic transition' (Lee 2003), show specific stages, as can be seen in Figure 1.2. The first phase is the long-term balanced pre-industrial situation, while the second corresponds to the implementation of the population dynamics due to economic and social changes. The latter is characterised by a decreased mortality rate (due to scientific and infrastructural improvements in the healthcare system) and by a birth rate which is stable at a high level. These trends result in an increase in the net growth rate of the population (measured by the vertical distance of the corresponding curves) and in a subsequent demographic explosion. This phenomenon reaches its highest point in the third phase, when the socioeconomic changes taking place match the ones characterising the transition in the economic process which was described previously. But only during the fourth phase do the birth rate and mortality rate finally stabilise: due to a rapid drop in the number of offspring per woman and to a slow extension of the average life expectancy, the values of the two rates come close to equalling each other, while the population growth percentage decreases and might even turn into a decline.

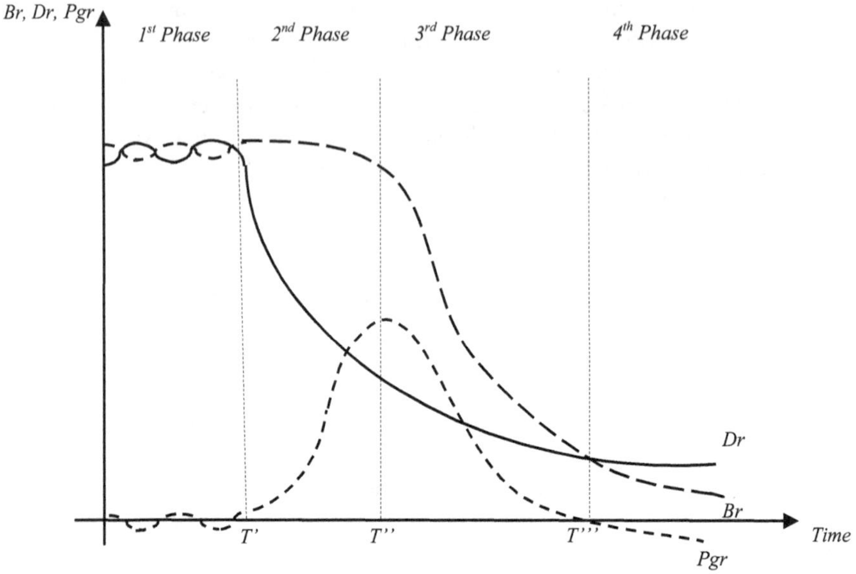

Br = Birth rate
Dr = Death rate
Pgr = Population growth rate

Figure 1.2 The demographic transition
Source: Author's elaboration

The population dynamics does not consist only of its absolute increase but also of the change in its age structure, a factor which is of highest importance for the economic system. Figure 1.3, which compares the age cohorts of an economy that has just started the process of demographic transition with the one that has already reached the most advanced phase, can be useful in understanding such a relevance. As pointed out previously, the second phase of the demographic transition shows a greater share of young people over the total population; this will mean a greater incidence of old people on the overall population in the third phase (thanks to the birth rate that tails off to the death rate value). Such demographic dynamics result in the need for a different distribution of social services produced in the economy. In fact, the high rates of population growth – which correspond to a major growth within the youngest groups of people – increase the need for investments in education and children's healthcare services. As people within this age group grow older and reach the point when they enter the job market, a new need joins the previous ones: that of creating jobs at a faster pace than the population growth rate. Finally, when 'the babies of the demographic boom' arrive at retirement and are more numerous than the working population, the social allocation of services will need to be devoted to this cohort.

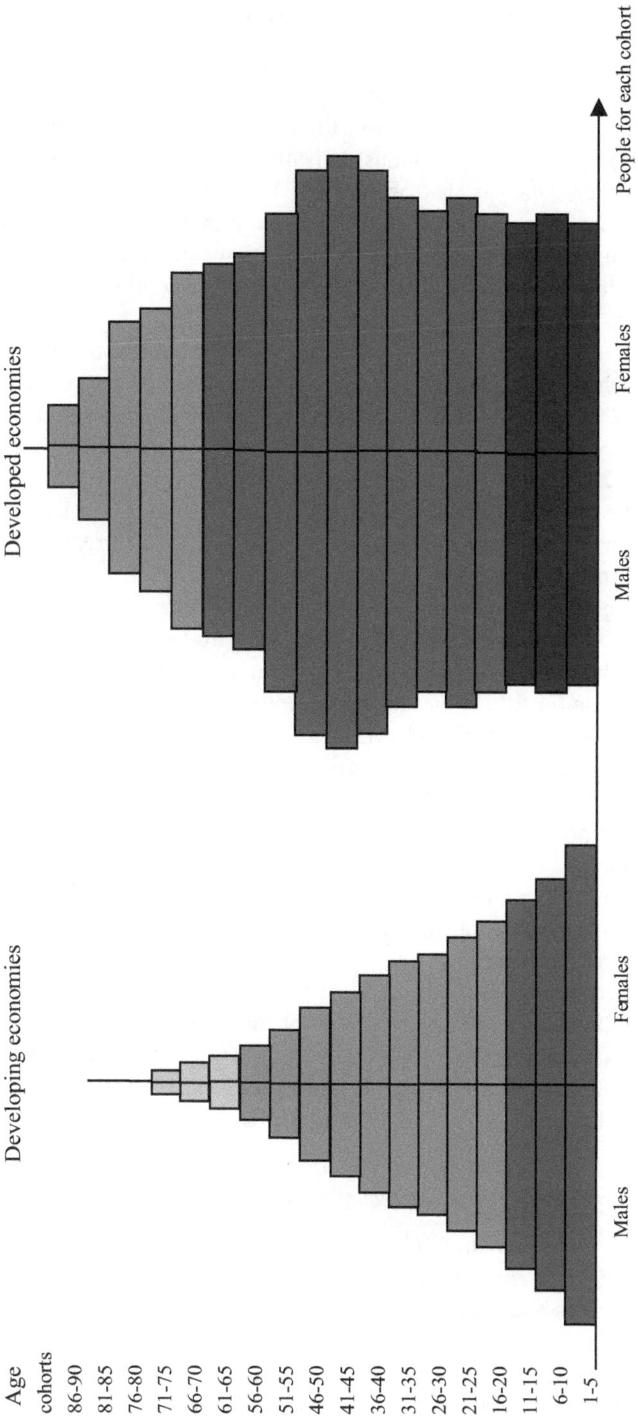

Figure 1.3 Structure of the population by age cohorts in the second and fourth phases of the demographic transition

Source: Author's elaboration

Technological progress and industrial revolutions

The changes recorded in the rural world right before the blooming of the industry enabled new organisational structures and operational procedures to gain a foothold in both the economic and social life. However, the exodus from the countryside to the cities and the process of industrialisation would not have been possible without the technical changes that occurred in Europe from the second half of the 18th century onwards. Unlike what had happened in the past, only during this period did the ability of humanity to conceive new inventions and introduce new production techniques succeed in achieving an intense and continuous flow of progressive technical changes in just few decades.

In the pre-industrial society, the manufacturing expansion was hampered by many factors, such as the availability of natural energy (obtained from either human and animal effort, or from inconstant and not very flexible resources such as water and wind) and the technical features of machines put into operation by such energies. Despite this, early in the 18th century a new belief came to the fore: a deeper knowledge of the production organisation and procedures in use in farms and in factories could in any case enhance the results obtained with current techniques. Moreover, alongside the changed management of agricultural activities, a new interest rose in agronomy and plant nursery capable of improving the procedures in agricultural production processes. Thanks to the introduction of new technical innovations into the processes of artisanal and manufacturing productions, instead, a fertile environment for further cutting-edge improvements was created.

The need to free the human production processes from the rhythms of nature and from its forces led first to the production of mechanical energy through the combustion of fuels such as coal. New machines were then introduced to support the workers and improve their performance beyond their physical capabilities, and new semi-finished and final goods were produced. Finally, communication infrastructure was created to move products and people from one place to another in a progressively shorter amount of time and at a cheaper cost. The introduction of production process and product innovations was also eased by promoting the principles of effectiveness and affordability to an increasingly larger audience: the endorsement passed mainly through the publication of the so-called 'manuals' codifying production's procedural routines and product use. In addition, new laws offered protection to innovative procedures and goods (patents) and to the organisations through which they were implemented (different types of firms).

The release of nature's grip: The production of mechanical energy

Energy constraint was the main hindrance for the expansion of output in the pre-industrial production systems. The amount of power used to accomplish production operations in factories and mills – which was mainly of muscular, hydraulic and aeolian nature – was contingent upon both the availability of capacity, the strength and possibility of preservation of natural energy resources. Every successful technical change relaxing one of these bonds increased the output produced. This was the case of the replacement of flat blades with curved blades in waterwheels and windmills: thanks to these innovations the water and wind horsepower increased, pushing up the production capacity of factories and mills per unit of time. It was just when machines producing mechanical energy with water reached the highest progression step of such a technology (with the hydraulic spinner in the factories of Bologna, Italy) that the point of no return represented by the creation of mechanical energy from heat was crossed. It was the invention of the Watt steam engine and its improvements, in the 18th century, that opened the era of the slackening of the energy hindrances imposed by nature and started the evolutionary process of power systems.

The 'power system' is a set of organised and interconnected components for the production, distribution and use of power. The devices of such a system are as follows:

i. The 'power source' – i.e. the natural resource storing the 'potential energy' (such as fossils, water, wind, solar radiation, food and fuels – which emanate heat or power when burned or harnessed) found in nature and used to produce 'mechanical power'.
ii. The 'converter' (or power unit) – i.e. the machine converting energy from one form to another. In pre-industrial power systems, the chemical energy produced by the bodies of workers and animals of labour and the kinetic energy of wind and water were transformed into the mechanical energy needed for the production in factories and mills, by 'generators' like muscles on the one hand and waterwheels and mill blades on the other hand. (See Figure 1.4.) Conversely, industrial power systems produce mechanical energy by transforming the chemical energy contained in fuels into heat energy: they use the combustion process of generators such as stationary steam engines in the case of manufacturing processes and internal combustion engines for vehicles. But in the industrial era mechanical energy is created also by transforming either the kinetic energy into electric energy (by means of water and wind turbines) or the heat energy into electric energy thanks to steam and gas turbines or electric generators. This kind of energy is essential for modern production systems because it can be switched to mechanical power by means of another converter: the 'electric motor'.
iii. The 'power transmission', which consists of a mechanism that transfers power to factory machineries via line shafts, belts, gear trains, clutches and electrical grids.
iv. The 'power load' – i.e. the use of power in factories, offices, homes and transportation and for the use of durable goods.

The 'water and wind power system' was typical of traditional societies because those economies obtained mechanical energy by means of hydraulic and wind engines (i.e. turbines and propellers). Thus, the source of energy, the energy production facility and the processing apparatus that the facility powered were inseparable: think of watermills or spinning mills, for example, and their structure and location. The introduction of the Watt steam engine resulted in an energy system

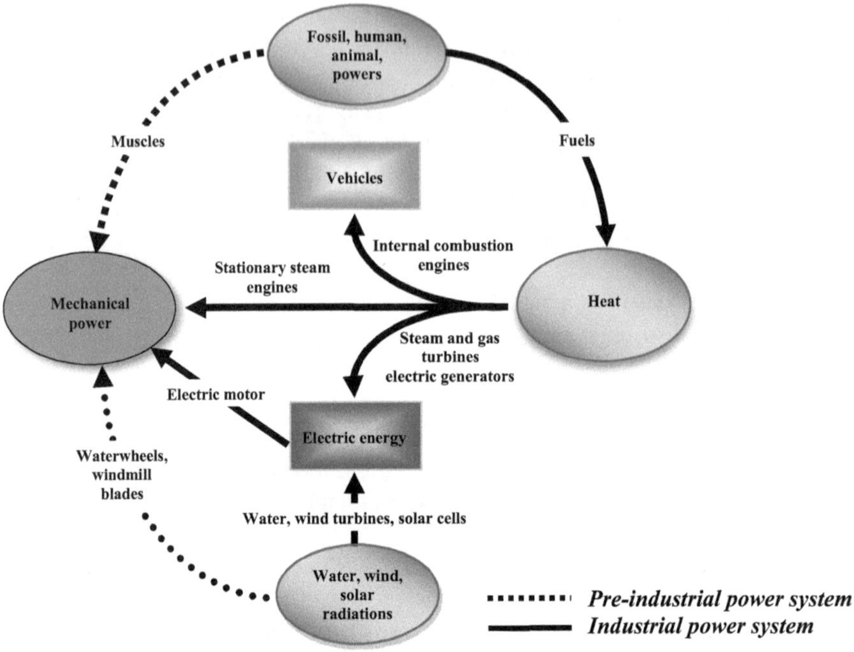

Figure 1.4 The mechanical power generation in pre-industrial and industrial power system

Source: Author's elaboration

providing mechanical power as desired. Through a set of pistons, cylinders and flywheels activated by the steam generated by a boiler, the machine was in fact able to turn thermal energy (created by an external process of hard coal combustion) into mechanical energy. The mechanical energy, in turn, was distributed to the factory equipment through flywheels and transmission belts. Its use in production processes marked for the first time the dissociation between engine and energy resource – a dissociation that led industrial production to be situated in structures large enough to contain steam engines surrounded by operating machinery. Placing factories near coalfields represented, at the beginning of the industrialisation years, a comparative advantage for the location of production plants due to the lack of transport costs for the fuel. Later, however, the use of the steam engine as a motor vehicle for railways (locomotives) succeeded in managing even factories located far away from the coalfields.

Although the 'coal power system' based on the Watt steam engine set the industrial development in motion (and thus the economic transformation as well), its widespread use was limited by two factors: first, the production of energy was still expensive and, second, the factory's layout (that is the arrangement of machines and manufacturing processes) must always be planned according to energy supply requirements. The high energy cost was due to the price of coal (because of the difficulty of its extraction) and considerable transport costs (because of its huge volume). The layout organisation constraint was due to the mechanism of energy transmission: in fact, the coal power system generated a dispersion which was economically acceptable only when a limited number of operating machines were in the immediate vicinity of the converter (or power unit).

In an attempt to reduce the first type of costs, factories started to use less expensive fuels. This led to the advent of new power systems, based on different raw materials ('oil, gas, nuclear power systems') and characterised by a growing energy efficiency. In fact, the process of shifting from one power system to another entailed the following:

i. The use of less expensive fuels – i.e. of resources available in greater quantities and capable of generating more energy per unit volume.
ii. The gradual dematerialisation of fuel for an equal amount of thermal energy as a by-product of this shifting process due to the gradual introduction of raw materials characterised by a greater power per unit of mass. Both trends reduced production and transportation costs.
iii. The creation of new converters capable of generating mechanical energy not only from heat (thermal energy) but also from other sources (chemical energy, electricity and hydropower).

The economic efficiency of power systems was achieved through the solutions proposed to solve the problem of energy dispersion during the transmission to operating machines and through the modularity of the service use. With the invention of both the Gramme dynamo (1869) and the electric motor (1888), significant progress was made in those directions. In fact, since the Gramme dynamo could convert the mechanical energy produced by different natural sources or fuels into electricity, it was possible to build power stations capable of producing low-cost electricity and distributing it across long distances with relatively low dispersion. On the other hand, the highest divisibility and flexibility in terms of use of the power was obtained thanks to the electric motor applied to every operating machine to turn electricity back into mechanical energy. Because of the introduction of electric motors, the dissociation between the power unit and the power load was achieved and the factories' internal organisation was henceforth focused entirely on the management of the production system, which was gradually mechanised and made more efficient in its operating procedures (various kinds of layouts were introduced).

The internal combustion 'heat engine' (1876), however, was the invention that afforded the highest performance and maximum flexibility in the production and consumption of mechanical energy. This thermal converter, based on gas or oil, made it possible to produce small amounts of energy for use not only in new means of transportation but also for many production purposes. This opened the way to the era of road transport, giving a boost to many industries and radically changing the lifestyle of the population. Moreover, the economic process broke free from the constraint represented by the possession of energy resources on one's own national territory.

The trigger for the industrial revolutions: The technological progress

Both agricultural transformations and the upgrade of power systems and machinery in spinning and textile factories represented the technological remodelling implemented by the leading sectors of the economy transitioning from a traditional economic to a capitalist one. The main result of these processes was the emergence of new production techniques and of a new organisational entity charged with the economic management of production processes (firm or farm, depending on the sector of activity). Together with the forces described previously, such an outcome was due to the technological advances.

'Technology' is a set of theoretical and operational knowledge, physical devices and routines acquired by a society to solve its socioeconomic problems. Thus, 'technological progress' is an ongoing, general innovative process involving scientific knowledge, its economic enforcement and resulting social consequences. However, it is not a homogeneous straight-line flow, as right inside specific momentous shifts can be marked, corresponding to the emergence of noteworthy innovations that offer the opportunity for further technical developments or new basic procedures. Thus, technological progress presents different qualitative periods, triggered by such core innovations which have been defined 'technological paradigms.' A 'technological paradigm' is a collection of solutions to socioeconomic problems based on specific principles (derived from the scientific progress) and material technologies ensued from them (Dosi 1982: 152). Thus, each technological paradigm does not represent merely a certain techno-production combination (production techniques) but also a specific scientific and social context. Furthermore, every technological paradigm also enshrines its own notion of technological development: it heavily steers the technological change, indicating not only the most urgent technical issues which need to be fixed but also in which direction the solution can be found ('technological trajectory').

The inventions (or innovations) triggering a technological paradigm are labelled 'general-purpose technologies' (GPTs) (Bresnaham and Trajtemberg 1992) – i.e. fundamental discoveries whose impact will be prolonged over time by virtue of the following proprieties (Lipsey, Carlaw and Bekar 2005: 97–105):

i. The 'pervasiveness', which means that they can be employed in many types of production processes.
ii. The 'capability of improvement' because they offer an ample opportunity for refinement and evolution over time.
iii. The 'capability of generating innovations', because they ease the process of inventing and introducing new models of production as well as new goods.
iv. The 'complementarity', as they can be used together with pre-existing technologies whose costs of use are thus reduced.

Such GPTs (the steam engine, factory plant, railways, production system management, electricity, and computer-led information and communication technologies – ICTs) have been used to stagger the technological development which structurally changed the production, consumption and social life of capitalistic society in periods characterised by technological paradigms called 'industrial revolutions' (Lipsey, Carlaw and Bekar 2005: Chapter Six).

Although scholars disagree on such a list of GPTs and on their time periods of influence, they agree on the starting point. The 'First Industrial Revolution', which took place between 1750 and 1820) in Great Britain and then in France and United States, was launched by the steam engine and the factory plant; in fact, the former made it possible to produce mechanical energy for the factory machines distant from the energy source, while the latter first started the mechanisation of the production systems and later its automation. Therefore, both innovations led to the progressive reduction of human intervention in production operations and to the control of the production processes carried out by a set of co-ordinated machines. The production systems management and railways pushed the newly industrialised economies toward the 'Second Industrial Revolution' (which took place from 1830 up to the early 20th century). These factors promoted the low-cost creation of a standardised amount of goods and services and their distribution far from the production site, respectively. In fact, starting from the mid-19th century, the production arrangement of tools and workers changed thanks to the introduction of the 'organisational chart' and different cost-reducing methods of production ('mass production'). At the same time, the increasing speed of trains made it possible to establish manufacturing plants far from coal mines, the concentration of populations in towns and the long-distance transportation of passengers and freight. In the last decade of the 19th century the 'production of electricity' enabled the utmost power divisibility and flexibility. This innovation launched a new phase in the economic transformation (the 'Third Industrial Revolution'), which, by supplying energy both to production and consumption activities, implemented the outcome of the two previous revolutions. Lastly, starting from the 1970s, the introduction of the 'computer-led ICTs' triggered the 'Fourth Industrial Revolution', not only reducing communication and access times but also further improving production and consumption.[11]

The chronological progression of the GPTs cannot provide a comprehensive assessment of the technological advances in the capitalist evolution, and this makes the identification of the timing and innovations introduced by the so-called 'industrial revolutions' more complex. In fact, even though single GPTs characterised the phases of the industrial upgrading, their use was sometimes limited. In the First Industrial Revolution, for example, the use of the steam engine was limited to mines and foundries in spite of being the most important invention (it became the basis for transport development in the rail and maritime systems only later). Nevertheless, for the textile industry, whose machinery was still fuelled by hydropower at the time of First Industrial Revolution, the introduction of the spinner brought about some important production improvements, also diverting the production towards the use of cotton because of its compatibility with such machines. Similarly, during the same period, metalworking experienced a new boost from Cort's conversion method, which turned cast iron into iron, and from the use of coke, which led to the introduction of very large furnaces. Finally, it must be remembered that, in addition to GPTs and other key sectoral innovations, the mechanisation of production processes and the spread of technical progress were the results of an intense development of machine tools, which during the earlier stages of industrialisation were often pedal operated.

As for the exclusive role of GPTs in promoting the industrial revolution, it must be considered that most of them emerged with the contribution of scientific knowledge. Although up to the first half of the 19th century the technological development was mostly independent from scientific change (Mokyr 2005), the following decades saw the role of science becoming more and more pivotal for the emergence of new innovations, especially in the steel and chemical industries. During the 'Second Industrial Revolution' scientific research focused on solving the technical problems of production such as, for example, finding the best combination of iron and carbon to obtain materials such as steel, which was essential for the success of new means of transport such as the train. Another case was the development of the 'American system of manufacturing', which led to the standardisation of products, the interchangeability of parts, and the continuous production cycle. Also, progress made in chemistry characterised the scientific research during the Second Industrial Revolution (such as the best way to create sulphuric acid and soda), but the discovery of electromagnetism was probably the most fruitful result of that period: in fact, it led to the inventions of the dynamo and the electric motor. Early in the 20th century, thanks to both the generator and the motor, electricity could be produced, thus making it possible to refine previous inventions and create new goods and services, effectively triggering the Third Industrial Revolution. Later, the advances in electronics led to the invention of the transistor in 1950: this marked the starting point for the 'Fourth Industrial Revolution', for it made it possible for any kind of device (electric motors, calculators, and operating machines) not only to simultaneously execute more than one program, but also to reduce the dimensions of the devices themselves. Its replacement with the microcircuit further advanced this miniaturisation process, allowing the development of multifunctional calculators operating at high speed. These features set in motion 'process innovations' in every sector (changes in machinery and production arrangements (OECD 2005: 47–52) as well as 'product innovations', such as the introduction of new instrumental and consumer goods (mobile phones, computers, etc.). In the tertiary sector microcircuits also led to the establishment of a telecommunications sector.

The spread of transportation and communication systems

The traditional socioeconomic communities generally lived isolated, not only because of their poor economic relations but also due to the difficulties entailed in moving from one place to another. Such difficulties were caused by the harshness of the territory, the lack of transport infrastructure and insecurity due to banditry. Roads and ports were constructed based only on the government's needs – i.e. either for political control and economic coordination or for reaching the various towns scattered throughout the territory in a faster and/or easier way. For centuries, the transport of goods over long distances fuelled the 'administrative market', the market managed and supervised by political authorities. Instead, the transport of goods over short distances supplied the local markets, where commercial exchanges were scarce and had to follow rules and prices dictated by local authorities. Long-distance transport was carried out on water (navigable rivers, canals, seas), while for short distances, itineraries mapped down through the centuries were used.

In Britain the outdated internal transport system was improved only when the production growth generated by the 'British Agricultural Revolution' and the industrialisation process created the necessity to sell the food surplus and the textile fibres of agricultural origin as well as to secure supplies of coal and raw materials. The construction of railways was made possible by the combination of rail tracks (already used in mines) and the steam locomotive (derived from the steam engine). The railway led to a wider possible range of transportation, of both goods and people. The overcoming of geographical obstacles reduced the travel times, while the expansion of the rail network reduced the transport unit costs for goods. These improvements encouraged not only the circulation and distribution of production resources over the territory but also business ventures and the birth and development of new production sectors within the steel and mechanical engineering industry: it was due to these structural changes that the dimension of intermediate product markets began a continuous process of expansion.

The development of the railway system led to solving certain technical and organisational problems that were limiting its sprawl. On the one hand, travel times to reach locations further and further away needed to be reduced as much as possible so that perishable goods such as foodstuff could be transported also. Moreover, the transport capacity of new vehicles had to be exploited to the maximum. In both cases, the achievement of the goal would make it possible also to obtain a substantial decrease in the unit cost of services. On the other hand, transport being a service provided territorially, the arrangement and management of the train traffic over a progressively broader area was necessary. The first necessity was dealt with through the construction of more powerful and faster locomotives, as well as through the replacement of old fuels with new ones, characterised by a high energy potential (coal was replaced by diesel, diesel was replaced by electricity). The second necessity saw the introduction of new corporate structure arrangements (for example the 'functions organisational chart' to manage railway companies).

Economically and technically speaking, however, the railway system set certain limits to its expansion: it required massive financial capital on the one hand, was hardly flexible as far as transport capacity was concerned (the carriages usually had standard dimensions) and was not very widespread in terms of territories covered because it tended to minimise the distances by preferring straight-line itineraries. Financial needs were responded to by encouraging public funding or the propagation of enterprises in which the capital was conferred (and thus owned) in shares – the 'stock companies.' In addition, the deployment of a certain type of market called 'stock market' was also promoted, in which investors could buy shares with their savings. The last two problems were solved by developing a transport system complementary to the railway: 'road transport'.

The construction of rural roads, which at first connected the rail stations to the villages and towns nearby, led to the widespread use of vehicles to transport goods (lorries) and people (cars). These vehicles had great flexibility in terms of mobility over the territory as well as great divisibility in terms of transport capacity. They were also able to travel on the road network without requiring traffic coordination. The road transport expanded quickly because the funds used to build the road network were usually public and also because the cost of such vehicles became more and more accessible over time. This was due to the new production techniques reducing unit costs of vehicles and also to the rise in individual salaries and the companies' available funds.

The development of these transportation and communication systems brought monumental changes to the economy and society. First of all, alongside the organisational and financial upgrading of railway companies, the providing of the transport service of goods and people needed to be supported by an effective system for communication of information on the train traffic ('information system'). Thus, first the telegraph was introduced, and later the telephone when the trains became faster and faster. Moreover, the technical and production evolution of both transport systems (the transport system of goods/people on the one hand and the transport of information – the information system – on the other) gave rise to new sector services (such as air transport and phone service), but it also triggered other sectors producing consumer services: take, for example, the tourism sector, mass communication sector and communication services for entertainment. The more the progress in the construction of transport vehicles reduced the unit cost of the service, the more rapidly the settlement of factories spread over the territory, thus decoupling from the place where raw materials were produced. In particular, their locations spread near conurbations with a wider workforce availability and sale markets. New town centres rose, and people changed their way of living as well as their way of working, becoming progressively freer of and more detached from rural habits and beliefs.

New technical and social rules to support the new economy

The capitalist economy was not generated just by sociodemographic changes, the continuing succession of scientific discoveries and the ensuing progress in production techniques, and the transformation of the production system. Alongside the factories' routines focused on efficiently obtaining products and the transformations of the rules of social coexistence, economic players' behaviours and populations' habits also changed to make this new economy work. For taking advantage of the evolution of such a new system and exploiting its welfare potentials, for example, the attitude towards the consumption of commodities changed also; in fact, the consumer emerged as a new economic being appointed to such a role.

Institutional changes and new organisations to 'drive the machine'

Institutional change represents one of the most important transformation processes of traditional societies. The 'institutions' are social rules managing either interpersonal relationships among single individuals or the operational performance of groups of people gathered in collective units for the pursuit of common goals. Such rules may be informal (i.e. non-written rules of behaviour, incorporated within beliefs, habits and traditions) or formal (i.e. instructions enacted by authorised entities through laws, codes, regulations). Since all institutions must be acknowledged as useful for relational and/or operational purposes and must be learned before being applied, they need time. All the rules concerning work, land use and trade become commonplace within a relatively short time under the impetus of events and thanks to laws and regulations supporting them; on the other hand, a change in social habits takes more time, as is shown by the drop in the birth rate of a population. As the function of institutions is to govern social processes and to make them progressively more and more efficient and/or effective, during historical periods characterised by epoch-making changes, such as the one we are analysing, institutions undergo a continuing evolution process.

The first type of institutional change which characterised the birth of the new economic system took place during the British agricultural and industrial revolutions and concerned the procedures used to obtain goods and services (routines). The changes that affected the structure of the traditional production operations as well as their procedures were caused by the use of new tools (seeder) and the 'Norfolk rotation system' in farming on the one hand, and the introduction of machines producing mechanical energy and operating machines in the industry to help workers on the other hand. In fact, following these innovations, the operational order of the machine service and worker's labour in the production process changed, alongside the way in which workers carried out their tasks (division of labour). The mechanisation process first, and the automation process later, imposed new rules on production arrangements, which gave rise to a succession of methods progressively more and more complex and efficient, sometimes codified in the manuals of business management.

While the first kind of institutional change supporting the emergent new economy was related to the technical structure of the production in both agriculture and industry, the second kind concerned the production unit: the farm and industrial company. Over the past couple of centuries, countries have emanated laws governing the establishment of companies, the contracts concerning the production and sale of their products/services and the terms of competition in both industrial sectors and final markets. Public authorities, however, have also issued laws and regulations aimed at protecting the goods at the disposal of the individual (property rights), creating structures for the coordination of economic activities (goods, financial and job markets) and defining public policies that direct the economy towards desired public objectives (development, growth, occupation, etc.).

The institutional change described previously gave rise to collective economic structures of various types (companies, consortia, markets, service networks), called 'organisations', which are typical of the capitalistic system (Hodgson 2015). An 'organisation' is a social unit made up of people, tools, and tangible and intangible objects, which is structured and managed either to meet its needs or to pursue its collective goals. All organisations have a management to structure relations between members and assign responsibilities and roles, which are endowed with the authority necessary to accomplish the task. Furthermore, all organisations operate by means of procedures based on efficiency criteria and coordination arrangements that can be of a horizontal (market) or vertical (bureaucracies) type. Some elective political organisations (parliaments, governments, public administrations) have as their specific task that of creating institutions, while some public organisations are charged with this task through international agreements signed by the states (WTO, supervisory bodies monitoring the quality of products, etc.). Also, companies and associations can set up institution building processes: this is the case, for example, of business routines or sport game plans. All of them are thus institutional sources – i.e. entities entitled, in practice or by right, to create institutions.

Towards the consumer society: Changes in social mores and new lifestyles

As has been mentioned elsewhere in this chapter, the capitalistic system emerging from the traditional society presented another distinguishing feature: it assigned consumption an independent role within the economic process. In the pre-industrial society, for most of the population, consumption was satisfied by producing everything on their own. Only people belonging to the aristocracy, the merchants, the army and the clergy could have spending power – i.e. money to buy goods and services that satisfied needs going beyond the subsistence level. In economies that embarked on structural changes, aimed at improving the material production and addressing it to buyers in markets, the direct link between consumption and production stopped and was substituted by an indirect but essential relation. In fact, while the quantitative and qualitative evolution of production made it possible on the one hand to offer more and more goods and services, on the other the people's needs, preferences and wishes could express a corresponding demand for those outputs. But, obviously, this concurrence was connected to a reciprocal and matching pair of conditions: that firms produced them in a technically efficient and economically sustainable manner and that consumers had just enough money to buy the goods and services produced. Such independent but correlated development of both represents a coevolution process that is a constitutive feature of the capitalist economic system.

The interface between these two spheres of economic activity is represented by the income earned by people participating in the production activity; this value represents, at the same time, the share of the production cost corresponding to the inputs that people provide to the production process (work and capital services) and the revenues (salary, rent, and profit) used by people to buy goods and services. Because of the two-pronged nature of the income, in the economic system it could happen that the two ways in which it is expressed do not match up, consequently leading to a surplus of the value of production compared to that of consumption or vice versa. In addition, as different wage earners (salaried workers, rentiers, and profit earners) have different spending propensities because of their saved earnings, the values of the three incomes' share have a different impact on consumption. Thus, the distribution of income among salaried, rentiers and profit earners becomes pivotal for the economic system to match production and consumption.

For this reason, historically, the purchasing power of the labour incomes grew, while the output prices decreased parallel to the industrial development, and both trends could be conducive to the survival of the capitalist economy. This way, consumption patterns could emerge and evolve.

The historical patterns of consumption – i.e. the economic and social dimension of the modes through which it expressed itself – kept changing continuously over time based on the citizens' purchasing power. This gave rise to the diffusion of consumption styles, a phenomenon affecting not only elites but the masses as well. Their establishment in developed and underdeveloped countries happened thanks to transnational companies and entailed the standardisation of products, which means that the same kind of good is sold everywhere and in the same way. From the standpoint of human beings, the main socioeconomic consequences deriving from the role of consumption as it has been described above are the following:

- Consumer societies have produced time savings spent on consumption and a higher amount of time spent on activities such as travelling and shopping.
- More money is spent for more goods while more time is spent spending money.

Concluding remarks: Modern economies as capitalist economies

This chapter has aimed to provide documentary evidence of the emergence of a new organisation of economic activities through a series of transformations in the economic, social and institutional fields of human life. The advent of the new economic organisation represented a break with the past. "At the heart of the Industrial Revolution of the eighteenth century there was an almost miraculous improvement in the tools of production, which was accompanied by a catastrophic dislocation of the lives of the common people. . . . The Industrial Revolution was merely the beginning of a revolution as extreme and radical as ever inflamed the minds of sectarians. . . . The transformation to this system from the earlier economy is so complete that it resembles more the metamorphosis of the caterpillar than any alteration that can be expressed in terms of continuous growth and development' (Polanyi 2001: 35, 42, 44).

The novelty wasn't due only to a new economic arrangement, an innovative social structure, an unaccustomed environment for human life and an unprecedented lifestyle. Alongside these structural changes in social life there was a reallocation of the social functions and of the roles played by different social players. In fact, the emergence of the entrepreneur and salaried worker marked the 'transfer of the organisation and control of production from the imperial and aristocratic strata of pre-capitalist states into the hands of mercantile elements' (Heilbroner 2008: 4). Such a process created 'the separation of a traditionally seamless web of rulership, extending over all activities within the historical formation, into two realms, each concerned with a differentiated part of the whole' (Heilbroner 2008: 5): the economic and the political spheres. 'The presence of two realms, each responsible for part of the activities necessary for the maintenance of the social formation . . .

establishes the basis for a problem: . . . the appropriate role of the state vis-à-vis the sphere of production and distribution' (Heilbroner 2008: 5). In addition, this separation was also accompanied and shaped by an institutional framework (supporting and protecting the economic activities) 'distinguishable in history by the predominance of a prudent, accountant-like comparison of costs and benefits, a perspective discoverable in the mercantile pockets of earlier formations but highly uncharacteristic of the tempers of their ruling elites' (Heilbroner 2008: 6). The qualification of the new economy as a component of a distinctive 'historical formation' ('capitalism') made by some economists and sociologists such as Smith, Mill, Marx, Weber, Weblen, Shumpeter and Braudel was largely due to these aspects.

In such a context of momentous transformations it is difficult to select nowadays, among the many features of the new economic system, the one that can identify and label it. Undoubtedly, the use of material capitals (that is of machinery or goods produced in previous production periods) and the adaptation of human labour effort and living conditions to the production feature represent the engine of such economies. Given these two elements and considering the constitutive role played by the economic sphere in the new 'historical formation', it is consequential to maintain that modern economies are capitalist economies.

Such a conclusion is important from the analytical standpoint not only because it definitely settles the nature of the modern economies but also because highlights the set of features characterising them. Such list provides, directly and/or indirectly, a paradigmatic set of axioms for the representation of modern economies and their explanatory models. Thus, no single model of the economic system based on abstract organisational functions or a generic human endogenous behaviour can represent or analyse modern economies.

Notes

1 However, this hasn't always guaranteed the replenishment of natural capitals in the past: the overdevelopment of pasture, intense land use, and deforestations aimed at expanding the agricultural areas have often generated an environmental degradation, leading to the fall of ancient civilisations.

2 With this, we do not mean to enter the dispute among historians regarding the relationship between population growth and the performance of agricultural production but only highlight the fact that a constant population growth required a higher amount of foodstuffs produced and, for the same number of workers and cultivated lands, a higher output per unit of production resource. On this problem, see Grigg (1982).

3 This mechanism took the population back to the starting level only if new lands were not farmed, if there was no technical progress in both agriculture and the fight against diseases, and if the marriage rate depended only on the real income.

4 The mechanism also seemed to be able to keep the populations' per-capita purchasing power constant in the long term despite the demographic growth. A comparison of the GDP in late medieval and early modern European economies shows that 'Roman per capita GDP two thousand years ago was the same as that of other pre-modern agrarian economies before modern growth'. (Lo Cascio and Malanima 2014) A discussion of this theory is in Temin (2013: 243).

5 The rotation order was sometimes different as it depended on the weather conditions and the latitude of the lands on which the technique was applied.

6 When the human intake in the transformation is prevalent, the machines will 'depend' on the worker; in the case of highly mechanised processes, on the other hand, the worker is the one 'serving' the machines (see Romagnoli 1996b: 22–3).
7 Going forward, the cultivation of potatoes also turned out to be a further step towards the increase of the agricultural output as they provide more than one harvest each year. Alongside this production advantage, the cultivation of potatoes was important for the strengthening of the industrial revolution in England because of their higher nutritional content and their convenience compared to wheat: they do not need to be transformed.
8 A German chemist who lived in the 19th century. He was considered the father of agricultural chemistry.
9 The presence of capitals and of paid work is generally considered a necessary requirement for the transition from the traditional economic system to the capitalistic one. Without dwelling on a discussion of the problem, it is nonetheless necessary to mention that the historical debate reached such a conclusion by answering questions such as 'When was capitalism born and why?' 'What are capitalism's distinctive features?' A summary of the debate and its answers can be found in Screpanti (2007).
10 The debate on the matter, especially among economists, has focused on the comparison between the agricultural output growth rate and the population growth rate: the dispute has been over the possibility of surplus if the former exceeds the latter and of stagnation if the reverse happens. The progress achieved in the agricultural sector has led academics to lean towards the first-case scenario, and famines have been blamed on the lack of sectoral renovation or on dysfunctions within the world markets trading foodstuffs. Only recently there has been a new interest in the problem of the consistency between the current dynamics of the population and present trends of capitalism, that of the sustainability for mankind of this model of capitalism.
11 The chronological review and structural features of the upgrading process that technology showed in the capitalist evolution enliven the discussion on the 'industrial revolutions'. For a different approach see Bruland and Mowert (2014: 85–96).

Bibliography

Bresnaham, T. and Trajtemberg, M. (1992) 'General Purpose Technologies: Engines of Growth', *NBER Working Papers, No. 4148*. https://doi.org/10.1016/0304-4076(94)01598-T

Bruland, K. and Mowert, D. C. (2014) 'Technology and the Spread of Capitalism', in L. Neal and J. G. Williamson (eds.) *Capitalism Volume II. The Spread of Capitalism: From the 1848 to the Present*, Cambridge: Cambridge University Press: 82–126.

Chayanov, A. V. (1966) *The Theory of Peasant Economy*, Madison: The University of Wisconsin Press.

De Agostini. (1997) *Grande enciclopedia della scienza e della tecnologia (Encyclopedia of Sciences and Technologies)*, Novara: De Agostini-La Repubblica.

Dosi, G. (1982) 'Technological Paradigms and Technological Trajectories', *Research Policy*, 11 (3): 147–62.

Georgescu-Roegen, N. (1971) *The Entropy Law and the Economic Process*, Cambridge, MA: Harvard University Press.

Grigg, D. B. (1982) *The Dynamics of Agricultural Change: The Historical Experience*, New York: Harper Collins Publishers.

Heilbroner, R. L. (2008) 'Capitalism', in S. N. Durlauf and L. E. Blume (eds.) *The New Palgrave Dictionary of Economics*, 2nd ed., London: Palgrave-Macmillan. http://doi.org/10.1057/9780230226203.0198. Available at http://www.dictionaryofeconomics.com/article?id=pde2008_C000053

Hirschman, A. O. (1977) *The Passions and the Interests: Political Arguments for Capitalism Before Its Triumph*, Princeton, NJ: Princeton University Press.

Hodgson, G. M. (2015) *Conceptualizing Capitalism. Institutions, Evolution, Future*, Chicago: The University of Chicago Press.

Lee, R. (2003) 'The Demographic Transition: Three Centuries of Fundamental Change', *Journal of Economic Perspectives*, 17 (4): 167–90.

Lipsey, G. R., Carlaw, K. I. and Bekar, T. C. (2005) *Economic Transformations. General Purpose Technologies and Long-Term Economic Growth*, Oxford: Oxford University Press.

Lo Cascio, E. and Malanima, P. (2014) 'Ancient and Pre-modern Economies GDP in Roman Empire and Early Modern Europe', in François de Callataÿ (ed.) *Quantifying the Greco-Roman Economy and Beyond*, Bari: Edipuglia: 201–19.

Marx, K. (1999) *Capital. A Critique of Political Economy* (German edition 1867, first English edition 1887), Marx/Engels Internet Archive. See emain.org.

Mokyr, J. (2005) 'Long-Term Economic Growth and the History of Technology', in F. Aghion and S. N. Durlauf (eds.) *Handbook of Economic Growth*, Vol. 1B, Amsterdam: Elsevier.

Mosley, K. P. and Wallerstein, I. (1978) 'Precapitalist Social Structures', *Annual Review of Sociology*, 4: 259–90.

OECD (2005) *Oslo Manual. Guidelines for Collecting and Interpreting Innovation Data*, Paris: OECD.

Olsen, K. (1999) *Daily Life in 18th-Century England*, London: Greenwood Press.

Polanyi, K. (2001) *The Great Transformation*, Boston: Beacon Press (first edition 1944).

Romagnoli, A. (1996a) 'Agricultural Forms of Production Organisation', in M. A. Landesmann and R. Scazzieri (eds.) *Production and Economic Dynamics*, Cambridge: Cambridge University Press: 229–51.

Romagnoli, A. (ed.) (1996b) *Teoria dei processi produttivi. Uno studio sull'unità tecnica di produzione (The Theory of Production Processes. A Study at the Factory Level)*, Turin: Giappichelli.

Screpanti, E. (2007) *The Fundamental Institutions of Capitalism*, London: Routledge.

Temin, P. (2013) *The Roman Market Economy*, Princeton: Princeton University Press.

Glossary

Agricultural production system is a set of organised activities performed to produce agricultural goods and services.

Biosphere is the set made up by all the earth's ecosystems.

Crop production techniques is a set of organised elements (seeds, peasant work, tools, soil) and of management procedures necessary to produce a crop unit.

Crop rotation is the organised sequence of crops on a plot of land during a period of many years.

Demographic transition is the process of population changes in quantity and structure experienced by the capitalist societies along with their development.

Ecosystem is a basic ecological unit assembling a community of organisms living in a specific area.

Enclosure is the historical process of field fencing in the British countryside that started the forced transfer of the farmlands from peasants to the landlords.

Entropy is the degree of equilibrium of an organised system.

Food chain is a sequence of living organisms in which each one feeds on the lower ones and is food for the higher ones.

General-purpose technology is a drastic invention affecting the technological trajectory by the emergence of a new technological paradigm and pushing epoch-making socioeconomic changes.

Income distribution is the splitting up, among the participants in an economy, of the value of the economic activities they perform.

Industrial revolutions are periods of the capitalist evolution characterised by technological paradigms.

Institutions are a kind of rule governing human behaviour in relational life. They can be classified as techno-organisational procedures, legal norms and behavioural principles.

Layout is a configuration of the arrangement of machinery, staff members and semi-finished products during the production process.

Natural capitals are elements constituting the earth's assets assembled during its chemical and physical evolution. They include minerals, rocks, air, gas, water and fossil fuels but also forests, polar and alpine glaciers, landscapes and biodiversity.

Organisation is a social unit composed of people, tools and tangible and intangible objects, structured and managed to meet its needs or to pursue its collective goals.

Power system is a technological system for power generation, transmission, distribution and load.

Process innovation is the introduction of production or delivery methods that are new or improved because they change techniques, equipment and/or software.

Product innovation is the introduction of goods and services that are new, improved in some components or having a new use.

Productivity is the value of the output produced by a production resource unit in a specific production process and context. It is measured by the ratio between the total output value and the amount of each input.

Purchasing power is the amount of goods and services that can be obtained by a specific amount of money (or by the wage value).

Technical advance is any technical improvement achieved in a production technique by the change in the amount and quality of materials, labour and machine services, and/or operating procedures.

Technique of production is a production method for a specific good or service unit of output, including the amount of materials, labour and machine services, and the standard operating procedure necessary to obtain it.

Technological paradigm is a pattern of solutions for technological problems which emerged in economies, based on scientific principles and operating procedures.

Technological progress is an ongoing, general innovative process involving scientific knowledge, the entire economic system and the society.

Technology is a set of theoretical and operational knowledge, physical devices and routines acquired by a society to solve its socioeconomic problems.

2 The long-run driving forces behind the evolution of capitalist economies

To study the capitalist advent and strengthening and the 'forces' that supported them it is necessary to understand what capitalism is. In 1943 Schumpeter wrote, 'The essential point to grasp is that in dealing with capitalism we are dealing with an evolutionary process. . . . Capitalism, then, is by nature a form or method of economic change. . . . The fundamental impulse that sets and keeps the capitalist engine in motion comes from the new consumers' goods, the new methods of production or transportation, the new markets, the new forms of industrial organisation that capitalist enterprise creates' (Schumpeter 2003: 82–3).

Although he traced the path for studying capitalism by putting in evidence of its evolutionary nature, the scholars investigating modern economies ignored this suggestion. In fact, during the Cold War, when the analysis of modern economic systems attracted the interest of researchers, their attention was focused mainly on the mechanisms coordinating economic activities (the plan or market) rather than on their evolutionary process and the forces generating and supporting them. This bias – frequently originated by an ideological support of the economic structure and institutions built by political and judicial systems in the United States and the Soviet Union – had a huge impact on the research conducted on modern economies with regard not only to their evolution but also to their very nature. As for their evolution, the attitudes toward the issue fluctuated between a complacent triumphalism over the extraordinary spread of the new socioeconomic system all over the world despite its opponents and a riotous resentment against the injustices and suffering caused to human beings throughout the two and a half centuries of its emergence and upgrading. As for their nature, the study of the capitalist economy was confined to the mechanism of coordination of economic activities, and this fostered an image of modern economies as entities outside of history and free from any evolutionary path. Among other things, on these grounds, the idea that economic development is a transition process from traditional societies toward a new socioeconomic system was also rejected.

Actually, the onset of capitalism is a historical event, first observed in Great Britain, then spread to Continental Europe, the United States and Japan and later also to other countries all over the world. Therefore, the diffusion of the new economy took place in more than one phase over two and a half centuries, while the 'point of no return' indicating its self-sustainability occurred only starting in

DOI: 10.4324/9781315679730-4

1820. In addition, alongside its evolutionary process, there were many upgrading sociotechnological changes which came about in succession (industrial revolutions), so that capitalism's upgrading may be thought of as an ascending path which is neither continuous and balanced nor regular; the proof of such a dynamics is provided by the trends of some variables representing the 'long-run dynamic forces' supporting it.

This chapter will revisit the appearance and spread of capitalism, starting from a presentation of the timing of the process, the instruments necessary to provide quantitative evidence of the phases and main results in terms of structural change and wealth. Therefore, the 'long-run dynamic forces' ruling it (Maddison 1991) are reviewed to highlight the support given to the strengthening and dynamics of the capitalist economy by human, natural and physical capitals as well as by institutions.

An overview of capitalist dynamics

The advent and upgrading of the capitalist economy resulted, throughout the period, in never-ending and sweeping changes in social and material conditions for the people living in countries that introduced the new model of production and institutional changes. Such transformations can be revealed, in terms of size and evolutionary trends, by using statistical data. As the advent of capitalism was experienced by single countries at different times and its upgrading has been a staggered process due to industrial revolutions, a historical picture of capitalist dynamics cannot overlook a convenient recognition of the starting point and divisions of the period. This is the reason why a statistical digression is necessary before reviewing those momentous changes.

The timing and measuring of capitalist advancement

The evolutionary process of capitalist economies is the result of the 'driving forces' – that is, of socioeconomic phenomena or elements that made it feasible; the appraisal of such a progression can be made through the statistical analysis of all these drivers. In fact, every phenomenon/element summarised by an indicator (i.e. a concept defining its state or level) presents several aspects that can be measured by corresponding index numbers (i.e. numerical values displaying their quantity).[1] In such a way each driver becomes a variable quantified by the values of the index numbers accounting for it. Thus, the time series (a set of data obtained over a period) of the index numbers show the trends of the variables, enabling to characterise both the capitalist advancement and the sequence of the intervals inside it.

A study of the evolution of capitalism requires the identification of a historical starting point for the phenomenon; this does not mean establishing a date for the beginning of the emergence and spreading of capitalism but rather discovering the period of those strong changes in world economic conditions which promoted a permanent self-sustained growth in all the countries experiencing them. As for the historical scouting, some pre-industrial periods when the rise of personal income in Europe occurred were recorded, but as they later were followed by an economic decline, they prevented the spread of a self-sustained process of improvement in welfare conditions and the advent of a new economic system (Fouquet and Broadberry 2015). However, 'historians describe the period from the seventeen eighties to the eighteen twenties as an epochal time of change' (Graff, Kenwood and Lougheed 2014: 16), during which, in Europe, many sociopolitical events contributed to facilitating the strengthening and diffusion of the new economy through the demolition of the privileges of old political and economic classes. Significant institutional changes going in this direction, as a matter of fact, included the introduction of the *Code Napoléon* (1804) and its dissemination beyond France in conjunction with the Napoleonic Wars as well as the British policies designed to reduce trade barriers.

As for the starting point for a permanent self-sustained economic growth, some economists (such as Schumpeter, Spiethoff, Tugan-Baranowsky and Maddison) have studied this matter. In particular, Maddison states that 'capitalist development since 1820 has a certain unity because economic growth . . . has been much more rapid than in the merchant . . . epoch from 1500 to 1820'. (Maddison 2007: 160) Thus, the analysis of the trends shown by the variables representing the 'long-run dynamic forces' can start with the first decades of the 19th century, statistical data permitting.

From that period onward, the emergence of the world's capitalist economies was staggered over time. Historically, Great Britain was the first to be industrialised during the second half of the 18th century, but it reached the 'point of no return' during the period 1800–1830, while industrialisation in France came about in 1814–1844 and in the United States between 1815 and the beginning of the Civil War in 1861 (Clark 2016). Another generation of economies approached capitalism during the second half of the 19th century; in the 1860s it was Japan's turn, in the 1870s Germany's and Italy's, and in the 1880s it came to Russia (all other countries in the so-called group of 'BRICS'[2] moved towards capitalism more recently, after World War II). Such waves of emergent capitalist economies were due to a succession of sociotechnological changes, creating both an upgrading of capitalism (as it has been shown in Chapter One) and advantageous historical conditions for the transition of some traditional economies towards the new socioeconomic system. Therefore, considering both aspects, the evolution of capitalism can be described as a progressive and expansive process characterised by a sequence of separate economic periods.

The time partition of capitalism's evolution according to this perspective attracted the attention of Angus Maddison, who dedicated an important part of his scientific carrier to this topic. In his opinion:

> Since 1820 one can identify separate phases which have meaningful internal coherence in spite of wide variations in individual country performance within each of them. . . . Phases are identified, in the first instance, by inductive analysis and iterative inspection of empirically measured characteristics. . . . Five phases (1820–1870, 1870–1913, 1913–1950, 1950–1973, and 1973

> onwards) I have identified within the capitalist epoch. . . . It is clear that growth momentum in the first phase (1820–1870) was much faster than that in the merchant . . . epoch; it accelerated somewhat in 1870–1913. 1913–1950 was the period when performance was worst. Extreme shocks struck three times between 1914s and the 1940s. Performance in the unprecedented post-war boom-the golden age, 1950–1973, was also very special in Western Europe and Japan. The nature of the growth process changed sharply after 1973.
>
> (Maddison 2007: 161 and 169)

As for the recent decades characterised by GDP growth rates of non-OECD countries higher than those of OECD ones, Maddison stated that they must be split into two periods because of a reversed configuration of world economy (OECD 2010). In fact, from 1973 to 1990 (an interval that he called 'cautious objectives') the welfare for the citizens of OECD countries improved comparatively due to the fact that the population growth rate in developing economies increased more than that of their GDP. Conversely, from 1990 onwards (a period labelled as 'shifting wealth'), the per-capita GDP growth rate of non-OECD countries was faster than that of OECD economies due to their success in controlling the population growth (see later in this chapter).

The six different periods[3] in the advancement of capitalism identified by Maddison represent phases of 'meaningful internal coherence' and of homogeneous trends in the world economic process revealed by the institutional sets and structural outcome of the capitalist economies. Such coherence and homogeneity in each period can be observed in the following institutions (Maddison 2007: 165):

i. The policies implemented to face the trade-off between the reduction of unemployment and the stability of prices
ii. The system of international payments
iii. The workings of the labour market
iv. The structure and freedom in international trade
v. The degree of liberalisation in international factor movements

The statistic description of the 'driving forces' and the identification of a timeline highlight the moments and different periods of the capitalist evolutionary path, thus enabling the evaluation of the structural transformations of the economy and of the contribution of the single 'long-run dynamic force' to the process.

The structural change of social and material human conditions

An overall view of the advent and progress of capitalism, compared to the pre-industrial society, shows many changes in the socioeconomic environment – i.e. in human social and material conditions. The onwards repositioning of the feeding constraint (which made sustainable population growth) by the production transformations introduced in the countryside opened the way to demographic expansion.

This phenomenon, together with further production and social processes, triggered a general increase in the production of material goods and services. Thus, the expansion of both the population and output determines associated trends in the capitalist dynamics. In any case, both processes are interconnected. On the one hand, the economic upgrading affects the demographic transition by causing a structural change in the variables ruling it (i.e. death and birth rates); on the other hand, the demographic dynamics affects the economic growth rate (regarding the quantity and quality of the labour force – see later in this chapter) and the welfare of everyone by lessening or increasing the amount of goods and services at their disposal.

The level of material welfare of capitalist societies can be seen as the result of the comparative dynamics of demographic and economic processes, in a long-run statistical perspective. As a matter of fact, all other things being equal, when the population growth rate exceeds that of the national income, economic conditions worsen for everyone, whereas when the two growth rates show the opposite trend, an improvement is registered. By and large we expect the latter to occur in all the countries moving forward in all the phases of capitalism's evolution. Table 2.1 confirms that a higher growth rate of the gross domestic product (GDP) with respect to the population growth was recorded in all the countries approaching capitalism in the first two waves of its evolution, with a widening gap between the two indexes during their best economic period (between 1950 and 1973). Similarly, latecomers China and India experienced this trend when their capitalism became irreversible between 1950 and 2001, after showing an inverse relation between the two growth rates in the period between the two World Wars (1913–1950).

Table 2.1 Average annual growth rate of population and GDP during capitalist phases for a group of selected countries

Phase	*1820–1870*		*1870–1913*		*1913–1950*		*1950–1973*		*1974–1990*		*1991–2018*	
Country	*Pop.*	*GDP*	*Pop.*	*GDP*	*Pop.*	*GDP*	*Pop.*	*GDP*	*Pop.*	*GDP*	*Pop.*	*GDP*
UK	0.79	2.05	0.87	1.90	0.25	1.19	0.50	2.93	0.24	2.16	0.53	2.11
USA	2.83	4.20	2.08	3.94	1.21	2.84	1.45	3.93	0.96	3.00	0.97	2.49
France	0.42	1.43	0.18	1.63	0.02	1.15	0.96	5.05	0.53	2.65	0.50	1.46
Germany	0.91	2.00	1.18	2.81	0.13	0.30	0.63	5.68	0.04	2.31	0.15	1.59
Italy	0.63	1.24	0.68	1.94	0.64	1.49	0.66	5.64	0.21	2.93	0.17	0.77
Japan	0.21	0.41	0.95	2.44	1.32	2.21	1.14	9.29	0.78	4.34	0.08	1.00
Russia	0.97	1.61	1.33	2.40	0.38	2.15	1.44	4.84	0.65	–	–0.10	2.28
Brazil	–	–	–	–	–	–	2.82[a]	8.30[b]	2.08	3.85	1.16	2.21
India	0.38	0.38	0.43	0.97	0.45	0.23	2.11	3.54	2.14	4.83	1.56	6.72
China	–0.12	–0.37	0.47	0.56	0.61	–0.02	2.10	5.02	1.56	8.06	0.71	9.63

Sources: For the phases 1820–1870, 1870–1913, 1913–1950 and 1950–1973 author's elaboration of data from Maddison (2003) *The world economy: historical statistics* (except for Brazil); for the phases 1974–1990 and 1991–2018 author's elaboration of data from *World Bank Open Data 2019*.

Notes: [a] period 1951–1973
[b] period 1961–1973

Table 2.2 Average rate of growth of per capita GDP during capitalist phases (%) and per capita GDP values at the end of the periods for a group of selected countries

Phase	*1820–1870*		*1870–1913*		*1913–1950*		*1950–1973*		*1974–1990*		*1991–2018*	
Country	*%*	*Value*[a]	*%*	*Value*[a]	*%*	*Value*[a]	*%*	*Value*[b]	*%*	*Value*[b]	*%*	*Value*[b]
UK	1.26	3190	1.01	4921	0.93	6939	2.42	20319	1.95	28553	1.48	42986
USA	1.34	2445	1.82	5301	1.61	9561	2.45	25794	1.90	36059	1.50	54542
France	1.01	1876	1.45	3485	1.12	5271	4.04	22843	2.17	32524	1.06	43664
Germany	1.08	1839	1.61	3648	0.17	3881	5.02	21903	2.32	32337	1.40	47502
Italy	0.59	1499	1.26	2564	0.85	3502	4.95	19626	2.72	30839	0.42	35392
Japan	0.19	737	1.48	1387	0.88	1921	8.06	22138	3.26	30074	0.91	48920
Russia	0.63	943	1.06	1488	1.76	2841	3.35	6059	–	9550	1.02	11729
Brazil	–	–	–	–	–	–	4.71[c]	6219	1.52	7984	1.19	11026
India	–	533	0.54	673	–0.22	619	1.68[c]	386	2.49	581	4.7	2104
China	–0.25	530	0.10	552	–0.62	439	2.91[c]	254	8.40	729	8.83	7755

Source: Author's elaboration of data from Maddison (2003) *The world economy: historical statistics* for the phases 1820–1870, 1870–1913 and 1913–1950 and from *World Bank Open Data 2019* for the phases 1950–1973 (only data marked with [b] and [c]), 1974–1990 and 1991–2018.

Notes: [a] value in 1990 internationally Geary-Khamis dollars
[b] *value in 2010 constant US$*
[c] *period 1961–1973*

To provide evidence of the improved material welfare conditions when the pace of the population growth is lower than that of the economy the researchers generally use as an indicator the so-called 'income per capita' – a rough and come under fire concept obtained by dividing the annual value of GDP by the population number of each country. Table 2.2 shows a time series of two index numbers depicting the upwards trends of such an indicator. On the one hand, the annual growth rates of the per capita GDP within each phase display positive (or increased) values when economies approached capitalism in their expansionary periods; on the other hand, the monetary values of the per capita GDP in the final year of each historical phase show ever-growing values during the capitalist advance. These two indexes provide evidence of the improved welfare enjoyed by citizens in different economic systems. They also enable the ranking of the latter in each period and the highlighting of some specific moments or trends of the phenomenon: the United States overtaking the UK economy at the end of the 19th century; the catching-up of French, Italian and German economies after World War II; and the undefeated welfare improvement of Japan between 1950 and 1973 and of China in the following phases.

Additional documentary evidence of citizens' improved socioeconomic conditions, which are associated with the demographic transition, is provided by the life expectancy at birth. Such an indicator, defining on average how long a newborn can expect to live given the nutriment conditions, the access to healthcare, the economic situation, lifestyle and death rate, is represented by an index number. The values of such an indicator during the advance of capitalism are shown in Table 2.3.

Table 2.3 Life expectancy at birth during capitalist evolution for a group of selected countries (total average)

Countries	*1820*	*1900*	*1950*	*1973*[a]	*1990*[a]	*2018*[a]
UK	39	50	69	72	76	81
USA	37	47	68	71	75	78
France	41	47	65	72	77	82
Germany	30	47	67	71	75	81
Italy	34	48	66	72	77	83
Japan	–	44	61	74	79	84
Russia	–	–	66[b]	68	69	72
Brazil	21	–	54[b]	60	66	75
India	–	24	32	50	58	69
China	–	24	41	62	69	76

Source: Author's elaboration of data from Maddison (2001) *The world economy. A millennial perspective* and *World Bank Open Data 2019* ([a]).

Note: [b]) *World Bank Open Data 2019*, year 1960

Together with the change in material conditions, important socioeconomic transformations occurred during the progress of capitalism. Following the progressive relocation of job opportunities in urban areas people moved away from the countryside to cities ('internal migration'). This phenomenon – which emerged because of the manpower surplus in agriculture and shortage in industry – caused the factories to become the engine of economies and new sources for jobs. Table 2.4 provides evidence of this process by showing the historical levels of urbanisation (i.e. the percentages of urban residents in the total population) in the sub-periods of emergence and evolution of capitalist economies. It confirms that when France and the USA started their transition towards capitalism with an urban population amounting to around 9–12 per cent of the total inhabitants of their countries, more than one fourth of the UK population (that had already accomplished this phase) was living in towns; this threshold was passed by France and the USA in 1880, together with Germany and Italy. Despite a different world economic environment, China and India also made the same step a century later.

It must be taken into account, however, that in spite of this conformity, 'the urbanisation process in developing countries is occurring more dramatically and rapidly than that in developed countries'.[4] (Chen, Zhang, Liu and Zhang 2014: 11) Furthermore, various countries had different urbanisation speeds, depending on the labour needs of industrial factories, the removal of rural-urban mobility barriers, supportive policies, markets and infrastructure investments, as well as on geography, history, cultural tradition, governmental management and institutional setting. Therefore, the UK maintained its primacy up until 1950, when three-fourths of its population lived in towns, with a slight decrease later; during the same period, the USA and Germany experienced their biggest leap forward, which enabled them to achieve an urbanisation level of nearly two-thirds of their populations. In France, Japan and Italy the urbanisation level was only slightly over 50 per cent, but in the 1970s they caught up with the USA and Germany, arriving at over 70 per cent (except for Italy, which remained below this value until the end of the entire period). At the turn of the century, the USA and Japan were close to the UK's

Table 2.4 Share of urban population over the total population

Country	*1830*[a]	*1880*[a]	*1910*[a]	*1950*[b]	*1973*[c]	*1990*[c]	*2018*[c]
UK	27.5	56.2	69.2	79.0	77.3	78.1	83.4
USA	12.3	35.9	41.6	64.2	73.6	75.3	82.2
France	15.7	27.6	38.5	55.2	72.3	74.1	80.4
Germany	9.1	29.1	48.8	68.1	72.4	73.1	77.3
Italy	19.0	28.0	40.0	54.1	65.2	66.7	70.4
Japan	–	–	–	53.4	74.2	77.3	91.6
Russia	–	–	–	53.7[d]	64.9	73.4	74.4
Brazil	–	–	–	46.1[d]	58.8	73.9	86.6
India	–	–	–	17.0	20.6	25.5	34.3
China	–	–	–	11.8	17.1	26.4	59.1

Source: Author elaboration from

Note: [a]) Bairoch and Goertz (1986) *Urban Studies*, p. 288;
[b]) *UNDESA (2014) World Urbanization Prospects;*
[c]) *World Bank Open Data 2019.*
[d]) *World Bank Open Data 2019, year 1960*

primacy, and nearly three-quarters of the populations in France and Germany were urban, while Italy stopped at 67 per cent.

Structural transformations in production and consumption

Together with the socioeconomic transformations, capitalism's dynamics evidenced a continuous restructuring of production plants, changed consumption patterns and a reshuffling of the economic players' roles. As for the first item, the emergence of new production processes and the introduction of new products and services had an influence on the general basic trends of capitalism's evolution, thus causing a continuous growth and qualitative restructuring of the total manufacturing capacity. In this process the quantitative restructuring of production sectors emerged as a consequence of the different growth rates of the output of new productions compared to old ones. The expansion in production and diversified sectoral dynamics changed the sectoral contribution to the gross domestic product, as the case of the agricultural sector shows (see Table 2.5). Despite the increased output and two production revolutions agriculture reduced its share of the GDP to insignificant percentages in all capitalist countries (with the exception of India and China). This shift from approximately 40 per cent (except for Italy) to 1–3 per cent in continental Europe and Japan between the end of the 19th century and now is the result of the two aforementioned historical trends. On the one hand, there was less radical technical progress after the high rates of innovation recorded during the introduction of new farming methods coming from the 'British' and 'green' revolutions and the industrialisation of all the processes of transformation of agricultural products; on the other hand, the proportion of agricultural food in consumers' total spending was lower while personal incomes increased (the so-called 'Engel's law', 1854 – see Leon 1967). This does not mean that agriculture has been a backward sector but that the speed of growth

Table 2.5 Contribution to the GDP (in %) of some productive sectors

Country	*Sector*	*1820*	*1870*	*1913*	*1950*	*1973*	*1990*	*2017*
UK	*A*	26	15	6	5	3	2	1
	I	32	40	38	47	44	30	19
	T&C	16	23	10	9	8	8	7
	C	–	–	19	13	11	14	26
	O	–	–	*27*	*26*	*34*	*46*	47
USA	*A*	–	21	17	6	3	3	1[b]
	I	–	21	27	39	34	30	18[b]
	T&C	–	12	11	8	6	7	9 [b]
	*C**	–	27	31	26	31	34	32 [b]
	O	–	19	14	*21*	*26*	*26*	40[b]
France	*A*	43	41	32	13	6	2	2
	I	40	33	41	48	38	28	17
	T&C	3	6	7	6	5	6	5
	C	11	16	20	12	13	16	18
	O	3	4	0	21	38	48	58
Germany	*A*	–	38	23	10	3	1	1
	I	–	32	44	51	48	32	28
	T&C	–	2	6	7	6	6	4
	C	–	8	9	13	11	–	16
	O	–	*20*	*18*	*19*	*32*	61	51
Italy	*A*	–	58	44	30	8	3	2
	I	–	19	24	37	43	30	24
	T&C	–	2	6	7	6	7	15
	C	–	16	16	14	16	18	12
	O	–	*5*	*10*	*12*	*27*	*42*	47
Japan	*A*	–	41[a]	30	23	6	1	1
	I	–	10	20	30	46	40	29
	T&C	–	1	6	8	6	6	6
	C	–	45	41	37	12	13	13
	O	–	3	3	2	30	40	51
India	*A*	–	–	60	49	41	28	18
	I	–	–	–	17	21	28	30
	T&C	–	–	–	17	4	7	9
	C	–	–	–	–	8	12	16
	O	–	–	–	17	26	25	27
China	*A*	–	–	–	–	39	29	7
	I	–	–	–	–	47	55	41
	T&C	–	–	–	–	10	5	–
	C	–	–	–	–	4	10	–
	O	–	–	–	–	0	1	52

Source: Author's elaboration of data from Palgrave Macmillan (2013) *International Historical Statistics* and other specified sources, US Department of Commerce (2018) and Italian Ufficio studi Confcommercio (2017).

Notes: Yearly average over five (sometimes ten) years

A: agriculture, forestry and fisheries; I: manufacturing, mining and construction; T&C: transport and communication; C: commerce (excluding financial and other services); C*: commerce and financial services

[a] 1885–89; [b] 2018

of the agricultural output is lower because of both technological progress and the relative dynamics of the demand for its products (Pasinetti 1981).

In the recent past the industry experienced the segmentation of its production processes into more separated firms, in particular the parting of the services previously connected to the factory processes; this created the reduction of the industrial dimension and an increasing growth rate of the service sectors. The contribution of the industry to the GDP increased without stopping up until 1950 in Germany, France and the UK, arriving at a share of around 50 per cent. Japan and Italy also continued to expand their industry between 1950 and 1973, but the maximum contribution of industry to their GDP stopped at 46 per cent and 43 per cent, respectively. Also, the USA showed the highest industrial contribution to the GDP in 1950, but with only up to 39 per cent; this percentage then decreased, as it did in all the countries. Early in the 21st century, all the highest-income countries aligned their industrial shares at around 30 per cent of their GDP, while both China and India were going through their growing periods (51per cent and 24 per cent, respectively).

While the contribution of industry to the GDP in advanced economies has had an inverted parabolic trend (because it increased and then, at the beginning of the 21st century, dropped to a value similar to that recorded at the advent of capitalism), the share of services has increased for the entire period considered in this analysis. Not only the separation of some service activities from industrial and agricultural firms which had formerly performed them but also the production of new services and a higher sectoral growth rate are supporting this trend. Generally speaking, this macro sector includes transportation, communication and commerce as well as financial activities and some other services not specified in Table 2.5. Considering that, by definition, the kinds of productions from the point of view of the nature of the transformation are three (agriculture, industry, and services – see Chapter Six), the contribution of services to the GDP can be estimated by the difference at nearly 67 per cent in all countries at the end of the 20th century (excluding China and India).

A second important change in the structure of the capitalist economy, experienced during its advance, is the transformation of consumption patterns. The expansion and diversification of productions brought a continuous increase of goods and services to be sold on markets. Thus, an equivalent increase in consumption corresponded to this quantitative and qualitative production growth. This means that the purchasing power (the real wage) of workers in evolving economies has grown to enable them to buy all the goods produced (or a part, in the case of exports). This trend was implicitly referred to above when discussing the increased welfare in the evolution of capitalism, but a further explicit verification can explain the scale of this phenomenon. 'In most historical studies, the real wage – the purchasing power – of an unskilled male labourer in the building industry is calculated to gauge trends in well-being within one country'. [As a proxy of such an indicator, some researchers proposed an index measuring] 'the number of times an unskilled building labourer is able to purchase the minimum required subsistence basket' (de Zwart, van Leeuwen and van Leeuwen-Li 2014: 75) of goods and services, with his wage. Table 2.6 provides evidence of the increased purchasing power of workers in the dynamics of capitalism, as real wages in their countries rose by 6–12 times, a range that is confirmed if the appraisal

Table 2.6 Number of subsistence baskets that a daily wage of building labourers buys (decade average)

Country	*1820*	*1870*	*1910*	*1950*	*1970*	*2000*
UK	16	21	23	36	62	167
USA	–	–	73[a]	103	173	209
France	17	16	27	12	31	–
Germany	10	13	27	23	72	140[b]
Italy	4	4	9	13	43	114
Japan	4	–	7	7	27	45
India	–	3	4	7	3	7
China	3	3	4	5	18	22[b]

Source: Author's elaboration from de Zwart, van Leeuwen and van Leeuwen-Li (2014), 'Real wages since 1820'.

Notes: [a]1920; [b]1990

in each country is made also considering the trend of the per-capita GDP (see Table 2.2). Apart from the performance of each country, it is noteworthy that, alongside the dynamics of capitalism, the increase in production has been flanked by an equal increase in the workers' purchasing power. This made it possible for the value of the output produced to be repaid by an equal value of consumption.

In a capitalist economy, however, the demand for goods and services is not originated only by household consumers; in fact, there are also firms requiring intermediate goods, machinery and raw materials as well as the public administration of the country and consumers and firms from other economic systems. Thus, if the rise in workers' purchasing power increasingly shifted the production towards consumer goods (whose share grew higher and higher), the new export markets made it possible to add a foreign demand to the household demand. As a matter of fact, an increased output sold abroad (export) is another important trend in the progress of capitalist economies; its origin is due to the agreements signed as part of the international relations among countries. For this reason, it will be dealt with later in the third part of the book.

Another important change in the evolution of capitalism is the reshuffling of economic players' roles and, in particular, the growing role of the government. While this topic is postponed to a later discussion (Chapter Five) it can be highlighted that 'in 1820 government spending was typically less than 10 per cent of GDP, but the proportion is now much bigger. In the advanced capitalist countries, governments intervene on a massive scale to operate a vast network of social transfers, which change the distribution of income and the pattern of private spending. Total government spending (including transfers) in our 16 countries is now nearly half of GDP' (Maddison 2007: 160).

The 'long-run dynamic forces' enabling the evolution of capitalism

'Long-run dynamic forces' are the boosting factors that triggered and sustained the dynamics of capitalism from the moment of its emergence. Although it is not possible to establish or calculate a direct causal effect between these elements and the outcome of economies, some convincing relations can nevertheless be identified. Some researchers have traced such forces in the demographic structure, the use of increasing amounts of natural, financial and physical capitals (encompassing technological and organisational progress) in the production process, and the institutional change involving both technical and social rules. All these 'long-run dynamic forces' were driving forces in the evolution of capitalism, and as such they also supported its strengthening, brought about its outcome and shaped its path (Bassanini and Scarpetta 2001).

The demographic sources of capitalism's dynamics

The comparative analysis of the interplayed dynamics of demography and economy presented above is an ex-post statistical result, which is ineffective in highlighting the contribution of demography to the advent and strengthening of capitalism. This kind of relation has been carefully investigated by demographers and economists, who have discussed the effects produced by quantitative and structural changes in population (the so-called 'demographic transition' – Caldwell 1976; Lee 2003) on capitalist economies along with their evolution. The most interesting discussions on this subject are those concerning the 'demographic dividend' (i.e. the extra source of economic growth emerging thanks to a population age structure where the cohorts of the labour force exceed those of youth and retired people – Bloom, Canning and Sevilla 2002), 'the case for immigration in developed countries' (due to the an amount of retiring people greater than that of the new entries in the labour market due to the ageing population – OECD May 2014) and the policies necessary to deal with them.

In discussing these topics, researchers refer to the 'human capital' as a demographic 'long-run dynamic force' affecting capitalism's evolution. Such an indicator first takes into account the size of the labour force (which makes it possible to measure the total work provided by the population to the economy) and its characteristics (providing information about its quality – i.e. the knowledge, abilities, aptitude, competences, practice). As for the amount of work there is historical evidence that economies implementing capitalism increased the worktime for workers. In effect, in traditional agriculture there was underemployment of the family members in relation to the land to be cultivated, and the worktime was discontinuous and staggered according to the weather and soil conditions. Other than that:

> before capitalism, most people did not work very long hours at all. The tempo of life was slow, even leisurely; the pace of work relaxed. . . . A thirteenth-century esteem finds that whole peasant families did not put in more than 150 days per year on their land. Manorial records from fourteenth-century England indicate an extremely short working year – 175 day – for servile laborers. Later evidence for farmer-miners, a group with control over their worktime, indicates they worked only 180 days a year.
>
> (Schor 1993)

Table 2.7 Annual and weekly hours worked per person employed in selected countries

Country	*1870*		*1913*		*1950*		*1973*	*1970*	*1998*	*2000*
	Annual	*Weekly*	*Annual*	*Weekly*	*Annual*	*Weekly*	*Annual*	*Weekly*	*Annual*	*Weekly*
UK	2,984	56.9	2,624	56	1,958	45.7	1,688	42	1,489	40.4
USA	2,964	62	2,605	58	1,867	42.4	1,717	38.8	1,610	40.2
France	2,945	66.1	2,588	62	1,926	44.8	1,771	44.8	1,503	35.7
Germany	2,841	67.6	2,584	57	2,316	48.2	1,804	43.8	1,523	39.9
Italy	2,886	63.3	2,536	62.4	1,997	47.8	1,612	42.9	1,506	38.4
Japan	2,945	–	2,588	–	2,166	–	2,042	–	1,758	–

Source: Author's elaboration of data from Maddison (2001) *The world economy. A millennial perspective* and from Huberman and Minns (2007) 'The times they are not changing': days and hours of work in Old and New Worlds, 1870–2000'.

Conversely, the advent of the industrial society increased the people's working time to such an extent that in around 1870 it arrived at about 280–300 days, with the worked hours per person employed in industrialising economies totalling between 2,840 and 2,965 (see Table 2.7). Starting from the early twentieth century the annual workload decreased mainly because of a reduction in the number of working days, and this trend continued until the weekly work fell below the threshold of 50 hours in the 1950s.[5] At the end of the 20th century Western and Japanese economies reached a weekly workload of between 40 (in the UK and USA) and 35 (in France) hours, thanks to technological progress and the new, more favourable labour laws.

As for the quality of the human capital – i.e. the knowledge and the skills of workers – the debate among historians highlighted that two interacting learning processes took part in promoting the technological advance during capitalism's progress: training and education. The first process was prevalent in triggering the industrial revolution because:

> eighteenth century Britain did have a cadre of highly skilled technicians and mechanics, almost all of them trained in the apprenticeship system rather than in formal academies, and these contributed materially to its technological development. The Continent, too, had its share of skilled and well-trained craftsmen'. . . . The job learning process was led by a supervisor or an experienced employee who, through a demonstration to trainees, transmitted knowledge on how to perform particular tasks or working procedures, and 'naturally gifted mechanics would teach themselves from whatever source was available as much as learn from their masters.
>
> (Mokyr 2005: 44)

The prevalence of training was due to the fact that the factory system needed 'human capital . . . instrumental in creating competence rather than useful knowledge itself, in teaching how to carry out instructions rather than writing them' (Mokyr 2005: 48). 'Over the 19th century, the importance of advantages in competence (tacit skills and dexterity) declined, and that of formal codified useful knowledge increased, eroding the advantages Britain may have had through its skilled craftsmen that other nations envied and coveted in the years before 1815' (Mokyr 2005: 47). This phenomenon increased the importance of education for the training as a provider of requirements, easing the 'learning by doing' process. In fact, 'the form of schooling that emerged in the 19th century generates specific cognitive, behavioural and social knowledge that are critical ingredients for the way industrial societies organize production and consumption, daily life in cities and nations, the size and fitness of the population for work, the creation and use of knowledge' (CISCO System 2007).

Assessing the contribution of training to technological advancement is difficult not only because it is impossible to quantify such expertise but also because it is used in production processes in combination with natural capitals (or raw materials) and/or physical capitals (or tools). The same applies to the knowledge possessed by the worker. Nevertheless, to assess how demography is acting as a 'long-run dynamic force' for capitalism's development, education is used as a proxy. The importance of schooling in the dynamics of capitalism is shown in Table 2.8, where there are two index numbers measuring the literacy rate of the total population and the average years of education of people living in upgrading economies. Some trends emerge from the comparison of the values of the two indexes in specific periods. First, it is evident that a high level of literacy at the beginning of the transition path between traditional societies and capitalism in specific situations (see the case of Germany between 1870 and 1910) supported an improvement of schooling, leading, in turn, to scientific progress. Second, the periods of high economic growth corresponded to a great increase in the average number of years of education (as shown by France and the UK between 1870 and 1910; Japan, Germany and the UK between 1950 and 1970; and Italy, China, Japan and India between 1970 and 2001). Lastly, the data show a catching-up process in the levels of schooling for the most dynamic economies (as the average years of education show in 2001).

Table 2.8 Literacy rate (% of total population) and average years of education for a group of selected countries

Phase	*1870*		*1910*		*1950*		*1970*		*2003*	*2000*
Country	*L r*	*Years*	*L r*	*Years*	*L r*	*Years*	*L r*	*Years*	*L r*	*Years*
UK	76	3.6	85[a]	5.9	90[a]	7.7	93[a]	10.2	99	13.1
USA	80	5.6	92	7.5	98	9.6	98	11.1	99	13.0
France	69	4.1	78[a]	7.0	87[a]	8.1	91[a]	10.0	99	11.8
Germany	67[a]	5.4	77[a]	7.0	85[a]	8.5	91[a]	11.1	99	12.9
Italy	32	0.8	53[a]	2.8	75[a]	5.0	81[a]	6.6	99	10.3
Japan	–	1.0	–	2.9	–	6.8	–	10.1	–	12.7
India	–	0.1	–	0.4	–	1.6	41[c]	2.0	61	4.5
China	–	1.0	–	1.2	–	1.7	65[d]	3.3	91	6.9

Source: Author's elaboration of data from Roser and Ortiz-Ospina (2017) *Literacy*, and from van Leeuwen and van Leeuwen-Li (2014) 'Education since 1820'.

Notes: [a] estimated data; [b] 1982; [c] 1981

The capitals triggering the advent and dynamics of capitalism

As previously mentioned, the labour force reveals its creative potential through the working time and levels of education and training, but it originates the production transformation in both agriculture, industry and services only in conjunction with raw materials and the service of the machinery; the last ones, in turn, display their productive capacities via their bulk and the technological progress they encompass. The financial resources, instead, providing the money necessary for the 'capital outlay' and the 'floating capital', make possible both the implementation of productive economic activities and their ordinary management – in short, just the production process. Thus, they can be considered 'long-run dynamic forces' whose contribution is essential for understanding the dynamics of capitalism.

The natural capitals considered here are the raw materials employed in the production processes in use when capitalism emerged and spread throughout different countries: land, minerals, rocks, gas, water, fossil fuels and timber. The assessment of their importance is feasible only by inductive reasoning because of both the shortage of statistical data and the impossibility of measuring the causal relationship between them and capitalism's evolution. For example, historians also disagree on the role played by coal in bringing about British industrialisation, but all they agree on its importance in driving the country's technological advance. Therefore, at this point of the analysis, it does not matter if the contribution made by specific abundant minerals was necessary to trigger the industrial revolution or if countries well endowed with natural resources performed better in transforming their economies than those without them. Nor does it matter if 'resource abundance' refers to either a geological endowment or a greater exploitation of a geological potential.[6] What is important is an assessment of whether the countries approaching and strengthening capitalism could count on the domestic availability of essential raw materials for their productions at that time.

As for the availability of natural capitals the historical evidence shows that during the British transition to capitalism a large amount of cropland was made ready for use thanks to the 'enclosures' that triggered together with other elements the English agricultural revolution. Even more, during the Industrial Revolution British factories had huge amounts of domestic iron, non-ferrous metals (copper, zinc, lead), whale oil and especially coal, the use of which was extended to heating because of timber shortage. With regard to the United States, Wright argues that 'the abundance of industrial minerals was a deeper cause of American industry's distinctive strength', so much so that US manufacturing production was intensive in natural resources between 1879 and 1940, while the US economy was, by a wide margin, the world leader in the production of natural resources (Wright 1990: 666–7). This leadership of the US in the possession of stockpiles of minerals for upgrading the economy (i.e. in their production, exports and home consumption) on the eve of World War I is confirmed in Table 2.9. A similar position (in some cases thanks to imports) for some of the minerals presented in this Table is also shown for UK, Germany and France. In addition the production of those countries was concentrated just on copper, coal, zinc, iron ore, lead and other minerals that were at the core of the industrial technology when they started and hastened their

Table 2.9 Production (P), trade balance (exports X minus imports M) and home consumption C of coal and copper (1913), iron, steel and lead (1920) by industrialised countries

	Coal[b]			*Coppera*	*Iron and steel*[b]			*Lead*[a]		
Countries	*P*	*X-M*	*C*	*P*	*P*	*X-M*	*C*	*P*	*X-M*	*C*
UK	287.4	73.4	214.0	214.0	29.8	–6.1	–6.1	23,421	–97,217	120,638
USA	508.9	20.7	488.2	546,644	147.0	0.1	146.9	891,783	–55,464	947247
France	40.2	–17.3	57.5	–	20.1	4.5	15.6	16,100	–82,052	98.152
Germany	274.3	23.7	250.6	24,902	18.4	–5.7	24.1	102,000	–6306	108,306
Italy	0.7	–10.7	11.4	2,917	1.2	–0.2	1.4	37,604	8,460	29,144
Japan	21.0	3.8	17.2	66,822	0.7	–1.0	1.7	4,093	–20,992	24,504

Source: Author's elaboration of data from Imperial Institute Mineral Resources Department (1925) *The Mineral Industry of the British Empire and Foreign Countries*: 16–17; 19; 112–32.

Notes: [a]) in long (British) tons; [b]) in millions of long (British) tons

process of transition. Lastly, it is important to note that, in the absence of available natural resources, the German, Italian and Japanese economies improved their exploitation of the scarce minerals produced and drove technological advances. Ultimately, 'coal-rich Britain focused on Newcomen engines, while coal-poor Switzerland found economic success in precision-intensive low-energy industries such as watchmaking and engineering' (Mokyr 1999: 22).

'Physical capitals' are tangible instrumental assets used as production inputs which are suitable for more than one production process (tools, machinery, vehicles and buildings, for example). From the technical standpoint, their function is to help the worker in production operations by speeding up or improving performance. Their contribution to the production transformation consists of an amount of machine service equalling the time necessary to perform the production tasks. Their qualitative characteristics (or technical specifications) are expressed through the level of technological progress with which they are endowed – i.e. through the speed and the accuracy with which they perform one or more production operations. From the economic standpoint, their use increases the number of tasks carried out by workers per unit of time, thus decreasing the production cost and product price, which makes the goods or services available to a greater number of customers. Moreover, the application of 'machine tools' to the production is a powerful channel for disseminating the technological progress from production to consumption. For all these reasons, physical capitals can be considered 'long-run dynamic forces' contributing to the advent and evolution of capitalism.

The contribution of physical capitals to capitalism's progress can also be measured to attempt to detect their overall effects on the economy, although this is a very difficult task. As the physical capitals used for production improve workers' performance, it would be easier to measure their effects on the output per unit of labour rather than per unit of hour worked.[7] Nevertheless due to statistical data, Table 2.10 shows the constant dollar value of labour productivity per hour worked in selected countries at the turning points of capitalism's advance. As expected, this

Table 2.10 Value of the labour productivity in selected countries (GDP per hour worked in 1990 international $)

Country	*1870*	*1913*	*1950*	*1973*	*1998*
UK	2.55	4.31	7.93	15.97	27.45
USA	2.25	5.12	12.65	23.72	34.55
France	1.38	2.88	5.82	18.02	33.72
Germany	1.55	3.03	3.99	14.76	26.56
Italy	1.05	2.13	4.38	15.92	27.90
Japan	0.46	1.08	2.08	11.57	22.54

Source: Author's elaboration of data from Maddison (2001) *The world economy. A millennial perspective*.

index number shows increasing values for each country during the period but with different growth rates. In fact, the growth rate of the productivity (which can be calculated as the difference between two consecutive values) reached nearly 100 per cent between 1870 and 1913 and between 1913 and 1950 (excluding Germany). Later it was between almost 2 and 5.5 times in the post–World War II period and almost 1.8 times (excluding the USA) in the last quarter of the 19th century.

The infrastructures are constituted by all the basic facilities that enable the development of the economic activities or that accelerate it. In the category are generally included ports, transport systems, telecommunication systems and utility distribution systems (electricity, water and gas). These facilities have represented a basic 'long-run dynamic force' in all the phases of the capitalist evolution because they are the framework bearing the production, consumption and exchange of the capitalist economy. In fact, the ports and the railways widened the markets and enabled the provision of raw materials for the industry of all the newly born capitalist economies, while the utility distribution systems supported the urbanisation of the industrial towns and the technological upgrading of the factories. The telecommunication system facilitated the transport and the information in both the phases of the capitalist evolution, but particularly in the actual one where its contribution to the GDP is near a half of the value.

Financial resources can be considered a 'long-run dynamic force' essential for both the success and the evolution of the capitalist economy because they are the assets by which the production investments and the management of the activity are carried out. There has been a long debate among economists on the 'primitive accumulation of capital' since it appeared initially as a precondition for the establishment of the industry; Smith ascribed it to the diligent labour of some among the workers who gradually built their wealth, while Marx charged it with the violent expropriation pursuant the enslavement, colonialism and accumulation of land (like the enclosures). As much as the creation of personal prosperity could have supported the establishment of the industry in some cases, the historical stylised facts show alternative sources of financing, and complex and varied supply experiences. In general, the kind of financial resources used to trigger industrialisation depended on the period in which the process started, thus on the stage of evolution of the banking system both in the industrialising country and in the other industrialised economies. In fact, in 18th-century England the entrepreneur could resort to his savings to create a factory because the fixed capital needed wasn't large:

> In prosperous days the building of mills for lease to one or more tenants was a profitable way of investing. Large landlords were especially active, but merchants, manufacturers, and others who had money to spare turned it into bricks, mortar, and machinery, and then sought tenants among 'persons desirous of commencing the woollen or worsted business with a small outlay of capital'. . . . A greater 'load was the need for large sums of operating capital, or "floating capital" as the bookkeepers called it'. . . . 'Bank loans might help to bridge the gap in time between outgo and income, but the firm must have some working capital of its own and must relate the scale of its operations to the amount of that capital'. Otherwise 'the merchants made a more important contribution; they supplied funds to some producer whose goods they were handling, or went into partnership, as in the case of Arkwright, Boulton, and Wedgwood; or they went into the new form of production themselves, as in the case of Benjamin Gott and some of his fellow cloth-merchants in Leeds, or of David Dale and his fellow Glasgow traders. Private bankers helped less. Like their joint stock descendants, they were commercial bankers, not investment houses'.
>
> (Heaton 1937: 3, 4, 5)

The contribution of saving to the industrialisation of England in the second half of the 18th century amounted to two-thirds of the capital necessary, but the residue consisted in foreign funds coming mainly from the Netherlands; thus, Britain borrowed when it was developing and then lent in the following century (Brezis 1995).

In the United States the financial driver for creating factories and supporting them by infrastructures came from the states. Although the US Congress in 1791 granted the Alexander Hamilton bank with a 20-year national charter to provide emerging entrepreneurs with financial support, only the state governments in the second decade of the 19th century created 200 banks equipped with special privileges to continue and expand the credit locally. Such an exceptional instrument was used when the transport infrastructures appeared necessary to support the growing factories. 'Road, bridge, and especially canal building was an expensive venture, but most state politicians supported using government-granted legal privileges and funds to help create the infrastructure that would stimulate economic development' (ushistory.org March 16, 2023). The situation changed in the middle of the century because the big companies borrowed funds from banks to create their factories and sold shares or bonds on exchange markets to finance their activities, just when the citizens shifted their saving preferences from physical assets to securities; an example of such a mechanism to implement and sustain the entrepreneurial activities has been the railroad companies (Laughlin 2012: 50).

In Continental Europe the financial resources for implementing the industrialisation come from different sources compared to the experience of Britain and the USA. When the process started some management companies, sponsored by the states, were created to finance infrastructure building (railroads, for example), whose shareholders were private banks. Instead, to finance the entrepreneurial activities already started in France, there were credit and investment banks up to 1870, but thenceforth the deposit banks were separated from the business banks that lent to the firms. In Germany, Belgium, Austria and Italy, instead, emerged and strengthened banks that were credit and investment banks as well as financial institutions maintaining relationships with foreign banks. These 'mixed banks' were authorised both to open deposits for people's savings and to loan long run to industrial companies. They also could own shares of the financed companies so that their deposit activity was instrumental to the investments' financing. Considering the derivation of financial capital used in Italy to finance industrial investment, an important part were foreign direct investments (FDI) of European industrial companies building factories in the country, and another part came through the national bank relations with the corresponding German and British ones (Segreto 2009: 186–96).

The financing of the industrialisation in Japan was more complex because the state was an active player in this process. 'Meiji Japan [from 1870 onwards] did not welcome FDI or foreign loans for industrialisation, except for the public-sector borrowing [in the form of public bond issuing] in late Meiji for the purpose of war execution and Postwar Management . . . [and of railway construction]. Initially, as a matter of principle, the government rejected the incurring of external liabilities for fear of foreign control. This was in sharp contrast to other latecomers, such as Russia and Italy' (Ohno 2018: 79). The agricultural sector represented instead an important source for financing public investments in infrastructures and subsidies to the industry via land taxes; in fact, such a duty represented in the period more than 40 per cent of the value of the investments in the industry. The most important source of the financial capital for industrial investments came from the private non-agricultural savings – that is, from retained earnings, resources of businessmen and merchants and family savings; such resources were directed to the investment through self-finance, collected funds and specific joint stock companies.

The institutional 'forces' enabling the capitalist dynamics

As mentioned earlier, the capitalist evolution underwent a continuous change within the institutional framework to deal with and support the transformations of the economy. This institutional change concerned all kinds of rules governing economic activities: the operating procedures implemented in the structuring of the organisations responsible for the production and trade of goods and services and in the realisation of the production process; the regulatory framework laid down by the state for the performance of economic activities (i.e. corporate law, contract law, etc.); and the rules to be followed by people when performing economic activities (such as behavioural principles). The importance of new institutions to enable the introduction and rooting of capitalist economy has been discussed in Chapter One when speaking of production techniques, organisations, property and markets laws, and social habits, but the role of institutions in the strengthening and upgrading of the new economic system must be further investigated to show how they acted as 'long-run dynamic forces'.

The inspection of the way by which the techno-organisational procedures supported the new economic system pivots on the workings of the firms. The technological advance of firms moves forward through innovations – i.e. activities which can be classified as product innovations, process innovations, organisational innovations and marketing innovations. With a new product the innovative activity consists of either a new planning routine (combining knowledge, technology, and design) or a rearrangement of the elements in the current one. Process innovation gives rise to significantly improved methods of production and/or delivery through changes in techniques and equipment; 'organizational innovation is the implementation of a new organizational method in the firm's business practices, workplace arrangement or external relations' (OECD 2005: 51). Marketing innovation consists of the implementation of a new model of promotion and placement for products or services. All these improvements, which entail the transformation of operating methods, are institutional changes in the production and supply system, which make it possible to reduce prices, increase output and improve products and services.

The mentioned virtuous effects obtained through the change of techno-organisational procedures enable the firms both to stabilise their market position and upgrade the economic system. Thus, such institutions act as long-run dynamic forces driving the capitalist advance by stimulating additional technological improvements in the economies that first introduced capitalism and then later spreading to the traditional economies as they transitioned towards capitalism. With regard to the first phenomenon, Bruland and Mowert say that innovations:

> [first] gave 'rise to new corporate forms. Second, these new corporate structures helped to transform the character of the innovation process itself, laying the foundations for the development of organized research and development in industries, universities and government. Third, technological innovation had a powerful impact on the structure of capitalism, enhancing the role of government and changing the relations between firms and States'.
>
> (Bruland and Mowert 2014: 83)

As for the expansion of technological progress beyond capitalist countries, its spread was promoted by the export of new products toward the economies that were unable to produce such goods and, later, by the export of the machinery and techniques used to produce them.

It is difficult to list the new techno-organisational institutions established in the different phases of the capitalist dynamics because every new product or service put into production entailed the implementation of a new planning routine, a new technique of production and a new process innovation. Also, each routine was changed whenever a new general-purpose technology implemented some process innovations or when a new method for the optimisation of production processes was introduced (just-in-time production, Toyota production system, etc.). Similarly, the introduction of different 'organisational structures' by the firm (bureaucratic, functional, divisional, matrix) produced a change in the setup, performance and monitoring of an established sequence of tasks ('workflow management systems'), as did the emergence of new relations with customers.

The second group of institutions acting as long-run dynamic forces involves the regulatory framework laid down by the state to support economic activities during capitalism's emergence and evolution. Since capitalism introduced new forms of organisation for producing and trading goods and services (firms and markets, respectively), the focus of the analysis is on the 'legal norms' regulating the creation and operation of these structures. In this respect it must be said that the emergence of capitalism in agriculture was facilitated by the state's regulatory framework, which released the estates from the exclusive control of the old classes and included those properties among the freedom rights that could be enjoyed by the citizens in the landowners' class. Thus, lands could be registered in a public cadastre as private properties (Harris 2014: 136–7), thanks to the legal regulations that governed the purchase, availability and transfer of such properties. This environment made possible not only the restructuring of agriculture but also the creation of the real-estate market and the use of such capitals as collateral for mortgages and loans. Conversely, 'the distinctive phase of the industrial economy, that is the creation of new wealth through the production, was run inside of an empty legal space up to the late 19th century. It was only ruled through the routines dictated by the technological progress and by the capital investments' as well as by the traditional types of commercial unincorporated companies, such as general and limited partnerships. 'The industrial entrepreneur was conceived as a merchant who purchased and sold goods, although she was performing a transformation activity' (Galgano 2005: 46). Up to that period, the trading phases connected to production were also subject to private regulations and expressly to the traditional 'lex mercatoria', a medieval code of professional conduct created by the trade guilds and implemented by nearly all European merchants.

State support to trade activities (and thus also to those of the entrepreneur) was granted with the deregulation of the contract introduced in civil codes (Harris 2014: 133–5). In the mid-18th century freedom of contract and contract enforcement were introduced into the legal system of industrialising states. With these new provisions private economic beings could create new forms of contract, whose obligations were legally binding for the contracting parties and, later, for all the economic players involved once the said new contract forms were introduced into commercial codes.

> The economic and social effects of this transformation are disputed. While some historians believe that it enabled a release of the entrepreneurial energy, the expansion of the market, a more efficient allocation of resources and economic growth, other view it as distributive, allowing the rising industrial capitalists to subsidize their activities and transfer wealth in their pockets at the expense of landowners and laborers.
>
> (Harris 2014: 135)

The full support of the regulatory framework of the state to the capitalist advance was granted when, at the end of the 19th century, commercial codes appeared on the scene. These put under state protection the production and commercial phases of the economy by transforming a professional code (the 'lex mercatoria') into a state code endorsing and regulating all business activities. The focus of this code shifted from property and the enjoyment of estates to contracts that enabled creating and adding value to the goods (Galgano 1976: 79–86). Within this framework, an important institutional change was corporation law.

Another important stage of the state support to capitalist economy was highlighted by Polanyi, whose perspective leads to the interaction and reciprocal support between the political and the economic spheres of social activities:

> Nineteenth century civilization rested on four institutions. The first was the balance-of-power system which for a century prevented the occurrence of any long and devastating war between the Great Powers. The second was the international gold standard which symbolized a unique organization of world economy. The third was the self-regulating market which produced an unheard-of material welfare. The fourth was the liberal state. Classified in one way, two of these institutions were economic, two political. Classified in another way, two of them were national, two internationals. Between them they determined the characteristic outlines of the history of our civilization.
>
> (Polanyi 1944: 2)

Just like every rule respected by people in doing their social activities is an institution, so are economic behaviours, and as every human behaviour performed by instinct is subordinated to social control to adjust it to public interest, so are economic behaviours. Thus, all the economic behaviour principles, even though linked to spontaneous deed, are institutions under the influence and control of the socioeconomic system where they are implemented. Being that capitalism was a new socioeconomic system empowering people and forcing them to make a lot of economic choices to survive, the economic behaviour principles that resulted, encouraged in such a framework, have been those related to his assets and domain: 'self-interest' and 'aptitude to exchange'.

'Self-interest' is a propensity to use efficiently (and thus profitably) the property owned by people carrying out production activities. Such a result can be achieved, in organising and accomplishing the production process, via compliance to personal basic rules of conduct like the attainment of the minimum cost of product or service units or the maximum return for the entrepreneurial activity (measured by profit, revenue or stock value). 'Aptitude to exchange' is the ability of the economic subject to obtain better conditions of welfare or of productive resource provision by contracting in the markets. Using this instrument it is possible to take possession of what is needed by giving up an equivalent, by implementing rules of conduct like the attainment of 'transaction/information cost minimisation'. Both 'self-interest' and 'aptitude to the exchange' can be considered 'long-run dynamic forces' supporting the capitalist advance because they facilitated the efficient development of firm management and market bargaining from the ground thanks to a widespread dissemination of positive practises for the evolution of capitalism.

Concluding remarks: Structural change as the dynamics of capitalist economies

The analysis of the evolutionary process characterising capitalism, taken forward in the chapter, comes to some conclusions: that capitalist economies present their dynamics as an intrinsic feature; that such a motion results from the action of forces outside and inside it (respectively demographic trends and political support on one hand and the disposal of natural, physical, financial and human capitals as well as of appropriate institutions on the other hand); that the patterns of change and upgrading produced by the driving forces lead to the structural transformation of economies.

Such features of capitalism are important for the identification of the methodology to be used in studying modern economies because they enable the listing of some cornerstones from which to start. As environmental conditions played an important role in upgrading capitalist economy, the historical and politico-institutional conditions matter it its analysis; in particular the degree of coevolution between economic, political and social spheres can sustain or prevent the achievement of economic aims. Given that the capitalist advance has been characterised by structural transformations of the economies, its evolutionary path can be represented only by an irregular course sketched in all the phases by the long-run driving forces.

In addition, some important consequences for economic theorising also emerge as a result of the analysis carried out in the chapter. Development and growth are economically different processes that cannot be managed by the same policies, inner drivers are important (in different ways) for both the processes and the capitalist advance also results in a continuous repositioning of economic organisations (firms, the state and national economies) as well as of economic players (workers, consumers, entrepreneurs).

Thus, to study the problem of modern economy, economics must take into consideration all the conclusions just highlighted.

Notes

1 The outcome of an economy in a current year, for example, can be expressed by an indicator named gross domestic product that, in turn, can be measured by different index numbers: GDP at current prices, GDP at constant prices, GDP at purchasing power parity, GDP related to the value recorded by the economy in a previous year taken equal to 100.

2 Acronym to define a group of five countries: Brazil, Russia, India, China and South Africa.

3 This time partition is an inductive result of the historical inspection aiming at distinguishing different periods inside capitalist evolution. These periods have nothing to do with capitalist 'long waves' or 'cycles' that are a theoretical representation and explanation of the laws of motion of capitalism. This argument is debated in Maddison (2007).

4 On the reciprocal influences of urbanisation and economic growth see Chen, Zhang, Liu and Zhang (2014).

5 This trend seems to be the same in new industrialising countries also, as 21st-century China and India are also experiencing the same levels recorded in the 1950s in Italy, Germany and Japan (between 2,000 and 2,200 annual hours worked per employee).
6 The discussion on these topics (the so-called debate over the 'resource curse theory' or that concerning the importance of coal for the industrial revolution of firstcomers) entails economic explanations, modelling, and cliometric analyses that go beyond the methodological framework and subject matter of this volume. On the subject see Roy, Sarkar and Mandal (2013), and Clay (2011).
7 This index number also depends on the skills and labour intensity of the worker.

References

Bairoch, P. and Goertz, G. (1986) 'Factors of Urbanisation in the Nineteenth Developed Countries: A Descriptive and Econometric Analysis', *Urban Studies*, 23 (4): 285–305.

Bassanini, A. and Scarpetta, S. (2001) 'The Driving Forces of Economic Growth: Panel Data Evidence for the OECD Countries', *OECD Economic Studies*, 33.

Bloom, D., Canning, D. and Sevilla, J. (2002) *The Demographic Dividend: A New Perspective on the Economic Consequences of Population Change*, Santa Monica: RAND, MR–1274.

Brezis, E. S. (1995) 'Foreign Capital Flows in the Century of Britain's Industrial Revolution: New Estimates, Controlled Conjectures', *Economic History Review*, 48 (1): 46–67.

Bruland, K. and Mowert, D. C. (2014) 'Technology and the Spread of Capitalism', in L. Neal and J. G. Williamson (eds.) *Capitalism. Volume II. The Spread of Capitalism: From 1848 to the Present'*, Cambridge: Cambridge University Press: 82–126.

Caldwell, J. C. (1976) 'Toward a Restatement of Demographic Transition Theory', *Population and Development Review* 2: 321–66.

Chen, M., Zhang, H., Liu, W. and Zhang, W. (2014) 'The Global Pattern of Urbanization and Economic Growth: Evidence from the Last Three Decades', *PLoS ONE*, 9 (8): e103799. https://doi.org/10.1371/journal.pone.0103799

CISCO System (2007) *Education and Economic Growth: From the Nineteenth to the Twenty First Century*. Accessed 17 March 2023 http://www.cisco.com/c/dam/en_us/solutions/industries/docs/education/Education-and-Economic-Growth.pdf

Clark, B. (2016) *The Evolution of Economic Systems. Varieties of Capitalism in the Global Economy*, Oxford: Oxford University Press.

Clay, C. (2011) 'Natural Resources and Economic Outcomes', in P. W. Rhode, J. L. Rosenbloom and D. F. Weiman (eds.) *Economic Evolution and Revolution in Historical Times*, Stanford: Stanford University Press: 27–50.

de Zwart, P., van Leeuwen, B. and van Leeuwen-Li, J. (2014) 'Real Wages Since 1820', in Jan Luiten van Zanden et al. (eds.) *How Was Life?: Global Well-being Since 1820*, Paris: OECD Publishing. http://doi.org/10.1787/9789264214262-8-en

Fouquet, R. and Broadberry, S. (2015) 'Seven Centuries of European Economic Growth and Decline', *Journal of Economic Perspectives*, 29 (4): 227–44.

Galgano, F. (1976) *Storia del diritto commerciale (The History of the Commercial Law)*, Bologna: il Mulino.

Galgano, F. (2005) *La globalizzazione nello specchio del diritto (The Globalisation in the Law Mirror*), Bologna: il Mulino.

Graff, M., Kenwood, A. G. and Lougheed, A. L. (2014) *Growth of the International Economy 1820–2015*, London: Routledge.

Harris, R. (2014) 'Spread of Legal Innovations Defining Private and Public Domain', in L. Neal and J. G. Williamson (eds.) *Capitalism. Volume II. The Spread of Capitalism: From 1848 to the Present'*, Cambridge: Cambridge University Press: 127–68.
Heaton, H. (1937) 'Financing the Industrial Revolution', *Bulletin of the Business Historical Society*, 11 (1): 1–10.
Huberman, M. and Minns, C. (2007) '"The Times They Are Not Changing": Days and Hours of Work in Old and New Worlds, 1870–2000', *Explorations in Economic History*, 44 (4): 538–67.
Imperial Institute Mineral Resources Department (1925) *The Mineral Industry of the British Empire and Foreign Countries*, London: His Majesty's Stationery Office. https://www,bgs,ac,uk/mineralsuk/statistics/worldArchive,html
Laughlin, E. A. (2012) 'The Rise of American Industrial and Financial Corporations', *Gettysburg Economic Review*, 6 (Spring): 42–57. https://cupola.gettysburg.edu/ger/vol6/iss1/5
Lee, R. (2003) 'The Demographic Transition: Three Centuries of Fundamental Change', *Journal of Economic Perspectives*, 17 (4): 167–90.
Leon, P. (1967) *Structural Change and Growth in Capitalism*, Baltimore: Johns Hopkins.
Maddison, A. (1991) *Dynamic Forces in Capitalist Development: A Long Run Comparative View*, Oxford: Oxford University Press.
Maddison, A. (2001) *The World Economy. A Millennial Perspective*, Paris: OECD.
Maddison, A. (2003) *The World Economy: Historical Statistics*, Paris: OECD.
Maddison, A. (2007) 'Fluctuations in the Momentum of Growth Within the Capitalist Epoch', *Cliometrica*, 1: 145–75. http://doi.org/10.1007/s11698-007-0007-3
Mokyr, J. (1999) 'Editor's Introduction: The New Economic History and the Industrial Revolution', in J. Mokyr (ed.) *The British Industrial Revolution: An Economic Perspective*, Boulder: Westview Press: 1–127.
Mokyr, J. (2005) 'Long-Term Economic Growth and the History of Technology', in F. Aghion and S. N. Durlauf (eds.) *Handbook of Economic Growth*, Vol. 1B, Amsterdam: Elsevier.
OECD (2010) *Perspectives on Global Development: Shifting Wealth*, Paris: OECD.
OECD (May 2014) 'Is Migration Good for the Economy?', *Migration Policy Debates*. https://www.oecd.org/migration/OECD%20Migration%20Policy%20Debates%20Numero%202.pdf
OECD/EUROPEANS COMMUNITIES (2005) *Oslo Manual: Proposed Guidelines for Collecting and Interpreting Technological Innovation Data*, Paris: OECD.
Ohno, K. (2018) *The History of Japanese Economic Development. Origins of Private Dynamism and Policy Competence*, London: Routledge.
Palgrave Macmillan Ltd (eds.) (2013) *International Historical Statistics*, London: Palgrave Macmillan.
Pasinetti, L. (1981) *Structural Change and Economic Growth. A Theoretical Essay on the Dynamics of the Wealth of Nations*, Cambridge: Cambridge University Press.
Polanyi, K. (1944) *The Great Transformation*, Boston: Beacon Press.
Roser, M. and Ortiz-Ospina, E. (2017) *Literacy, Published Online at OurWorldInData.org*. https://ourworldindata.org/literacy
Roy, B. C., Sarkar, S. and Mandal, N. R. (2013) 'Natural Resource Abundance and Economic Performance – A Literature Review', *Current Urban Studies*, 1 (4): 148–55. http://doi.org/10.4236/cus.2013.14016
Schor, J. B. (1993) *The Overworked American. The Unexpected Decline of Leisure*, New York: Basic Books.

Schumpeter, J. A. (2003) *Capitalism, Socialism and Democracy*, London: Taylor & Francis e-Library (first edition 1943).

Segreto, L. (2009) 'Private Bankers and Italian Industrialisation', in Y. Cassis and P. Cottrell (eds.) *The World of Private Banking*, London: Ashgate: 177–203.

UN Department of Economic and Social Affairs, Population Division (2014) *World Urbanization Prospects: The 2014 Revision*. CD ROM Edition. https://esa.un.org/unpd/wup/CD-ROM/WUP2014_XLS_CD_FILES/WUP2014-F01-Total_Urban_Rural.xls

ushistory.org (2023) 'Economic Growth and the Early Industrial Revolution', *US History Online Textbook*. Accessed 16 March 2023. https://www.ushistory.org/us/22a.asp

van Leeuwen, B. and van Leeuwen-Li, J. (2014) 'Education since 1820', in J. L. van Zanden, et al. (eds.) *How Was Life?: Global Well-being Since 1820*, Paris: OECD Publishing. http://doi.org/10.1787/9789264214262-9-en

Wright, G. (1990) 'The Origins of American Industrial Success, 1879 1940', *The American Economic Review*, 80 (4): 651–68.

Glossary

Demographic dividend is 'the economic growth potential that can result from shifts in a population's age structure, mainly when the share of the working-age population is larger than the non-working-age share of the population' (UN definition).

Economic development is the transition process ferrying a traditional society toward capitalism.

GDP (Gross Domestic Product) is the value (calculated at market prices) of all final goods and services produced in an economic system during a year.

Human capital is the amount of working time of the labour force and the amount of knowledge, competence, skills and training endowing a worker with profitable working abilities.

Income per head is a measure representing the ratio between the GDP value and the population number of a country.

Index number is a numerical value displaying the quantity of the features of an economic aspect.

Indicator is a concept defining the state or the level of economic aspects.

Innovation is a dynamic process substituting the current technology with a new one through changes in products, production process, organisation or marketing.

Physical capital is every tangible, manufactured instrumental asset used as input for more than one production process.

3 A methodological framework for studying capitalist economies

As noted in previous chapters, there is a basic trend in the historical process of capitalist economy development which emerges despite the various phases and variants that have appeared all over the world: the increasing complexity of its activities, relations and organisations. In fact, on the one hand technological developments offer new production methods that increase the quantity and variety of goods and services available while, on the other hand, social transformations and economic improvements make it possible for a growing number of people to purchase these goods and services. These processes are working to expand the overall number of production relations and the intensity of each participant's links to the economic process. In addition, as the number of these participants is increasing, their individual behaviour becomes more complex and interdependent. What enables capitalism to develop along these lines is its extraordinary organisational and coordination ability. Actually, as unpredictable, irregular and tumultuous this process of dimensional development and structural differentiation of the economy may be, it has been able to establish itself and to evolve in what we may call a 'systematic' way, gradually transforming previous traditional economies and protecting the new ones from a self-destructive chaos. Thus, the core features of capitalism which emerged with it also include the coordination of economic activities and the adaptation of subjects and organisations to these changes, along with interdependence, fast-growing links among economic subjects and the creation of new goods, services and organisations.

Although such elements emerge as prominent features in an inductive analysis of modern economies, current modelling has never included them either in the representation of the situation being studied or among the axioms on which the economic explanation is based. In fact, modern economies are generally portrayed as a set of abstract 'exchange' contracts carried out by isolated economic subjects driven by their natural instincts. In addition, they are studied using interpretive models where the basic concepts are too abstract or simplistic to be effective key instruments for the explanation of such a specific and new reality as capitalism is. This incongruity prevents economic analysis from being effective, so to fully understand modern economies an appropriate methodology is needed. 'Systems analysis' may be this instrument because it enables the congruence between reality and its representation. In fact, it is based on relational networks and their evolution

DOI: 10.4324/9781315679730-5

(forming the system's complexity), elements that are undeniable features of the capitalist economy. Moreover, 'systems analysis' also makes it possible to take into account the set of institutions that have emerged with the evolution of modern economies in order to manage and co-ordinate their complexity – i.e. economic laws, technical procedures and economic behaviours.

Therefore, this chapter presents some basic concepts of the 'systems analysis' methodological approach, by focusing in particular on the consequences its application to economic phenomena may have on the interpretation of both the economic agent and the system's dynamics. With regard to the economic subject, this methodology replaces the traditional *Homo economicus* with a social being referred to by Potts as *Homo hetero-economicus* (Potts 2000). As for capitalist dynamics, the way the system works may be described as a process of coevolution (to which political and private social domains also contribute), creating a time consistency (momentum), rather than a mathematical equilibrium. The creators of this momentum are institutions, which enable the working of the system and its evolution. Modern economies can thus be seen as complex adaptive systems – that is, systems constituted 'of a large number of parts that have many interactions . . . and are composed of sub-systems that in turn have their own subsystems, and so on'; thus, the 'complexity takes the form of hierarchy' (Simon 1996: 183–4). Such systems are adaptive because they evolve thanks to the contribution of all social domains; have structures, speeds of growth and outcomes which may be significantly different; and provide welfare to their citizens in various ways via several capitalism models.

Stylised facts as cornerstones to represent capitalist economies

The way by which each discipline explains a phenomenon depends on its representation, while the effectiveness of a representation depends on the inclusion of the distinctive features of the phenomenon. Thus, a view of modern economies capable of inspecting their structure and working must solve this problem. According to Kaldor, 'Any theory must necessarily be based on abstractions. But the type of abstraction chosen cannot be decided in a vacuum: it must be appropriate to the characteristic features of the economic process as recorded by experience. Hence the theorist, in choosing a particular theoretical approach, ought to start off with a summary of the facts which he regards as relevant to his problem' (Kaldor 1961: 177–8). Each economic research design 'should be free to start off with a stylised view of the facts – i.e. concentrate on broad tendencies, ignoring individual details' (Kaldor 1961: 178) because the 'stylised facts' of a phenomenon represent all empirical events whose existence is not controversial. 'Stylised facts' emerge from the systematic observation of reality and often represent, in an emblematic way, its breaking points with the past, its tendencies, or its characteristics. As modern economies have been characterised in previous chapters as specific socioeconomic organisations different from all the others preceding them, it is appropriate to follow Kaldor's methodological suggestions. The next step of this chapter will thus be a short overview of the stylised facts of capitalist economies.

Stylised facts about the nature of capitalist economies

As already discussed the birth and affirmation of capitalism triggered three interconnected processes of change: 1) social transformation reshaping the nature of human beings and the structure of society; 2) the spread of new technological knowledge, along with an extraordinary improvement in production and consumption conditions; and 3) the development of new institutions. Within this framework many elements of discontinuity from previous socioeconomic organisations emerged. An intense demographic dynamic, the advent of new social and economic roles (salaried workers, the unemployed and the entrepreneur), the spread of new social lifestyles in both the work environment (technical division of labour, competition) and leisure time (consumerism) are just some examples of discontinuity from the first process of change. As for the second process, some novelties were the shift from natural energy exploitation to energy production; the rapid spread of new production techniques, new goods and services; the creation of synthetic materials (plastic for example); and the building of fast, widespread systems and means of transport and communication. Concurrently, the institution-building process brought about the introduction of new production routines, new laws for every aspect of social life, and new values, habits and customs (see Chapter One). All these elements, characterising the new socioeconomic organisations in the historical perspective, appeared as 'stylised facts' emerging from capitalism's dynamic tendencies to expand its activities and increase its complexity.

The 'stylised facts' just mentioned are very important from an epistemological standpoint because they form the inductive basis for any economic study on capitalist economies and their components. The historical evidence on human conditions in the age of capitalism, for example, shows that the socioeconomic change which followed the English agricultural revolution provided human beings with new economic roles. Thenceforth they experienced a detachment from nature; the disappearance of self-sufficiency in acquiring the means necessary for survival; a reliance on their personal endowment of skills, talents and assets for making a living; and self-determination and individual responsibility in making decisions. Detachment from nature was essentially triggered by the loss of the so-called 'common rights' (free pasture, farming and wood-gathering) that made it possible for agricultural societies to benefit freely from the use of natural resources. This 'expropriation of the means of production' and survival severed the ties of the symbiosis between the organisation of human life and the order of nature too. The resulting impossibility of self-sufficiency became more and more pronounced, since with technical and social progress there is a discrepancy between the knowledge and skills at an individual's disposal and those necessary for dealing with the economic and social needs of everyday life (constantly rising in their average level and individual ambition). In other words, each person began to need other people's work and expertise to survive. In such an irreversible framework individuals' self-determination, autonomy in making decisions and awareness of other people's need to account for their own actions became essential for the emergence of the salaried worker, the entrepreneur and the consumer. This is why these facts cannot be ignored in either the description of economic organisations/phenomena or the formulation of axioms and principles of economic analysis.

Similarly, the web-structured nature of the economy should find a place in portraying and theorising modern economies. The historical study of capitalism shows that connections have become the engine of this socioeconomic organisation, which works thanks to the flow, accumulation and the co-ordinated use of such tangible and intangible goods. The algorithms to be used for the purpose are nothing more than institutional processes, both in technical and social domains, given that cooperation, competition and coordination are the ways in which all subjects' behaviours make the economy work.

Tangible and intangible resources must also play a role in representing and assessing theoretical principles regarding modern economies, as capitalist stylised facts also include both an unprecedented amount of scientific output channelled into technological progress and a growing series of inventions and innovations whose impact on production is a total novelty. In this way, by removing (to a certain extent) the natural boundaries affecting human life in relation to the endowment of energy, travel time and the possibility to create new materials for the improvement of production or consumption (see, for example, chemical products or alloys), the human race came to have more devices at its disposal to improve its material and cultural conditions.

Bedrocks to inspect capitalist economies

The three main stylised facts discussed in the previous paragraph can be used to deduce the characteristics of the economic agent who acts in a capitalist environment with the following traits.

i. The economic agent is a social being connected with other social actors to acquire the means to survive.
ii. Each economic agent is a commodity and knowledge owner who increases both endowments through connections.
iii. Economic agents experience an escalating power of self-determination as their number of social connections increases.
iv. The behaviour of each economic agent depends on other agents' behaviour and endowment.

Therefore, we can consider capitalist economic agents as beings 'trading with, communicating with, or bargaining with their immediate neighbours' (Kirman 1997: 342). The same applies to economic organisations, which are collective economic subjects (as the firm and the state) as well as coordinating structures such as the market. In the case of firms, 'neighbours might be similar firms within the same industry, but these firms will, in turn, be linked either through customers or suppliers with firms in other industries' (Kirman 1997: 342).

From the main stylised facts, concisely and conveniently connected, some characteristics of a capitalist economy may also be inferred, such as the following:

i. A capitalist economy is a set of subjects and connections.
ii. Each connection represents the means providing economic subjects with tangible and intangible resources.
iii. The forms of each connection represent just as many institutions (contract draft and trading protocols are two examples of this).
iv. Connections among subjects are the way in which the transfer of an owned information is transformed into learning (human capital, technologies), while an endowment of goods and services is transformed into produced or consumed wealth. Both processes expand all forms of capital and improve the organisational membership of each economic subject.
v. Sets of consistent connections form webs of economic subjects and/or activities, aimed at either creating organisations providing goods and services (firms, public utilities networks, sectors, filières) or enabling all kinds of exchange (intermediate and consumer markets).

Since 'the individuals in the economy learn and their behaviour evolves (and) this, in turn, leads the network structure within which they function to evolve over time' (Kirman 1997: 351), capitalism can be thought of as a set of web structures were subjects learn and rebroadcast learnt contents through improved behaviours. This mechanism produces both an increasing complexity of the economy (due to the growth in the number of connections and individuals) and its evolution (because of the greater endowments of goods and knowledge).

These results should shape the epistemological and methodological bases of the models representing and explaining modern economies. However, economics textbooks contain images of the economic agent and organisation that don't match the stylised facts just summarised. Actually, as far as the economic agent is concerned, analytical axioms are characterised as follows:

i. Economic agents are one-dimensional individuals endowed with a certain amount of money (or productive resources), complete knowledge, computational abilities and pure hedonism.
ii. They live in a space characterised by stimulus-response functions (Potts 2000: 11).
iii. They are isolated from other similar subjects.
iv. The only connection among economic subjects is the contractual one – i.e. that which occurs via a market.

Moreover, traditional textbooks tend to define and characterise the economic system as follows:

i. 'A set of institutions for decision making and for the implementation of decisions concerning production, income and consumption' (Gregory and Stuart 2004: 19) – i.e. a set of rules introduced to allocate scarce resources.

ii. Something which emerges as a summation of the behavioural outcomes of all economic agents.
iii. The result of the market coordination of single economic decisions.
iv. An unhistorical model of general equilibrium.

Last sets of analytical starting points ('axioms') do not originate out of stylised facts through inductive reasoning but from an explanatory paradigm whose theoretical assumptions are consistent with an optimising and self-efficient model of economy, based mainly on exchange. Since important features of capitalism (such as human abilities on the one hand and technical and scientific aspects on the other) and the relational and connective structures operating in it are cut out of this framework of ideas, the analysis of modern economy results ineffective.

Using the 'systems theory' to represent capitalist economies

The 'systems theory' is a transdisciplinary methodological approach for researchers studying patterns and principles of systems – i.e. organised sets of regularly interacting components grouped for analytical or operational purposes. Among systems theorists there are scholars such as Bertalanffy (1968), Simon (1962), Koestler (1978) and Boulding (1978), together with many others who have contributed to this field of study. The basic idea of this approach is that each phenomenon can be represented as a system – i.e. as a web of interconnected elements (endowed with specific qualities) which have common patterns, concerted behaviours and shared properties. Acting as a purposive unit, the system interacts with the environment, causing both inner and outer complexity as well as dynamics.

This perspective, based on interdependent and interconnected elements, sets and processes, goes beyond the static view of self-centred subjects, groups and structures separated from the environment. Therefore, considering the emergence and evolution of capitalism as pictured by its 'stylised facts', systems theory seems to be a method consistent with the image that the new socioeconomic organisation has displayed throughout its evolution. This is the reason why a digression into its basic concepts and principles is necessary.

Basic concepts in systems analysis

A set *(S)* is a mathematical object including elements *(E)* and connections *(C)*:

$$S = (E, C) \tag{3.1}$$

Each element stands for a specific kind of entity and presents its own features. The elements of a system are therefore different from one another. Let *E(S)* be the group of the elements constituting the *set* (system) and *n* be their number. By definition *n* (5 in the formula 3.2) is the *system order:*

$$E(S) = (a, b, c, d, e) \tag{3.2}$$

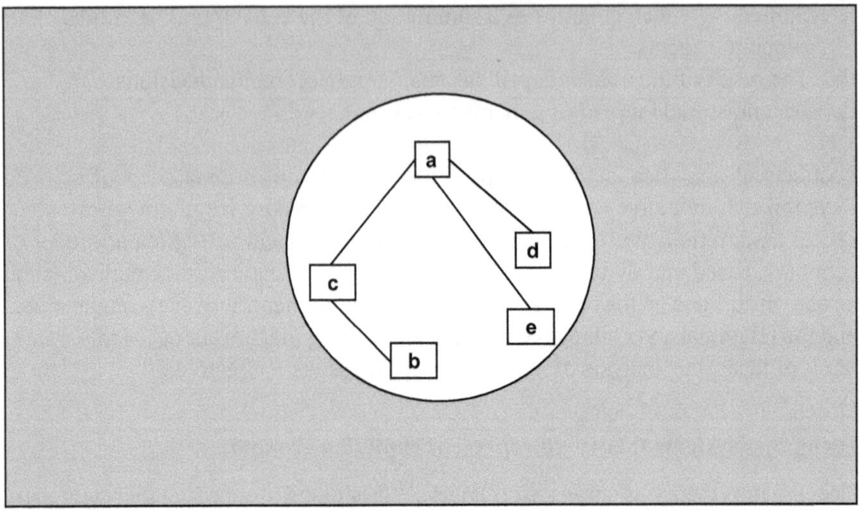

Figure 3.1 A system of order 5 having a specific binary system

Source: Author's elaboration

If the different elements *i* are joined two by two they are *contiguous* and the resulting set of connections *C(S)* is a *binary system*:

$$C(S) = (ad, ac, ae, cb) \quad 3.3$$

In every binary system, the grouping of the contiguous elements of any *i* may be defined *neighbourhood of i* (for example *ad, ac* and *ae* are the neighbourhood of *a*), and the number of connections including a specific element indicates its *degree* (for example in Figure 3.1 the degree of *a* – representing the centre of the system – is 3, of *c* is 2 and, for all the other elements, is 1). In addition, *b* is defined as *marginal* as it is the furthest element from the centre of the system (*a*) in terms of connections.

For every element *i* of a system the *moment M(i)* represents the *total amount of single connections necessary to reach all the other elements*. Thus, for each element appearing in Figure 3.1, the moments are:

$$M(a) = 5, M(b) = 9, M(c) = 6, M(d) = 8, M(e) = 8 \quad 3.4$$

Moments can be used to calculate the *degree m(S) of centralisation (or of concentration) of a system* according to this formula:

$$m(S) = [M(max) - M(min)] / M(min) \quad 3.5$$

We can assert that $0 < m(S) < 1$. When *m(S) = 0, the system presents maximum decentralisation* because each element is connected with all the other elements of the system, while *m(S) = 1 means maximum centralisation of the system* due to the

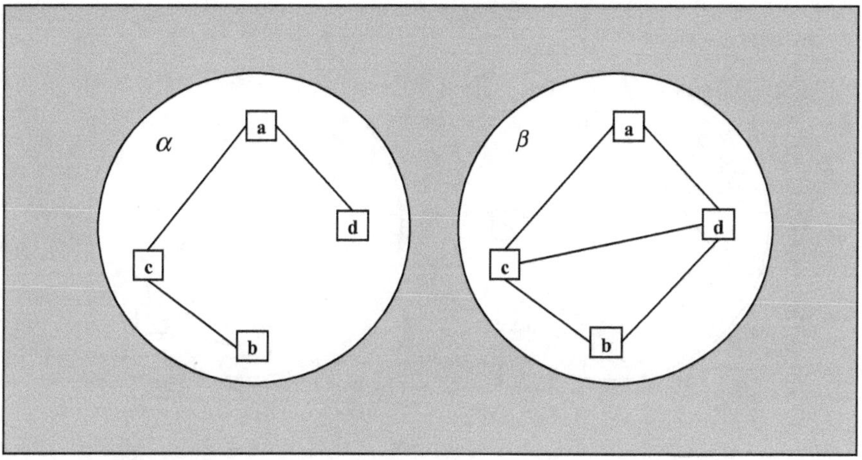

Figure 3.2 Systems with different degrees of concentration

Source: Author's elaboration

fact that there is only one element. Given the values of the moments which the different elements in Figure 3.1 have, the degree of centralisation is:

$$M(S) = (9-5)/5 = 0.8 \qquad 3.6$$

The more centralised (concentrated) a system is, the more hierarchical it is. The more connections there are among the elements of a system, the more decentralised it is. To show this relation let us consider the two sets α and β in Figure 3.2 and calculate their two degrees of concentration:

$$\alpha)\quad M(a)=4,\ M(b)=6,\ M(c)=4,\ M(d)=6 \qquad 3.7$$
$$m=(6-4)/4=0.5$$
$$\beta)\quad M(a)=4,\ M(b)=4,\ M(c)=3,\ M(d)=3 \qquad 3.8$$
$$m=(4-3)/3=0.33$$

The α system is more concentrated than β because its elements *b* and *d* present only one connection, while both these elements have more connections in the β system. Thus α is a more hierarchical system compared to β, which is in turn more polyarchic.

By definition, *the dimension of a system is represented by the total number of its connections C(S)*. Let α be the hierarchical system and β be the polyarchic one in Figure 3.3. The increase in an element determines a linear increase in the connections in α and an exponential increase in β if the new element is consistent with the others in terms of connections (strictly subordinated in the first case and the

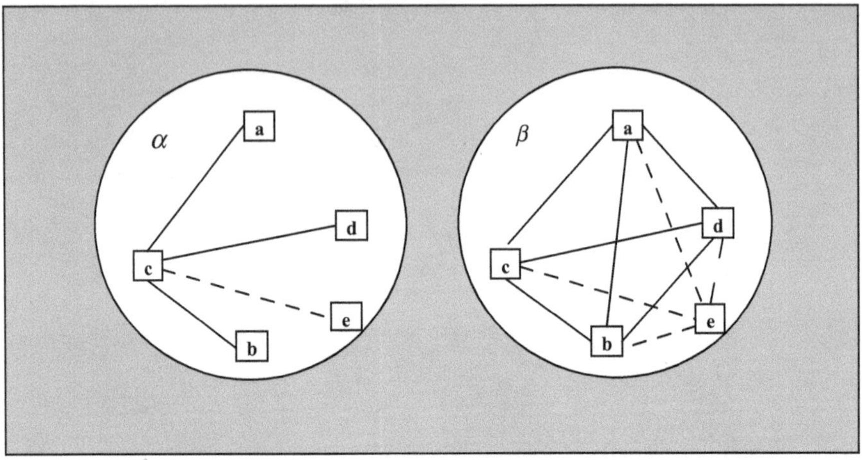

Figure 3.3 Dimension of a system

Source: Author's elaboration

contrary in the second). Thus, the dimension of both systems expands, respectively, according to the formula:

$$C\,(\alpha) = n - 1 \qquad 3.9$$

$$C\,(\beta) = n^2 - n \text{ (at full blast)} \qquad 3.10$$

The state of a system S (A) is a specific connective arrangement that can be represented by a *matrix of adjacencies*, where rows and columns correspond to the elements of *E* while the values 1 or 0 stand, respectively, for the presence or absence of the connection between two elements. In Figure 3.3 the states of the systems α and β are in this order:

$$\mathbf{S}\,(\alpha) = \begin{matrix} 0\,0\,1\,0\,0 \\ 0\,0\,1\,0\,0 \\ 1\,1\,0\,1\,1 \\ 0\,0\,1\,0\,0 \\ 0\,0\,1\,0\,0 \end{matrix} \qquad \mathbf{S}\,(\beta) = \begin{matrix} 0\,0\,1\,0\,0 \\ 0\,0\,1\,1\,0 \\ 1\,1\,0\,1\,1 \\ 0\,1\,1\,0\,1 \\ 0\,1\,1\,1\,0 \end{matrix}$$

Given the *state of a system S(A)*, the connective arrangements diverging from it because of one connection (called 'adjacent to it') are its *neighbourhood.* Every change in state in the neighbourhood is called a *strategic tweak or adaptation.* Finally, a system is called *null* when the adjacencies matrix *S(A)* is null, whereas a system is *complete* when the adjacencies matrix *S(A)* presents zero values only for the main diagonal (Figure 3.4).

The concept of 'state of the system' is related to the concept of *organisation.* If an organisation can be theoretically defined as 'organic composite of separable

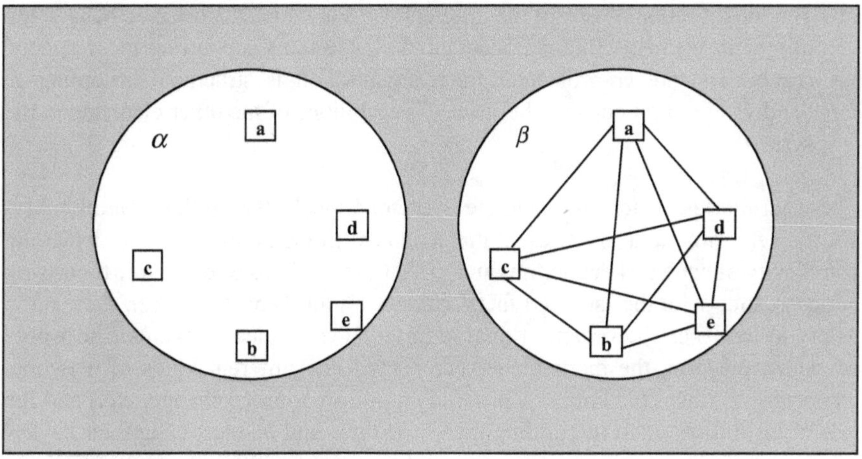

Figure 3.4 Null and complete systems

Source: Author's elaboration

parts', and if this entity can be viewed as a system presenting a specific state *S(A)*, each organisation is thus a species of system (Potts 2000: 75) – i.e. an actual form of system.

Capitalist economies as hyper-structures

As a consequence of these axiomatic foundations the systems analysis approach provides some corollaries concerning the research subject, such as:

i. Each system presents the following features:
   a. A function within a process.
   b. The organiser – i.e. the creator of the system.
   c. The way in which the system is co-ordinated (which can be deduced from the degree of concentration).
   d. The structure of the system, which results from its state or from the connective arrangement.
ii. The elements forming a system can also be seen at a reduced level as systems, and similarly each system can emerge as an element at a higher grade. Therefore, 'the system-element duality is the recognition that the definition of an element or of a system depends entirely upon the level at which it is viewed' (Potts 2000: 69).
iii. The material is thus a hyper-structure (Simon 1962) – i.e. 'a system of systems, or a system of systems of systems . . . where we may then speak of an x-level hyper structure as the number of layers of emergence within' (Potts 2000: 69).

iv. The 'organisation' is one of the different ways in which the oriented behaviours of system elements (human agents and all the tools supporting these agents' capabilities) are co-ordinated. Each organisation is structured according to the division of labour and the level of capabilities of the other elements in the system.

These corollaries, which complete the epistemological bases of the systems analysis, are very important to represent the economy. In fact, they enable to depict the complexity of capitalist economies and to shape the axioms of economic theorising in accordance with the 'stylised facts' characterising them. Moreover, they allow to put in evidence the organisational nature of the entities or agents (the whole economy, the firm, the market, the sector, etc.), the different kinds of networks characterising them (technology, production, information, exchange, etc.) and the role of institutions both in building their structures and in addressing their behaviours according to specific goals. Conversely, from the methodological standpoint, systems analysis is able to inspect modern economies in a functional, holistic and dynamic way. It enables the researcher to select all the facts and agents related to the phenomenon being studied and to enclose them within a recognisable unit for a specific heuristic/operational aim (function). In so doing it defines the system as a targeted entity, be it an organism (a consumer), a piece of machinery (an internal combustion engine), a production unit (the factory) or a connective network (communication system). Each targeted entity is an indivisible acting unit (a holistic organism that is higher ranked than the sum of its parts) whose dimension and structure can be modulated. The systems analysis truly represents a methodological instrument suitable for the study of the evolutionary path of capitalism and its subsystems; in fact, when each economic entity is carrying out the function for which it has been organised, it changes its state and evolves together with its neighbourhood, actually showing a dynamic trajectory.

The first important consequence of the application of the systems theory to the analysis of modern economies is the characterisation of the agent. As pointed out in previous paragraphs, the *Homo economicus* of textbooks is an unreal being imagined without considering the stylised facts concerning the individual in a capitalist society. Actually, 'he is a set of elements in a preference and technology field' (Potts 2000: 113) who can be considered merely as a calculating individual, given that no theory of choice has been provided for him in traditional microeconomics (Potts 2000: 113–16). Conversely, in a systems analysis approach (i.e. that of the *Homo hetero-economicus*) economic agents are provided with an algorithm of choice, as well as with the features highlighted throughout this chapter. Actually, they are 'a set of elements plus a specific set of connections between them' (Potts 2000: 113) and 'a set of conditional and sequential operations, such that we refer to a decision algorithm or a choice heuristic' (Potts 2000: 116–17), where learning and adaptability emerge as basic behavioural features.

As for the economy, the image of the reality highlighted above supports the idea of an economic system based on hyper-structure and system-element duality where, for example, 'routines build skills, skills build competence, competence builds firms, firms build industries, industries build economies and so on' (Potts 2000: 68). In addition, such an image of economy facilitates the identification of some species of systems, owing to the domain of economy, characterised as organisational subjects and based on a specific function. This is the case of the systems of commodities, cognitive and skilled agents, technologies and institutions (Potts 2000: 75). This approach also confirms that economic activities reflect also non-economic priorities, because the social reality of capitalism is a complex intertwining of the actions carried out in different domains (economy, politics, privacy) either by private economic subjects alone or in connection with the state or by organised social groups without a profit interest (Aoki 2007).

In the end this epistemological and methodological landing has many consequences on the economic analysis. On the one hand it tries to bridge the gap between the reality of modern economies and their theoretical representation. In fact, the importance of an economic theorising depends, together with the application of the logic, on the relevance of axioms put at the base of the deductive reasoning, which is guaranteed by the acceptance of stylised facts. Last elements also ensure at the same time the historical accuracy of the economic interpretation, avoiding another pitfall of the irrelevance of theorising. On the other hand, this approach supports 'relativism' in economics; in fact, both the historical foundation of economic theorising and the intervention of researchers in shaping the system according to their research goals confirm the viewpoint that the theories and models explaining capitalist economies are historical and problem solving-oriented ones. However, the impossibility to use unhistorical or neutral economic models does not imply that scientific trustworthiness is impossible, because such a feature of economic theorising relies on the application of logic.

The 'institutional system' and the dynamics of capitalist economies

After discussing the ability of the systems analysis to represent the structural features of the components of the capitalist economy, the same ability for other intangible constituting elements characterising it – self-coordination and non-chaotic evolution – must be questioned. Both organisational activities emerge thanks to 'institutions' – that is, thanks to 'a system of established and prevalent social rules that structure social interactions' (Hodgson 2006: 2; see also Shotter 1981; North 1990). According to the 'efficient institutional view' (Ogilvie 2007) institutions emerge as a voluntary choice of agents only when they are an efficient way of organising life in social domains – i.e. when they minimise economic costs (transaction and informational costs) in a specific context while providing advantages for the entire society in terms of output maximisation and wealth. In addition to being efficient, institutions are effective as they are purpose-built guidelines that channel social interactions; thus, they have a logical structure, in the sense that 'there are certain functions that institutions have to serve' (Chang 2007: Chapters One and Two).

The systemic structure of institutions can be confirmed by the fact that they constitute the procedural rules supporting the structure and operation of capitalism. As capitalism is a complex intertwining of actions carried out in different domains (economy, polity, privacy) the rules governing relational behaviours and operational paths (i.e. institutions) associated with this intertwinement can also be considered a hyper-structure. Moreover, as the systems built within this hyper-structure change their state in their neighbourhood (because of adaptation) like any other system, institutions can be considered responsible for the evolutionary path of capitalism and its subsystems. Thus, institutions guarantee on the one hand the efficient/effective organisation of all activities carried out by individuals and on the other the quantitative/qualitative change of the systems they put into operation.

To better understand why this type of system is essential for capitalism and why it triggers its dynamics, an in-depth analysis is necessary.

The 'institutional process' as the 'fuel' for capitalist economies

As an institution is a purpose-built guideline its 'function' is the aim on which the social behaviour or interaction is focused while its 'form' is the set of rules considered appropriate for the social purpose. The actual working of this set of 'established and prevalent social rules' is called the 'institutional process' because it consists of the ways in which the institutional function is carried out by the institutional form. Thus, the institutional process is none other than the set of rules supporting goal-oriented social actions and organisational routines which are implemented in a hyper-structure (Chang 2007).

To understand how these goal-oriented social actions and organisational routines are structured we can imagine a team (for example a football team) playing a sequence of matches (a championship) performed in compliance with guidelines (game regulations). The 'game form', fixed for every match but variable as time goes by, describes the 'game aims', the set of players and the 'game rules'. The 'players' (people and organisations), while planning the strategies to win a match, have three kinds of rules of conduct to comply with (Aoki 2007):

iv. The 'game rules' – i.e. the set of actions to be performed while pursuing the game aims, the permitted and prohibited ones and the sanctions and rewards connected to some actions. This set of rules is a 'consequence function' established by the national football league.

ii. The 'state of the game' – i.e. the set of all successful game schemes consisting of the relevant features of how the plays are repeatedly performed. These rules emerge from the strategies implemented over time by successful coaches.

iii. The 'plan of action' – i.e. the organisation of the actions by the team coach that the players perform (with limited rationality) in compliance with the state of the game and their own beliefs regarding the behaviour of the players of the other team.

Each kind of rules of conduct makes it possible to glimpse different kinds of bounded paths for social actions in a specific domain of competence; the game rules define all the actions constituting the game, the state of the game reveals the different setups of successful permitted actions and the player's plan of action shows the game arrangement deemed to be the best at the particular time. At a glance each bounded path could represent a type of institution as it identifies proper behavioural rules. To confirm that, however, the concept must be fully investigated in order to know what the characteristic features are.

Depending on each game form the players must strategically choose and arrange a set of permitted actions to win the match; therefore, they absorb both the consequence function and a procedural mixture of successful permitted actions before playing the game. This means that institutions represent 'punishment/reward compliant' procedural behavioural principles that are embedded within the common knowledge about the sport. Institutions thus convey a 'mental representation', resulting from a 'time interval' between the introduction and the full application of new institutions on one hand and their 'learning-by-doing process' on the other hand; such an interval enables them to exist and to be codified, transmitted and replicated. Institutions are two-sided entities because, in addition to the 'mental representation', they are also 'constitutive': they assign a special status under which a person or an object can 'perform functions that they couldn't perform solely in virtue of its physical structure' (Searle 2005: 22) Finally, as formal rules represent legislative or technical instructions and informal ones social conventions or habits, the state and society are entitled to create them. Therefore, only the procedural behaviour principles incorporating all these qualities ('punishment/reward compliance', 'mental representation' through 'temporal dimension' as well as 'learning-by-doing acquisition', and 'functional capacity') can be considered institutions.

Following on from this closer inspection of the features of institutions and without exhausting the discussion of the concept (see about it Hindriks and Guala 2014) the idea that they could be merely constraints stated by the 'game rules' must be rejected; institutions are a set of procedural rules, and among them only a part is conditional upon punishment/reward principles. The 'state of the game' has the requirement to be considered as an institution in the short run because it stands for the successful ways to win the match. As for the 'plan of action', this is an adaptation of the state of the game to the environment where the match is played; in the event of success, it will be repeated becoming a new 'state of the game'. Therefore, only the 'state of the game' emerging endogenously and changing in the long run because of successful plans of actions can accurately represent institutions – i.e. 'self-sustaining salient patterns of social interactions, as represented by meaningful rules that every agent knows and that are incorporated as agents' shared beliefs on how the game is played and to be played' (Aoki 2007: 6).

Once it is established which kinds of rules can be labelled as institutions and how they channel sociotechnical activities, it is apparent that the 'institutional process' is the driving force for the working of capitalism. After all, both 'mental representation' and 'functional capacity' are the proof of institutions' ability to address and entrust the management of social activities while their efficiency and effectiveness are proof of their capacity for self-sustainment. Furthermore, as the institutional process is embodied in social actions and technical procedures the 'established and prevalent social rules' cannot be separated from relational behaviours and routines in the different fields of social life. This means that each set of activities carried out in different social fields (economy, polity, private, etc.) can be wholly described and explained only if the conventional organisations constituting a hyper-structure level are associated with their connected level of institutions. For example, for economy the inspection of the different systems of activities (economy itself, sector, market, firm, etc.) must also consider the corresponding systems of institutions (respectively, commercial law, competition law, contract and consumer protection laws, corporate law, etc.). Consequently, since each element of a system can be considered a system in the hyper-structure of economic activities this is also the case for the system's elements in the hyper-structure of corresponding economic institutions.

The coevolution of Institutional systems as trigger of capitalist evolution

The debate on the institutions that enabled the appearance of capitalism emerged since the dispute over the origins of capitalism stimulated the interest among the scholars of different disciplines. The historical study of British and Western experience up to now has shown two approaches. On the one hand, there is the 'economic perspective', which states that the new economy was entirely a result of the actions promoted, taking advantage of the self-interest and propensity to exchange, by efficient institutions such as the property rights, credit markets, patent system and apprenticeship (Korpi 2001) or by a 'spontaneous order' (Hayek 1976). On the other hand, the 'cultural point of view' contends (following Weber on the role of the Protestant Reformation and Calvinist doctrine in Western Europe – Weber 1930) that values, beliefs and culture affected the 'institutional building process' of different environments, providing for different institutional trajectories.

On the matter Mokyr points out that in Great Britain the respect for contracts and reputation contributed, together with efficient institutions, to the characterisation of a model of trustworthiness (the 'gentleman') on which the cooperative environment for the development of the commercialisation and for the modernisation of the British economy grew (Mokyr 2008). Despite Mokyr's relativism about the institutions that triggered the advent of capitalism in Great Britain, the institutions identified as decisive for its emergence by the 'economic approach' (the property rights, credit markets, patent system and apprenticeship) have been generally considered not only effective for the problem solution but also basic for the emergence of capitalist economies everywhere and whenever. This conclusion would seem to be the last word on the topic of the institutional features of modern economies. But it isn't, because – historically – the institutional requirements that enabled the emergence of capitalism in Great Britain and some other Western countries ('first-comers') were different from the institutions characterising the working of a capitalist economy in full swing. Similarly, the creation of new institutions ('institution-building process') by current traditional economies in transition to capitalism questions the effectiveness of the replication of the institutions ruling the advanced modern economies ('institutional transfer'). Consequently, the problem of a consistent interpretation of economic institutions in different times and places of the capitalist evolution calls for an assessment of the institutional change process, which is able to explain the emergence, evolution and change of economic institutions.

There are many theories on institutional change, which differ in their interpretations about the sources, implementation and outcomes of institutional changes. (Person 2000; Dixit 2004; Williamson 2000; Kingston and Caballero 2009). In the systems analysis perspective institutional change may be thought of as a process of 'adaptation' of the institutional 'state of system' within its neighbourhood – i.e. as a 'strategic tweak' from a steadiness of the behavioural beliefs and procedures shared by individuals to another prevailing one, emerging from the agents' interaction. Consequently, institutional change is a historical and time-consuming process; the first trait depends on the number of connections characterising the outward equilibrium while the second is the result of the implementation of new connections. Therefore, since values and norms are shaped by individuals in a specific time and space, new institutions may result in different institutional organisations for the same function because of this distinctive feature. In such a framework institutional transfer may thus be ineffective in principle despite its sponsorship by international economic organisations ('Washington Consensus').

The systems analysis methodology is well-suited to pay attention to the main stylised facts which have emerged on the institutional change of capitalist economies (Chang 2007; Aoki 2007) – i.e. its internal origin, the proper internal growth of competition between old and new rules and the need for a complementary coevolution of other sociotechnical domains. Let's take a look at these aspects. Institutional change is an endogenous process triggered either by the transformation of old institutions or by the appearance of new ones. The source for this change is the development of groundbreaking procedures or new skills driving successful new strategies of action which, if repeated and co-ordinated, create sets of rules different from the previous ones. The technical advancement which took place with the evolution of capitalism can be considered an example for the rising competition within a settled institutional arrangement. In fact, the introduction of new technical routines for either different ways of conducting existing economic activities (such as the use of herbicide in the cropping methods implemented by the green revolution) or new methods (such as the sequence of different layouts-assembly line production systems – in industry in the so-called 'Fordism') stimulated the competition against old technical behaviours due to the effectiveness of the newer.

But such competition among agents implementing new and old practices is not always sufficient to spur the emergence of a new institutional set because sometimes it creates the destabilisation of the shared beliefs and balance of powers: despite the interplay between old and new institutions in shaping overall institutional quality, changes in the former cannot result in the adaptation to the latter until other interacting processes intervene. In fact, the evolution of economic institutions in the European capitalism of the 19th century, for example, shows the contrast between agricultural and industrial entrepreneurship; such divergence was decided by the political emergence of a bourgeoisie class, who imposed the commercial codes systematising the economic procedures and behaviours used in the everyday routine and introduced an industry-biased tax system. Historical trends thus evidence the groundlessness of the 'efficient view of institutions' hypothesis, which sees institutional change as a cooperative process in a unique field of social activities.

Even the fact that new institutions are an entirely endogenous process is questionable; the historical stylised facts show that institutional change in a specific domain is the result of a coevolving process – i.e. of an adaptive path followed by different but interacting domains (Aoki 2007: 24–6). In fact, the change in economic institutions during the capitalist evolution was also due to the transformation of cultural, political and legislative institutions because economic activities are carried out by interactions among entities belonging to one or more social fields (Aoki 2007: 11–13). An example of such a trend could be the 19th and 20th century laws which produced labour contracts restricting working hours and women's and child labour. These measures, promoted by the European States together with previous volunteer associations and hand in hand with the structural transformation of the socioeconomic system, attempted to validate the new economic structure and reduce the social and political costs stemming from the unequal distribution of power between employers and employees in different industries.

As a final comment on capitalist institutional change it must be pointed out that, if the implementation of this process in each social field requires a coevolution of other/social domains, the working and speed of evolution of modern economies also depend on the coevolution of policy, administration and private domain (culture, habits, etc). The reciprocal adaptability of interrelated domains is necessary for the advancement both of each social domain and of all the social systems.

Concluding remarks: Capitalist economies as complex, adaptive and evolving systems

The methodological framework described throughout the chapter for the representation of modern capitalist economies presents them as complex adaptive and evolving systems (Foster 2005) – i.e. as historical forms of economic organisation characterised by a 'restless nature' (Ramlogan and Metcalfe 2006: 121). This trait is important not only in relation to the way modern economies can be analysed but also for the economic system concept. When analysing a modern economy, the use of the systems analysis methodological approach makes possible a consistent assessment of the whole and its parts. As for the concept, the fact that the economic system is defined as an actual historical entity identified by its own constituents and hyper-structures means that:

i. The increasing levels of complexity correspond to different degrees of advancement in the path of transition from pre-industrial societies to capitalism. The economies characterised by different levels of capitalist development are thus partially capitalist ones.
ii. The development processes of two economies started at two different times of the world capitalist evolution are structurally different in both local and environmental conditions, as shown by the experiences of 'first-comers' and 'latecomers'.

iii. The coevolving processes characterising each development path can produce different 'models of capitalism'.
iv. Consequently, the so-called 'socialist' economic organisations must also be considered capitalist ones; the 'market socialism' label coined for the Chinese economy is nothing more than a 'model of capitalism'.

In this methodological approach an economic system is a complex entity (whose 'complexity is a problem in dynamics that transcend the complicated nature of the economic world') changing from within, 'and change from within depends on the emergence of new knowledge' (Ramlogan and Metcalfe 2006: 115–16). The economy is thus a knowledge-based system whose activities must be conceived as processes in an evolutionary path and whose fields of interest are 'the growth of knowledge, the development of the instituted framework of the system, and changes in the beliefs that stimulate action in a coevolutionary manner'. (Ramlogan and Metcalfe 2006: 122) In addition, from the point of view of the agents such a system presents these features:

i 'The agents are heterogeneous and interact directly with each other.
ii. the interaction and the information of agents are "local".
iii. The agents' behaviour is governed by simple "rules of thumb".
iv The aggregate behaviour of the system is not that of an "average" or representative agent.
v this aggregate behaviour "emerges" from the complicated interaction between the individuals' (Kirman 2008: 2).

Thus, such a perspective not only overcomes the fragmentation of economics (Kleiner 2009: 3) but also switches its traditional individualistic perspective into a 'systemism', which overcomes holism (Bunge 2000).

Bibliography

Aoki, M. (2007) 'Endogenizing Institutions and Institutional Change', *Journal of Institutional Economics*, 3 (1): 1–31.
Bertalanffy, L. Von (1968) *General Systems Theory. Foundations, Development, Applications*, New York: Braziller.
Boulding, K. (1978) *Ecodynamics: A New Theory of Social Evolution*, Beverly Hills: Sage.
Bunge, M. (2000) 'Systemism: The Alternative to Individualism and Holism', *Journal of Socio-Economics*, 29: 147–57.
Chang, H.-J. (ed.) (2007) *Institutional Change and Economic Development*, Tokyo: United Nations University Press.
Dixit, A. K. (2004) *Lawlessness and Economics*, Princeton: Princeton University Press.
Foster, J. (2005) 'From Simplistic to Complex Systems in Economics', *Cambridge Journal of Economics*, 29 (6): 873–92. https://doi.org/10.1093/cje/bei083
Gregory, P. R. and Stuart, R. C. (2004) *Comparing Economic Systems in the Twenty-first Century*, Boston: Houghton Mifflin Company.

Hayek, F. A. (1976) *Law, Legislation and Liberty Vol. II: The Mirage of Social Justice*, London: Routledge and Kegan.

Hindriks, F. and Guala, F. (2014) 'Institutions, Rules and Equilibria: A Unified Theory', *Journal of Institutional Economics*: 1–22. Available on CJO 2014 http://doi.org/10.1017/S1744137414000496

Hodgson, G. M. (2006) 'What Are Institutions?', *Journal of Economic Issues*, 60 (1): 1–25.

Kaldor, N. (1961) 'Capital Accumulation and Economic Growth', in F. A. Lutz and D. C. Hague (eds.) *The Theory of Capital*, London: Macmillan: 177–222.

Kingston, C. and Caballero, G. (2009) 'Comparing Theories of Institutional Change', *Journal of Institutional Economics*, 5 (2): 151–80.

Kirman, A. (1997) 'The Economy as an Evolving Network', *Journal of Evolutionary Economy*, 7: 339–53.

Kirman, A. (2008) 'Economy as a Complex System', in S. N. Durlauf and L. E. Blume (eds.) *The New Palgrave Dictionary of Economics*, 2nd ed., London: Palgrave Macmillan. *The New Palgrave Dictionary of Economics Online*. Palgrave Macmillan, 22 January 2016. http://www.dictionaryofeconomics.com/article?id=pde2008_E000246; http://doi.org/10.1057/9780230226203.0443

Kleiner, G. B. (2009) 'A New Theory of Economic Systems and its Application to Economic Policy Studies', *Russian Research Center Working Paper Series No. 13*, The Institute of Economic Research, Hitotsubashi University, Tokyo.

Koestler, A. (1978) *Janus: A Summing Up*, London: Hutchison.

Korpi, W. (2001) 'Contentious Institutions: An Augmented Rational-Actor Analysis of the Origins and Path Dependency of Welfare State Institutions in the Western Countries', *Rationality and Society*, 13 (2): 235–83.

Marx, K. (1887) *Capital. A Critic of Political Economy* (German edition 1867), Marx–Engels Internet Archive. Seearxistss.org

Mokyr, J. (2008) 'The Institutional Origins of the Industrial Revolution', in E. Helpman (ed.) *Institutions and Economic Performance*, Cambridge, MA: Harvard University Press.

North, D. C. (1990) *Institutions, Institutional Change and Economic Performance*, Cambridge: Cambridge University Press.

Ogilvie, S. (2007) 'Whatever is, is Right? Economic Institutions in Pre-industrial Europe', *Tawney Lecture 2006, CESIFO Working Paper*, 2006. https://www.cesifo.org/DocDL/cesifo1_wp2066.pdf

Person, P. (2000) 'The Limits of Design: Explaining Institutional Origins and Change', *Governance: An International Journal of Policy and Administration*, 13 (4): 475–99.

Potts, J. (2000) *The New Evolutionary Microeconomics*, Cheltenham: Edward Elgar.

Quesnay, F. (1766) 'Analyse de la formule arithmétique du tableau économique de la distribution des dépenses annuelles d'une Nation agricole', *Journal de l'agriculture, du commerce & des finances,* tome II, 3ème partie (juin): 11–41.

Ramlogan, R. and Metcalfe, J. S. (2006) 'Restless Capitalism: A Complexity Perspective on Modern Capitalist Economies', in E. Garnsey and J. McGlade (eds.) *Complexity and Coevolution. Continuity and Change in Socio-Economic Systems*, Cheltenham: Edward Elgar, 115–46.

Searle, J. R. (2005) 'What is an Institution?', *Journal of Institutional Economics*, 1 (1): 1–22.

Shotter, A. (1981) *The Economic Theory of Social Institutions*, Cambridge: Cambridge University Press.

Simon, H. (1962) 'The Architecture of Complexity', *Proceedings of the American Philosophical Society*, 106: 476–82.

Simon, H. (1996) *The Science of the Artificial*, 3rd ed., Cambridge, MA: MIT Press (first edition 1969).
Walras, L. (1874)' *Éléments d'économie politique pure, ou théorie de la richesse sociale (Elements of Pure Economics, or the Theory of Social Wealth)*.
Weber, M. (1930) *The Protestant Ethic and The Spirit of Capitalism*, English translation by T. Parson, New York: Charl'es Scribner's Sons (German edition 1904–5).
Williamson, O. E. (2000) 'The New Institutional Economics: Taking Stock, Looking Ahead', *Journal of Economic Literature*, 38: 595–613.

Glossary

Axiom is a universally accepted statement, principle or rule that is believed to be true without any proof.

Consequence function is the set of decided rewards and sanctions ready for disciplining the behaviours that occur in the performance of social actions or organisational routines.

Epistemology is the critical study of the grounds (principles and axioms) of a disciplinary scientific knowledge.

Form of an institution is the set of rules considered suitable for achieving the social purpose.

Function of an institution is the aim on which the social behaviour or interaction is focused.

Game form is a set of instructions provided for performing a social activity, which include the 'game aims', the set of participants and the 'game rules'('consequence function').

Hierarchy is a centralised organisational structure.

Hyper-structure is a mathematical concept whose properties make it possible to represent the reality as a system of systems of different levels so that the image of a phenomenon depends upon the level at which it is viewed.

Homo economicus is an isolated being endowed with a given income who carries out economic activities by following natural preferences and economic behavioural principles.

Homo hetero-economicus is a social being characterised by connections, competition, and adaptation who carries out economic activities.

Institution building process is the changing of old institutions or the implementation of new ones to facilitate or stimulate the emergence of new social actions or technological routines.

Institutional process is the actual working of rules of conduct supporting goal-oriented social actions and organisational routines within a hyper-structure.

Institutional transfer is the replication of a set of institutions ruling the advanced economies in developing countries seeking to implement a development process.

Methodology is a set of methods needed to scientifically explain a phenomenon.

Plan of actions are the arrangement of actions that the participants in a social activity carry out based on the state of the game and their beliefs about the behaviour of other participants.

Polyarchy is a decentralised organisational structure.

System is an indivisible acting unit made up of a group of interconnected elements and characterised by an order (number of elements), a dimension (number of binary connections), a state (a specific connective arrangement) and a degree of concentration.

State of the game is the successful schemes of behaviour representing the relevant features of the ways the social activities are repeatedly performed.

Stylised facts are uncontroversial relevant empiric facts showing the trends of a phenomenon.

Washington Consensus is a set of policies recommended by World Bank, the International Monetary Fund and the US Treasury Department to developing countries so they can achieve the structural adjustment of their economies.

4 Representation and appraisal of modern economic systems

The image of modern economies as complex, adaptive and evolving systems, emerged from the methodological perspective presented in the previous chapters, provides a framework both for understanding their evolution over two and a half centuries and for studying their hyper-structure and functioning. Notably, the use of systems analysis enables the synthetic portrayal of the historical dynamics outlined in Chapters One to Three as a capitalist advance due to coevolving processes characterised by a series of tweaks; moreover, it allows the examination of the economic systems and their components (studied in the second part of the book) as a set of organisations co-ordinated by networks of institutional relations.

Current economic thought tends to ignore the concept of economic system, so the approach adopted in this book for the analysis of modern economies could appear unfitting. Nevertheless, the representation of the economy as an entity on its own with respect to its components dates back to the downing of economics. In fact, after Quesnay's description of the way a traditional agriculture-based economy operated (Quesnay 1766) the economic theory proposed Marx's scheme of reproduction and accumulation under capitalism (Marx 1867–1884, vol. 1, chap. 23; vol. 2, chaps. 20 and 21 edition 1999) and Walras's investigation of equilibrium in economies conceived as sets of markets (Walras 1874). Later, between the 1930s and 1980s, economists inconclusively set against market and administrative planning as better forms of organisation and coordination for a modern economy. The fall of the Berlin Wall put an abrupt end to the wrangling, curtailing interest in this topic as well as in the building blocks of capitalism, just as the surviving economic arrangement (the market) seemed to be asserting himself as the sole, undisputed model representing modern economies. In the end an unhistorical, mathematical and micro-founded image of the economy based on a set of exchanges was established as the model representing every modern economy; meanwhile, a technological revolution, new forms of production and new institutions were demonstrating that modern economies are far more than a mere exchange mechanism.

To investigate modern economies under the perspective of systems analysis a representation consistent with the stylised facts characterising them is necessary, as well as a deep analysis of the nature of their organisational forms and coordinating

DOI: 10.4324/9781315679730-6

routines. An archetype of this representation (see Patinkin 1973; Emmett 2013) was sketched by Frank Knight in the 1930s:

> The general character of an enterprise system, reduced to its very simplest terms, can be illustrated by a diagram showing the exchange of productive power for consumption goods between individuals and business units, mediated by the *circulation* of money, and suggesting the familiar figure of the *wheel of wealth*. . . . Seen in the large, free enterprise is an organization of production and distribution in which individuals or family units get their real income, their 'living', by selling productive power for money to 'business units' or 'enterprises', and buying with the money income thus obtained the direct goods and services which they consume. This view, it will be remembered, ignores for the sake of simplicity the fact that an appreciable fraction of the productive power in use at any time is not really employed in satisfying current wants but to make provision for increased want-satisfaction in the future; it treats society as it would be, or would tend to become, with progress absent, or in a 'static' state.
>
> (Knight 1951: 61, 60)

A further step in the direction of synthetising an economic system was provided by the diagram known as the 'circular flow of income' (Gilibert 2008). Being consistent both with the methodological framework of this book and with the stylised facts observed during the evolution of capitalism, this portrayal of the mechanics of the economic process reveals its subjects and connections (real or monetary flows) side by side the basic functional organisations of the economic system and the types of economic activities. In addition, the representation of modern economies by the 'circular flow of income' enables the appraisal of the output of the system by identifying macroeconomic variables – i.e. the aggregate indicators of output and structure of the economy statistically measured.

The theoretical relevance of the representation of a modern economy by means of the 'circular flow of income' lies in the fact that such a model assumes the institutional structure of the economic process embedded in the configuration of flows (markets rules, technologies and fiscal policies), and by this way it manifests a role of the state in the economy. Indeed, initially the state defines, in the interest of society, the requirements necessary for the activities carried out in the economic process to be acceptable, attributing to them the qualification of 'formal, informal, shadow, and criminal' economic activities, thus splitting them in just as many categories. Then it sets the general orientation of the economic system through the laws and policies ruling the economy (for example, by structuring the fiscal system). So, considering the political and economic role of the state, the purposive and instrumental nature of a modern economy emerges as a machinery built to provide social welfare. This distinctive but neglected feature must be considered by the discipline dedicated to its study, as economics is.

A systemic representation of capitalist economies

The review of the stylised facts characterising capitalism shows that the core features of this socioeconomic system are the creation of new forms of organisation (to produce an increasing number of goods and services and to exchange and use them) and the ability to widely co-ordinate economic activities and subjects. Thus, the concept of organisation proves to be a powerful device to understand the structure of modern economies, side by side with the related concept of coordination – i.e. the establishment of a set of institutions essential for the performance of the economic process. Both elements are shown in the so-called 'circular flow of income', a sketch depicting the economic process of modern economies.[1]

An image of the capitalist economic process: The 'circular flow diagram'

The capitalist 'economic process' – i.e. a sequence of organised and co-ordinated activities carried out in modern economies by people to provide themselves with goods and services – originated from the previous socioeconomic system. In fact, the progressive dismantling of the self-consumption economy gave way to an economic organisation where the production process and consumption were autonomous phenomena, the exchange took place by a network of connections between them and the state carried out the general oversight of the economy. Throughout the advance of capitalism, on the one hand production became a complex capital-intensive activity (involving more and more instruments, skills and competences) carried out by ever larger organisations, and on the other hand consumption became a technologically interrelated activity increasingly connected to mankind's social needs as well as its biological requirements. Via independent trajectories, production and consumption advanced more or less harmoniously, thanks to the market connections, the monitoring and cooperative role of the state and the institution building process implemented in all the other social fields coevolving with the economy. This structure is the core of the 'circular flow diagram'.

Consider a very simplified economic system, where the economic process is carried out only by one kind of producer creating a consumer good later bought by families. Suppose that this 'final product' is a type of food produced on farms; furthermore, suppose that farms are managed by entrepreneurial farmers who rent fields from non-working landlords and hire workers. Finally, suppose that each farmer is equipped with the tools and seeds necessary to carry out their activity as well as with an amount of money to pay for the 'means of production' (labour and land). This simple economic process includes two 'subjects' performing different but complementary tasks: the farms that 'produce' a certain amount of food by farming the land and using salaried workers, and families that live by consuming the food produced by the farms. In terms of systems analysis this economy is a system of order 2 and dimension 4 as it has two 'elements' (farms and families) linked by two different pairs of connections: 'real flows' (the means of production and goods) and the corresponding monetary payments ('monetary flows') as in Figure 4.1.

Regarding the functioning of the system, production is carried out thanks to the presence of 'resource markets' transferring land and labour from the families that own them to the farms using them in exchange for rent (R) and salaries (W), as represented by the lines under the ovals in Figure 4.1. On the other hand, consumption is driven by the market for 'final products', where the farms supply food and

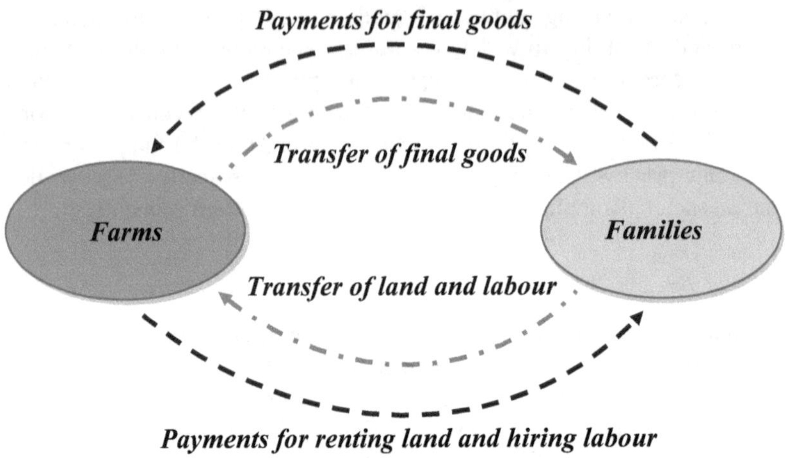

Figure 4.1 The economic process of a very simplified capitalist economy

Source: Author's elaboration

families purchase it using the money received as 'income' (wages and rents), as represented by the lines above the ovals in Figure 4.1. These elliptical figures form two 'circular' and opposing flows: a real flow of resources (labour and land) from the families to the farms and a flow of final products (food) from the farms to the families as well as a monetary flow consisting in the payment of rent and salaries by the farms to the families, who can pay for the goods by means of these revenues.

Bearing in mind the basic structure of a capitalist economy and the functioning of its economic processes the industrial production must be introduced in the previous representation. In Figure 4.2 the simplified economic system still includes two economic subjects (firms and households), but production is organised into three kinds of firms (legally incorporated – i.e. companies whose capital is divided in shares owned by a number of different people, the shareholders): the first one produces a certain amount of raw materials or agricultural products (Firms 1), the second creates semi-finished or intermediate products (Firms 2), while the third obtains finished products (Firms 3). Since firms use owned assets (i.e. machinery) as means of production, they expect to be rewarded for the economic risk they run for them in the managerial activity; it is therefore acceptable to introduce a 'profit' as risk insurance cover earned by the owners of the firms – i.e. the households that bought shares of the business social capital when the firm was created by their savings.

The functioning of this simplified economic system is shown in Figure 4.2, limited to monetary flows. At the beginning of the production process each type of firm has a stock of assets (establishment, plant and money) sufficient for production. Each firm hires workers paying them salaries (W) and distributing the profits to shareholders (Π) after the products have been sold (the dashed lines in Figure 4.2). For firms producing raw materials, the cost of production includes only labour, while for other firms it also includes the cost of raw materials or intermediate resources, produced by firms higher up the production chain (the payments are represented by dotted lines

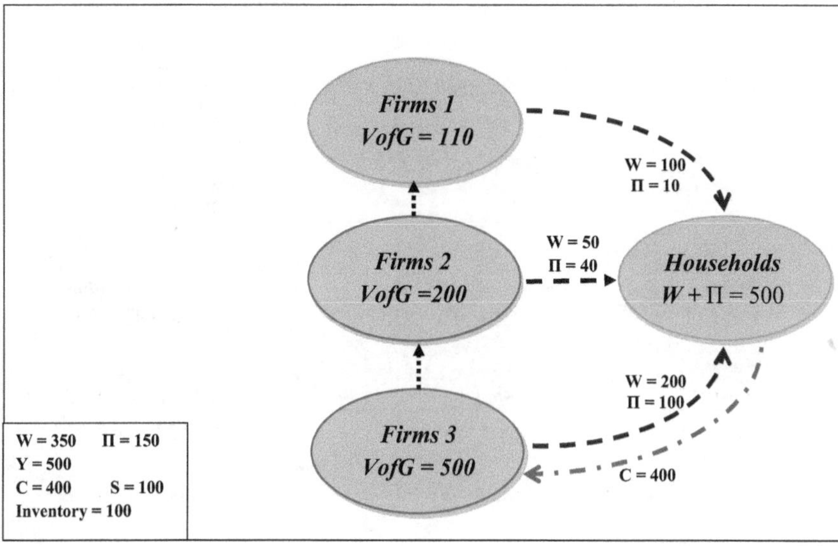

Figure 4.2 A simplified economic system

Source: Author's elaboration

in Figure 4.2). The profit is an extra-cost item (i.e. a mark-up) which determines the final value of the goods and services produced (VofG). Suppose that the total value of production in the system is 500 monetary units (whether £ or $, € or ¥) and 500 is also the 'income' (Y) the households receive as the sum of wages (350) and profits (150). Since the demand for final goods and services (consisting of consumption C) amounts to 400, the remaining part of the income (100) represents the savings (S); this means that the unsold part of the output (100 money units) must be stored by the firms as inventory (I). It should be remembered that the income produced by an economy is not its 'wealth'; wealth is the stock of assets in an economy which are used several times in a series of economic processes while income is the yearly flow of output obtained from the wealth in the system.

Figure 4.3 provides a picture approaching a modern economy. It shows the functioning of a closed capitalist economy – i.e. a system without economic relations with other nations. In this case the economic system also shows the role of another subject of an economy (i.e. the state), which reveals the third economic function: income/wealth withdrawal to provide the economy with communal goods and/or services. Actually, this economic function is allowed to the state only by virtue of its original power and comprises two economic activities: tax collection (i.e. the legal imposition of monetary payments by firms and households [T_f and T_h flows, dashed grey lines in Figure 4.3] and the activation, by means of these revenues, of the demand for the goods and services (C_g) and of employment in the public sector (W_g) necessary to provide general services and infrastructures. Thus, using these resources the state implements the production of goods and services for a value equivalent to the outcome of its organisational departments.

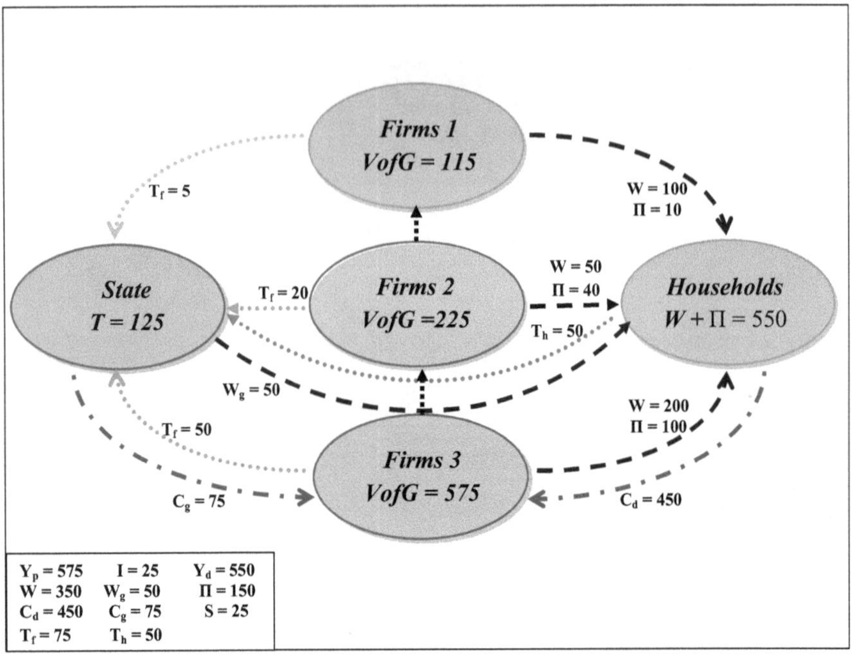

Figure 4.3 A closed economic system

Source: Author's elaboration

Modern economies, however, are increasingly open to commercial, financial and labour flows to and from other national economies. Therefore, 'exports' (the sale of goods and services abroad with a monetary inflow for firms) and 'imports' (a monetary outflow by firms and households to pay foreign firms for goods and services bought) must also be considered. This is shown in Figure 4.4, where domestic exports comprise only finished products and services (X), while imports are goods and services purchased by all kinds of firms (M_f) and households (M_h).

The 'open economic system' shown in Figure 4.4 is a good representation of modern economies because, on the one hand, it takes into account all their distinctive features and, on the other, it enables basic economic concepts to be identified. From the structural point of view this figure shows both the organisational dimension of the three functions characterising capitalist economies (production, consumption and the taxation through which the state administration can provide general social services) and the corresponding roles played by human beings in carrying out economic activities (as producers, consumers and taxpayers). Regarding the operation of an economic system Figure 4.4 demonstrates the ability of institutions through human aptitudes (behavioural principles), sociotechnical rules and laws to co-ordinate economic activities to make the system work. Thus, the functional components and the institutional connections constituting the capitalist economic system can be recapped in Figure 4.5, where the dotted black line

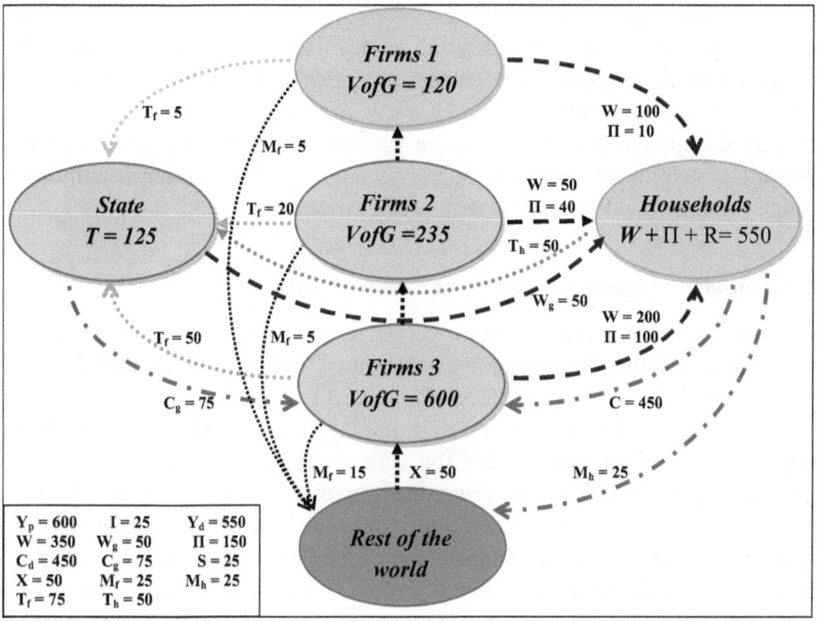

Figure 4.4 An open economic system (1)

Source: Author's elaboration

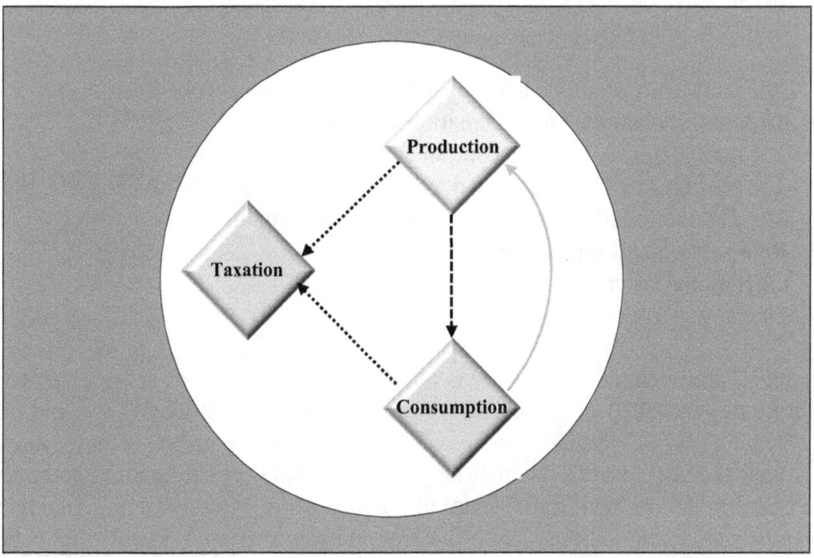

Figure 4.5 The functional representation of the economic system

Source: Author's elaboration

represents reciprocal real flows (the means of production and goods) and the grey continuous line shows the corresponding money flows. Both represent the markets through which the circulation of resources, goods and services occur, while tax payments are shown by black spotted lines.

Lastly, the circular flow of the income scheme enables the macro variables of an economic system to be identified and the accounting of the economic activities of a country to be carried out. These items are analysed later.

The organisations as basic components of modern economic systems

The structure of a modern economic system summarised in the 'circular flow of income' demonstrates the role of organisations. The set of interrelated firms carrying out production, the multifaceted choice of goods and services balancing household needs and its income through the consumption, the many intertwined intermediate and final markets and the economic activities of governments are organised economic actions. However, the aforementioned four organisations and their functions (production, consumption, the circulation of economic resources, goods and services, and taxation/provision of public services) have important differences in terms of the coordination of activities and cooperative behaviour right inside. An in-depth analysis of the concept of organisation is therefore needed before further examination of these four forms of economic organisation.

Albeit with differing interpretations of the term (Ouchi 1980: 129), it is generally agreed that an organisation is a well-established social unit, comprising people, materials, tools and intangible assets, that is managed in a co-ordinated manner in order to pursue a collective aim. Therefore, any generic organisation is characterised by the following:

i. The function it performs and its legal standing, as established.
ii. The subject charged with its creation and rule.
iii. The quality and skills of its components.
iv. The positions and tasks assigned to people according to the division of labour.
v. The distribution of responsibilities and decision-making.
vi. Relations of authority, control and power.
vii. Operational criteria.
viii. Operational routines.

Chapter Three defined organisations as the forms of a system as they are configurations (or states) of a specific set of elements and relations. Thus, the first two features in the previous list, recalling the purposive nature of any system, highlight the will of an individual or group of people (or subject that embodies their determination, such as the state) to pursue an aim by creating and managing an organisation. In addition, these features indicate that all kinds of established organisations are endowed with a specific institutional status in compliance with the law, even though their origin is 'naturally' connected to human propensities (like trade propensity or self-interest pursuit, for example). Feature number 3 in the list shifts the attention to the components of an organisation (people, materials, tools and intangible assets), which should be considered as groupings or baskets of different skills and characteristics. Although the potential resources of each component are an endowment for the organisation, they are generally exploited only partially by the organisation. Features 4–6 represent the processes of the organisation as a set of operations, with tasks (engineered and scheduled according to the technical division of labour and associated with both decision-making and responsibilities) assigned to people based on their skills. Thus, the 'organisational chart' shows operational routines while the 'organisational structure' shows the relations of authority, control and power – i.e. the degree of concentration or decentralisation of the organisation. Regarding the operational criteria of an organisation (item number 7 in the list), two different aspects can be appraised: 'effectiveness' and 'efficiency'. 'Effectiveness' represents the ability of an organisation to achieve its aims: this outcome can be evaluated in terms of goal-attainment measured as a percentage. Conversely, 'efficiency' is the ability of an organisation to obtain the achieved output with the minimum quantity of resources; this result is assessed by different indices consisting of input/output ratios (inputs productivity, net revenues per product, etc.). The ensuing measures depend both on the quality of the technical components of the organisation (other things being equal, better tools generate higher output), their coordination (seeking the optimum use of tools and workers) and the cooperation between people. While it is technically possible to calculate efficiency values for the materials and instruments used and for the operations carried out in the organisational process, this cannot be done for individuals: once embedded in a flowchart, they act efficiently only if they cooperate.

The cooperative behaviour of the members of an organisation is due to the trust in those who exercise authority, control and power over the individuals involved in the organisational process. The 'expectation of reciprocity' in the contribution/reward system (the higher the effort, the higher the pay for an individual) and the 'impartial application' of this principle to everyone motivate cooperation. Where the evaluation of the task performed (for functional or technical reasons) is ambiguous or uncertain, an extra reward/incentive (whether monetary or not) is necessary to persuade people to cooperate. Another element affecting cooperative behaviour is the 'degree of coherence' between the collective goal of the organisation and individual wishes: where there is incoherence, an incentive to cooperate is necessary. Therefore, organisations bear costs ('transactional' in the exchange or 'organisational' in a social organism) to induce individuals to act efficiently: the smaller the trust and coherence, the higher the transactional or organisational costs.

The coordination of an organisation is how its components are connected to efficiently achieve its aims. There are two different coordinating methods: hierarchical or vertical and heterarchical or horizontal (Crumley 1995). In the former case each component has one-directional connections with a superior and subordinate: generally, she receives directives from the former and sends directives to the latter. In the case of a heterarchical organisation the connections between components are two-directional and each component can be a centre of connections. Once established and repeated coordinating methods become a routine, hence an institution. As institutions are purposive each organisation can be the source of a state of art (the state of the game) in a specific field of social activities.

By combining some structural features of an organisation (the degree of trust and coherence) with the different forms of internal coordination (vertical and horizontal) three types of social organisations are obtained: a bureaucracy, a clan or a market. Bureaucracy is a form of organisation characterised by hierarchical coordination (with a high level of authority, control and power) and by routines, where only partial trust in superiors and the coherence between individual and collective aims is offset by incentives and/or inspection and monitoring costs. A bureaucratic organisation may be exhibited by firms, government administrations and teams. The clan is a bureaucracy where there is no need for incentives because of the absence of mistrust and incoherence; this is the case with religious congregations, families and armies. The market is a horizontal form of organisation where the exchange of goods and services is authorised and organised according to terms and conditions that establish generally interdependent duties for each of its components. In this type of organisation there are no problems of cooperation (the buyer and seller both have an interest in carrying out the exchange), but there are 'transactional costs' offsetting the asymmetric information. Thus, except for the market all the general functions of an economic system are carried out by hierarchical organisations.

The purposive nature of modern economic systems

The in-depth analysis of the concept of organisation completes the presentation of the theoretical instruments necessary to analyse the structure and functioning of modern economies. The historical examination has shown the novelty of the capitalist economic system, the systems analysis approach revealed its complexity and a dynamic concept of institutions made known its functioning and transformation. Now, the concepts of organisation and coordination enable its arrangement and hyper-structure to be studied, giving rise to a comprehensive definition of the economic system in line with the methodology adopted in this volume.

Following systems theory, the modern economic system is an instrument by which capitalist societies manage social welfare; thus, it is by nature a sort of machine built on social principles and in order to achieve the chosen aims of society. This general function is carried out by means of specific system's configurations of the economy resulting from four kinds of component (that are as much as organisations: production, consumption, the circulation of economic resources, goods and services and taxation/provision of public services) interrelated by networks of connections between them (the rules of coordination presiding over its functioning: the institution). Both the components and connections bestow on the economy a specific systemic endowment, whose value lies in the resources used (people, tools, tangible and intangible resources) and in the institutions established. The contribution of resources to the output of an economic system depends on their qualities: the intrinsic worth of people's work is based on their knowledge and skills (as well as the level of exploitation in economic activities); the qualities of production plant rest on the degree of mechanisation, technological obsolescence and innovation, and on the amount and suitability of the services supporting economic activities (such as transportation, communications, power plant and public services); lastly, the qualities of tangible and intangible resources depend on the amount of natural resources, real estate, financial capital and intangible assets (intellectual property, goodwill and branding of a country's businesses). The contribution of institutions depends instead on their levels of quality (i.e. of effectiveness and efficiency). If resources and institutions provide an economic system with value, both are necessary for the features and outcome of modern economies (for example the level of income that can be achieved). There is insufficient awareness of this dual nature of the economic system since most current definitions focus on institutions alone.[2]

The institutional framework of capitalism is a central topic in the literature on economic systems (see Gregory and Stuart 2004), but only the different ways of coordinating economic activities in modern economies (market or plan) have been investigated ever since the discipline came into being. In the framework of this volume, the problem must be dealt with in a wider perspective by applying the dynamic concept of institutions (Chapter Three) to the nature of a capitalist economic system. The technical and behavioural rules governing both the arrangement and the co-ordinated operation of a modern economic system have a twofold purposive role. On the one hand, they underpin the organisation of the four structural components of a capitalist economy which perform its essential 'functions' (production, consumption, the circulation of economic resources, goods and services, and taxation/provision of public services) and keep the system alive. On the other hand, they provide some institutional 'forms' in order to drive the economy towards the achievement of the social aims of society. Therefore, two groups of institutions co-ordinate economic system activities: one 'systemic' and the other 'socially goal-oriented'.

Although these two kinds of institutions are utterly interwoven, they can usefully be described individually. According to the above distinction, the vital functions towards which 'systemic institutions' drive decision-making processes[3] are the following:

i. The creation, management and development of the firm and its structural and territorial aggregations (sectors and clusters). The following are institutional forms suited to this function are:

    a. Corporate and property law.
    b. Competition law and industrial relations regulations.
    c. Incentives to investment and innovation.

ii. The promotion of jobs, the protection of personal purchasing power and welfare conditions in order to increase consumption. This function requires the following:

    a. Employment law and retirement regulations.
    b. Customer protection law and customer credit law.

iii. The support of all types of markets defending the equality of the contracting parties against information and power asymmetries. Institutional forms to achieve this aim include the following:

   a. Corporate law and advertising regulations.
   b. Financial market regulation and the regulation of information markets.

iv. The provision of procedures for making public choices, for guaranteeing an equitable and impartial tax system and for promoting a socially oriented, countercyclical role for the state. The rules that go in this direction include the following:

   a. The principles of the tax system and the national budget regulation.
   b. Incentives to promote and support a social welfare system.

Conversely, 'socially goal-oriented' institutions drive the economic process of the system as a whole toward the priorities of society, for example by directing healthcare or education toward the private or public system, favouring either joining in or leaving a free trade area and promoting banks or the stock exchange as the central operator in the financial system.

Regarding the determination of economic priorities, Gregory and Stuart maintain the solution 'differs from economy to economy', depending on how social decisions are taken and in particular on the 'various arrangements through which individuals can express preferences by voting' (Gregory and Stuart 2004: 45–6). This mechanism is important, but it concerns the short-term economic aims (generally focused on 'socially goal-oriented institutions') – that is, the policies to manage the economy day-by-day. To understand the role of economic activities inside of the society and what kind of social welfare the economic system tries to foster a close attention must be paid to the 'systemic institutions' – that is, to the long-term features that shaped the economy. These traits reveal the basic choices made and carried through over time concerning the structure and management of production, consumption, the role of the state and of markets. Such economic priorities are generally the ones the state – that is, the subject to whom the creation and regulation of the economic system may concern – commit to put into effects; they are frequently enshrined in the constitution and embedded via an institutional framework in the structure and management of the economy. Thus, the aims of modern economic systems can be deduced from their constitutional economic principles; however, generally, prescriptions or guidelines exist for the law giver issuing 'institutional forms' (laws), which are not always complied with.

A list of economic matters governed by constitutional disciplinary articles is presented in the Table 4.1, where the first column reports the economic functions that each national society wanted to shape in a specific way by steering the matters that are in the second column. Not all the top ten economies whose evolution has been presented alongside the previous chapters are considered in the table due to the absence of a constitution (as in the case of United Kingdom) or of articles concerning economic matters (as in the case of United States). Even though 'systemic

Table 4.1 Constitutional articles setting up principles for the economic activities in selected countries

Functions of the economic system	*Subject of constitutional principles*	*France*	*Germany*	*Italy*	*Japan*	*Russia*	*Brazil*	*India*	*China*
Management of property and organisation of production	- Private property safeguard and constraints	D17	14, 15	41, 42, 43,	29	8, 9, 35, 36	5	300	10, 11, 13
	- Entrepreneurship and business activity			41,44,		34			18
	- Cooperative			45			21	43	17
	- Public enterprise	P9		41,			21		12, 16
Organisation and management of working activities	- Work right	P5,	12	1, 4	27	7, 37		41,43	42
	- Work safeguard	P10–11		35,36	27	37	7	24	43, 45
	- Woman, child work protection	P10–11, P13		37	27		7		
	- Trade uions regulation and collective bargain	P6, P8,		39	28		7		
	- Strike right								
	- Unemployment		9(3)	40		37	9		
	and social policies	P7,	7, 91e	38		39, 41, 43	7		
Public finance organisation	- Public finance criteria		91a, 109, 110						
	- Fiscal duty principles	D13,		53	30	57			56
	- Taxing system criteria		106	75	84, 85		152		
	- Budget management criteria and rules		111–115	81	60, 86, 87, 90			112	89, 117. 118
Economic system's and sector's organisation	- Economic order principles			41		75	170, 174		6, 7, 9, 10, 14, 15,
	- Public regulation for saving and credit			47					
	- Agrarian reform			44			184	48	
	- Agricul. Management								8

Source: Author's elaboration from: *Constitution du 4 octobre 1958, Deutscher Bundestag (2019) Basic Law for the Federal Republic of Germany,* Government of India *The Constitution of India*, National People's Congress (2018) ***Constitution of the People's Republic of China***, Prime Minister of Japan (1946) *The Constitution of Japan,* Senato della repubblica (2012) *Constitution of the Italian Republic,* Supreme Federal Court (2019) *Constitution of the Federative Republic of Brazil*, The State Duma (2018) *Constitution of the Russian Federation.*

Note: D is for Déclaration des Droits de l'Homme et du Citoyen de 1789, and P for Préambule de la Constitution du 27 octobre 1946.

institutions' can be considered of constitutional relevance, the founding fathers of some constitutions thought that the guidance about specific 'socially goal-oriented' matters (like education and healthcare systems) could be necessary to pursue the desired welfare. The analysis of the table shows that all these countries are aware that to support capitalist economies the private and public property and entrepreneurial use of resources is necessary, as well as work safeguard and protection. Someone provides guidelines also to manage the public budget (Germany, Italy, Japan, India and China) or to build social policy systems (Germany, Italy, Russia and Brazil).

Along with economic principles and laws, technological procedures and personal behavioural principles direct the activities in an economic system. The former are efficient algorithms developed by technicians to obtain a result in the production process (of a product, a service or a project), for the public administration, in the use of durable consumables (driving a car, using a computer) and when buying or selling a product. Conversely, personal behaviour is a spontaneous human tendency (or a calculated manner to act) in economic activities, reflecting self-interest and attitudes towards trade.

From the representation of the economic system to national accounting

In addition to information on the structure and functioning of modern economies the 'circular flow of income' also provides data on their performance, enabling the assessment of different sets of economic activities. However, to unambiguously ascribe these activities to generic economic subjects (entrepreneurs, consumers, the state) the breakdown of economic activities into three separate categories (production, consumption and taxation) is insufficient. Producers/traders and customers are parties to the purchase agreement, but which subject is entitled to record the value of the transaction? To decide this issue – i.e. how accounts should be kept – 'economic activity' and economic subjects need to be more closely defined, an analytical step that paves the way to evaluating economic systems. Data collected by a 'system of national accounts' leads to statistical indices which show the trends of economic variables or general phenomena and from which economic forecasts can be made using statistical and econometric tools.

'Economic units' and legal categories of 'economic activities'

Generally speaking, the definition of 'economic activity' is tautological and partial. The term is used to cover all the actions driven by 'economic reasons' that are carried out to provide people with material welfare; thus, the production, purchasing or selling of goods and services are economic activities performed in exchange for money (or substitutes), this being the sole motivation pushing to go through with them. Conversely, non-economic activities are carried out for non-economic motives, including social, religious, cultural, psychological or sentimental reasons. As such, the term 'economic activities' excludes all actions unrelated to a market and hence denies that non-market production, distribution and consumption can provide societies with material welfare. However, in modern (and traditional) economies, many activities such as production for personal and family sustenance, the 'informal' activities carried out within households (jobs performed in exchange for something other than money[4]) and the state provision of social services are non-market activities which improve the material conditions of people. Therefore, a different perspective should be adopted to define economic activities and match the facts with science.

Since economies seek to provide societies with social welfare, all the actions carried out to create goods, services or capital for distribution and consumption are 'economic activities'. Such a definition rests upon the four categories of economic activity making up the schematic representation of the capitalist economic process (production, consumption, trade and the activities carried out by the state in relation to them) and on the activity conducted by the state acting as nonprofit institutional unit involved in the organisation and regulation of the economic system. This is the perspective of the System of National Accounts (SNA), which gathers statistical data to measure economic phenomena. This technical publication provides 'a comprehensive and detailed record of the complex economic activities taking place within an economy and of the interaction between the different economic agents, and groups of agents, that takes place on markets or elsewhere' (EC, IMF, OECD, UN and WB – *European Commission, International Monetary Fund, Organisation for Economic Co-operation and Development, United Nations, and World Bank 2009:* 1). In addition to the fact that economic activities are not restricted to market transactions, the publication defines them with regard to 'economic units' – i.e. the subjects at the centre of decision-making who are legally responsible for all the economic behaviour associated with a specific economic activity, such as production, consumption, the accumulation of assets and the transactions required to carry them out.[5] In modern economies these subjects are 'institutional units' of two types ('households' and 'legal entities'), endowed with legal personality and able to carry out a specific economic activity. In particular, legal entities

> are either entities created for purposes of production, mainly corporations and non-profit institutions, or entities created by political processes, specifically government units. The defining characteristic of an institutional unit is that it is capable of owning goods and assets, incurring liabilities, and engaging in economic activities and transactions with other units in its own right.
>
> (EU, *IM, OECD, UN, and WB 2009:* 2)

Thus, the 'economic subject' is an institutional unit acting in the economic field as producer, consumer, tax collector or taxpayer.

The System of National Accounts – recognised as an internationally agreed coordinating framework for economic statistics in accordance with accounting conventions and economic principles – anchors the definition of economic activities and subjects; therefore, it deserves some considerations. The economic subject as a legal unit is consistent with the fact that the economic system is a mechanism built and managed by the state for achieving social aims in the economic field. Therefore, if the institutional framework of a state shapes the traits of economic units, the behaviour of the three types of economic subject (producer, consumer and public administration) in their transactions must be consistent with the legal framework established by the state. Every individual (and legal entity) can act in one or more of these roles according to economic aptitude (self-interest, trading propensity, free riding, etc.), but only in compliance with the legal framework for each role. This legal framework, built by states to protect and empower economic subjects, extends to economic activities on behalf of the general interest of communities. Not all economic actions imagined can be carried out because some are forbidden or restricted by the states. Therefore, the actions carried out in the capitalist process require the authorisation of the state and only those permitted are acknowledged as 'economic activities'.

According to the legitimacy and legal requirements for their implementation, 'economic activities' can be broadly broken down[6] into four legal categories and subsets of the economic system (or so-called 'economies' – see Figure 4.6) defined as:

T. The 'formal economy' – i.e. the set of actions carried out in the economic process that are both legitimised by the law and performed according to the law. These categories include all authorised economic activities, which are registered and traceable.

ii. The 'shadow economy' (or 'grey/underground economy'[7]) – i.e. the set of economic activities carried out in violation of the procedures or rules under the law, mainly for the purpose of evading tax or regulatory requirements. This category includes all authorised actions (entrepreneurial activities, jobs, money transfers, trades and purchases) rendered deliberately untraceable and thus unregistered.

iii. The category of the informal economy is defined in various ways despite the attempts to unify the different concepts that are used. In the Chapter Twenty-Five of the *System of national accounts* the informal sector 'may be broadly characterised as consisting of units engaged in the production of goods or services with the primary objective of generating employment and incomes to the persons concerned' (*E C, I M F, O E C D, U N, and W B 2009 : 474).* This category includes informal own-account enterprises, labour relations based on casual employment, kinship, or personal and social relations rather than contractual arrangements, but also some nonprofit, non-market institutional activities (such as those of foundations, social and sports clubs, artistic and cultural organisations). These activities are generally untraceable but can be measured by indirect statistical methods.[8] This subset includes also economic actions performed without remuneration for altruism. To sum up the informal sector is defined as a subset of unobserved activities, as the starting point is the definition of the economic activities as observable and measurable ones. An alternative definition could be that the informal activities are permitted economic activities carried out on purpose without any kind of reward (domestic labour, voluntary work, gifts and nonprofit, nonmarket institutional activities.

iv. The 'criminal economy', production, consumption or exchange actions that are against the law. They include drug and human trafficking, cybercrime, smuggling, illicit trade in firearms and in wildlife and fraudulent medicines.

Few comments on this classification are necessary to complete the picture of economic activities. Only the first three categories are genuine economic activities because criminal actions are against the law. But the law can change, so activities in this group may become economic (for example after the decriminalisation of certain drugs); some shadow activities can also shift toward the formal economy through the abolition of regulatory requirements. Interestingly, through legislative changes the opposite is also possible. Outplacement of economic activities can also occur between the informal and shadow or formal economies, where some activities are carried out by market transactions (for example, when clothes are cleaned by a launderette in the formal or shadow economy rather than a domestic worker).

An accounting summary of the outcome of an economic system

To evaluate the output of a modern economy, all the economic activities carried out by economic subjects must be recorded following the national accounting system (Demski 2008). Accounting records the value of the transactions carried out to produce, consume and provide public goods and services. The 'circular flow diagram' enables these data to be collected and arranged as monetary flows in the accounting

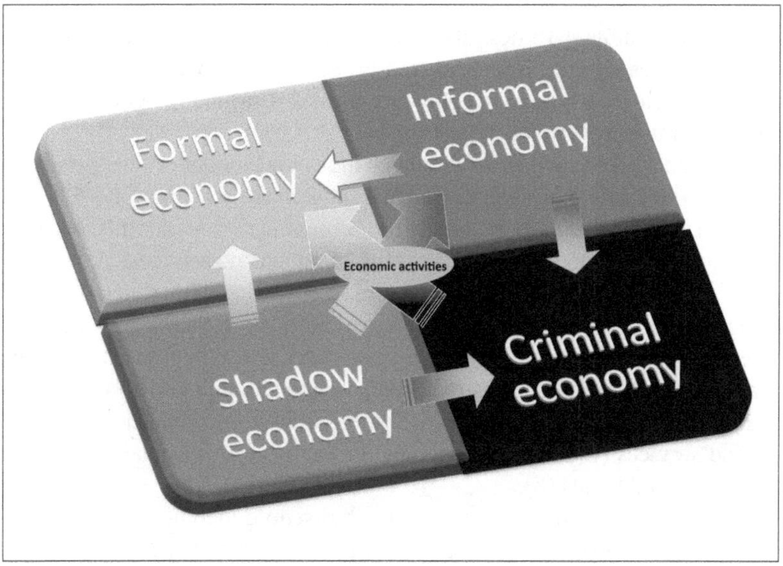

Figure 4.6 Categories of economic activities grouped according to legal criteria

Source: Author's elaboration

period and to be recorded as entries of the 'balance sheet'. Budget entries are made by grouping them according to structural functions in the economic system; this procedure highlights both 'aggregate demand' and 'balance sheets for institutional sectors'.

The output of an economic system, represented by the total net value of its final production, is generally called 'gross domestic product' (GDP), an aggregate composed by both the output of the private and public sector (respectively Y_p and Y_g). In an open economic system such values result from the cost of resources provided by all the domestic and foreign participants to the production process: for granting the private firms with the essential productive resources they bestow, the domestic employees receive wages (W), the owners of their shares profits (Π), the foreign firms that sell intermediate goods and services the equivalent value of imports (M_f)[9] and the state providing general public services and infrastructures the value added taxes (T_f). On the other hand, the output of the state (Y_g), that consists of public services as a rule freely delivered by the state to citizens (for whom there aren't financial flows in the Figure 4.7), is obtained by the contribution of employs (whose salary is W_g) and by the goods and services bought to carry out the state activities C_g. Thus, GDP can be defined as the total value of final goods and services (Y_p + Y_g) produced in an economy calculated at market prices. In the definition 4.1a such economic entity is showed from the point of view of its creation.

$$GDP = Y_p + Y_g = \left(W + \Pi + R + M_f + T_f\right) + (W_g + C_g) \qquad 4.1a$$

$$725 = 600 + 125 = \left(350 + 150 + 0 + 25 + 75\right) + \left(50 + 75\right) \qquad 4.1b$$

The values in formula 4.1b describe the open economy represented in Figure 4.4 where inventories (I) are Firms 3 unsold production of final goods and services, while in the following Figure 4.7 they are unsold instrumental goods of Firms 2 that will be future investments (I).[10]

The introduction of such a distinction changes the amount of final products and services obtained in the private sector (600 units in the first case and 575 ones in the second), but the total production of the economic system doesn't, because the value of investment goods adds up that of final goods and services.

In the Figure 4.6 domestic households receive incomes (that include also rent, R, being 0 in the example) in the amount of 550 currency units and, after paying income tax (T_h = 50, representing in a certain sense the household payment for general public services and infrastructures), use the remaining 'disposable income' (500 units) for two economic activities: the purchase of domestic and imported goods and services (C_h, M_h) and 'savings' in the form of financial assets, such as bank deposits and bonds (S).

The previous detailed description of the household income use introduces the financial activities in the economic system (saving/deposit accounts and loan by bonds). The financial activities consist not only of the production and distribution of financial services (deposit and bonds) but also of the money circulation control; thus, the financial sector performs the tasks of providing the money and

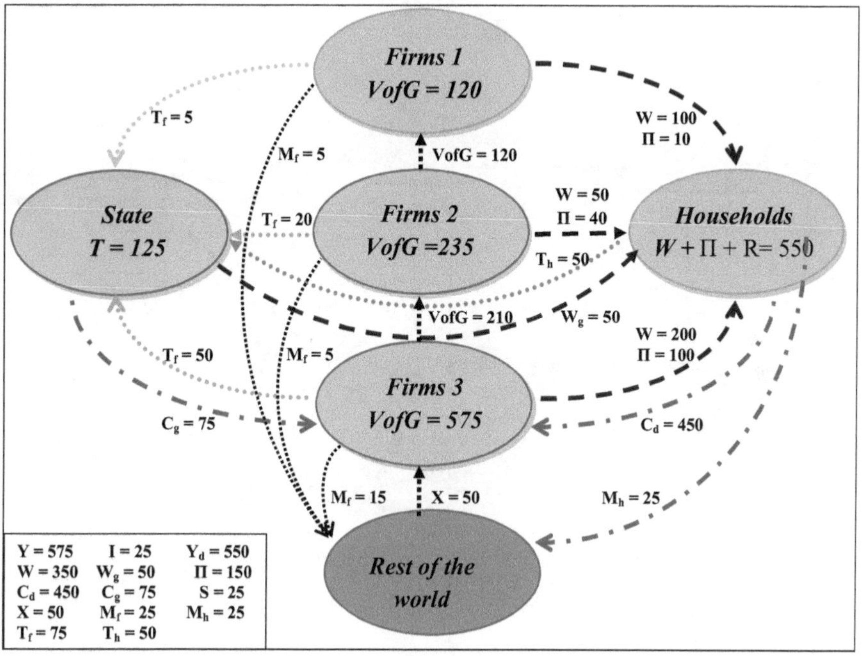

Figure 4.7 An open economic system (2)

Source: author's elaboration

the other financial services to enable the functioning of the economic system. The central bank, commercial banks and the stock exchange are the kinds of firms providing such services that belong to the production system of an economy. The financial flows channelling the loan and deposit services constitute corresponding markets whose contractors can be the state, firm and households (Figure 4.8).

After the representation of the economic system is completed by introducing the financial sector, the equivalence between the household disposable income (Y_h) and their expenditure is:

$$W + W_g + \Pi + R - T_h = Y_h = C_h + M_h + S \quad 4.2a$$

$$350 + 50 + 150 + 0 - 50 = 500 = 450 + 25 + 25 \quad 4.2b$$

From the previous equivalence results that domestic consumers demand is only a part of the output produced in the economic system (C_h); in fact, they buy goods and services also from abroad (M_h) and save a part of their income (S). The household savings deposited as financial assets become a financial loan that entrepreneurs will request to pay investment goods (I) – that is, machineries able to increase the production capital to be used by the firms in the following periods. As well as the demand for final goods and services and for investment products, the output

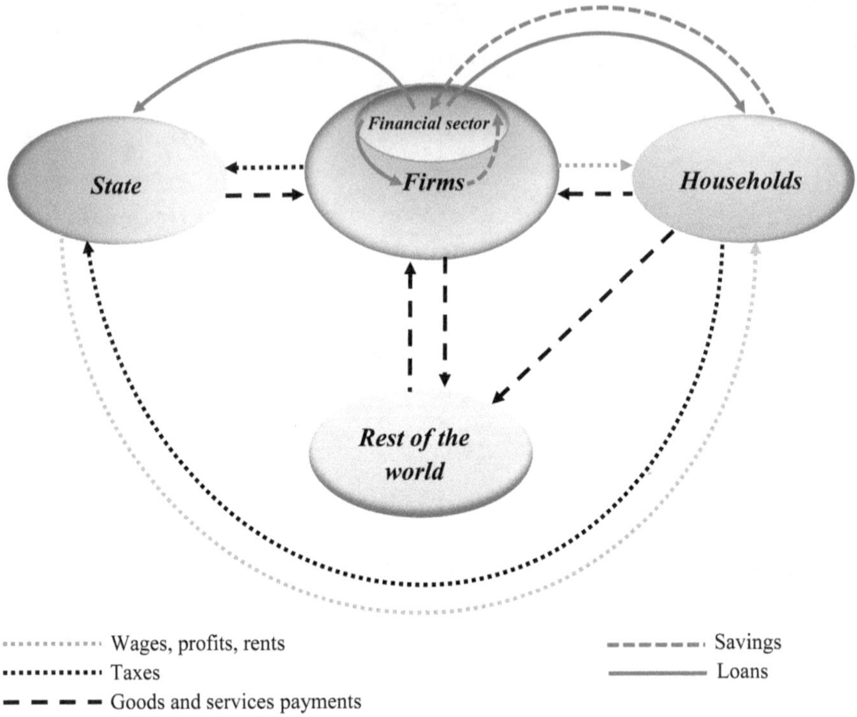

Figure 4.8 An open economic system including financial sector

Source: Author's elaboration

of domestic private firms is sold to the public administration (C_g) and to foreign consumers (X). Given that Y_g is freely delivered to citizens and firms, the output of the economy sold at market prices is only Y_p, and its value can be considered both as the sum of the items of expenditure for production and as the whole value of the use of different buyers.

$$W + \Pi + R + T_f + M_f = \mathrm{Y_p} = C_h + C_g + I + X \qquad 4.3a$$

$$350 + 150 + 0 + 25 + 75 = 450 + 75 + 25 + 50 \qquad 4.3b$$

This is the 'income equation' that says the output produced in an economic system is equal to 'aggregate demand' – i.e. to the sum of four components, which are the private and public demand for goods and services (C_h and C_g), the demand for investment goods (I), and foreign demand or exports (X).

The 'income equation' 4.3 and the equivalence 4.2 can be rewritten as:

$$W + \Pi + R = T_h + C_h + M_h + S - W_g \qquad 4.2c$$

$$W + \Pi + R = C_h + C_g + I + X - T_f - M_f \qquad 4.3c$$

So that substituting 4.2c in 4.3c we obtain 4.5a by the 4.4a and 4.4b rearrangements:

$$T_h + C_h + M_h + S - W_g + T_f + M_f = C_h + C_g + I + X \qquad 4.4a$$

$$T_h + T_f - W_g - C_g = I - S + X - M_f - M_h \qquad 4.4b$$

$$\left(T_h + T_f\right) - (W_g + C_g) = I - S + \left[X - (M_h + M_f)\right] \qquad 4.5a$$

$$\left(50 + 75\right) - \left(50 + 75\right) = 25 - 25 + \left[50 - \left(25 + 25\right)\right] \qquad 4.5b$$

Equation 4.5a shows the 'financial report' of the economic system during the budget period (lasting generally one year). It records *all assets and liabilities* accrued in managing the economic activities by distinguishing them in three '*accounts*', based on the kind of transaction and on the membership to the system: the 'state account' registers non-market transactions carried out between the state and household and firms in its territory, the 'private sector account' records market transactions between national household and firms and the 'rest of the world account' lists market transactions between national institutional units (household, firms and state) and those of the rest of the world. Thus, the 'balance' for the account of the institutional sectors results from the inflow of the taxes collected by the state from households and firms (T_h and T_f) and the corresponding outflows of government expenditure (*Cg and Wg*) in the case of state accounts and from the payments that national firms received from foreign households for the goods and services sold to them (X) and payments made by national households and firms to foreign producers (M_h and M_f) in the case of the rest of the world's accounts. A further type of monetary flow consists in payments from firms for the production resources owned by households (*W*, **Π**, *R*) and payments for the goods and services households buy from national firms (C_h); these are the only transactions not shown in equation 4.5a because they are clearance accounts, since the giver (the household) is also the receiver of the cash as income. But since the value of purchased goods and services is less than Y_h because of the unsold production of national firms (I) and the income spent is less than the income received because of savings (S), the values of I and S appear in the accounts of the private sector as the difference between assets and liabilities.

The balance of institutional sectors reveals both the accounting situation of the main macroeconomic components of an economic system (taxes T, public expenditure G, investment I, savings S, exports X and imports M) and the interdependence of the three macro-subsystems of the economy. In fact, simplifying *assets and liabilities* of the accounts of the equivalence 4.5a in the form of equivalence 4.6 we obtain:

$$(T - G) = (I - S) + (X - M) \qquad 4.6$$

In this equivalence all sectors have a zero-value balance so that all the system presents an accounting equilibrium. But this feature is a permanent situation for the annual balance sheet so that the disequilibrium of a sector must be offset by the disequilibrium in another or both sectors. For example, if the balance of the public sector were T < G, the balance of private sector must be I < S for the same amount and 0 that of the rest of the world; in such a situation a part of private savings has been used to buy bonds issued by the state to fund its deficit. Thus, if investments trigger the enlargement of the economic system, public deficit could adversely affect economic growth. Hence, similar structural features presented by the circular flow of income of an economic system point out the short-term functioning of the economy.

Concluding remarks: The picture of the capitalist economy as the foundation of economics

In scientific inquiries made by the scholars of different disciplines the representation of the subject of analysis is the step charged of the identification of the field of application for the suggested explanation. Usually, this assignment consists of the identification of the matter, phenomena, behaviours and elements involved in a specific environment. In particular, the matter refers to living organisms (individuals or organised forms like in biology), to physical matter (like in chemistry or astronomy) or social organisms (the family and social groups like in sociology or anthropology). As human beings create material goods, such elements must be included in economic matters of analysis as instruments and intermediate and final products taking part in production, consumption, and distribution. The economic system and its subsystem are thus a matter of economics, and their representation is necessary in order that the explanation for economic phenomena and behaviours makes sense.

The ways by which this preliminary but constitutive step is achieved in economics are different. On one hand some scholars maintain that 'economic representations . . . refer to the different ways the economy is conceived and portrayed. . . . They comprise different understandings of the economy: what it is, where it exists, how it operates, how it is constituted, how it is related to the other aspects of the natural and social world, what problems might exist and how they can be solved, what the goals of economic activity are, and much, much more. Each economic representation contains answers to these questions . . . and thus constitutes a form of economic knowledge' (Ruccio 2008: 899). On the other hand, the matter is identified by a model describing briefly the core of the economy, generally the market, and some related processes represented by a set of variables and logical or quantitative relationships between them. Both the approaches don't perform the task satisfactorily because they represent the economy in light of the theory proposed to explain it; in this way the representation of the matter isn't exogeneous but functional to the explanation.

The circular flow diagram, including the material and organisational elements, comply with the requirement of providing a pre-theoretical image of the matter of economics and of identifying the systemic phenomena and behavioural problems the economic subjects must face; in fact, all of these steps come into view in the representation of the economic system deduced from the historical stylised facts.

To tell the truth such a representation doesn't consider that the human production and consumption system is a part of the biosphere (see Chapter One) and that the increasing exploitation of raw material is raising entropy, putting the life of future generations and the survival of the economy at risk. Nonetheless, the problem doesn't invalidate the effectiveness of the circular flow diagram; the treatise of such aspects requires an additional inspection of the effects of this economic system on the 'natural capitals' that goes forward the aim of the book.

Notes

1 This representation of the structure and workings of the economy is a return to the 'reproductive approach' of the classical school of economics (for the origin of this representation and for the following improvements and in-depth analysis see Gilibert 2008).

2 See, for example, Gregory and Stuart: 'An economic system is a set of institutions for decision making and for the implementation of decisions concerning production, income, and consumption within a given geographic area' Gregory and Stuart (2013: 44).

3 The decision-making process in an economy is carried out by economic subjects (firms, households and the government) following the prescriptions of the institutions. The economic literature includes different lists of decisions to be taken. According to Knight, 'The general task of organising the economic activity of society may be divided into a number of fundamental functions. . . . The first is to decide what is to be done, that is, what goods and services are to be produced, and in what proportion. It is the function of setting standards, of establishing a social scale of values, or the function of social choice; the second is the function of organizing production, in the narrow sense, of getting done the things settled upon as most worth doing; third is distribution, the apportioning of the product among the member of society; the fourth is really a group of functions having to do with maintaining and improving the social structure, or promoting social progress' (Knight 1951: 7–8). According to Gregory and Stuart, 'economic systems differ along (five) dimensions' that require alternative institutions to be chosen. Thus, the decision-making process concerns the following:

i. 'the organisation of decision-making arrangements: structure
ii. mechanisms (rules) for the provision of information and for coordination: markets and planning
iii. property rights: control and income
iv. a mechanism for setting goals and inducing people to act: incentives
v. procedures for making public choices: the role of government' (Gregory and Stuart 2004: 19).

4 These activities can be carried out by own-account workers, who own and operate one-person businesses and work alone or with the help of unpaid workers, generally family members and apprentices. See http://www.businessdictionary.com/definition/informal-sector.html.

5 Further definitions and related concepts are given in the *System of National Accounts* at pp. 61–2.

6 The *System of National Accounts* ascribes economic activities to institutional units grouped together in sectors. Its aim is to present institutional sector accounts whereas the objective of this paragraph is to identify the nature of the economic activities; thus, the taxonomy presented can sometimes diverge from the *System of National Accounts*, especially in the case of the Non-Observed Economy – i.e. the interaction of formal, informal and shadow economies (see EU, *IM, OECD, UN, and WB 2009*: 471 and 474).

7 For a different interpretation of the shadow economy see Schneider and Enste (2000).
8 For a discussion of this topic see EU, *IM, OECD, UN and WB* (2009: 474–8).
9 Thus, the value of $M_f = 25$ also changes into income, but it is earned by foreign households.
10 The value of inventory, equal to 25, is the difference between the value of the intermediate goods produced by Firms 2 (equal to 235) and the value sold to Firms 3 (equal to 210).

References

Constitution du 4 octobre 1958, Déclaration des Droits de l'Homme et du Citoyen de 1789, Préambule de la Constitution du 27 octobre 1946, Charte de l'environnement. https://www.legifrance.gouv.fr/contenu/menu/droit-national-en-vigueur/constitution

Crumley, C. L. (1995) 'Hierarchy and the Analysis of Complex Societies', *Archaeological Papers of the American Anthropological Association*, 6 (1): 1–5.

Demski, J. S. (2008) 'Accounting and Economics', in S. N. Durlauf and L. E. Blume (eds.) *The New Palgrave Dictionary of Economics*, 2nd ed., London: Palgrave Macmillan.

Deutscher Bundestag (2019) 'Basic Law for the Federal Republic of Germany', *Federal Law Gazette*, 28 March 2019. http://www.gesetze-im-internet.de/gg/BJNR000010949.html

Emmett, R. B. (2013) 'Introduction' to the transaction edition of Frank Knight's *The Economic Organization*, Transaction Books. https://ssrn.com/abstract=2165805

European Commission, International Monetary Fund, Organisation for Economic Co-operation and Development, United Nations, and World Bank (2009) *System of National Accounts 2008*. https://unstats.un.org/unsd/nationalaccount/sna2008.asp

Gilibert, G. (2008) 'Circular Flow', in S. N. Durlauf and L. E. Blume (eds.) *The New Palgrave Dictionary of Economics*, 2nd ed., London: Palgrave Macmillan.

Government of India (2015) *The Constitution of India*, New Delhi: Jainco Art India.

Gregory, P. R. and Stuart, R. C. (2004) *Comparing Economic Systems in the Twenty-First Century*, Boston: Houghton Mifflin Company.

Gregory, P. R. and Stuart, R. C. (February 28, 2013) *The Global Economy and Its Economic Systems*, Boston: South-Western Cengage Learning.

Knight, F. (1951) *The Economic Organisation*, New York: Kelley (first edition 1933).

Marx, K. (1999) *Capital. A Critique of Political Economy*, Marx/Engels Internet Archive (German edition 1867, first English edition 1887). Seearxistss.org

National People's Congress (2018) *Constitution of the People's Republic of China*.http://www.npc.gov.cn/englishnpc/constitution2019/constitution.shtml

Ouchi, W. G. (1980) 'Markets, Bureaucracies, and Clans', *Administrative Science Quarterly*, 25 (1): 129–141.

Patinkin, D. (1973) 'In Search of the "Wheel of Wealth": On the Origins of Frank Knigh's Circular-Flow Diagram', *The American Economic Review*, 63 (5): 1037–46.

Prime Minister of Japan (1946) *The Constitution of Japan*. https://japan.kantei.go.jp/constitution_and_government_of_japan/constitution_e.html

Quesnay, F. (1766) 'Tableau économique', *Journal de l'agriculture, du commerce & des finances*, tome II, 3ème partie, juin: 11–41 (English edition in E. Monroe, *Early Economic Thought*, Cambridge, 1923: 336–48).

Ruccio, D. F. (2008) 'Economic Representations', *Cultural Studies*, 22 (6): 892–912. http://doi.org/10.1080/09502380701865115

Schneider, F. and Enste, D. (2000) 'Shadow Economies Around the World: Size, Causes, and Consequences', *IMF Working Paper No. 26*. https://www.imf.org/external/pubs/ft/wp/2000/wp0026.pdf

Senato della repubblica (2012) *Constitution of the Italian Republic*, Rome: Parliamentary Information, Archives and Publications Office.

The State Duma (2018) *Constitution of the Russian Federation.* http://archive.government.ru/eng/gov/base/54.html

Supreme Federal Court (2019) *Constitution of the Federative Republic of Brazil*, Brasilia: Supreme Federal Court.

Walras, L. (1874) *Éléments d'économie politique pure; ou, Théorie de la richesse sociale, Volumes 1–2*, Lausanne: Corbaz (English edition: *Elements of Pure Economics*. Homewood: Irwin, 1877).

Glossary

Balance sheet is the document showing 'the values of the stocks of assets and liabilities held by institutional units or sectors at the beginning and end of an accounting period' (EU, *IM, OECD, UN, and WB 2009:* 4).

Bureaucracy is a form of organisation characterised by hierarchical coordination with a high level of authority, control and power and by routines, where the degree of trust in superiors and the related coherence between individual and collective aims is offset by incentives.

Clan is a bureaucracy with no need for incentives because of the absence of mistrust and incoherence.

Consumer is an economic subject whose function is to consume final products and services to satisfy his or her needs and desires.

Consumption is the use of final products and services to satisfy household needs and desires.

Criminal economy is a set of production, consumption or exchange activities that are against the law.

Economic activities are all the legal actions carried out inside an economic process to create goods, services or capital to distribute and consume them in order to provide societies with material wealth.

Economic process is a sequence of organised and co-ordinated sociotechnical activities (production, exchange and consumption of goods and services) carried out by people within an economic system.

Economic resources are tangible or intangible elements that can be used to produce goods and services and/or to create economic wealth.

Economic system is a co-ordinated group of organisations and working procedures arranged and flanked by a political/administrative authority to provide society with social welfare by means of the economic process.

Economic subject is an institutional unit (household or legal entity) endowed with a legal personality to carry out a specific economic activity such as production (a company), consumption (a consumer) or taxation (the state) by means of market or non-market transactions.

Effectiveness is the ability of an organisation to achieve the intended or expected result – i.e. the relation between given means and achievable ends.

Efficiency is the ability of an organisation to perform its activity according to a quality parameter – i.e. an input/output ratio relation.

Exchange is a social activity intended to give up one thing for something else.

Exports are goods and services produced in a national economy that are bought by foreign economic subjects.

Firm is an economic subject whose function is to produce goods and services.

Formal economy is the set of all economic activities that are authorised and thus registered and traceable.

Gross domestic product (GDP) is the value (calculated at market prices) of all the final products and services produced in the economic system during a year.

Imports are the goods and services produced abroad that are bought by subjects of a domestic economic system.

Incentive is a reward (whether monetary or not) necessary to persuade people involved in organisational processes to cooperate.

Income is the flow of earnings by people from their work (wages, salaries) and/or from the economic use of their tangible or intangible assets (real estate, shares, bonds).

Informal economy is the set of self-produced goods or the use of goods, services or labour without payment.

Institutional unit is the subject (household or legal subject) of the decision-making process related to the economic activities and/or of its execution and its legal responsibility too.

Investment is an economic activity consisting in the purchase of machinery in excess of replacement to extend company plant.

Market is a system of exchange activities for goods and services authorised and organised according to certain terms and conditions.

Organisational structure is the way in which activities such as task allocation, coordination and supervision are managed in order to achieve organisational aims.

Means of production are the resources (establishments, materials, equipment, workers, energy and licences) necessary to carry out a production process.

Production is the organised process of transformation of raw materials, intermediate goods and labour and machinery services through which new goods and services are obtained.

Profit is the difference between the revenue and the costs for resources obtained by the firms as a result of their production activity.

Rent is a regular payment to an owner for the use of a property.

Savings is the part of income not used by an economic subject to purchase goods and services.

Shadow economy is the set of economic activities carried out in violation of procedures or rules under the law.

System of national accounts (SNA) is an agreed-upon international format to collect statistical data to measure economic phenomena.

Tax is a pecuniary charge imposed by the state on economic subjects in order to finance its activities.

Transaction costs are the costs to be added to the market price in order to handle unforeseeable aspects or non-compliance with legal obligations as stipulated in a contract.

Wealth is the stock of tangible and intangible assets in an economy that can be used over time to carry out production processes or to satisfy the consumption needs of the owner.

Part II

Structure and operation of modern economies

5 The state

Counterpart, partner and subject of the capitalist economy

The state is the legal, administrative and political organisation of a territorial community that is endowed with a lawful coercive power and that pursues public goals. Such an organisation, emerged worldwide in different historical periods, has developed in the last two centuries through diversified paths that can all be ascribable to the so called 'modern state' (Spruyt 2002). The variety of forms in which it has been structured hinges on the changes of both the social spheres (domestic, economic and communitarian lives) and international relations. The last form recently brought to the surface is the so-called 'global state', which 'doesn't represent a new form of the state resulting from the reduction of those historically present, but a set of simultaneous different forms of state hierarchically powered . . . that risk recurrently to be a trouble for each other, due to this multiplication' (Gherardi and Ricciardi 2009: 14). The features distinguishing the 'modern state' of the last two centuries are the 'rule of law'[1] and the 'welfare state'.[2] It was due to the fulfilment of the rule of law at the end of the 18th century that the modern state was entrusted with the protection and respect of citizens' rights and liberties and that individuals empowered by such entitlements became appointed with economic activities. But it was thanks to the welfare state that one century later the principle of solidarity, making universal the previous privileges, became a guideline for state legislation and policy, and that opportunity equality, equitable distribution of wealth and public responsibility for people unable to provide themselves for necessities informed state behaviour. Thus, due to the foundations of the modern state, on the one hand the functioning of the economy shaped up to be as a self-directed organisation, and on the other hand the state took it upon itself to ensure that the workings of the economic system guaranteed the enjoyment of economic rights and outcomes by all citizens.

Taking the cue from these crossed prerogatives, an intense debate to mark the spheres of influence of both the entities on economic activities developed over time in economic and political practice as well as in the corresponding theoretical fields. The solutions that emerged historically and culturally show a continuum of configurations within the subordination of the economy to the political interests and the subjection of the state activities (legislative, judicial and administrative ones) to the economic perspectives and outcomes. Although different at first sight, both the extreme configurations pursue the same aim: to decide the economic priorities, to structure the economic organisations and to shape the economic institutions mainly

DOI: 10.4324/9781315679730-8

according to the interest of only one entity. The paradox derives from the fact that both the state and the economy operate for the common good although from two different perspectives. The state is, by its legal nature and by historical reasons, the organiser of the economic system, the lawgiver of the routines that rule its working and the provider of the social acceptance of the economic activities. Because of these prerogatives the state is the designer of the environmental framework where the economic activities develop, and the guarantor of their compliance with the public interest (see Chapter Four). Nevertheless, the economy represents the set of economic behaviours and activities fulfilled by individuals, working on their own or in organised groups, that originate the welfare of the state. Thus, given the common interest and the intertwined activities, the state and the economy cannot be opposites; they are bound to coevolve to realise their respective goals (Romagnoli 2009). The evolution of the capitalist economy presents examples of successful and failed coevolution between the state and the economic system, side by side different roles played by the state in the various phases (Chang and Rowthorn 2003; Deane 1989). As British 'industrialisation proceeded the state was intervening more deeply and more effectively in the economy than it had ever done before. There was indeed a revolution in the technique and philosophy of government that was at least as significant in shaping and accelerating the first industrial revolution as the other transformations which we have come to regard as part of it' (Deane 1979: 231). 'Elsewhere, government played an important role in inhibiting industrialisation (as in France or China), in creating industrialisation engineered from above (as in Germany and Japan) or in encouraging and subsidising private sector industrialisation (as in the USA)' (Harris 2004: 204). In this chapter the forms of state intervention in the economy are discussed as a background for an in-depth analysis of the state acting as the third subject of whatever economic system.

State-economy interactions in a historical perspective

The relationship between the state and the economy has been present since the Renaissance as the coexistence of two powers characterised by mutual independence or subordination of one to another. But the advent of the modern state and of capitalist economy highlighted the need for cooperation among them to upgrade the corresponding spheres. This need gave rise to a variety of state-economy configurations situated between the states governed by economic technocrats subjected to economic interests and the states implementing economic bureaucracies centrally co-ordinated and managed according to political interests. During the last two centuries different forms of state intervention in support of the economy to promote, strengthen and rescue the economic system occurred, both in compliance with political strategies to sustain ruling groups or in favour of the economic and civil upgrading to redirect the economic activity towards social aims. Thus, the explanatory keys to understand the state-economy dialectics and the changing role played by the state in the economy during the capitalist evolution must be searched by inspecting historically the three different functions that the state has performed in the economic sphere: the creation of economic institutions to support the economy, the implementation of policies for the economy's rebound and the interventions for economic and civil upgrading.

The state as an economic institutions builder

The state-economy relations in a capitalist society can be better understood going back to examine the prior configurations that appeared in the early history of the modern era. The economic success of the late medieval European long-distance trade was due to the cosmopolitan nature of the merchant social group, which took upon itself the worldwide distribution of goods produced mainly by local artisans who were made-to-order producers and retail powerless. The merchants enjoyed craft guild internal regulations because they buffered on balancing the trade fluctuations, and merchant's courts and 'commercial techniques' that were developed as part of the so-called 'law merchants' (Kadens 2015). The control of the production and trade provided them with long-established trust as well as ample independence from political power. Although they supported the administrative institutions and shared the political power of nobles in the cities of origin, they did not develop their own political management or strategy to become a hegemonic political class. This was the reason for their medieval independence but also for their subordination to the sovereign power when an emergent individual or family took possession of a territory or city and established a princedom or an absolute state.

When at the beginning of the 17th century the absolute monarchies succeeded, the sovereigns realised that the trade control and the support to such business could strengthen their political power. Thus, they deprived merchant guilds of their competences to bestow them on the state, and the practise of commercial activities became a sovereign prerogative that could be granted each time to private individuals. The belief that the profit could be obtained only if the sovereign granted it prevailed, and new forms of corporation (India Companies) started their business by his gracious permission, potentially supported by the state army that paved their way toward new markets (Galgano 2005: 46). In this mercantile system (Mercantilism) the legal context of commercial activities lost its autonomy too; in fact, the commercial law must be part of the public law as it pertained to both politics and policy. When, at the advent of absolute state, the trading activities dropped under the state control, the production organisation and its subordination towards commerce did not change; the workshops kept on working in the same medieval way and under the same institutional framework, as the statutes of apprentices were still applied to regulate the job, and the regulations specified in detail how goods should be manufactured (Ogilvie 2004). The earlier restrictions on the mobility of labour and on the use of capital remained, sided by 'complicated system of protection which placed a variety of restrictions on the free flow of overseas trade' (Deane 1979: 222). In such a context 'one very important task of the state has been to create well-functioning markets by providing a legal framework, standard, credit, physical infrastructures and – if necessary – to function temporarily as an entrepreneur of last resort. Early economists were acutely aware that national markets did not occur spontaneously, and they used "modern" ideas like synergies, increasing returns, and innovation theory when arguing for the right kind of government policy' (Reinert 1999: 268).

When the modern state experienced industrialisation, the interaction between state and economy appeared in the form of antagonism. In fact, the introduction of capitalism moved the barycentre of the economy from the exchange of goods (commerce) to their production so that all the state restrictions to production management, built previously to protect trade, revealed themselves at once as barriers to industrial development. The unfitness of the mercantilist institutional order for ruling and supporting the capitalist economy brought about the request of dismantling it. This appeal was borrowed by the political and social philosophy of 'liberalism' that assumed it as a source of the liberal economic creed, together with other principles contained in the Adam Smith's works. The economic paradigm that arose from this concurrence conceived economic activities as the display of the 'system of natural liberty' of the individual 'left perfectly free to pursue its own interest his own way and to bring his industry and capital into competition with those of any other man' (Smith 1904: IV.ix.51). In this context the relation between the state and the economy went in with a clear segregation of duties; starting from such a definition it remained to the political-administrative entity nothing else but a way to pursue peace conservation, the protection of person and properties against force and fraud, and the management of administrative activities in a sparing way.[3] The split was strengthened by the alleged association of the economic efficiency with utilitarian individualism on one side and of economic harmfulness with the governmental economic administration on the other side (Evans 1991: 4–5).

The states introducing capitalism granted all the entrepreneur's wishes at once as in revolutionary France or staggered over time as in Britain. France started the abolition of the traditional economic institution at the beginning of the 1789 revolution,[4] while Britain made it in the first half of the 19th century.[5] Germany followed the path in the second half of the 19th century like Italy and Japan, where the 'Meiji Restoration' started in 1867 (Mikami and Hirota 1999: 149). The elimination of guilds[6] and old institutions entailed the abolition of the regulations on the production of goods, of the restrictions on worker apprenticeship and on the mobility of labour. Following this dismantling process, plenty of peasants flowed into the industrial cities; the freedom of entrepreneurial and trade activities resulted in consequential effects as well as the constitution of a goods national market. Speaking of which, a lot of duties still had to be paid after 1815 to transfer agricultural and handcrafted goods in some parts of Europe; this was the case for Italy and Germany. However, by 1834 in Central Europe an area of free exchange with a common custom (the unified goods market called Zollverein) was introduced sooner that the political union of these states gave rise to the German empire in 1871.

The demolition of old economic institutions was not sufficient to comply with the new economy; an institution's active state policy was necessary to create a more capitalism-enhancing legal framework ensuring 'the facilitation of market transaction; the security of property rights; technological innovations; and the pooling together of capitals for investments in firms' (Harris 2014: 133). To carry out such a state 'fine-tuning' function in France, for example, in 1807 the Commercial code was issued, which regulated some company types being used since the 17th century; in 1844 the patent law was issued, in 1857 the brand law, in 1865 the cheque law. In Britain the demolition of old institutions was made by substituting them with new laws (see note 4). The interventions of the state to tune the institutional framework to the economy have gone with all the noteworthy changes that marked out the capitalist evolution. Thus, alongside the 19th century the so-called 'commercial codes' went in this direction, causing, after the Mercantilist period, a further national differentiation of the rules governing the economies.[7]

Starting from the end of the 19th century a new phase of the economic institution upgrading was committed to the national states to support the enlargement of the economies beyond the national borders. The expansion of the international trade solicited the creation of shared institutions providing the legitimation of national economies as a trade partner, the recognition of their sole rights and the sharing of the rules of the game. The first requirement was fulfilled by the trading states through their participation in the 'gold standard',[8] a monetary system whose currency values were based on a quantity of gold for each coin unit, defined by the issuing central banks and guaranteed by their golden reserves. To make the international exchanges safe and on equal terms, the companies needed an international protection of their sole rights (inventions and brands) and a shared law for the cheque, the promissory note and the purchase agreement. The Paris Convention in 1883, the Geneva Convention of 1930 and the Vienna Convention of 1980, respectively, didn't succeed in coming to an agreement so that different national commercial codes emerge; nevertheless, neither did the single states succeeded on the mission in the USA. As to the trade conditions the states had more success; they signed trading agreements reducing customs (as the General Agreement on Tariffs and Trade signed in 1947), created customs unions (like the European Common Market signed in 1957) or monetary unions (like the European Monetary Union activated in 2001), and established in 1995 the World Trade Organisation. This lending place created an independent international organisation appointed to issue trading rules and procedures, rule the globalised international trade and administer dispute resolutions. Considering the institutional framework built by these international conferences and by those aimed to design a world financial market, the results obtained by the states acting as international economic institution builders are the creation of a 'new merchant law' – that is, 'a new set of laws, made by entrepreneurs without the intervention of the legislative powers of the states [but adopted by the parliaments], aimed to rule evenly the globalised markets beyond and over the states' (Galgano 2005: 57). But this role of the states to build international institutions to promote both the trade and international coordination of economies will be further explored in the final two chapters of the book.

The state as the supporter and rescuer of the economy

In the time of 'liberalism', when the segregation of state and economy roles was postulated by the '*laissez-faire doctrine*'[9] and the two organisations were seen as rivals,[10] another kind of state intervention in the economy sided the institutional building: the support for economic activities through the creation of infrastructures, the financing of private investments and direct aid to private sectors.[11] As the industrial production set up itself, the infrastructures (bridges, roads, canals, ports, and rails) became particularly important both to stock the firms with materials and to widen their selling markets. Such engineering works couldn't be attractive for private entrepreneurs because their realisation needed a great outlay of capital and a lot of time both to be accomplished and to yield a profit, and because the returns of such investments would be enjoyed by all the community. These are the reasons why the states paid attention to the provision of such major works intervening directly or lending money to private entrepreneurs involved in their realisation. Regarding these aspects the case of Japan is emblematic of the direct intervention because:

> The Government gradually developed various elements of an infrastructure for national development. A Nation-wide postal/telegram network was established, and a series of civil engineering works was started to expand land transport and water supply networks. In the late 1890's, national railway construction was started. In 1870 the Ministry of Engineering was created to manage these infrastructure development programs. . . . During the first few decades after the Restoration, the government invited thousands of foreign educators, engineers, and other experts to provide assistance in managing the government-led civil works, and in running government-owned factories and educational institutions. The Ministry of Engineering allocated about 42 per cent of its total budget to salaries for foreign experts from 1870 to 1885. This shows the strong eagerness of the new government to obtain western invented modern technologies.
>
> (Mikami and Hirota 1999: 149, 150)

The same involvement appeared in the United States. Prior to the American Civil War, the federal and state authorities supported initiatives in turnpike, waterway and canal construction as well as in the establishment of banks. As to the state expenditures on railroads in the South:

> Public investment should be credited with more than 55 percent of total investment in that area (based on the total value of its railroad in the Census 1860). . . . 4.7 percent of total public expenditures were federal, 56.7 percent were state, 26.0 percent municipal, and 12.6 percent country. In addition to direct expenditures, there was aid in the form of services of public officials and property, grants of rights of way, public lands and building sites, materials, tax exceptions, banking facilities, and other privileges. . . . The role of the state in American economic development in the nineteenth century was surely more than minimal. The effects of the action and presence of government on growth were significant and were manifested throughout the period.
>
> (Broude 1959: 12, 25)

In such quotations an added intervention of the states in support of firms emerges that goes beyond infrastructure. As a matter of fact, starting from the Napoleon wars on, in European developing countries not only strong government support for military considerations was granted to industries such as shipbuilding, steam shipping and even railway transportation but also to steel and mechanical production; in the German empire such an intervention expanded to chemicals and electricity (Lee 1988: 359), and in Japan it went beyond to also include paper and spinning (Mikami and Hirota 1999: 149, 151).

A new phase of the state intervention in support of the economy appeared in the 20th century, characterised by two different forms put into action before and after the Second World War. In the first period the companies rescue through the acquisition of ownership and management, and the creation of demand through the public spending prevailed, while in the second emerged the state-owned enterprises (SOEs). In the first 40 years of the century the inability of the economy to be self-sufficient, because of the disruptions connected to the First World War and the aftermath of the 1929 crisis, pushed the West European governments to take over banks and industrial companies that went bankrupt. The social and political tensions and the risk of widespread unemployment solicited the provisional rescue of such firms, but when in the 1930s the mistrust towards the private entrepreneurship and the market appeared, 'a first massive wave of nationalisation was undertaken, particularly in those Western European countries most affected by recession' (Toninelli 2008: 682). Moreover, the 1930s was a decade during which the governments of USA and Europe implemented expenditure policies intended to promote the production of firms and employment through the demand of weaponry and the implementation of public works. This phase went with an out-and-out interference of the state over the economy in authoritarian countries like Italy, Spain and Germany, where it was necessary to pursue the aims of political power. Such interference became incorporation in the Soviet Union, where all economic activities were in the hands of the state that owned and managed them. The nationalisations made before the Second World War were generally intended, in Western economies, as a temporary acquisition of non-performance companies, in view of their return to private entrepreneurs once restored. Thus, the propagation of state-owned enterprises (SOEs) between the end of the Second World War up to the 1980 represented a new sub-phase in the relation between the state and the economy, characterised by public policies addressed to the promotion of the welfare state and of a steady growth of the economy.

The state as the designer of the social protection

All the pre-industrial societies presented institutions providing social protection for poor relief, aid to orphans and illegitimate children and healthcare to disadvantaged people. Such charities were voluntary organisations, generally of religious origins (confraternities), that emerged in Middle Age Europe. Among the oldest brotherhoods devoted to sick-person carriage to hospitals, to dead people's burial, to donation raising for providing poor brides with down and to disadvantaged people's shelter was created in Italy in 1244. It is the Arciconfraternita della Misericordia di Firenze (the Mercy Archconfraternity of Florence), a still active laic organisation that was acknowledged in 1329 as a public institution devoted to the social protection of the municipality. This social institution was imitated at the time and during the following centuries elsewhere in Italy and in Europe, starting a decentralised urban system of social protection privately managed. The extension of social protection to a whole country occurred only with the Poor Relief Act issued by the British Parliament in 1601. This law entrusted the organisation and the management of such services to the parishes, bestowing them also with the authority to allot the disadvantaged people to different shelters. Pursuant to this law the people who were lame, impotent, old or blind were cared for in the almshouses, the able-bodied poor were set to work in factories; the idle poor or vagrants were put in houses of correction or in prison, and the poor children were addressed to apprenticeship.

> While Poor Laws existed in many cities in early modern Europe, the English system was unique in its scale and geographical ubiquity. English poor relief post-1834 differed from most continental systems . . .; its source of finance of a local tax on income from property . . . allowed more redistribution
>
> (Powell 2020: 19)

On the contrary the continental laws on poor relief were financed by voluntary donations, income from capital, subsidies from local and national governments and taxes, and that made social protection more uncertain and variable. Furthermore, the poor laws of pre-industrial societies regulated social protection from the public interest's perspective through the private management of the system.

The situation changed when, with the advent of the modern state, social protection became over time a citizen's right. Two different categories of factors contributed to this change of perspective. On the one hand, the introduction of capitalist economy transferred to individuals all the responsibilities and encumbrances connected to their life cycle, making uncertain and seesawing their economic life. Therefore, he had to face the social consequences of the capitalist economy (like unemployment, job turnovers, the business cycle, and the market rules) as well as the 'social contingences' connected to life (for example, sickness and old age; see Briggs 1961: 228). On the other hand, the emergence of the individual as a protagonist of the modern state highlighted the specific conditions of people acting as a citizen, a worker, a member of a family, all roles invoking rights whose enjoyment must be guaranteed by the state. Thus, on the one hand, 'social protection' went beyond poor and disadvantaged people to concern everyone in all phases of life; on the other hand, the reason for the protection provision shifted from the charity to the legal right.

As industrialisation and new social conditions evolved, the institutional activity of the state about social protection intensified, pushed by the intention of protecting social values, reacting to socialist party campaigns or implementing governmental social programmes. To protect the human dignity of children, youth and adults in the workplace, the British Parliament issued the 'Health and Morals of Apprentices Act' of 1802 that introduced limits to the work hours for apprentices in cotton mills and the 'Ten Hours Bill' of 1847 establishing the maximum duration of the working day (Powell 2020: 20). Also, in Prussia a law limiting the employment of children was issued in 1839, which joined the other legal interventions regulating factory activity in industrialising countries (Stefan 2015: 27). In the second half of the 19th century, the class struggle and trade unions and socialist parties' requests forced the governments to implement social protection instruments to face the occurrences. The German chancellor Bismarck[12] proposed between 1883 and 1903 a programme of 'social legislation' (Health insurance bill of 1883, Accident insurance bill of 1884, Old age and disability insurant bill of 1889, Workers protection act of 1891 and Children's protection act of 1891) to protect people from life events. Such social institutions were also imitated by France and Great Britain.[13] Although the German and British institutions were similar for the events taken into consideration, they then differed with respect to the model of protection: the first one was based on workers' contributions to access benefits delivered in the form of insurance, and the second on widespread solidarity and thus state payments.

The state as promoter of civil and economic upgrades

The social institution's building process started in Germany and Great Britain at the end of the 19th century, expanded to other emergent economies during the first 40 years of the 20th century. The health insurance system was among the first social protection programmes implemented by the states. It has been introduced by Germany in 1883, by Italy in 1888, by the USA between 1880 and 1890, by Norway in 1909, by Great Britain in 1911, by Netherlands in 1913 and by Japan in 1938, based on compulsory insurance whose premium was paid in the form of contributions by employees, employers and the state according to due percentages. Speaking of which again, another 'form of social security insurance introduced was insurance for industrial accidents, while unemployment insurance be the last. Between these two categories are placed another two types of insurance, respectively for old age and invalidity' (Stefan 2015: 33). The models of social protection generally outlined by the lawgivers of the states 'relied on collective occupational social insurance funds, with a focus on providing job and income security for male industrial workers through separate insurance schemes across industries and firms' (Kanchoochat 2019: 10). The state commitment on the matter of social protection, mainly concentrated in building institutions than in financing the services, was a reaction to the political, social and economic events that occurred in the period. The programmes that were adopted, aimed primarily at protecting the workers, were, in connection to the healthcare system, a complementary support for economic activities because they enabled the capitalist economy to gain social approval. Besides the evidence of a trade-off between economic welfare and social welfare in the absence of social protection, such programmes highlighted two other features of the capitalist economy. The first is that the production of social benefits, both through private insurance companies and public agencies, is complementary to all other production because it creates 'means of production' necessary to obtain social approval for the production system; in fact, in some countries such services are produced by the same companies hiring the workers

(USA, Japan and other Eastern Asia economies). The second is that the contributions paid by employers for such insurance services can be considered a 'mandatory consumption' to maintain a certain standard of living.

The historical period we are considering has been important not only for the expansion of social protection programmes but also for the increasing awareness that they must be improved and extended. The debates on the extension of the guarantees in the workplace, on wages and economic conditions allowing a dignified existence and on assistance and protection for other life emergences shifted the attention of public opinion from social and economic protection of workers and disadvantaged people to civil and economic upgrades for citizens and their families. At the same time the discussion about the role of the state in providing social protection opened to state social benefits – that is, to the generalisation of such programmes to all the citizens as an acquired right. All these debates resulted in the realisation of the 'welfare state'[14] in most part of Western economies from the end of the Second World War up to the eighties. The 'welfare state' is a set of institutions, policies, administrative activities and public expenditure implemented by the state to promote and provide citizens with economic and social well-being. Beyond the definitions, the nuances of the term and the interpretations according to whom such state intervention was the consequence of the 'market failure',[15] the welfare state implies the implementation of the principles of opportunity equality,[16] equitable distribution of wealth and public responsibility for the people unable to provide themselves for necessities. Such principles became part and parcel of some post-war constitutions of first comers and latecomers as well as of the so-called 'socialist countries'; on one side they have stressed the mandatory social function of economic activities and on the other side have specified in some market economies the extent and the limits of some economic rights (the social use of property, the safeguard of work, free entrepreneurship consistent with social utility – see Chapter Four, Table 4.1).

The development of social protection programmes starting from the beginning of the 19th century is presented in the Figure 5.1, where the world adoption of each single programme (protection of children and family, and of maternity, protection from sickness, unemployment, work injury and old age) results each year from the percentage of the world population covered by the service, owing to their provision in national economies. The protection from work injury presents the most rapid increase in all the periods, having already been benefited from in 1940 by 47 per cent of the world population and 75 per cent in 1960. Protection from old age, maternity and sickness have had a similar development, but the adoption of such programmes covered nearly 25 per cent in 1940 and 55 per cent in 1960. Protection from unemployment has been the most delayed as it covered 16 per cent of the world population in 1940, 32 per cent in 1960 and only 52 per cent in 2020. Only protection during maternity, from sickness, from work injury and from old age have a percentage of implementation between 93.50 per cent and 99.50 per cent in 2020.

The expansion of social security services in some industrial economies during the period under consideration is shown in Table 5.1, which shows the share of GDP spent in such services in particular years. The paltry values recorded in the first two columns corresponds to a simply institutional intervention of the state, while the comparison between the values of the last two columns reveals the economic policy

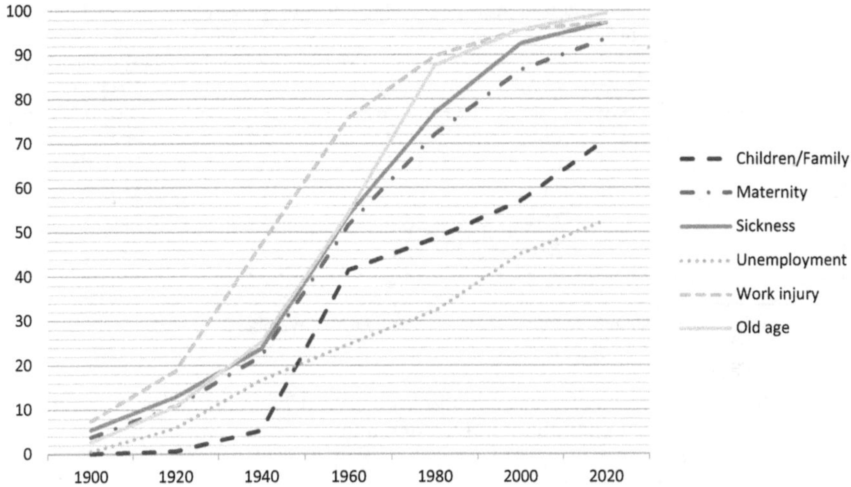

Figure 5.1 Development of social protection programmes measured by the population share of all countries adopting them starting from 1900

Source: Author's elaboration from: ILO, *World Social Protection Data Dashboards*, accessed the 20th of November 2021, https://www.social-protection.org/gimi/WSPDB.action?id=19

Table 5.1 Share of the GDP spent for 'social security programmes' in selected countries

	1880	*1900*	*1930*	*1960*
UK	0.86	1.00	2.24	10.21
USA	0.29	0.55	0,56	7.26
France	0.46	0.57	1.05	13.42
Germany	0.50	0.59	4.82	18.10
Italy	–	–	0.80	13.10

Source: Author elaboration from: G. M. Stefan (2015: 31)

measures, which were certainly due also to the debates on the extension of social protection programmes and the transition to the 'welfare state'. In addition, the leading position of the countries having higher attention towards the problem emerges from the higher development pace of the GDP share for these services.

As to the expansion of the state intervention in providing 'social benefits', the current expenditure of government to support the provision of services about sickness, unemployment, retirement, housing, education or family circumstances has sharply increased with the stabilisation of the 'welfare state'. Considering the share of the GDP spent for social security programmes by the governments of a set of industrialised countries up to 1960 (Table 5.1) and the government expense to produce benefit services from 1980 to 2020 in the same countries (Table 5.2), the general upwards trend of this entry of the public balance sheet emerges concentrated between 1945 and the 1980s. Moreover, it is evident that in the last decade of the

Table 5.2 Government expenditure for 'social benefits' in percentage of the GDP for selected countries

	1980	*1990*	*2000*	*2010*	*2019*
U K	15.6	14.9	16.9	23.3	20.6
U. S. A.	12.9	13.2	14.1	19.1	18.7
France	20.1	24.4	27.7	31.1	31.0
Germany	21.8	21.4	25.5	26.0	25.9
Italy	17.3	20.6	22.6	27.0	28.2
Japan	10.0	19.9	15.4	21.2	23.0

Source: Author's elaboration from OECD. Stat extracted on 23 November 2021.

period only Italy and Japan proceeded in this trend despite the crises that affected all the countries under examination (Ocampo and Stiglitz 2018).

The state as a subject of the economy

The historical review of the role of the state during the evolution of capitalism just presented highlighted some stylised facts whose importance is basic in understanding the structure and the workings of the economic system. The state has been required to create economic institutions that could make easy the introduction and the strengthening of the new economic system; the fulfilment of such a task has been a due diligence because the state is the holder of the legislative power. In performing this function, the state implemented a process of coevolution with the economy that, in case of mutuality, validated and addressed the workings of the economic system too. The state has also been rescuing the economy to protect the citizenry from economic crises throughout the evolution of capitalism; thus, it has been intervening in economic affairs, acting as an agent of last resort that tried to find a remedy for the performance of the economic mechanism below expectations. Finally, the state has been planning some forms of social protection programmes and has been contributing to the costs of their implementation to promote civil and economic upgrades pursuant to one among its constitutive functions: the redistribution of income. Such exclusive competence, which will be discussed in this paragraph, linked to the previous ones, shows that the state has the complete nature of an economic subject.

The systemic structure of the state and its economic functions

The state is, by definition, a non-profit legal institutional unit (or set of units) established by political processes on a territory where 'there may be many separate government units when there are different levels of government, specifically central, state, or local governments' (EC, IMF, OECD, UN, and WB 2009: 78). From a structural point of view the state is a complex system whose elements are autonomous and interconnected organised components, carrying on specific functions contributing to achieve the common interest of a territorial community. The parliament, the judiciary and the government are the three components executing, respectively, the legislative, judicial and administrative functions, but when their activities concern the economy they also contribute to the economic function of the state: the legislative power builds the economic institutions, designing both the environment and the behavioural rules for consumers, producers and the government. The judicial one enforces them towards all economic subjects (by the courts) and the government (by the court of auditors); the government makes economic activities of consumption, production and redistribution of income.[17] When the state is dealing with economic activities to provide social benefits, the social security funds, hospitals and schools can also constitute government units having administrative autonomy (institutions); on the contrary, when the state produces goods and services it uses ministerial bodies (agencies) or autonomous legal entities (state owned enterprises). Based on such distinctions the public economic activities are generally gathered into two aggregates: the economic activities of the 'general government sector', which include non-profit institutional deeds of organisation and regulation of the economic system pertaining to the three powers of the state, and the production activities through 'public enterprises' managed as administrative divisions of the government (agencies and institutions). Instead the 'public sector' consists of the general government sector and the 'public market corporations' or SOE (see Figure 5.2).

The state consumes goods and services to carry out the different institutional activities that are pertaining to it; thus, it buys non-durable goods and services like

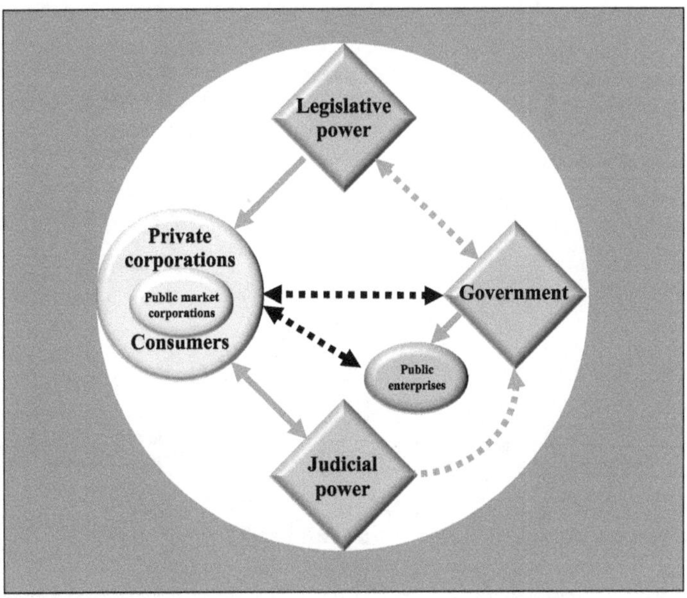

Figure 5.2 The systemic structure of the state as an economic subject

Source: Author's elaboration

fuel, paper, electricity and water to make the central and local administrations work. It also buys durable goods (like devices, equipment, tools, cars, trucks and office furnishings) and buildings to install the activities. Finally, it hires people as workers in its administration bodies (civil servants: magistrates, soldiers, local authorities, police officers). Thus, the provision of services to citizens by the legislative, judicial and administrative bodies as well as by homeland security, complying with the political function of the state, is none other than a production process managed differently from that of a company; in fact, the state buys the means of production at market conditions but delivers the output free or receiving a small repayment ('duty') lower than the cost of production. The production activities through 'public enterprises' takes place in the same way as well: the provision of 'social benefits' implies, based on the indirect or direct intervention, government funding for block grants or operating costs in the case of the public administration providing the service (schools, hospitals) and the fees and social security contributions[18] as repayments. The state disbursements in performing political and economic tasks are recorded as expenses in the state (public or government) financial account and itemised as 1) compensation to employees; 2) social benefits; 3) rents; 4) interests for the loan received and dividends for the issued public debt bonds; and 5) block or capital grants and other capital outlay (as for roads, administrative buildings, hospitals, schools and weaponry), while the repayments are recorded as revenues.

The general upwards trend of the 'public sector' expense in the top-ten world economies during the period 1880–2011 is shown in Figures 5.3; the countries are grouped in three images according to the starting period of development, and the

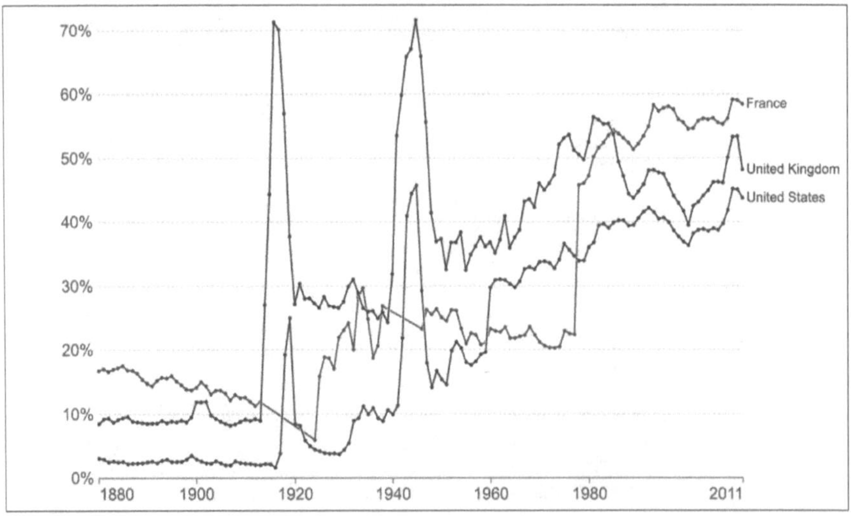

Figure 5.3a Public sector spending in percentage of the GDP from 1880 to 2011 in 'first comers'

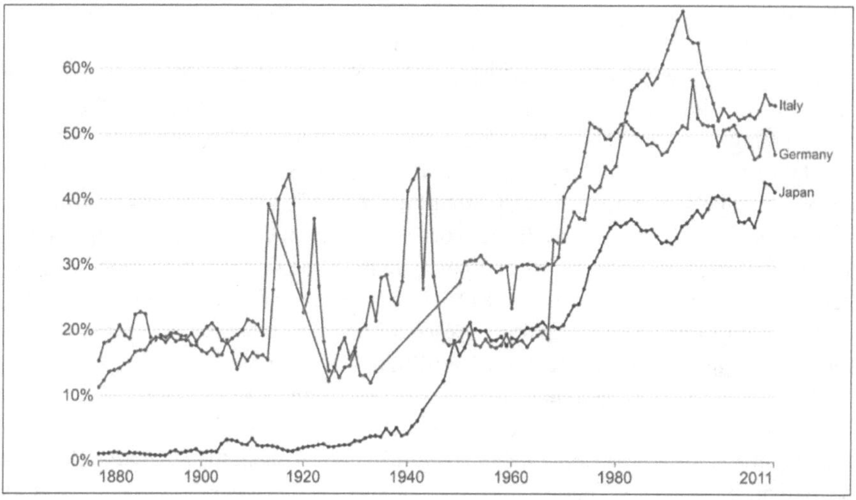

Figure 5.3b Public sector spending in percentage of the GDP from 1880 to 2011 in 'latecomers'

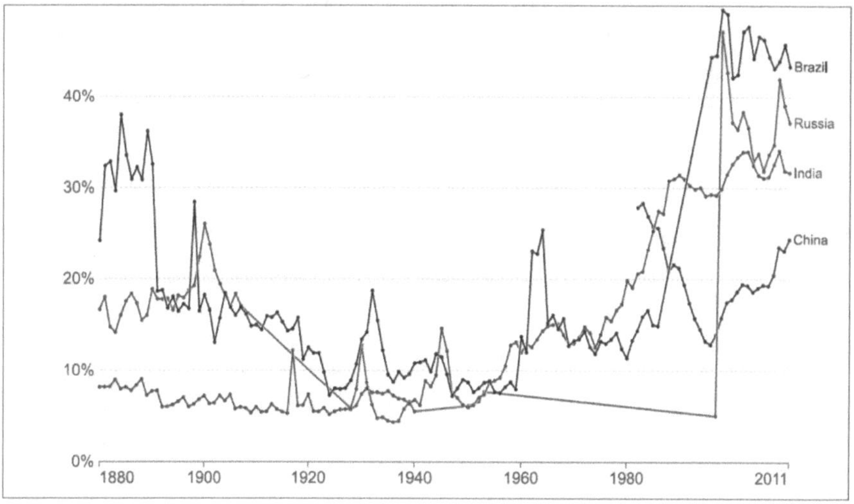

Figure 5.3c Public sector spending in percentage of the GDP from 1880 to 2011 in BRIC

Source: Author's elaboration from Ortiz-Ospina and Roser (2016) https://ourworldindata.org/government-spending

values of the variable are measured in percentage of the GDP. Four broad phases characterise all the economies. The first goes up to the First World War and presents a constant value of the economic intervention of the state lower or converging under 10 per cent for the 'first comers', swinging between 15 per cent and 20 per cent in the second group of countries (with Japan always near 3 per cent) and declining in the third group of economies for Brazil from 30 to 15 per cent, for Russia between 20 and 10 per cent, and for India from 8 to 5 per cent. The second phase starts and ends with the World Wars, being affected by them; in fact, the countries involved in the wars present peaks equal to 70 per cent of the GDP for the United Kingdom, to 25 per cent and 45 per cent for the United States, to 45 per cent for Italy and Germany during the Wars and a generalised up and down for all the economies due also to the interwar economic crisis. The third phase is represented by the period between the late forties to 1980; the public expenditure increased in all the countries, reaching in 1980 a percentage of the GDP swinging between 35 per cent for Japan and United States to 50 per cent for France, United Kingdom, Germany and Italy. The last period presents one more increase for all the groups for 20–25 years followed by a decrease of the public intervention in the economy.

After the post-war increment that led to UK, France and Italy having a 'general government outlay' equal to 35 per cent–38 per cent of the GDP in 1980, such economies experienced a rising trend of the variable in the following decades despite an up-and-down pace. Germany behaved as the other European countries too even if the government outlay remained at 25 per cent of the GDP up to the reunification and jumped to 38 per cent in 1995, declining later to reach 28 per cent at the end of the period. USA and India reached slowly a value of the variable of 23 and 16 per cent, starting respectively from 19 per cent and 11 per cent, while in the last three decades Russia and Brazil quickly increased their government expense reaching the values of 37 per cent and 31 per cent (Figure 5.4).

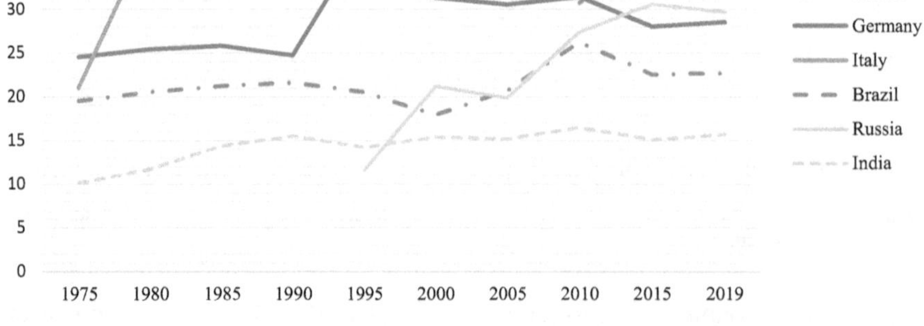

Figure 5.4 General government expenditure in percentage of the GDP for selected countries in the period 1972–2019

Source: Author elaboration from Ortiz-Ospina and Roser (2016) https://ourworldindata.org/government-spending

The public expenditure for the economic upgrade and welfare services

The rising trend of the 'public sector expenditure' after the Second World War was due to different reasons: on the one hand, due to the multiplied need for administrative services by society and the economic system and to the transition from the provision of some 'social benefits' to the creation of the 'welfare system' and, on the other hand, due to the prosecution of the best practices of state intervention began by the governments in the thirties and forties to sustain income and recover the economy following the crisis and the war. Such antecedents, theoretically strengthened by the spread of the Keynesian theory, favoured the entry of state and local administrations in the production of other services or goods. Different managerial models were used for the purpose: the in-house public enterprises to supply 'social benefits' and 'utilities' and public market corporations (the state-owned enterprises) to produce goods and services believed as fundamental for the structure or rescue of the economy. In this context the economic role of the state was legitimated as the engine of the development process in lower-income countries but also as the promoter of a balanced income growth in higher-income economies. In both the cases 'economic policies' and 'economic programming' were the instrument to support the state in such functions.

Within this historical and theoretical framework, the provision of 'public utilities' was an important instrument to promote the improvement of both social and economic conditions of the citizenry. Indeed, such activities, which include the production and distribution of electricity, gas, and water; the city transportation service, intercity rails, and coaches; and telecommunications and the postal service constitute final services characterising an upgraded lifestyle for citizens and intermediate resources necessary for production as well. The reasons for the state and local authorities' management of such productive activities are several. Firstly, these productions need plants characterised by networks of pipes and mandatory routes as well as entrances in networks (stations, repeaters and junction boxes) that entail huge investments and long-run returns; thus, only the state can support such an economic burden and/or guarantee the pursuit of general interest instead of personal gain. Secondly, given their importance of both production and lifestyle, public utilities must be present in all territories of the state even where the returns are lower than the cost of the service, and they must be available for all citizens, even for those who cannot pay for the service; only the state can offset such diseconomies.

Another instrument of intervention of the state in support of the economy used between the end of the Second World War and the 1980s not only in higher-income countries (Amatori 2017) but also in developing ones was the state-owned enterprises (SOEs). The emergence of mixed economies in Western European countries was due, side by side, to the structural weakness and failures of the economies recovered from the war to the convergence of four sociocultural approaches:

> The French tradition supporting a strongly centralized and authoritative bureaucracy; . . . the new vision of the state, either under the economic profile or the legal-administrative one, that matured in Germany in the second half

> of the nineteenth century; . . . the current of scientific socialism inspired by Marx, which advocated the socialization of the means of productions; . . . the influence of Keynesian economics in the twentieth century, which undoubtedly supplied the most important contribution to the theoretical foundation of the mixed economy.
>
> (Toninelli 2000: 11–12)

The importance of SOEs for the world economy in the third quarter of the 20th century has been calculated in terms of GDP and investment shares of public enterprises for industrial and developing countries. For the first group of economies the output of SOEs fluctuated between 7 per cent and 15 per cent of the GDP, while the share of total investments varied between 11 per cent and 23 per cent. In the second group of countries, by contrast, the SOEs contribution to the country income was highly diversified between few per cent points and the 30 per cent; as to the contribution to the total investments it was near 5 per cent in some countries in certain sub-periods and arrived near 50 per cent in others, with peaks of nearly 70 per cent in Algeria (Short 1984: Table 5.1). Although the SOEs worked in a lot of productive sectors, extractive industries (minerals, oil, and gas), electricity, manufacturing and transport/communication were those presenting the highest concentration. The public share in the production and distribution of electricity, gas and water in Western Europe economies was mostly due to SOEs (the share was 90 per cent in UK and France and 65 per cent in Italy, see Toninelli 2010), in the transport and communication services it fluctuated between 58 per cent in the UK and 69 per cent in Belgium, and as to manufacturing Italy had more than one quarter of the output produced by SOEs (Short 1984: Table 5.2).

The 'welfare state building' represented probably the main expensive entry of the government financial statement for high-income economies. Between the 1970s and the 2000s the average government expenditure on social security, health and education amounted to 29.6 per cent of the total public expenditure in East Asia, 37.6 per cent in Latin America and 52.6 per cent in OECD Countries, while in terms of the GDP shares it was 6.2 per cent in East Asia, 5.7 per cent in Latin America and 15.9 per cent in OECD Countries. The degree of financial and managerial participation of public administrations to the provision of services depended on the different models implemented. In this respect five have been the models of 'welfare state' experienced around the world:

- The Nordic model, adopted by Norway, Sweden, Finland and Denmark, was based on universality, social inclusion and redistribution of income. The public social spending for the provision of services wavered between 25 per cent and 26 per cent of the GDP for the first two countries and 28 per cent for the others, while the OECD value was 20 per cent. In economic terms these countries experienced high per-capita income levels, low inequality, high tax level based on the individual (not on a family), active labour market policies, upgrade of worker skills and reintegration of unemployed people.

- The continental model, introduced by Germany, France, Belgium, Austria and the Netherlands, was based on collective compulsory social insurance funds, independent from both the state and the contractual mechanisms. The benefits were addressed to the workers and connected to both the job and the contributions paid. The state relied on industry employer association and trade unions to supervise and finance the mechanism of vocational training: the centre of recruitment, training, skill upgrading, and reintegration of unemployed people. The economic results were highly skilled workers, high rate of economic growth and high salaries but large fragmentation and complementary private schemes for pension and health security.
- The South European model, implemented by Italy, Spain, Portugal and Greece, was based on a dualistic social insurance and fragmented social assistance models centred on the presence of a large public sector and a diversified private industrial sector. The social protection was high for both the categories of workers and lower for the other ones. In the last part of the seventies and the eighties the social protection was upgraded thanks to a universal national health service and pension system as well as unemployment insurance, family allowance, safety nets and the promotion of gender equality. The economic results were 'the combination of extended households, high rates of (mainly traditional) self-employment, large informal economies, tax evasion, and an institutional week administrative apparatus' (Kanchoochat 2019: 11).
- The Anglo-Saxon model, implemented by the United Kingdom, the United States, Australia, Canada, Ireland and New Zealand, was centred on market-based social security schemes, means-tested benefits and few social transfers, sometimes in the form of tax breaks. The economic result was that the access to social benefits was an individual trait depending mainly on the income earned, thus on the distribution of income.
- The East Asian model, adopted by Japan, the Republic of Korea, Singapore, Taiwan and Hong Kong, was based on low 'social protection' when measured in terms of state intervention to compensate social problems. The reason was that social welfare activities were embedded in the corporate structure. This meant that 'the focus was more on the production-enhancing elements (e.g. health and education) and less on the redistributive and protective aspects of social policy. In other words, social protection in the early phase of development was provided by 'welfare through work' (Kanchoochat 2019: 14)'. In the case of Japan, the welfare enjoyed by the employees was paid by employers (including retirement allowance), and the disbursement amounted to 20 per cent of the cash earnings of an employee in 2001. Such a model was labelled 'corporate welfare' in a 'productivist welfare capitalism'. This model created a close alliance between employer and employees.

Whichever model of 'welfare state' was implemented, it stood for a good opportunity of coevolution between state and economy that enabled going beyond the trade-off between personal profit and social welfare. The effectiveness of such a best practice to achieve a better standard of living has been acknowledged by a

United Nations Economic and Social Council resolution issued in 1966, which ascribed it to 'the interrelation between economic and social factors and the importance of incorporating social development into economic development' (Kwon 2005: 3–4).[19]

The public revenues, or the management of the fiscal function

The outlay made by the state to carry out its administrative and economic functions is financed by compulsory reductions of the income and wealth of citizens. The legal reason why the state imposes such a one-sided disbursement is that the fulfilment of everyday life and economic activities by the citizen of a state can be achieved thanks to the public administrative and economic services. The way by which the citizens are levied, established by law, depends on the different economic activities conducted and administrative service required. When personal or legal subjects practice a job or business, own real estates or receive rents or dividends, or produce and exchange goods and services, they must undergo a 'tax levy' on their income revenues and properties to contribute to the general administrative and indivisible outlays that the state bore for the collective consumption of the society (justice, defence and public administration). The 'tax rate' – that is, the percentage of the tax with reference to taxable income – is generally increasing for consecutive tax brackets of income; this creates a rising average rate for higher incomes and thus a wealth redistributive effect of the tax system. The corporation, property and dividend taxation, on the contrary, pay a flat tax. When personal or legal subjects ask public administrations or their agencies for a service they produce (education, healthcare) or for a license or a permission to use or take advantage of public resources (driving license, extraction of minerals, hunting or fishing), they must pay a 'fee'; such a levy, lower than the beard cost of production, rewards the individual consumption of public services and infrastructures made for their own benefit. When the state provides to employers and employees the entitlement to receive future 'social benefits' in the case of unemployment, accident, injury and sickness, old age, disability, and family charges, it demands the payment of 'contributions' in the form of an insurance premium. The indirect taxes for the exchange of goods and services in the territory of the state or for imports and exports paid by the buyers (value added taxes and customs) are flat taxes related to the kind of goods; also, in the case of specific good production like fuel, alcohol and tobacco a levy is due ('excise'). All the levies (the 'income', 'property' and 'dividend taxes'; the 'production' and 'value added taxes'; the 'fees'; and the 'contributions') constitute the so-called 'fiscal revenues'. In the balance sheet account of the general government sector there are also 'non-fiscal entries' due to returns coming from 'grants', the 'use or the sale of public goods' and from the 'public bonds issue' (see Figure 5.5).

The historical evolution of government revenues presents, just as the total government outlay does, a sharp increase after the Second World War and a continuous change in the pattern of taxation (that is in the shares that the different kinds of levies represent in the total revenue). The tax burden turns out to be higher as development proceeds, and the composition of government revenue relies on

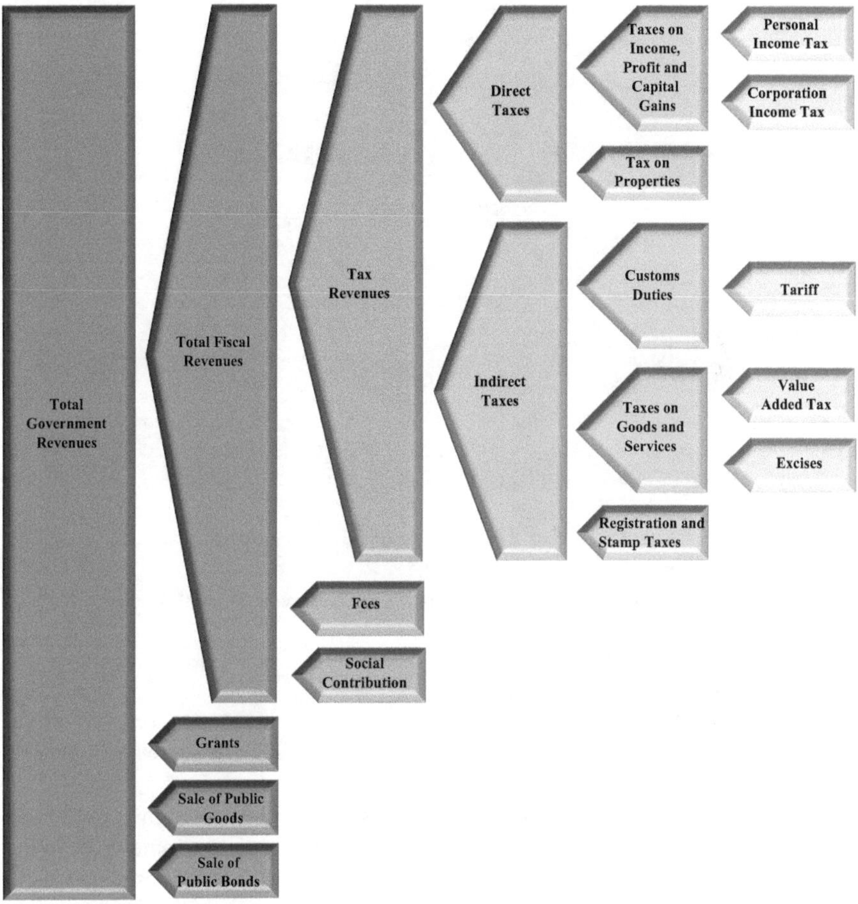

Figure 5.5 The structure of government revenues

Source: Author's elaboration

income taxes more in high-income countries than in developing ones, where the value added and the trade taxes give the highest shares of revenue. The share of the government revenue as a percentage of GDP more than doubled between 1920 and 1980 and for some high-income economies exceeded 40 per cent all over the last four decades (Belgium, Denmark, France and Sweden) or reached such a threshold at the beginning of the 21st century (Austria, Finland and Italy). Figure 5.6 shows both the higher tax burden for some European economies with respect to the USA and Japan due to the private management of some social benefits and the general lower values for developing economies. The prevailing rising trend of the total fiscal revenue is another feature of the past four decades for all the economies, even if some trend inversions emerged in case of national political or economic events (like in USA, Japan and Russia). Starting from 1990 in France, Italy and Germany

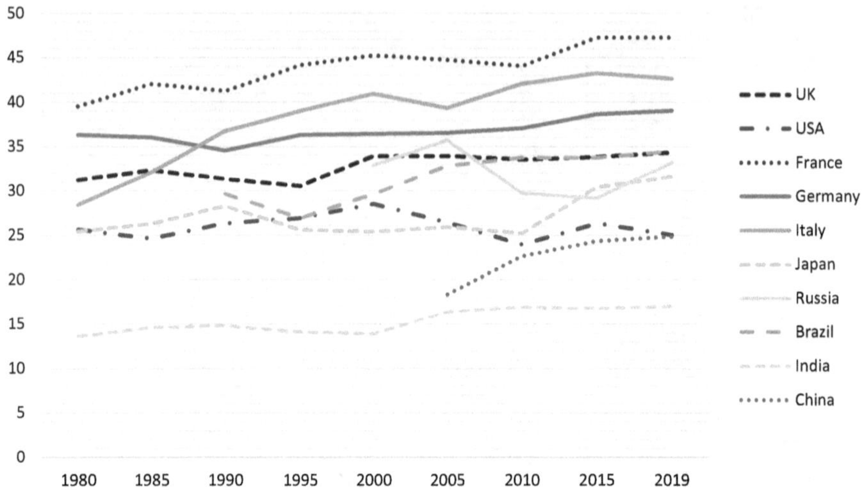

Figure 5.6 Total fiscal revenues as a percentage of GDP for selected countries from 1965 to 2020

Source: Author's elaboration from 'UNU-WIDER Government Revenue Dataset'. Version 2021. https://doi.org/10.35155/UNU-WIDER/GRD-2021

the variable raised by 5 per cent points lining up the economies, respectively at 47.2 per cent, 42.6 per cent and 39 per cent of their GDP. The increase in the UK was 4 points up to 34.4 per cent, the same value as Brazil.

The relevance of direct taxes on the total fiscal revenues are shown in Figures 5.7 and 5.8, presenting the trends of personal and corporation income taxes in the last 60 years. In both representations it is evident that up to the eighties there wasn't a clear trend due to the fluctuations of the variables; however, it emerges that in the USA the amount of personal income taxes and corporate ones increased from 55 per cent to 65 per cent of the total, in Japan from 52 per cent to 54 per cent, and in Italy, where the share was lower, from 27 per cent to 35 per cent. In the UK there was a reduction from 55 to 51 per cent, while in France the sum remained at 20 per cent to 21 per cent and in Germany near 40 per cent. Starting from 1990 the situation changed due to a different composition of direct taxes in favour of corporate and profit earners; in the USA and Japan such revenue shares decreased, reaching nearly 58 per cent and 39 per cent of total fiscal revenues, respectively. The decreased relevance of corporate and profit taxes associated to an increase of personal income taxes shifted the direct taxes from 22 per cent to 34 per cent in France, from 45 to 48 per cent in the UK and from 35 per cent to 38 per cent in Italy. In Germany there is no concentration of direct taxes, and the sum remained near 40 per cent of the total tax revenues. To sum up, the share of direct taxes on total fiscal revenues in the period increased in France by 28 points, in Italy by 11 points and in the USA by 3 points and decreased in Japan by 13 points and in the UK by 7 points. In addition, it is interesting to note that the USA present the highest

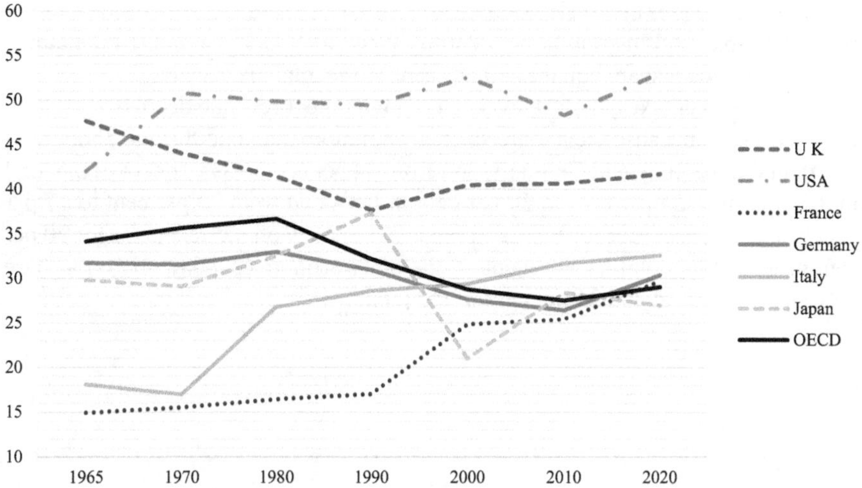

Figure 5.7 Tax on personal income and properties as a percentage of the total fiscal revenues for selected countries from 1965 to 2020

Source: Author's elaboration from OECD general government revenue https://stats.oecd.org/index.aspx?lang=en

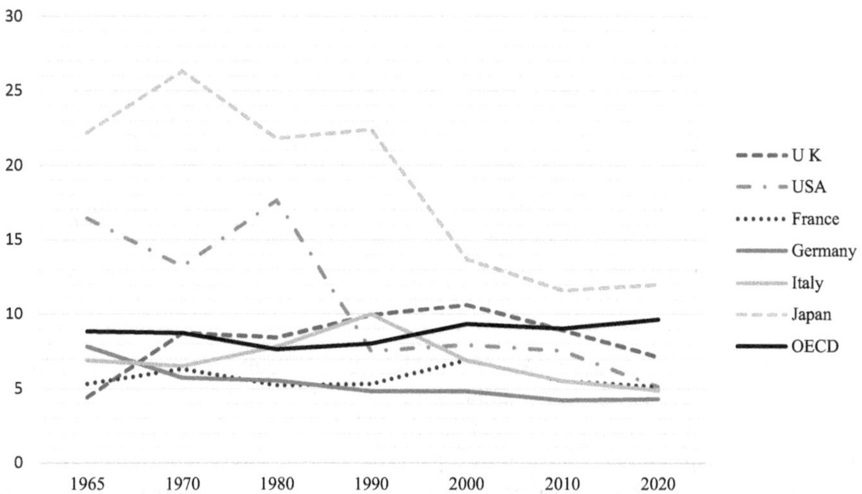

Figure 5.8 Tax on corporate profits as a percentage of the total fiscal revenues for selected countries from 1965 to 2020

Source: Author's elaboration from OECD General government revenue https://stats.oecd.org/index.aspx?lang=en

share (58 per cent of the total), followed by the UK and France, equalised at 48 per cent, and Japan and Italy at 38 per cent to 39 per cent. Only Germany maintained for all the period a share equal to 40 per cent of the total tax revenue.

As for indirect taxes, their relevance on government revenue decreased starting from the 1980s because their share shifted from more than one-third to about one-fourth in France, Italy and Germany, and from 34 per cent to 31 per cent of the total in the UK, from 26 per cent to 20 per cent in USA and from 22 per cent to 17 per cent in Japan. So, except for USA and Japan, which rely on indirect taxes for 20 per cent or less of the total fiscal revenues, the other economies today rely on a share between 25 per cent and 31 per cent of the total.

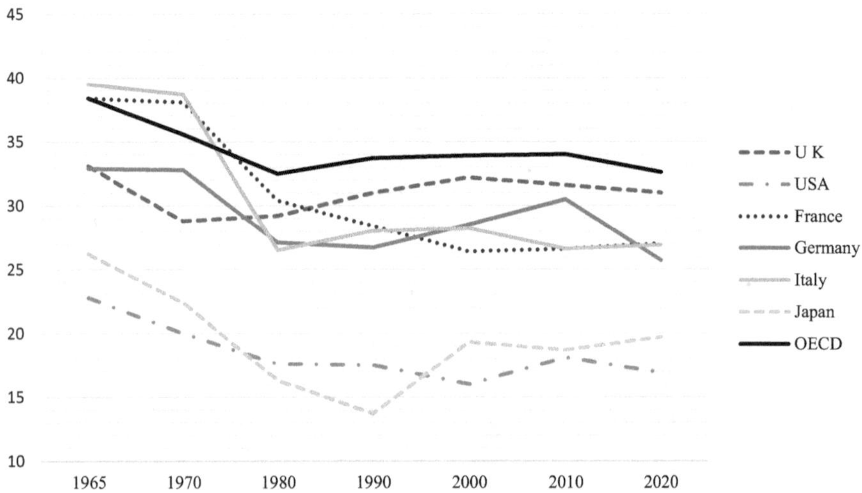

Figure 5.9 Value added and sale taxes as a percentage of the total fiscal revenues for selected countries from 1965 to 2020

Source: Author's elaboration from OECD general government revenue https://stats.oecd.org/index.aspx?lang=en

The share of social contributions over the total fiscal revenues presents a trend having two reverse points. Up to the eighties the variable increased for all the countries by 11 per cent to 12 per cent points in the USA and Germany, by 5 per cent to 7 per cent points in Japan and France and by 2 per cent points in UK and Italy. Then a slow decrease or a constant path was there up to the new century, when a new increase of the contribution share over the total fiscal revenue was reclaimed. As a result, the relevance of such an entry shifted for Germany from 26 per cent of the total to 39 per cent, for Japan from 22 per cent to 41 per cent, for the USA from 13 per cent to 24 per cent, for the UK from 15 to 21 per cent, for France and Italy from 34 per cent to 32 per cent and 31 per cent, respectively. Considering the relevance of this revenue entry, Japan and Germany rely on it for 40 per cent of the total revenues, France and Italy for a third of the total, and the UK and the USA for 23 per cent to 25 per cent.

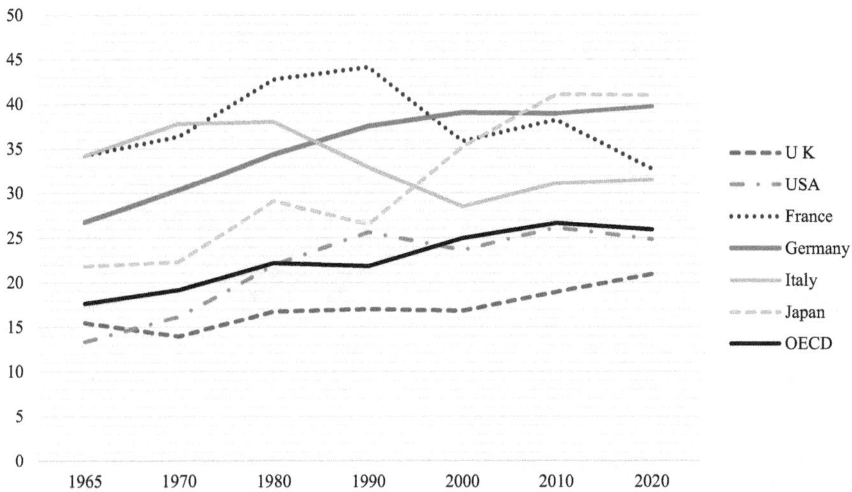

Figure 5.10 Social contributions as a percentage of the total fiscal revenues for selected countries from 1965 to 2020

Source: Author's elaboration from OECD General government revenue https://stats.oecd.org/index.aspx?lang=en

The sovereign debt and the fiscal crisis of the state

The increase of the public expenditure, recorded in the higher-income countries during the last decades, has not always been offset by the total government revenue. Although the fiscal policies of the governments tried to achieve this aim by changing the pattern of taxation and the tax rate brackets, the deficit emerged in the balance sheets starting from the eighties. There are circumstance and structural reasons behind this phenomenon. The economic contraction of the eighties and of the period after 2007 solicited the state intervention in support of the economy, and that caused the increase of the expenditure; at the same time, it reduced the taxable income, and this fact had a negative impact on the fiscal revenue. Thus, such cyclical reverse trends resulted in an increasing public account deficit, as Figure 5.11 shows for the top six economies during the mentioned critical periods. Even though the deficit declined in the nineties and in the last decade, it remained throughout the period under a negative value of 2 per cent for all the countries; the only one exception was Germany, which presented a continuous recovery starting from 1995 and in 2015 changed to a positive account balance.

The negative trend of the public deficit, worsened starting from the new century, shows that the phenomenon isn't a cyclical event but a structural one. In fact, the worsening of the balance sheet from the revenue side has been caused, alongside the economic crises, by some structural features of the economy. Characteristics like the shadow economy, self-employment, the idleness of assets and financial globalisation have facilitated some attitudes towards the collection of taxes, such as tax evasion,

Figure 5.11 Public account sheet balance for selected countries in the last forty years

Source: Author's elaboration from OECD *Data*

https://data.oecd.org/gga/general-government-debt.htm

avoidance or dodging, and tax havens. Tax evasion is the illegal behaviour of a taxpayer consisting in the partial or total non-fulfilment of due payment. The shadow economy (legal economic activities carried out without observing some compulsory legal obligations), self-employment and the idleness of assets can allow the hiding taxable incomes due to undeclared work or to occasional capital rents or gains. In addition, in the era of free trade areas and globalisation, both the transfer of financial assets towards the so-called tax paradises in search of lower tax rates and the difficulty of identifying the national market shares of multinationals cut the fiscal revenues of the states. Tax avoidance increases the amount of such failed revenue because, although it is a legal behaviour, it enables taxpayers to utilise the tax regime to their own advantage to reduce the amount of the tax that he will pay. It is difficult to calculate the revenue losses due to these phenomena because of their random nature; however, some evaluations have been produced. As to the value added tax evasion Germany, France, Italy and the United Kingdom have recorded fluctuating values starting from the nineties with an increase before the new century (Germany and Italy excluded) and a decrease later (UK excluded; Table 5.3).

As to the evasion of income taxes in the shadow economy and self-employment activities, the evaluation is more difficult. Despite a study calculating an average value in percentage of GDP for the OECD countries equal to 3.2 in the period 1999–2010 (Buehn and Schneider 2012), for the United Kingdom the value of the variable equalled 1.8 per cent, for the United States 0.5, for France 1.7, for Germany 1.9, and for Italy 4.0. The legal transfers on financial capitals toward the fiscal havens reduce the tax revenue too, but also in this case it is difficult to know in which measure. As a result, the tax evasion affecting the public revenue is responsible for part of the deficit because it represents non-fulfilled due payments. As the

Table 5.3 Value added tax evasion in selected countries

	1994–96	*2000–04*	*2010–14*	*2015–19*
UK	3.8	17.0	10.0	10.9
France	4.8	13.0	11.0	7.1
Germany	8.8	6.0	13.0	8.7
Italy	34.5	25.0	27.0	25.7

Source: Author's elaboration from Nam, Parsche and Schaden (2001: 11) and European Commission (2021)

amount of public expenditure is approved generally by the parliaments through the budget law only if it is funded by simultaneous revenues, tax evasion is also responsible for a part of the loans needed to counterbalance the deficit.

The state generally relies on international financial institutions or on the stock exchange to have loans. In the second case the state issues treasury bills – that is, bonds entitled to have a certain annual yield rate and the capital reimbursement to maturity. Due to the increasing deficit of public accounts starting from the nineties and the need to renew the debt and fall into additional ones, the public (or sovereign) debt increased in percentage of the GDP (Figure 5.12).

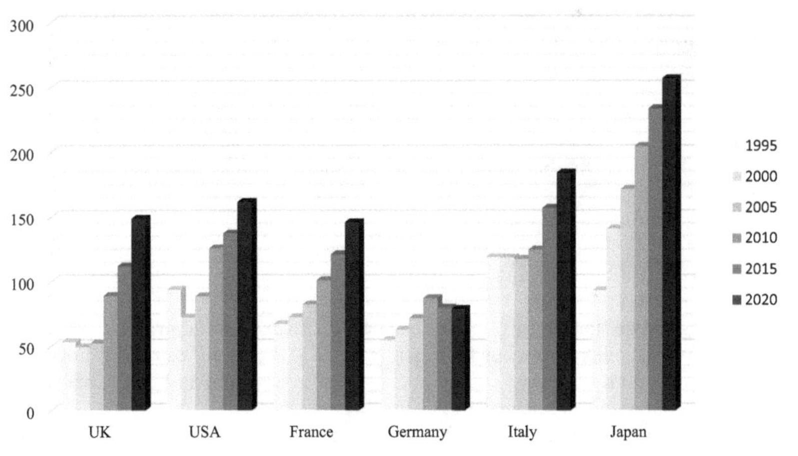

Figure 5.12 Gross debt of the general government for selected countries from 1995 to 2020

Source: Author's elaboration from OECD data

https://data.oecd.org/gga/general-government-debt.htm

Concluding remarks: Modern state and capitalist economy as coevolving adaptive systems

The political authority and the economic activities, after a period of relative separation in Middle Age Europe and a prevalence of the absolutist regimes over the merchants during mercantilism, in the capitalist socioeconomic system have been bound not only to confront each other on their respective roles in the management of the economic activities but also to wonder about their own existence without the support of the other interlocutor. This contention caused in the last two centuries a continuous encounter clash between the state and the entrepreneurs, mainly driven forward by ideological arguments because, as the historical analysis has shown, both powers have actually resorted to mutual support in case of an emergency for one of them.

This dispute has been fostered by theoretical slogans like '*laissez-faire*', *'free trade'*, *'state-market incompatibility'*, and more recently *'privatisation'*, *'deregulation'* and *'liberalism'*, all words praising the freedom of economic activities against the restrictions of the intervention of the state. As these epithets were stated, not only the traditional economic functions of the state necessary to the economic activities were overshadowed, but also its historical political function vanished behind its bureaucratic inefficiency. The myth of a lumbering, bureaucratic state versus a dynamic, innovative private sector was established.

The results of the historical analysis on the economic role of the state in the evolution of capitalism don't match such a narrative, not only for the past but also for the present (Mazzucato 2013). Not only does the state act as a player of last resort behind the market failures and the system failure when the banks are 'too big to fail'; it is also the driver of innovations and the entrepreneur pushing new industrial processes, showing once again that the modern state and the capitalist economy are coevolving adaptive systems.

Notes

1 The 'rule of law' is the basic principle of the state authority and power that has been pinpointed by philosophers and jurisconsults of the 18th and 19th centuries in the laws or in the jurisprudence. By this principle every person – lawmakers, law enforcement officials and judges included – is subject to the law. The set of principles regulating citizens' rights and obligations and state duties and organisation are established in the state's constitution.

2 The 'welfare state' is a form of modern state that promotes and protects the economic and social well-being of citizens by organisms and policies aimed at fulfilling the principles of opportunity equality, equitable distribution of wealth and public responsibility for people unable to provide necessities for themselves.

3 'The sovereign has only three duties to attend to; three duties of great importance, indeed, but plain and intelligible to common understandings: first, the duty of protecting the society from the violence and invasion of other independent societies; secondly, the duty of protecting, as far as possible, every member of the society from the injustice or oppression of every other member of it, or the duty of establishing an exact administration of justice; and, thirdly, the duty of erecting and maintaining certain public works and certain public institutions, which it can never be for the interest of any individual, or small number of individuals, to erect and maintain' (Smith 1904: 184–5).

4 In 1791 in France the so-called 'Le Chapelier law' was issued, which repealed the system of corporations and introduced trade and entrepreneurial freedom, in accordance with the 'Man and citizen rights'.

5 'Much of this regulation was abolished in the first half of the nineteenth century. The wage-fixing and apprenticeship requirements of the Statute of Artificers were repealed

in 1812–13. The new poor law replaced the old poor laws in 1834. The East India Company's Indian monopoly was abolished in 1813. The Bubble Act was repealed in 1825, the corporate and note issuing monopoly of the Bank of England in 1826, the corn laws in 1844, the usury laws in 1854 and the navigation laws between 1850 and 1854' (Harris 2004: 206).

6 'Many European guilds only broke down in the wake of the French Revolution, as France abolished its own guilds in 1791 and exported this institutional reform to neighbouring polities – especially to the Low Countries, parts of western Germany, and northern Italy. In other European societies, such as the Austrian Habsburg Empire, Iberia, and Scandinavia, guilds survived well into the nineteenth century, breaking down finally only after 1860' (Ogilvie 2019: 16). For the dates of guilds' abolition in European countries see Table 9.4, page 535 of Ogilvie (2019).

7 'The American model of regulatory state emerged in the last quarter of the nineteenth century after the establishment of the Interstate Commerce Commission (ICC) in 1887 and (. . .) forty-seven federal agencies having social and economic regulatory functions have been created' (Toninelli 2000: 12–13; see also Eisinger 1988).

8 Such a system was introduced by the Bank of England in 1844, by the Bank of Germany in 1871, by the Bank of France in 1878, by the USA in 1879 and by the Bank of Japan in 1897 and lasted up to the First World War.

9 *Laissez-faire* is a faddy slogan of 19th century politics and economics summing up the need for the government banning from the economic activities. It was considered proved by the 'doctrine of the invisible hand' that shows how the individualistic behaviour of economic subjects determines economic welfare. But this interpretation was actually a misunderstanding of a piece of the *Wealth of nations,* because 'Adam Smith used it to justify free trade. His followers developed further the philosophy of *laissez-faire*, the view that the business of government was to live things alone and adopted wholeheartedly the view that the unrestricted operation of private enterprise was the most effective way of securing the maximum rate of economic growth' (Deane 1979: 220).

10 The state and the economy appeared as rivals in managing economic activities for their ways of coordination and working. The state is a hierarchical organisation whose mode of operation is by directives, while the economic organisation is a polyarchic arrangement of decentralised equivalent subjects coordinated and activated by the market through exchange contracts. Thus, the intervention of the state in the economy, whether to structure the economic organisations or shape the economic institutions and to issue regulations about economic activities or even to manage them, is considered as an illicit encroachment harmful for the economy and wounding for the individual freedom. This interpretation of the role of the state in economic affairs originated the idea that, as for the management of economic activity, the state and the market are incompatible (Dutt, Kim and Singh 1994).

11 Government's actions affecting the economy can include 'attempts to modify the physical environment and the level and skill of the labour force, the introduction of new techniques, and the direct undertaking of business ventures, as well as support of industries in the private sector' by 'taking initial risks, leading the way, and removing bottlenecks; and creating a favourable climate which had salutary effects on expectation in the private sector' (Broude 1959: 11).

12 In a speech in 1884 Bismarck said, 'The real grievance of the worker is the insecurity of his existence; he is not sure that he will always have work, he is not sure that if he will always be healthy, and he foresees that he will one day be old and unfit to work. If he falls into poverty, even if only through a prolonged illness, he is then completely helpless, left to his own devices, and society does not currently recognize any real obligation toward him beyond the usual help for the poor, even if he has been working all the time ever so faithfully and diligently. The usual help for the poor, however, leaves a lot to be desired, especially in large cities, where it is very much worse than in the country' (Frölich, Kaplan, Pages, Rigolini and Robalino 2014: 36).

13 The Children and Young Persons Act of 1908 introduced pension for the over 70 years. In 1909 Labour Exchanges were set up to help unemployed people to find work. In 1911 the National Insurance Act ensured free medical treatment. The National Assistance Act in 1948 was established for the protection of the homeless, the physically handicapped and unmarried mothers. The National Insurance Act of 1946 was established to protect workers who were left injured or disabled as a result of work-related accidents.

14 The term 'welfare state' and its contents have been for long debated, starting from the public letter by A. E. Zimmern published in 1934 and the debate followed by the publication of a book by W. Temple in 1941 and of the report by W. Beveridge in 1942. According to Briggs, 'A "welfare state" is a state in which organised power is deliberately used (through policy and administration) in an effort to modify the play of market forces in at least three directions: first by guaranteeing individuals and families a minimum income irrespective of the market value of their work or their property; second, by narrowing the extent of insecurity by enabling individuals and families to meet certain "social contingencies" (for examples, sickness, old age and unemployment) which lead otherwise to individuals and families crises; and third, by ensuring that all citizens without distinction of status or class are offered the best standards available in relation to certain agreed range of social services' (Briggs 1961: 228).

15 'Social policy is still considered by many as a "residual category" of safety net to be introduced in response to the adverse side effects brought about economic imperatives. . . . In this view the size of the economy is attributed to market efficiency, while welfare measures assume only the task of redistribution, completely *unrelated* to the size of the economy. Such perspective thus imply that the protection of those adversely affected by markets or contingencies is always achieved at the expense of achieving additional gains' (Kanchoochat 2019: 5).

16 In this respect the public system of education is important. A state commitment to implement it has been taken between the end of the 18th century and the first forty years of the 20th one.

17 The powers, motivation and functions of the state are different from those of other economic subjects. 'Governments use their powers to pass laws affecting the behaviour of other economic units. They are able to redistribute income and wealth largely by means of taxes and social benefits. The accounts for the general government sector show how goods and services provided to the community as a whole or to individual households are financed mainly by revenue raised. The range of goods and services government provides, and the prices charged are based on political and social considerations rather than on profit-maximization' (EC, IMF, OECD, UN, and WB 2009: 435).

18 For deepening the economic definition and the accounting structure of the state see EC, IMF, OECD, UN and WB 2009: 78–82 and 435–54.

19 'This resolution was developed in more detail by a group of experts on social policy. The chairman of the group of experts was Gunnar Myrdal, who argued for a unified approach to social and economic planning in developing countries. The group criticised the tendency in economics to draw a distinct line between economic and social phenomena, separating social development from economic development (UNDESA 1971: 4). It argued that social factors, such as excessive concentration of wealth and income, inequalities in educational opportunities and inegalitarian social and power structures, impede development and should be dealt with by social policy. In other words, economic development requires social policy' (Kwon 2005: 4).

References

Amatori, F. (2017) 'State and Enterprise: The Case of SOEs in Europe in the Twentieth Century', in D. Felsini (ed.) *Reassessing the Role of Management in the Golden Age. An International Comparison of Public Sector Managers 1945–1975*, London: Palgrave Macmillan: 9–16.

Beveridge, W. (1942) *Social Insurance and Allied Services. Report*, London: HMSO.
Briggs, A. (1961) 'The Welfare State in Historical Perspective', *European Journal of Sociology*, 2 (2): 221–55.
Broude, H. W. (1959) 'The Role of the State in American Economic Development 1820–1890', in H. G. J. Aitken (ed.) *The State and the Economic Growth*, New York: Social Science Research Council: 4–25.
Buehn, A. and Schneider, F. (2012) 'Size and Development of Tax Evasion in 38 OECD Countries: What Do We (Not) Know?', *Cesifo Working Paper No. 4004*. http://www.kspjournals.org/index.php/JEPE/article/view/634State intervention
Chang, H.-J. and Rowthorn, R. (2003) 'Theories of State Intervention in Historical Perspective', in H.-J. Chang (ed.) *Globalisation, Economic Development and the Role of the State*, London: Zed Books Ltd: 17–43 (first publishing 1995).
Deane, P. (1979) *The First Industrial Revolution*, Cambridge: Cambridge University Press (first edition 1965).
Deane, P. (1989) *The State and the Economic System. An Introduction to the History of Political Economy*, Oxford: Oxford University Press.
Dutt, A. K., Kim, K. S. and Singh, A. (1994) 'The State, Markets and Development', in A. K. Dutt, K. S. Kim and A. Singh (eds.) *The State, Markets, and Development. Beyond the Neoclassical Dichotomy*, Aldershot: Edward Elgar: 3–21.
Eisinger, P. K. (1988) *The Rise of the Entrepreneurial State. State and Local Economic Development Policy in the United States*, Madison: The University of Wisconsin Press.
European Commission, Directorate-General for Taxation and Customs Union (2021) *Study to Quantify and Analyse the VAT Gap in the EU-25 Member States: Report 2009*. https://data.europa.eu/doi/10.2778/018525
European Communities, International Monetary Fund, Organisation for Economic Co-operation and Development, United Nations, and World Bank (2009) *System of National Accounts*, New York.
Evans, M. (1991) 'The Classical Economists, Laissez-Faire, and the State', in M. Moran and M. Wright (eds.) *The Market and the State. Studies in Interdependence*, New York: St. Martin's Press: 1–23.
Frölich, M., Kaplan, D., Pages, C., Rigolini, J. and Robalino, D. (eds.) (2014). *Social Insurance, Informality, and Labour Markets: How to Protect Workers While Creating Good Jobs*, Oxford: Oxford University Press.
Galgano, F. (2005) *La globalizzazione nello specchio del diritto (The Globalisation in the Law Mirror)*, Bologna: Il Mulino.
Gherardi, R. and Ricciardi, M. (eds.) (2009) *Lo stato globale (The Global State)*, Bologna: CLUEB.
Harris, R. (2004) 'Government and the Economy, 1688–1850', in R. Floud and P. Johnson (eds.) *The Cambridge Economic History of Modern Britain*, Cambridge: Cambridge University Press: 204–37. https://doi.org/10.1017/CHOL9780521820363.009
Harris, R. (2014) 'Spread of Legal Innovations Defining Private and Public Domain', in L. Neal and J. G. Williamson (eds.) *Capitalism. Volume II. The Spread of Capitalism: From 1848 to the Present'*, Cambridge: Cambridge University Press: 127–65.
Kadens, E. (2015) 'The Law Merchant: The Tyranny of a Construct', *Journal of Legal Analysis*, 7 (2): 251–89. https://doi.org/10.1093/jla/lav004
Kanchoochat, V. (2019) 'Social Protection and Welfare State Building: Fast and Slow Lessons', *UN-ESCAP Social Development Working Papers, No. 7*. https://hdl.handle.net/20.500.12870/1225

Kwon, H. (2005) 'Transforming the Developmental Welfare State in East Asia', *United Nations Research Institute for Social Development, Social Policy and Development Programme, Paper No. 22*. https://www.files.ethz.ch/isn/102838/22.pdf

Lee, W. R. (1988) 'Economic Development and the State in Nineteenth-Century Germany', *The Economic History Review*, 41 (3): 346–67.

Mazzucato, M. (2013) *The Entrepreneurial State. Debunking Public vs. Private Sector Myths*, London: Anthem Press.

Mikami, Y. and Hirota, H. (1999) 'Japanese Industrial Development and the Role of the State: A Short History', *Technical Report of the Technological University of Nagaoka*, 21: 149–65.

Nam, C. W., Parsche, R. and Schaden, B. (2001) 'Measurement of Value Added Tax Evasion in Selected EU Countries on the Basis of National Accounts Data', *CESifo Working Papers, No. 431*. https://www.cesifo.org/en/publications/2001/working-paper/measurement-value-added-tax-evasion-selected-eu-countries-basis

Ocampo, J. and Stiglitz, J. (2018) *The Welfare State Revisited*, New York: Columbia University Press.

Ogilvie, S. (2004) 'Guilds, Efficiency, and Social Capital: Evidence from German Proto-Industry', *The Economic History Review*, 57 (2): 286–333.

Ogilvie, S. (2019) *The European Guilds: An Economic Analysis*, Princeton: Princeton University Press.

Ortiz-Ospina, E. and Roser, M. (2016) 'Government Spending', *Published Online at OurWorldInData.org*. https://ourworldindata.org/government-spending

Powell, M. (2020) 'The Eureka Moment? The Creation of the British Welfare State', *Social Work and Social Science Review*, 20 (3): 12–33.

Reinert, E. S. (1999) 'The Role of the State in Economic Growth', *Journal of Economic Studies*, 26 (4–5): 268–326.

Romagnoli, A. (2009) 'Stato ed economia fra co-evoluzione e momenti di ordine temporaneo' ('State and Economy Between Co-evolution and Provisional Order Situations'), in R. Gherardi and M. Ricciardi (eds.) *Lo stato globale (The Global State)*, Bologna: CLUEB: 280–96.

Short, R. P. (1984) 'The Role of Public Enterprises: An International Statistical Comparison', in R. H. Floyd, C. S. Gray and R. P. Short (eds.) *Public Enterprises in Mixed Economies: Some Macroeconomic Aspects*, Washington, DC: International Monetary Fund: 110–96.

Smith, A. (1904) *An Inquiry into the Nature and Causes of the Wealth of Nations*, London: Methuen & Co (first edition 1776).

Spruyt, H. (2002) 'The Origins, Development, and Possible Decline of the Modern State', *Annual Review of Political Science*, 5: 127–49. http://doi.org/10.1146/annurev.polisci.5.101501.145837

Stefan, G. M. (2015) 'European Welfare State in Historical Perspective: A Critical Review', *European Journal of Interdisciplinary Studies*, 7 (1): 25–35.

Temple, W. (1941) *Citizen and Churchman*, London: Eyre and Spotswood.

Toninelli, P. A. (ed.) (2000) *The Rise and Fall of State-Owned Enterprise in Western World*, Cambridge: Cambridge University Press.

Toninelli, P. A. (2008) 'From Private to Public to Private Again: A Long-Term Perspective on Nationalisation', *Anàlise Social*, 43 (189): 675–92.

Toninelli, P. A. (2010) 'Energy Supply and Economic Development in Italy: The Role of the State-Owned Companies', in A. Beltran (ed.) *A Comparative History of National Oil Companies*, Bruxelles: Peter Lang: 125–42.

UNDESA (United Nations Department for Economic and Social Affairs) (1971) *Unified Socio-Economic Development and Planning: Some New Horizons*, New York: United Nations.

Zimmern, A. E. (1934) *Quo Vadimus? A Public Lecture Delivered on 5 February*, Oxford: Oxford University Press.

Glossary

Economic policy is the set of economic measures adopted by central and local governments to support the economic system in achieving specific economic aims (inflation, unemployment reduction, international trade promotion, poverty reduction, reduction of the income inequality, increase of the economy rate of growth).

Economic programming is an instrument developed by the state acting as an agent co-ordinating public action and private activities to ensure stability and order in the growth of the economy and to achieve balanced social and economic aims.

Fee is a kind of levy paid for receiving a service produced by the public administrations. The outlaid amount of money is lower than the beard cost of production because the state acknowledges the access to the service of utmost importance for the citizenry.

General government sector is the set of state administrative units, organisations and 'public enterprises' providing institutional activities of organisation and regulation of the economic system and production of services.

Guilds were formal associations of qualified artisans (craft guild) or merchants (trade guild), working in Europe between 1200 and 1800 under the guild jurisdiction, that were endowed with the exclusive right to practise a certain job by virtue of privileges granted by the political authorities.

Laissez-faire is a faddy slogan of 19th century politics and economics summing up the need for the government banning in economic activities.

Law merchants or Lex mercatoria was a set of trade rules, commercial techniques and negotiable instruments decreed according to the best practices applied by merchants and enforced by merchant courts in the medieval and Renaissance periods.

Levy is the money paid by persons or legal subjects receiving an income, requiring services produced by state administrations, obtaining public licences, or carrying out economic activities of production or consumption of goods and services. It is a compulsory disbursement under the form of direct and indirect taxes, fees and social contributions.

Public enterprises are agencies managed as administrative bodies of the government and institutions having administrative autonomy

Public sector consists of the 'general government sector' and the state owed enterprises ('public market corporations').

Rule of law is the set of principles regulating citizens' rights and obligations and state duties and organisation in the 'modern states'.

Social benefits are the social services protecting from life emergencies and upgrading social conditions, like old-age pension; the healthcare system; unemployment benefits; accident insurance; disability allowance; survivor's pension; maternity, family and children assistance; and education.

Social security contributions are 'compulsory payments paid to general government that confer entitlement to receive a (contingent) future social benefit. They include unemployment insurance benefits and supplements, accident, injury and sickness benefits, old-age, disability and survivors' pensions, family allowances, reimbursements for medical and hospital expenses or provision of hospital or medical services. Contributions may be levied on both employees and employers' (OECD Accessed on 18 January 2022).

Social legislation is the set of laws seeking to protect and assist the workers and the weaker members of society (children, the jobless, the invalid, the disabled and elderly people) by guaranteeing their rights and by providing them with social benefits.

Social policy is the set of economic measures adopted by central and local governments to provide social benefits.

Social protection is, according to ILO, 'the set of policies and programmes designed to reduce and prevent poverty and vulnerability throughout the life cycle. Social protection includes benefits for children and families, maternity, unemployment, employment injury, sickness, old age, disability, survivors, as well as health protection. Social protection systems address all these policy areas by a mix of contributory schemes (social insurance) and non-contributory tax-financed benefits (social assistance).'

Tariff is a kind of levy imposed by law on the value of import or export goods.

Tax is a kind of levy paid by a person earning an income in the form of wage, pension and rent (income direct tax) or by a legal subject conducting business (corporate income direct tax), or by who owns real estates (real property tax) or receives dividends (dividend tax), or by producers or specific goods (excise tax), or by the buyers of goods and services (value added indirect tax).

Tax avoidance is a legal behaviour of taxpayers consisting in utilising some tax regime conditions to their own advantage to reduce the amount of the tax that they will pay.

Tax evasion is an illegal behaviour of the taxpayer consisting in the partial or total non-fulfilment of the due payment.

Welfare state is an economic and social result obtained by the intervention of the state, carried out by building institutions, managing directly or indirectly the provision of social benefits, and implementing social policies designed to guarantee to all citizens social security and a standard of living adequate for their health and well-being.

6 Production

A transformation process steered by materials, assets, labour and institutions

Production is a set of economic activities designed to produce goods and services to satisfy the needs of the society, carried out by personal or organisational units (firms) forming the corresponding functional aggregate of the economic system. Such activities consist both of transformation and circulation processes. The transformation process is an arranged sequence of oriented events that incorporates the inputs into the output through the change of the structure of the material and immaterial resources used. 'Industrial structure is really about two interrelated but conceptually distinct systems: the technology of production and the organisational structure that directs production. These systems jointly must solve the problem of *value*: how to deliver the most utility to ultimate consumers at the lowest cost. Industrial structure is an evolutionary design problem. It is also a continually changing problem, one continually posed in new ways by factors like population, real income, and the changing technology of production and transaction' (Langlois 2003: 353). The sequence of technical and organisational transformation events, which comes in succession from the natural resource to the final output, can be split off economically many times at different points of the execution if the semi-finished output can be traded as such; the emergence of a firm production chain and intermediate markets constituted a recurrently growing trend of the production processes as the capitalist economy upgraded. The circulation is instead represented by the processes at the service of the transformation – i.e. the provision of resources (the logistic) and the delivery of output involving both intermediate and final markets.

Until the advent of capitalism, the production process of goods and services has been organised according to epochal technical principles but conducted by familiar groups following administrative or corporative organisational rules or by public entities; therefore, it was an economic activity fluctuating between the dependence and the relative autonomy from the political/administrative sphere. In traditional societies, for example, the artisan and commercial workshops produced following technical routines under the coordination of the guilds, which bargained the interests of the members with the political power. The agricultural production was instead organised in farms working according to the crop rotation and the crop techniques in the framework of the villain's system rules, under the control of the

DOI: 10.4324/9781315679730-9

feudal political powers. When new requirements emerged from society, the farms and the workshops conformed with them through rearrangements of their activities, learning from scientific and technical discoveries and soliciting the support of the political authorities.

Under the capitalist socioeconomic system, the management of the production process has been entrusted to a specific organisation (the firm), distinct from both the family life and the public administration spheres. Such economic entity, characterised by the increasing working abilities of its resources and by the rising complexity of the productive methods and organisation, multiplied the number of goods and services produced; this improvement was due not only to the upgrading of 'physical technologies' but also to the creation of compliant 'social technologies' (new managerial methods to develop strategies upgrading the market position of firms, new laws regulating economic activities and markets and new lifestyles) (Nelson and Sampat 2001). Thus, in the capitalist economy the production became a transformation process increasingly complex and lengthened, progressively partitioned by intermediate markets and all along managed by committed organisations following managerial methods.

Although the firm (that is, the subject that structures, manages and designs the strategies inside the functional sphere of the productive organisation) is the decision-making unit of the productive system, there are two other entities shedding light on the working of this part of the economy: the 'factory' and the 'operating environment. The factory – that is, a component of the firm, represents the unit where the technical transformation occurs; its evolution came along with the technological progress requiring a consistent division of labour, the creation of new capabilities through the training and development of human capital and the establishment of routines. The operating environment represents structural production units, composed of sets of firms, identifying the competitive environment of firms producing the same output or a partnership built to control the production chain and to achieve common objects for all the participants.

After the analysis of the upgrading process of physical and social technologies supporting the evolution of the industries and the general features of the production process, the chapter will present a specific investigation on the three units characterizing the organisation of production in the capitalist system.

Production as a result of physical and social technologies' coevolution

The capitalist production emerged and evolved thanks to the interaction of two different processes: the recurrent upgrading of production technologies and the spreading out of intermediate and final markets. The introduction of machines and the diffusion of mechanisation have been characterised by an uninterrupted upgrading of technological levels – that is, of the specific working capabilities to perform operations that were done in the past by workers and of operating instructions. This process moulded the way by which human beings handed over the productive

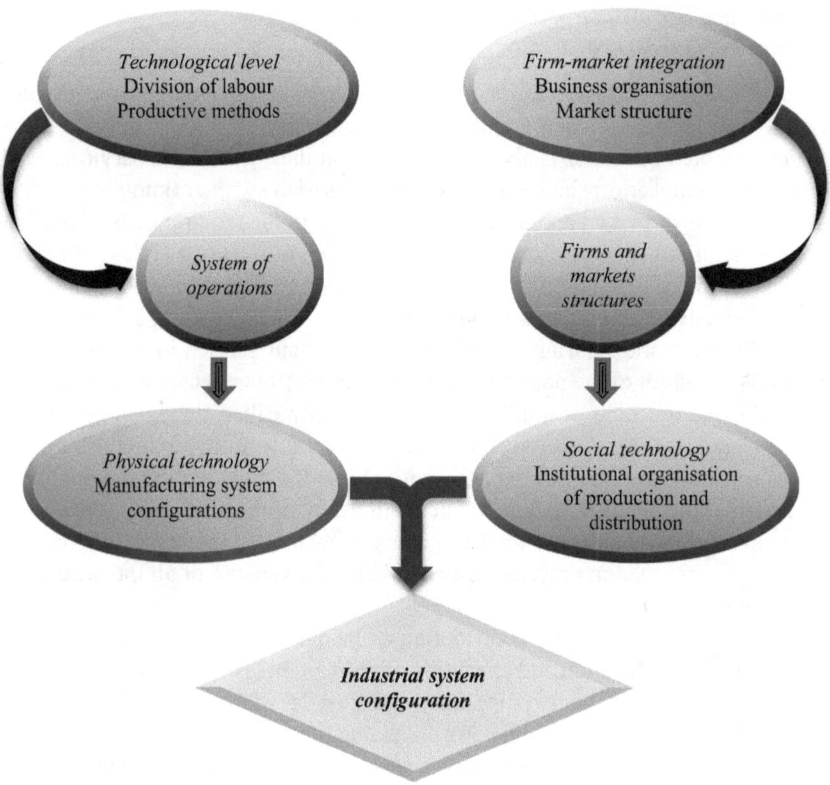

Figure 6.1 Determinants of the industrial system configuration

Source: Author's elaboration

tasks (division of labour) as well as the sequence and the structure of the productive operations necessary to obtain goods or services (productive methods). The systems of operations resulting from these 'in time arrangements of the creation process' describe the evolution of the production 'physical technology' – i.e. of the configurations of the manufacturing systems.[1] The increasingly widespread methods to manage the firm-market integration and the market pervasiveness, on the other hand, shaped both the organisation and the management of the firms (business organisation management) and the coordination of the productive system with the distribution one (market operation) (Langlois 2007). Both the production and management procedures enabling the functioning of production organisations (the firm and the operating environment) and that of the distribution (the market) are institutions that amount to 'social technologies' (Figure 6.1). Thus, the historical evolution of production processes (manufacturing system configurations) and of firms and markets working (institutional organisation) can be represented by the 'industrial systems configurations', resulting from the coevolution of physical and social technologies (Nelson 2003).

Mechanisation and division of labour behind the physical technologies of production

The production is a transformation of inputs into output implemented and, directly or indirectly, brought to completion with the human participation. This means that a certain amount of labour is always needed to produce goods and services. Such physical or mental effort showing the competences of the worker (knowledge, skill, and training) is turned on and modulated according to the requirements of the productive operations to be performed (accuracy, speed, reliability and flexibility) and to the level of the technological capabilities of the tools used to accomplish such tasks (productivity, flexibility and quick lead time). Thus, the competences implemented by the worker during the release of the labour service to the production process are a subset of the potential owned resources ('human capital'). Moreover, the productive outcome of a unit of work (generally called 'labour productivity' and measured by the ratio between the total output value produced and the amount of labour needed to obtain it) depends not only on the quantity and the quality of the human effort but also on the technical efficiency of the machinery (because of the complementarity between worker and machine) and on the organisational efficiency of the production process (responsible for the synergy of all the productive components).

In traditional societies the contribution of labour to production was prevalent not only in the organisation and execution of production tasks but also in the provision of the mechanical energy (supplied by the muscles of the body), the movement of materials and transport, loading and unloading of the products; thus, the production was 'labour-intensive'. The worker specialisation ('division of labour') was mainly of a professional kind as each employee could perform all the tasks necessary to obtain the final output. The guilds of artisans and merchants, for example, trained each new member in all the operational procedures of the crafts to enable them to produce a complete good or service ('professional division of labour').

By contrast the capitalist production, introducing increasingly the machine tools to assist the worker in performing a task more rapidly and carefully or to substitute him in doing operations, adapted the role of staff members and their contribution in the execution of the tasks to the machinery; such process gave rise to the 'technical division of labour'. The good and service process of production was split into many tasks more and more simple, and each one was assigned to a worker provided with specific competences. As each machine tool could generally perform one or few tasks and as the economic efficiency of its use needed its least idleness, every skilled worker remained allocated to the same utensil and to the same task all the working day. Historically, the worker specialisation was first limited to a complete phase of the production process (spinning or weaving for a fabric, for example) and then to a simple task (turning of screws or making shoelaces). Little by little the mechanisation moved forward, the labour contribution reduced and restricted to simple and iterative tasks and the interdependence between machine and worker overturned; thus, the production became more and more 'capital-intensive'. Such a form of division of labour became extreme in the Fordist-Taylorist model, a productive system based on the 'assembly line': a sequential organisation of workstations with special-purpose tools handling and/or assembling the semi-finished parts of the product, moving onwards thanks to conveyors, forklifts and cranes. In the assembly line the workers, specialised in executing so many simple tasks so he was nearly unskilled, accomplished a few movements repeatedly.

As time went by the industrial machinery became a complex operating system where the production, integrating new technological features and productive methods with market requirements and managerial systems, reshaped the technical division of labour accordingly. The result was obtained step by step through the introduction of production systems as 'computer-integrated manufacturing' (that is, management of the production process entirely controlled by computers) and of managerial methods of production optimisation as 'world class manufacturing': both opened, in the last quarter of the 20th century, to the implementation of the 'human resource management', a personnel management model that considers labour as a resource of productive organisation that must be motivated to do this role through specific policies. The application of such an approach only partially relaxes the Fordist-Taylorist model of the technical division of labour; in fact the worker, although appreciated as a skilled and responsible resource, now more than ever results to being integrated in the process of business value creation through comparative advantages, being a component who could make more efficient new technological equipment by adapting to it.[2] In this context human resource management risks to treat labour like an element of this technological machinery.

Production mechanisation entailed the change of operational procedures side by side with the evolution of machinery and division of labour. In fact, the technological advance[3] in production did not mean only the simple introduction of machine tools and the reorganisation of the contribution of workers to execute the tasks but also a total reshaping of the production process. In this framework the routines, bringing to completion the technical efficiency of the production process and enabling the definition of the productive standards, showed their pivotal role inside the 'physical technologies': to push the upgrading of the capitalist production.

Business organisation and market structure as social technologies of production

The improvement of 'physical technologies' couldn't be carried out lacking the 'social technologies' transformation: in fact, to support the production upgrading through technological advance, a change in the other organisational functions of the economic system, as well as in the other social spheres, has been necessary. The 'social technologies', defined as the 'forms of business organisation, management practices, market mechanisms and structures, public policies, legal and regulatory structures, etc.' (Nelson 2003), are just the institutional framework enabling the conversion of the technological output into consumer goods and services. They represent the environment to which the firm must comply to operate but also the source of shocks it must buffer to survive. Thus, the evolution of the capitalist productive organisation has been feasible thanks to the coevolution of 'physical technologies' and 'social technologies' (von Tunzelmann 2003). Such a process, springing both from the firms and the state, provided, throughout the evolution of industry, different solutions for the coordination of technological evolution and corresponding market organisation; each one among these patterns gave rise to different phases of capitalism – i.e. 'proprietary capitalism', 'corporate capitalism' and 'network capitalism' (von Tunzelmann 2003: 368–9).

Before the advent of industrialisation some textile manufactures were made in the countryside or villages according to the 'putting-out system' (Lazerson 1995), a production organisation where an entrepreneur/merchant, owning raw materials and equipment to hire out, provided with them subcontractors who produced at home the goods and were piece rate paid. Once the finished products are picked up, the entrepreneur/merchant took it upon himself to sell them. 'Proprietary (or personal) capitalism' stepped into the breach of this production system. It represented the first phase of industrialisation, characterised by systems of small-scale factories scattered on the territory that supplied their distinct products in local markets that were small because of the high inland transport costs. The organisation of the manufacturing process, grounded on physical technologies using water and steam-powered machines to transform cotton and metals into goods or semi-finished products, was based on 'machine-assisted labour'. In fact, as the capital owned by entrepreneurs was limited due to the cost of machinery and as the possibilities of taking out a loan were lacking, the worker providing skilled professional labour was the main factor of production. Thus, 'in the low-fixed-costs economy of the period, profitability depended not on the ownership of tangible assets but on specialised knowledge and the ability to adapt' (Langlois 2003: 357). Therefore, the social technologies promoted by the state were mainly biased to encourage innovation and dissemination of knowledge and favour learning by doing through technical training, as well as to protect profit-seeking activities. The centre of the industrial system was, however, represented by the 'all-purpose generalist merchants' who, 'rather than concentrating on a narrow range of commodities or on a single aspect of trade, . . . tended to diversify fairly widely. . . . Only by aggregating demands for a variety of types of goods could they generate sufficient scale to employ their overheads resources adequately' (Langlois 2003: 356). Thus, the centre of the economy was the trade that the merchants, pushed by their interests, tried to implement. The market governed the coordination of the industrial system as an 'invisible hand', and unexpected alterations due to swings in demand, or specific customer needs, or required modification of a product component, were buffered by merchant inventories or by the abilities of the factory workers.

'Corporate capitalism' took advantage both of new means of transport and of the third industrial revolution. The railway construction enlarged the market space, enabling the firms to increase the scale of production of engines and wagons and foster the development of other sectors (iron and steel industry and infrastructural components) but encouraged the introduction of new vehicles too (coaches, trucks and cars). As for the physical technology upgrading, the introduction of chemicals, electricity, oil and plastics on one side pushed the production of new goods and services; on the other side it totally changed the structure and organisation of the manufacturing process ('manufacturing system configuration'). In fact, the increasing mechanisation of production raised the capital intensity of the factories, featuring them as 'labour-assisted machinery' organisations having high fixed costs (due to plant investments) but lowering unit costs (because of high throughput).

To grab the technological and market opportunities the firm needed to have more capital stock and to be organised according to new management methods and legal institutions: as soon as these requirements were settled, the corporation emerged. The increased capital endowed the firm with multitasking machinery more and more complex, whose application needed both the specialisation of the machine tools and their coordination within the production process by means of 'systems of operation'. During the 19th century the 'American system of manufacturing' appeared, which introduced machine tools for shaping wood, metals, etc. (like the lathe and the milling machine) and the production of 'interchangeable parts' that are semi-finished outputs exploitable as components of several products. Moreover, the technical routines changed with the introduction of the 'workflow management systems', consisting of the coordination of productive tasks in a sequence to produce output better and as quickly as possible and of the 'assembly production line', a line of machines and workers within which the semi-finished outputs moved and was wrought to become goods.

Such technological changes pushed the firm towards the increase of its dimension and complexity, phenomena that were faced by business organisation and management methods. An example of such social technologies is the 'functions organisational chart', which is a representation of the firm organisation where people are positioned in the different departments according to the job they perform. Another one is the set of 'organisational management techniques', which are procedures showing, through analytical techniques, indicators and standards, how firm resources and processes can be efficiently managed in the different fields of operation (finance, human resources, marketing, etc.). The coordination of both the manufacturing system and other firm functions was assigned to professional experts on firm organisation and management (the managers), who governed scientifically (in a predictable way) all the relations of the productive apparatus with the other corporate departments and with the markets. In these activities they were assisted by other social technologies provided by the state through relevant legislation. First is the corporate law, which through the regulation of the legal entity, nominal capital split into shares,[4] limited liability, shareholders and managers' rights and accounting methods structured its legal standing. Then the laws on stock exchange and the investment bank created the financial channels for the emergence and operation of corporations. Finally, antitrust laws regulated the operative environments in which the corporations implement their strategies. By their ability, the managers buffered the market shocks by matching the firm technological features (the high throughput of standardised final goods – i.e. the 'mass production') with customer needs, also thanks to a rising use of advertisement and a commercial legislation favouring corporations in the market. Thus, their ability to govern the coordination of the industrial system showed that they acted as a 'visible hand'.

Such industrial structure collapsed in the 1970s because the features of the manufacturing system could not match with the customers' requirements for an increasing variety and the differentiation of goods and services, resulting from higher incomes and changed tastes. In fact, large vertical integrated corporations, whose earning power was connected to huge throughputs of standardised goods, presented not only technological rigidity caused by inconvertible committed plants but also the impracticability of economic dismantling and reclamation for invested capitals and sunk costs. The exit strategy they found to cope with the manufacturing system restructuring was the vertical disintegration of production, outsourcing and the implementation of standards – that is, quality benchmarks for components or goods. The emergence of the ICT revolution, based on semiconductors, computers and information technologies supported these strategies, both by introducing a physical technology upgrade (computer-integrated manufacturing enabling the decomposition of the manufacturing system configuration in modules) and social technologies (like new methods of business organisation and management and globalisation – see Kusiak 2018). The information technologies produced declining transport and transaction costs both in intermediate and final markets (pushing the firms towards the business coordination through the market) and supported the creation of networks in all fields of human activities; thus, the current economic phase typifies itself as 'network capitalism'. The firm has been transformed too by information technologies and networking propensity, becoming an external integrated 'project-based firm' (Kapás 2008), characterised by information-assisted automation (von Tunzelmann 2003: 372). 'In many respects, the structure of this model looks more like that of [the craft-production] era that like that of the era of managerial capitalism. Production takes place in numerous districts firms, whose outputs are co-ordinated through market exchange universally understood. It is in the sense that the visible hand of management is disappearing. Unlike [the craft-production] structure, however, the new economy is a high-throughput system, with flows of work even more closely co-ordinated than in a classic [corporate company characterised by] Chandlerian hierarchy' (Langlois 2003: 373).

The production as a hyper-structure: Production unit, firm and operating environment

The evolution of the industrial system configurations just presented highlights important stylised facts that deserve careful considerations. Firstly, the production is a time process resulting from the combination of technological evolution and human learning abilities, both ensuing from long upgrading processes characterised by research and formation, respectively. Secondly, the attainment of the output requires a continuous adjustment of workers' competence and service due to the increasing direct contribution of machine service to the output, as well as a restructuring of the operations and of their sequence. Thirdly, these processes of interaction, coevolution and increasing complexity confirm the systemic nature of the production apparatus; because of such features each capitalist model of the process of production can be represented as a system whose components are machines and workers (sided by the material and immaterial inputs and the power resources used to make the machine work) and whose connections are the procedural relations among them (that is, the routines). Such representation facilitates

Table 6.1 Kinds of industrial system configurations

Industrial system configuration	*Physical technologies*		*Social technologies*		*Typical kind of firm*	*System coordinator*
	Division of labour	*Productive methods*	*Business organisation*	*Market structure*		
Putting-out system *(Labour-intensive production)* Simple instruments	Professional	Domestic system of production	Coordination of independent sub-contractors	Market negotiation	Cottage industry	Agent as coordinator and merchant
Personal capitalism *(Machine-assisted labour production)* Machine tools	Technical: complete phase expertise	Single production processes	Coordination of specialised and able-to- adapt workers	Market (as invisible hand) Property law Labour market	Small-scale factories scattered on the territory	All-purpose generalist merchants
Corporate capitalism *(Capital-intensive & labour-assisted machinery production)* Assembly production line Computers	Technical: single task expertise Human resource management	Workflow management systems World class manufacturing	Functions organisational chart Organisational management techniques Corporate law Limited liability	Financial markets (stock exchange, investment banks) Antitrust law	Corporation	Manager (visible hand)
Network capitalism *(information-assisted automation production)* ICT technologies Modular product architecture	Technical experts and specialists' team	Computer-integrated manufacturing	District/ network firms	WTO ISO	Project-based firm	Market (invisible hand)

Source: Author's elaboration

the acknowledgement of the structural features of the phenomenon, but it would be too generic to understand the economic problems of its organisation and functioning; in fact, the process of production is actually a hyper-structure with three units of decision regarding the different organisational processes: technical transformation, economic management of the output and firm enhancement.

The phase of technical transformation – that is, the core of transformation – can be considered the first unit of the production process, displaying in different organisational forms when it is implemented in the different sectors (the field, the factory, the office). But the output emerging from the production process is the result both of physical technologies and of organisational activities ensuring on one side the efficient execution of the transformation process and on the other side effective processes of resource provision and output distribution at the best market conditions. The functional component of the economic system whose assignment is to organise such activities by applying organisation programmes, laws and market procedures (social technologies) is the firm. The firm is an economic subject, endowed with the legal standing, that by reason of such condition organises and manages the production in all the sectors (agriculture, industry and services). To organise the production and the other connected activities the firm is structured as a vertically integrated organisation, continually interacting with the resource providers and with users of its products and services through market bargaining. Thus, the firm can also be conceived as a system whose components are the organisational departments (administration, marketing, finance, production, etc.) carrying out specific functions and whose connections are the routines implemented, based on the recommendations of 'organisational and management methods'. As the transformation unit represents one among the components of such system, the firm can be considered as a system of higher level with respect to the unit of production. The firm, in executing its activities, lives always in close contact with other firms to such an extent that its behaviour affects them and is affected by theirs. This interaction emerges from the firm strategies aimed to keep and reinforce its own market position or to create technological webs; even they can be considered systems of firms or operating environments that are at a higher level with respect to the firm. Thus, in terms of systemic representation the production organisation of an economy appears as a hyper-structure showing three different units of analysis: the production unit, the firm (managerial unit) and the operating environment (goal-oriented operative configurations of firms).

The transformation process and the production operating unit

The transformation of inputs in output represents the core of the goods and services creation. In fact, the characterisation of the plant structure and of the transformation process defines the amount of material, the worker and machine interventions and the routines in all the kinds of production.[5] Nevertheless, the structuring and management of the output production are pertinent matters of the firm; as such an organisation is entitled to assist the technological process of transformation and to introduce the output on the intermediate or final markets, given that it is important to inspect this double-directional relation between the technical transformation and the firm activities to understand the technical nature of the production process. Thus, what is following is a deep inspection on the different kinds of production transformation and of the unit of production.

The transformation process as a foundation of production

Broadly speaking the process of transformation is a sequence of operations designed to change the nature and/or the form of inputs to produce an output that will be a good or a service once the process of production is finished. It is a complex and diversified process shaped differently in relation to the technological level, the kind of production and the business approach to the problem. The agronomists, chemists, engineers and experts in business process management, interested in the operation scheduling, consider first the technical conditions for transformation fulfilment. The order for the realisation of production operations is not always a decision of the operation manager's choosing, because sometimes it depends on the kind of transformation occurring in different industries; it is a forced path when an exact order of operations is technically required to make possible the transformation ('compulsory technological cycle'); it is elective when there are degrees of freedom in organising the order of operations fulfilment due to the prevalence of assembly activities characterising the production ('optional technological cycle'). Given the first kind of technological cycle, the production process can be 'linear' when the semi-finished product created from a row material fully moves from one phase to the following alongside the transformation, and 'divergent' when it is shared in more outputs containing portions of the originating semi-finished product by an allocation taking place alongside the phases of the production process ('joint production'). Instead, the transformations have optional technological cycles present 'convergent production processes' because more than one kind of semi-finished product from different production processes contribute to the output creation. Thus, the 'biological', 'chemical' and 'melting' (changing in physic state) transformations occur via 'linear production processes', the 'commodity transformations' give rise to a 'divergent production process' and a large number of 'physical transformations' are carried out by 'convergent production processes' (Figure 6.2).

The 'biological transformation' occurs when the production process consists of the cultivation or breeding of living organisms (vegetables, animals or cellular entities) that become the output of the process at a certain point of their life; this is the case of industries such as the agriculture, livestock farming, forestry, fishing and biotechnological activities.[6] Due to this feature, such a process is diversified with respect to the other kinds of transformation; the semi-finished products are organic elements affecting the sequence of operations by dictating an express order of execution to comply with natural variables, climatic trends, and biological rhythms. Moreover, the transformation also needs biological capital in addition to workers and machines; better yet, such capitals are constitutive for these production processes. In fact, the agricultural and forestry production processes have a dedicated

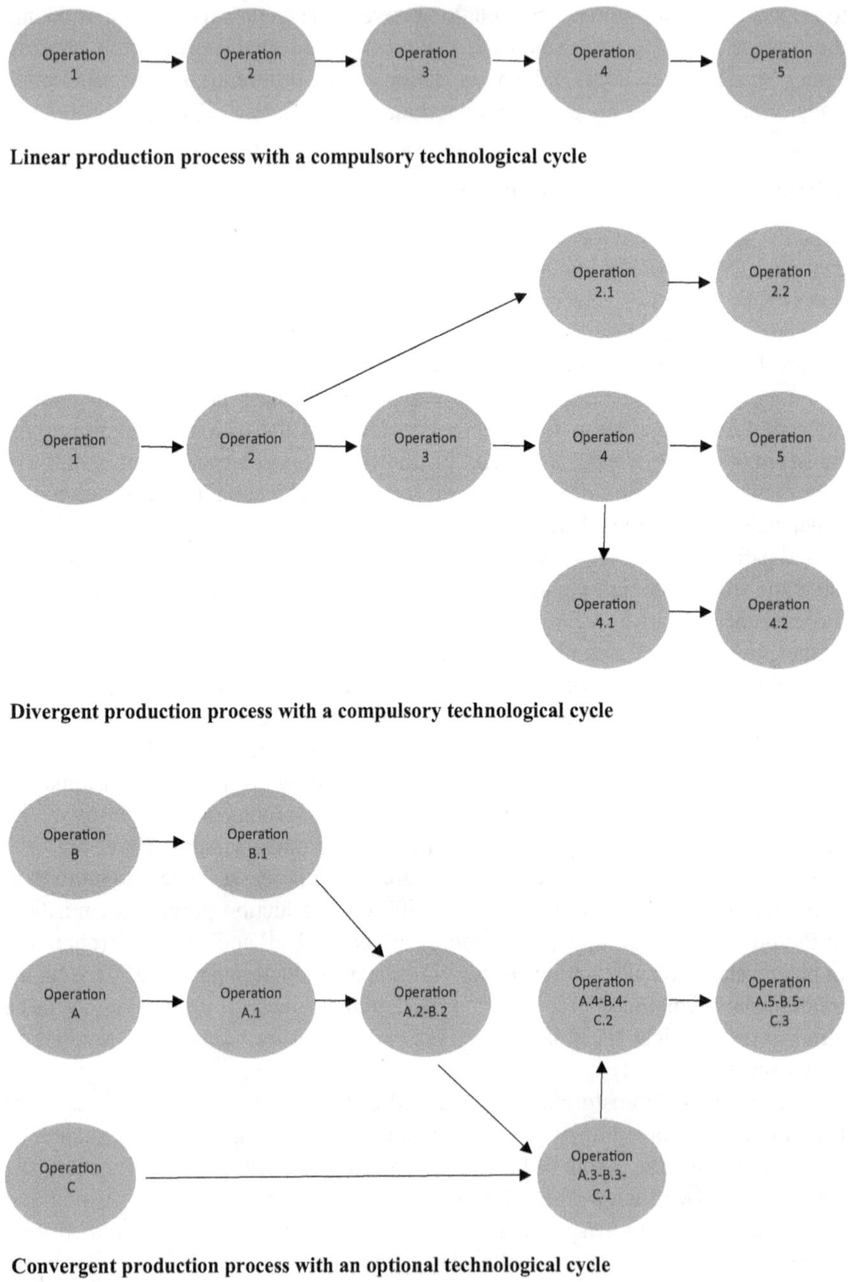

Figure 6.2 Technological structure of production processes

Source: Author's elaboration

plot of land (fields, grazing lands, woodlots and woodlands) as fundamental and distinctive input used for all the production period, while fisheries have fish pools. Such biological capitals underwent an upgrading during the capitalist evolution, just as workers and machinery did; this is the case of estates, whose improvements are due to sprinkler and plumbing systems.

The 'chemical transformation' is typical of all the industrial activities that produce chemical products, such as artificial materials, plastics and substances (refinement products, pharmaceutical, hygienic, sanitary and cleanser ones) through the chemical change of the inputs; it is due to the chemical reactions and to the nature of inputs that the production processes are linear or divergent. The 'physical transformation' occurs in all the productions where the output presents a different form and composition with respect to the inputs used due to activities of melting/decomposition and assembly. The activities of mining and metallurgy present linear or divergent production processes, while in the case of assembly productions (mechanic, automotive, construction and infrastructure, electricity, electronics and so on) the sequence of production operations is mainly uninfluenced by the technical features of the transformation, but it is established by the arrangement of machines (layout).

The process of production of services is characterised by an 'economic transformation' of goods to increase their value by enabling them at a disposal in a specific place (transport, wholesale and retailing) and in a particular condition of usage (repair and dry cleaning), or by an 'economic activity' aimed to produce advantages and relief for people by specific tangible actions (healthcare, tourism, food service) or intangible ones (education, information, entertainment, finance and insurance). Both kinds of service present processes of transformation of inputs into outputs depending on the prevailing capital used. In addition, the service delivery often coincides with its production; thus, the client is a component of the arrangement process.

From the previous analysis emerges that the 'in line' and 'assembly' productions are the possible creation methods of semi-finished products to organise the sequence of production operations. The first method presents bound procedures of execution and a semi-finished product passing through several stages where it is operated on a continuous basis until it becomes a single or a joint output; the second one shows minimal constraints and is characterised by semi-finished products that are often interchangeable parts or standardised components of a final output that can be processed separately in departments or 'islands' without an order of execution before being merged by the assembly. Whatever the technological cycle, the sequence and the arrangement of its phases is represented by a 'technological chart'.

The production operating unit and the production technique

The production unit is the functional sub-organisation of the firm in charge of executing technical transformation by arranging a set of production resources for all the outputs produced; thus, it is a system whose components are machines, workers, potential biological plants[7] and materials and whose relations are the

Table 6.2 Features of the technical process of transformation

	Technical conditions for the transformation fulfilment	*Production operations order*	*Sequence of production operations*	*Nature of the transformation process*	*Kind of production activities*
				Biological process	Agriculture, forestry, fishing
			Linear production processes	Chemical process	artificial materials, plastics, pharmaceuticals, sanitary
		Compulsory tech. cycle		Melting process	mining, metallurgy
	Production procedures		Divergent production processes	Melting/decompo-sition process	Metals, glass, oil, gas
Technological cycle		Optional tech. cycle	Convergent production processes	Physical transformation	mechanic, automotive, construction, infrastructure, electricity. electronics
			In line production		
	Semi-finished products creation methods	Technological chart			
			Assembled production		

Source: Author's elaboration

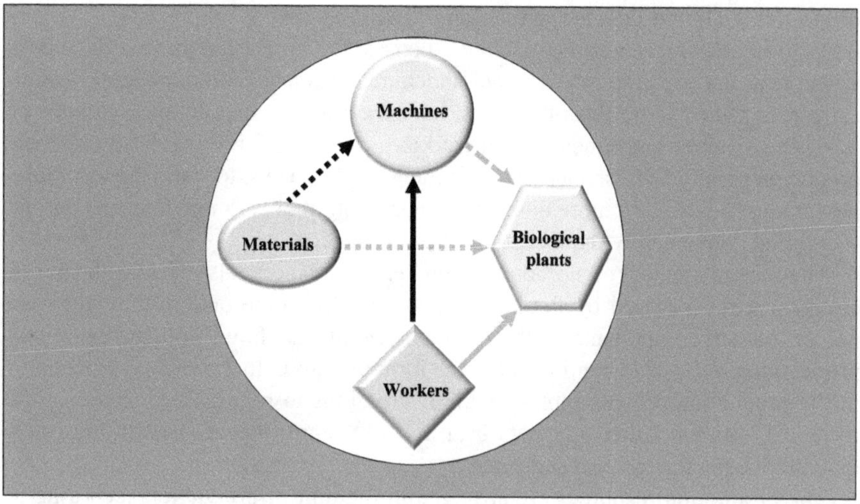

Figure 6.3 The production unit system

Source: Author's elaboration

procedures implementing the transformation. In Figure 6.3 the routines represented by grey arrows characterise the relations inside biological units of production, where both physical and human capitals converge on the dominating biological plant; the black ones represent instead all the other kinds of production units. The endowment of productive resources is provided by the firm, not only because the production transformation represents one among its activities but also because the firm is the legal holder of the entrepreneurial function, consisting in the organisation and management of all the activities that are necessary to produce and deliver the output.

As to the role of resources in the transformation process, the capital assets (machines, workers and biological plants) provide 'time service' that process the materials during the production transformation. The use of such capitals go beyond the single output production process because they deliver the service for a period established by the technical capacity in the case of physical capital, by laws for human capital, or by the level of availability (property, rent) for biological capital. Thus, such assets can be considered endowments or 'funds' of service (Georgescu-Roegen 1976) conferred to the production transformation for a defined time interval. All the capitals of the production unit are endowed with specific features qualifying them; thus, each production unit presents a distinctive technological level, whatever is the sector where it takes place (field, breeding farm, workshop, factory, laboratory, office). Moreover, associated to the qualitative features of the endowment of production resources there is their quantity so that each production unit presents a distinctive production capacity. The disposal of the endowment of time service capacity of each fund corresponds to the total cost borne for obtaining the asset, and the cost of each unit of its application is calculated based on its time of use. As such unit cost is the fraction of the total cost of the asset and the total time of use; the greater is the machine idleness, the greater the time service cost. Given that, and considering that each machine takes a specific time lapse technically determined to perform the tasks, machine idleness can be avoided only by using the machine continuously in a workday, but to perform a task for a specific product generally it is used a fraction of the workday. Thus, to avoid the asset idleness it must be used for more units of the same output or for more than one output, staggering conveniently the inception of each usage.

The second element of a production process is the materials – that is, the physical resources processed by fund service that turn into the output; thus, they are not permanent components of the production unit but 'flows' joining the output production process and coming out in the form of output. In the end the procedures in the production process represent the instructions to be followed to obtain the technical transformation of inputs in a unit of output; they consist in the tasks, quantitative parameters and sequence.

The production resources are arranged in the unit of production according to the outputs that the firm decide to supply. Thus, for each product the unit output production plan must be organised starting from the 'technological operations cycle', which identifies a set of technological operations and a group of ordered times per operation (Jovanovic, Milanovic and Djukic 2014: 514). Such a theoretical recipe, which provides a set of fixed coefficients of production (amount of each input for a unit of output) quantified by the task parameters and by the execution times, is built on the base of the features of the technical transformation and of the 'production organisation'. Such an arrangement is the organisational setup of a single output production plan within the unit of production working time; the activation of production processes of a certain good is 'consecutive' when one unit output production process starts at the conclusion of the previous one; it is 'in parallel' when some processes start and go forward simultaneously and 'combined' if the inception of each unit production process is staggered alongside the unit output production process time at a suitable gap. The first arrangement determines the highest cost of the capital asset service when the machines fulfilling a task are used for a fraction of the unit output production time, the second one presents the same situation because each parallel process multiply the number of funds and the third arrangement cancels the idleness of all the machines used.[8]

The different kinds of production organisation depend both on the number of different outputs produced and on their technological cycles, but also on the throughput of each output. The last two variables affect the arrangement of the plant machinery (called 'layout'), which thus appears in three forms: 'product layout', 'process layout' and 'fixed-position layout'. In 'product layout', used in the case of 'in-line production processes' with high throughput, the machines are arranged in the same sequence of the transformation to enable the continuous movement and stop at work centres of the in-process material up to the final stage of production (the case of the refinery products is shown in the Figure 6.4). The 'process layout', suitable for the 'assembled production processes' in cases of a large range of

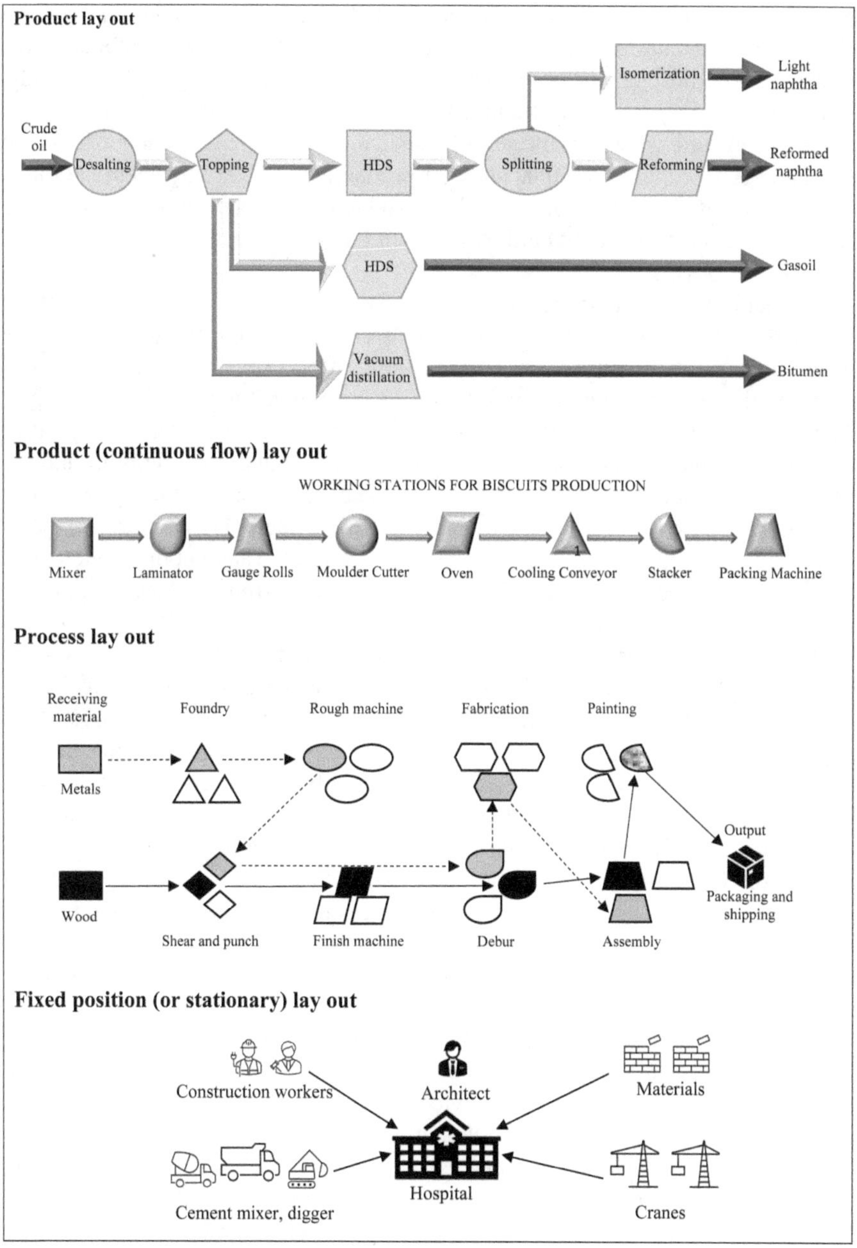

Figure 6.4 Kinds of layout

Source: Author's elaboration

manufacturing productions or of service productions, locates together in the same site similar machines separated according to their performing task or function (as in the cases of hospitals or of kitchen cabinets production in Figure 6.4). Finally, in the 'fixed position layout' the machines and workers move around a required construction yard, where a static semi-finished material increases, and the tasks are gradually fulfilled up to the final stage of production. This arrangement is typical for 'assembled production processes' of productions whose output presents big sizes or weights (agricultural cultivations, building and infrastructure construction, ships and planes).

Although the layout arrangement for productions like biological and chemical industries and construction productions is determined by the technological cycle when this constraint is lesser or is absent the pros and cons of the three kinds of configuration are evaluated in the light of the economic comparative advantages. As machinery, workers and biological plants constitute the long-lasting capital of the firm, the layout arrangement also represents its medium long-term production capacity in terms of scale and variety. Thus, the criteria used for the layout choice are the 'flexibility' of the machine configuration to face new or more customer needs and the 'scalability' – that is, the ability to adjust the amount of output to deal with the intensity of the demand. Both abilities increase from the first layout to the last one, but the capital investment also does.

The analysis of the organisation of the production operating unit shows the complexity of the process that involves the combination of managerial decisions, the technological constraints and the organisational management. The provision of capitals, the number of outputs and the relative throughputs are variables defined by the managers that, by these determinations, set both the capacity and the technological level of the unit of production and the output that must be obtained. The technicians provide technical guidelines, namely the information about the feasibility and scheduling of the transformation process (technological chart). The unit executive director, who is the person in charge of organising the layout and the unit output processes, develops the production planning on the base of previous data and objectives and following the idleness and downtime reduction criteria. Then the production process can start.

What has been described is a schematised representation of the steps underlying the production planning that is developed before the implementation of a production process in agriculture, industry and service. The current sectoral productions present certainly specific arrangements of this outline, and some instruments (computers) and applications (business programmes) nowadays help the directors in making decisions. Nonetheless this representation offers important stylised facts. The first is that the production transformation is a purposeful organised process where the operations are combined according to a time path dependency and where machines and workers intervene for a certain length of time, following scheduling and sequencing procedures. The second stylised fact is that the objective of the unit of production is to produce the output established by the managers applying the idleness and downtime reduction to lower the unit output cost as an organisation efficiency criterion. In this framework time operates not only as a 'yardstick' to measure the service provided to the production process by the capitals (human, biological and physical ones) but also as an 'active ingredient' to obtain the output. Due to such a feature time is a 'real' factor (O'Driscoll Jr and Rizzo 1985: 59–62); in fact, it presents the properties of heterogeneity (two equal periods inside the production period are different because the handled tasks are different) of dynamic continuity (because the task's time must be spent in performing the task to handle the following one) and of causal effectiveness (because each interval changes the semi-finished product). Consequently, from the theoretical point of view, the production is an irreversible, organised, predictable and thus repeatable process. The third stylised fact is that the 'coefficients of production', which are the quantity of inputs necessary to obtain one unit of output, are technically determined and constant in each unit of production; thus, the recipe to produce a specific output is unique in every technological environment.[9] In fact, the materials needed for each operation of the process of transformation are decided in befitting units of measure by the technical feasibility study (technological cycle), while the times of operation of the assets are fixed, ones arranged by the production planning. Both are fixed because the efficiency connected to the technological cycle elaboration provides the exact amount for the materials needed for a unit of output, and the time to execute a task remains constant in a work shift. Once the plant configuration is decided the time for the execution of each operation is also established; thus, the technique of production in real terms is determined. Only the production arrangement provides information to calculate the cost of the service for the capital assets, and as the market provides the price of materials then the 'technique of production'[10] is determined in monetary values.

The firm as the economic unit: Governance, organisation and management

The firm has emerged alongside the chapter as the joining link between the output production process and the realisation of the socioeconomic value created within it. In doing this function the firm turned out to be an organisation evolving, in the long run, in tune with the upgrade of physical and social technologies, by matching the manufacturing system configurations and the institutional arrangement of markets and legal systems. The proof of such a bent is the turnover of the firm archetypes (factory, corporation and project-based firms) and of physical and human capital intervention in the production process (mechanisation and division of labour) along the evolution of capitalism. At the same time, in the previous paragraphs the firm appeared as the business hub managing all the activities needed for the output production process and its distribution, via a thick web of relations inside and outside its boundaries. Besides such a structural complexity developed in performing its role, it showed its ability to adapt and comply with the environment where it was working through coordination and strategies. All these stylised facts, which are useful pillars to characterise the firm in the different phases of the capitalist evolution, prove the firm systemic structure; however, to examine the topic in a more in-depth manner, all the components and the relations that characterise it must be organised and sketched.

The systemic structure of the firm

A lot of literature has scrutinised the different structural features of the firm and its evolution during the capitalist advent and spread in search of its main constitutive element; organisation and governance have been identified as original ones, but entrepreneurial function and legal peculiarities also held this position. However, most often each feature has been deepened as separate from the other ones (even when a historical perspective has been adopted for the analysis) and considered as the main fundamental component of the firm; thus, the nature of the firm has been identified each time as a single aspect or element, not to mention when single behavioural principles or theoretical concepts have been used for purpose (Dietrich and Krafft 2012). To go beyond the advice of distinct or abstract features of the firm as constitutive elements explaining its archetypes, a systemic representation of such an entity based on stylised facts can bridge the gap.

Production and distribution of goods and services are carried out by organisations, established and administrated in accordance with 'corporate law', whose aim is to manage profit-making, non-profit or charitable allowable businesses in this scope. Such organisations are legal business entities, generically labelled firms, that are endowed with memberships or autonomous 'legal capacity' under which they can own assets and stipulate provision and sale contracts and with organisational structures to perform their activities. Thus, considering the stylised facts previously reviewed, the firm can be represented as a system whose elements are the legal standing, the organisation and the resources and connections set by the incorporation deed that defines the organisational roles, the corresponding rights and the hierarchical organisational of operating routines. Each element type identifies a constitutive/operating level of the firm which, in turn, can be represented as a system because it is composed of elements and connections; thus, the firm can be defined a 'complex adaptive system' (Figure 6.5)

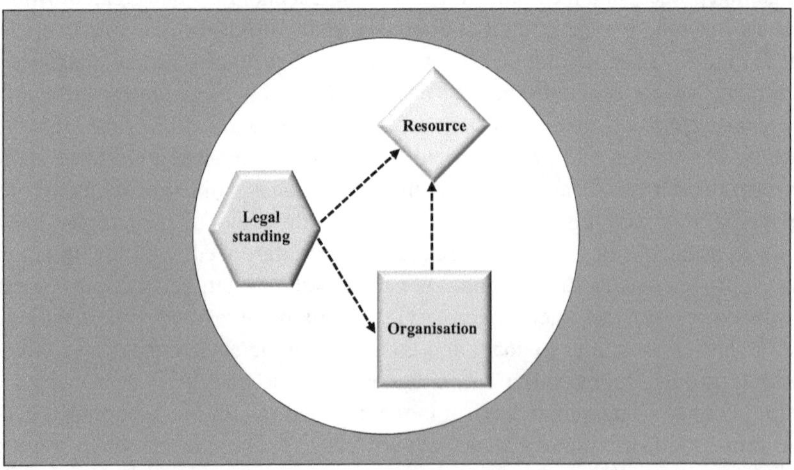

Figure 6.5 Elements and connections in the firm system

Source: Author's elaboration

that can be portrayed as a hyper-structure (see Chapter Three and Potts 2000: 68–71).

The 'legal standing' awards the firm with rights and duties, but it also imposes specific prescriptions for its creation regarding, especially, the definition of the risk capital connected to the entrepreneurial function and the prevention of conflicts among stakeholders. By the first kind of regulations the lawmakers try to promote upgrading the economy through an increasing use of private assets in entrepreneurial activities and to protect the personal properties from the firm failure risk. To pursue these aims the lawmakers of the different countries have created many types of business entities that can be broadly generalised by the following ones:

i. The 'sole proprietorship' (or individual entrepreneurship) is a type of firm without legal entity whose assets belong to the person who manages it by unquestionable decisions, receives firm profits, pays the corresponding taxes and faces the failure of all personal assets ('unlimited liability'). It is the first type of firm appearing when industrialisation started. It can also be established to manage agricultural and handcrafted activities as well as for small commercial and professional service supplies.
ii. 'General partnership' is a type of firm (without legal entity) where all the participants in economic activities provide capital on equal terms, jointly manage the firm and are liable for debts; in the presence of a 'limited partnership', someone turns down the managerial right in return for the limited liability. In both cases the firm taxes are paid by partners.
iii. A 'limited private company' is a type of firm endowed with a legal entity whose capital stock is divided into shares that cannot be traded to the public and where the shareholders are endowed with limited liability.
iv. The 'public company' is a type of firm endowed with a legal entity, generally taken by corporations, whose capital stock is divided into shares traded in the stock market, which entitle the owner to participate in shareholders' meetings, receive profits, enjoy limited liability and trade stocks; the company pays the earned income taxes.
v. The 'cooperative' is a type of firm endowed with a legal entity referred to specific businesses (working, retailing, services, building constructions) owned and managed with limited liability by the members through democratic procedures and control.

To prevent conflicts among stakeholders and enable them to regularly organise and manage the activities of the firm, the legal norms try to create role and power certainty for all the participants. The roles depend on different forms of business entities as well as on the functions and rights of the components. The co-partners who set up the company and risk the personal and/or the awarded capital jointly practise the direction of the firm activities or their control in different forms; in the presence of managers, who are in turn charged with firm management in the case of limited companies, they share such functions as they designate and control them according to corporate law. The employees carry out their job complying with the employment contract but under the hierarchical coordination and control of managers; the trade unions, which are appointed by employees, negotiate their salary and work conditions with the managers. The other stakeholders (resource providers, distributorships, financers and bondholders) support the production and distribution process, keeping the terms of supply and distribution contracts drawn up with the managers of the firm; thus, they have horizontal relations with the managers. The 'legal standing system' of a firm includes all the stakeholders and two legal connections: the incorporation deed that rules, among other rights, the relation between the holders of the capital and the managers, and the contracts signed by the managers and the stakeholders providing resources and delivering the output. The configurations of the 'legal standing system' for different legal types of firms (called 'corporation governance') present the hierarchical structure of the roles and powers in managing the firm built around the managers (employees) and the horizontal one (distributors, resource providers and bondholders); the shareholders commit such a prerogative to the managers. This configuration for a public company is displayed in Figure 6.6.

Despite the corporate governance configuring hierarchical relations between shareholders and managers, conflicts among them cannot be avoided. The reason is due to the different interests of the two groups of stakeholders: the first one is represented by financiers of the entrepreneurial activity, whose aim is to increase the value of the invested capital by both the appreciation of the share value (in the long run) and the distributed profits, while the second one is constituted by corporate directors interested in better earnings for the firm during the period of appointment (three or five years).

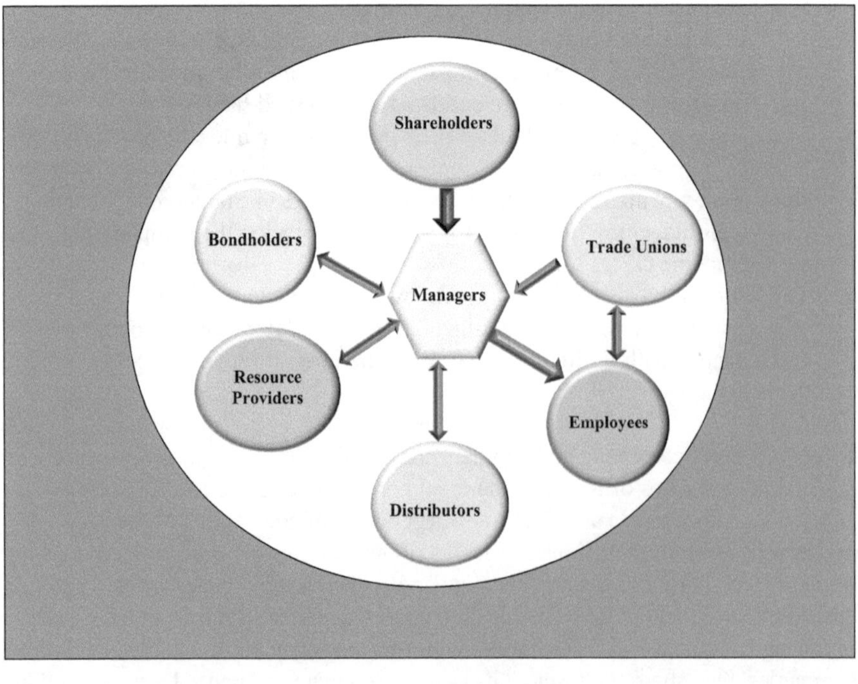

Figure 6.6 Elements and connections of the firm legal standing system

Source: Author's elaboration

To increase the long-term performance of the firm means to make investments, and that produces indebtedness that reduces share value and distributed profits; thus, a trade-off emerges. As the managers run the firm activity, they can also enjoy information asymmetry with respect to shareholders and climb over their dependent position implementing short-term objectives. The introduction of incentive stock options as managers' payments to foster the achievement of long-run objectives produce the opposite result: the managers try to manage the firm in order to obtain short-term boosts of stock values to sell their stock option immediately and have higher revenues.

The 'organisational system' represents the structure of the 'operating units' by which the firm tries to achieve its objectives. The operating units are collections of people, resources and procedures organised to cooperatively carry out or control the different functions or partitions of the operational process of the business: thus, they are firm sub-systems charged with specific, appropriately measured objectives that represent the output of their processes (number of products, services, paperwork, results, behaviours, sales). They work by adopting the criteria of minimum resource use and instrument idleness as well as of process improvement. The operating units of a firm organisation can represent the main areas of decision and activity or the production process of single outputs (productive division); in the first case the 'organisational system' of the firm turns out to be made up of the following departments carrying out the corresponding functions: management, productive operations, human resources, marketing, sales, accounting and finance, research and development. Such departments, co-ordinated by the managers (see Figure 6.7), carry out

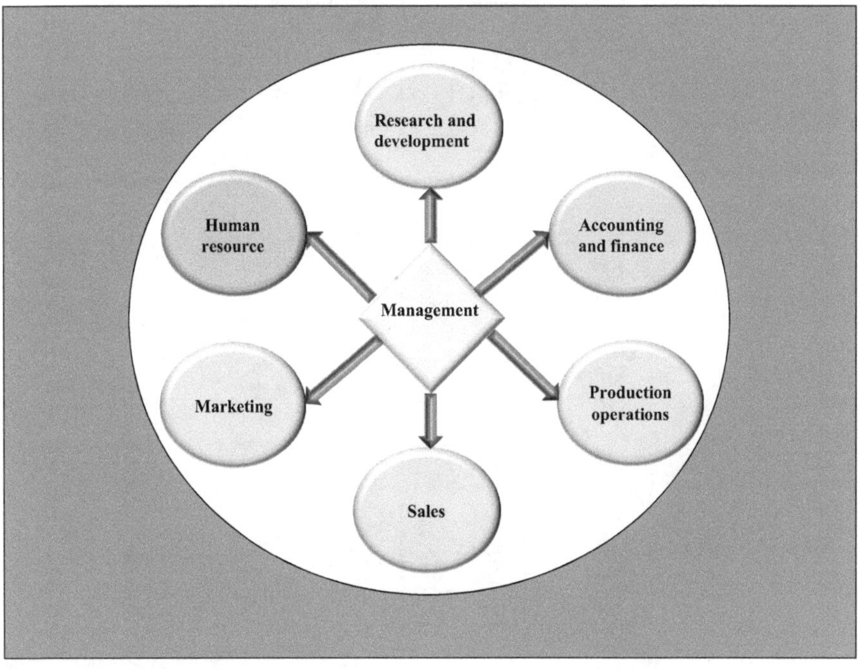

Figure 6.7 Elements and connections of the functional organisation system of the firm

Source: Author's elaboration

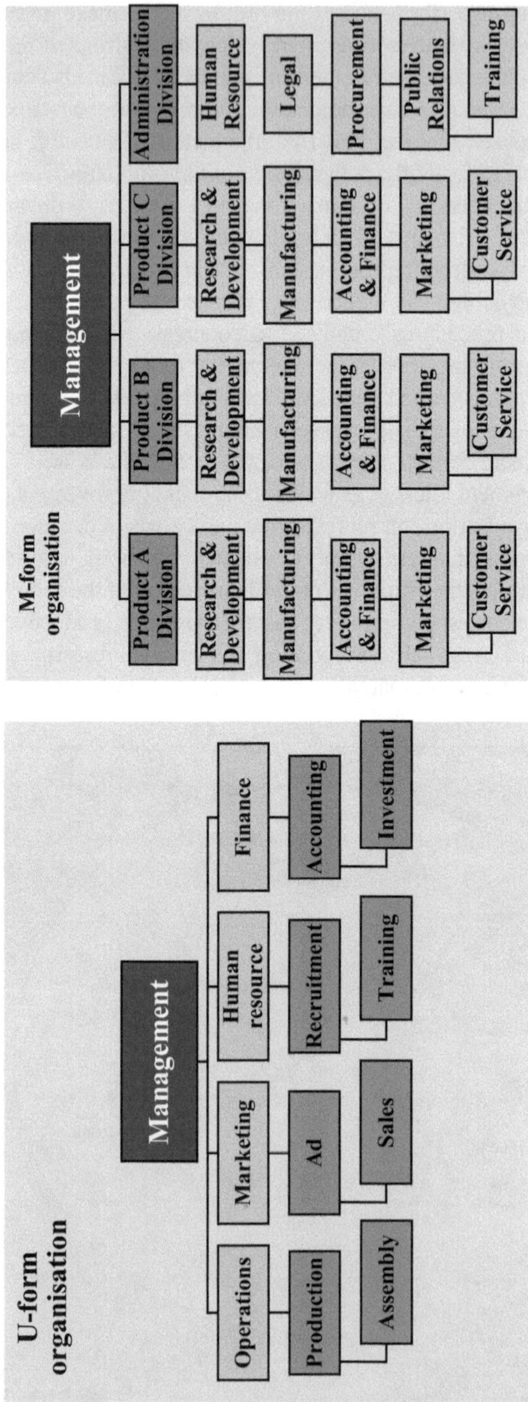

Figure 6.8 Functional and divisional organisation structure of the firm

Source: Author's elaboration

their activity according to the set roles and powers of the staff, and the operational relations among the operating units shown in the 'organisational chart' (the diagram representing the relation of one firm official, department or function to another).

The hierarchical allocation of power, shown in the Figure 6.7, is in force even though the operating units of a firm organisation structure represent a productive division. A division is a sub-company organisation, directed by a person in charge, producing a kind or set of products/services through a devoted autonomous organisation and management also regarding the functional activities supporting the production process (finance, sales, marketing, etc.). But the configuration of control through the levels of management is lesser in the models of divisional organisation structure ('multi-divisional form', or M form) than in the functional one ('unitary form', or U-form) because each divisional manager is independent in organising and managing the divisional production process from the parent company; in some configurations such independence is mitigated by the presence of a firm division managing common services like human resources, procurement, accounting, legal, public relations, etc. (see Figure 6.8).

The firm's 'resource system' represents the endowment of physical capitals (such as plants, equipment and buildings), current assets (accounts receivable and inventory), human resources, financial assets (sovereign and corporate bonds,[11] preferred equity), and intangible assets (operational knowledge and methods, patents, trademarks, copyrights and goodwill; Figure 6.9). Such resources, organised

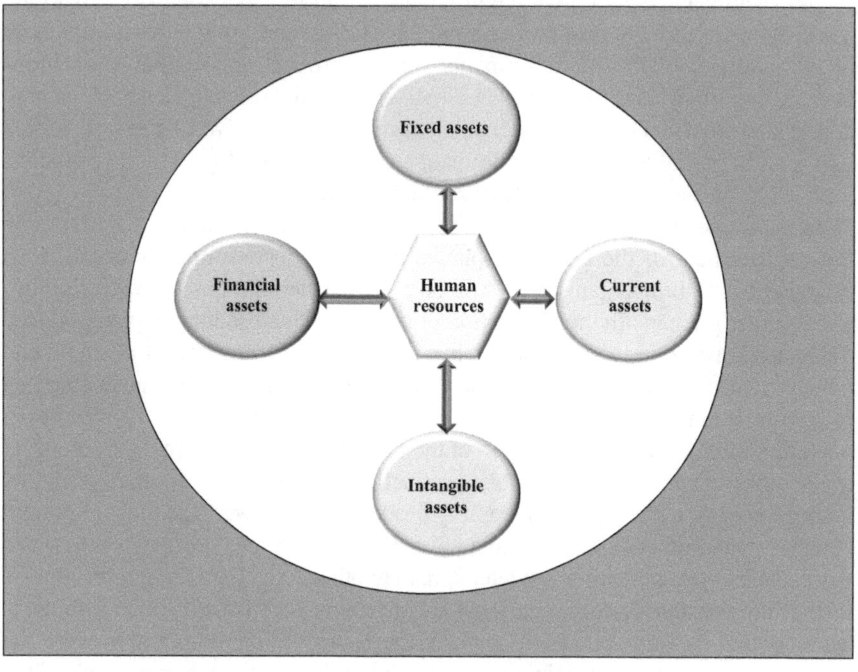

Figure 6.9 Elements and connections of the firm resource system

Source: Author's elaboration

and used by management and employees (human resource) in accordance with the operational routines developed by the firm in its production and distribution activities, give rise to the 'operational configurations' of the firm.

The evolution of the firm through organisational efficiency

The succession of the three firm archetypes (the factory, the corporation and the project-based firm) was undoubtedly characterised by the adoption of ever-new external physical and social technologies but also by their internal elaboration to make them consistent with the structural features of the firm. As the business entity is a purpose-built organisation, such an adaptation process could be achieved making 'efficient' all the processes carried out to pursue the aim it has been created for; thus, the 'efficiency' of the firm has been functional to the firm organisation's 'effectiveness' (see Chapter Four). Such effectiveness can be proved through parameters that can be quantified by indexes measuring the achievement of the organisation target. In the case of the firm the main parameters are its 'survival' and the 'stabilisation' of its market position. Such aims are intrinsic features for all firm archetypes because they are long-run focused organisations, but the indexes by which the effectiveness has been measured have been adapted over time. With the advent of the corporation, for example, firm survival was evaluated by indexes different from short-term profit earnings characterising the factory because of a more dynamic and competitive environment. To survive in a context of enlarging markets meant that the firm had to increase its sales and grow at least at the rate of the market growth; the investments and the product and market innovations became important steps to succeed in it (Malerba 2006; Malerba, Nelson, Orsenigo and Winter 2016). Thus, the indexes measuring the objective of the firm turned into a set of partial targets (flexibility and scalability, rate of growth, investments, innovation, sales, market share, launch of new products,[12] etc.).

In the framework of the evolving firm, the attainment of efficiency started with the improvement of the use of resources in the production operating unit, then it spread to the firm organisation structure and to the relations between the firm and its outer partners. In the production organisation the 'production plan' reduced the material wastefulness for each unit output, while the removal of machine and labour idleness made more efficient the use of capital. This result was obtained by the combination of the mechanisation and division of labour with some changes in operating routines; the configuration of the firm production arrangement according to the more suitable activation of the production processes, besides the 'workflow management systems' and the 'assembly production line', were the most important changes in the procedures implemented by the firm. Such 'process innovations' that reduced the output unit cost later spread to other firm operational units, thanks to the introduction of 'organisational management techniques'. Such efficiency leanings that marked the transition from the factory to the corporation were the consequences of the increasing company dimension and complexity and of the empowerment of department/division directors. In fact, as in the new organisational chart the executives were charged with the achievement of the function aims set by the management; they were authorised with the needed managerial power to organise and carry out the activities. Thus, they had to introduce methods to efficiently manage the department ('organisational innovations') that in this context was considered as a 'cost unit' in the firm financial report.

The search for the efficiency through the 'output unit cost reduction' also hit the contractual relations drawn up with outer stakeholders, bringing the firm to ensure the quick, safe and less expensive provision of materials and component parts or the distribution of output. The strategy implemented to achieve the expected result was to pursue the 'vertical integration' of providers and/or distributors – that is, the grouping of the partners acting independently in backward and/or downward stages of the supply chain, under the ownership of the manufacturing company. Although the 'integrators' succeeded in making efficient also their relations with suppliers and sellers and in expanding in activities different from their core production, their strategy led to the tying up of financial capitals and to the technological rigidity of the group company; thus, such a managerial method fell in disuse in late 1980s.[13] More so, starting from 1990s the managerial strategies to obtain company efficiency in a framework of financial recovery relayed on group disintegration (Kaiser and Obermaier 2020) and on market transactions or 'outsourcing'. On one side the sale of backward and/or downward companies, as well as of some inner productive phases, restored the consolidated financial statements, because the selling price of such assets turned out higher than their value as a group/company component. On the other side resorting to the market produced efficiency in all the productive phases of the company because, comparing the cost of a component produced in-house and its market price when obtained by another producer enabled the company to decide whether to make or to buy it (and then to sell the corresponding group company). In this case the evaluation of the output unit cost reduction as efficiency criterion was made by the 'transaction cost minimisation' index.

Such an efficiency strategy was made possible thanks to institutional changes. The International Organisation for Standardisation (ISO) started to provide agreed-upon requirements and methods to obtain high-quality components and outputs so that the firms receiving such certificates for their products and services could be admitted as technically safe participants to the world trade; in this way the provision of components or products and services could be satisfied by many suppliers among whom to choose the best offer price. But another strategy to obtain both a form of vertical disintegration and a reduction of the unit cost of production keeping control of the supply chain is the 'outsourcing' – that is, an agreement by which a company relegates to another company the responsibility and risk of the realisation of some production stages, functions or services previously carried out internally.

Besides the organisational efficiency based on unit output cost reduction, in an industrial and service context where complex kinds of specific output are required, a new firm organisation emerged based on projects. 'Project-based management' consists of the coordination, within a flattened organisational hierarchy, of the knowledge and skills of organisation members to create the capabilities of the team working to obtain a particular result; thus, the efficiency of the organisation isn't 'process oriented' (that is, tending towards the minimum use of resources as in the traditional U- and M-form methods) but 'output oriented' (tending to shape the tasks and procedures in the most befitting way for the achievement of the project result). Although project-based management emerged in some sectors (architecture, engineering and construction, 'engineer to order manufacturing' [the creation of a unique product as required], feature film production, software industry, and professional services), the adoption of such an organisational method not necessarily corresponds to the new firm archetype called 'project-based firm'. In fact, the 'project-based firm' is more than the project-based management; it is a legal business entity established temporarily as the administrative and contract maker (labelled 'hollow' firm by Teece, Rumelt, Dosi and Winter 1994: 20) for the creation of a one-off project by a specific organisational team that presents:

> the flattening of organizational hierarchies, the weakening of its boundaries in favour of networks of collaborations, and the restructuring of competition between firms within and across industries. Both the nature of the firm as a hierarchically controlled system of work organization combining legal personality, centralized authority, investor ownership and transferability of shares, and the arm's length, adversarial nature of interfirm relations in markets are, in this view, becoming transformed into more fluid, overlapping organizational arrangements in which both internal and external boundaries are breaking down and cooperation between firms is growing.
>
> (Whitley 2006: 77)

The operating environment of the firm

The structure of the production system of developed economies has changed during the evolution of capitalism not only in response to the modifications in physical and social technologies but also due to the increased number of relationships among the firms. Such interplay sometimes results in particular 'firms' whose business activity is the ownership and control of capital stocks of operating firms (the holdings) or in the joint management by a group of firms of the same specific output (the consortium) or a particular one (the joint venture). However, the interplay of the firms also gives rise to aggregations that represent structural sub-units of the production system or systems of a higher level with respect to the firm. The first kind of aggregation includes the firms producing the same output and the second one, the firms producing inputs of relevance for strengthening the position of a single firm. In fact, besides the 'sector' that represents the traditional environment within which the firms producing similar goods or services compete to share the sectoral output sales, some firm coalitions have been created over time to improve the efficiency of a integrating firm (corporate group) and control the productive chain; at the base of these strategic coalitions there is the need for reinforcing the competition ability of the leading firm. Holdings, consortium, joint ventures and corporate groups represent collective systemic elements of the productive system that side by side the single production economic units constitute its 'operating environment'; instead, the sectors are subsystem of production.

From the sector to strategic partnerships

The operating environment of firms consists of production economic units making different goods and services but also of partnerships whose objective isn't the production but the acquisition of the ownership and control of a group of subsidiary corporations engaged in operating businesses. This is the case of the 'holding company' whose social object is the ownership and control of the capital stock of other corporations. Such a 'parent company' oversees the management decisions of the subsidiaries and can also own real estate, patents, trademarks, stocks and other assets. Together with subsidiary companies it forms a corporate group functioning as a single economic entity due to only one control; despite of it being constituted for fiscal reasons it is regulated in different ways according to the laws of the countries.

There are other production partnerships operating as a single economic entity in the operating environment. This is the case of a 'consortium' – that is, a coalition of companies established by articles of incorporation – that are working together to achieve a common productive or distributive objective. Each member operates independently of its own business operation that isn't a matter of consortium activity; thus, it is the only one responsible for it, but it pools resources for consortium activities and can't intervene in the business operations of other participants. A famous for-profit consortium is Airbus, whose participants (British Aerospace, Aérospatiale, Construcciones Aeronáuticas SA and DASA) are both subcontractors to and shareholders of the consortium. Another example of such a partnership is Hulu, whose participants are Comcast, Time Warner, the Walt Disney Company and 21st Century Fox. An example of a consortium whose object is to distribute and publicise a product is the Italian 'Consorzio del Parmigiano Reggiano', which provides marketing and promotion for the cheese produced by the participants. Differently from the consortium a 'joint venture' is a business arrangement to accomplish a specific task independent from the other businesses of the participants, who share the ownership and governance of the venture as well as the risks, the profits and the losses that it produces. Such partnership can be carried out by any legal deed mainly for technological advances or specific projects.

Besides the particular production entities just presented the production system is composed of firms of different forms engaged over time in an increasing interplay with other firms producing both similar goods and services and different ones; it is a matter of competitors in the first case and of partnership in the second one. The competition among firms producing goods or services that are substitutes is a stylised fact representing a feature of capitalism, likewise the fact that the firms also try to reduce or remove it through advertising and innovation of the output; such rivalry – that is, the mechanism to maintain the achieved position on the 'market' or improve it – sometime turns into a cooperation in the case of cartels. The interplay with firms that are partners is generally cooperative, but it can turn into antagonistic policies when the interests of the prevailing firm require control of the relations and the evolution of the partners; this is the case of integration in a group or the control of the production chain.

The environment where the firm competition comes true is the 'sector' – that is, the aggregation of firms producing similar goods and services that operate interdependently to carve up the sales. Some economists have studied the concept, and according to their results the requirements to gather the firms in a sector are the similarity of the production processes so that their output could be replaceable by that of other producers (substitutability from the offer side) and the interdependence of the firms entailing that the actions implemented by one cause the reaction of the others. The classification of the firm in a sector occurs through the collection of data on the prevailing added value (more than 50 per cent) obtained in its establishments (units of activity) relative to a specific output. The institutions providing economic statistics created various systems for the statistical classifications of economic activities: United Nations' International Standard Industrial Classification of all Economic Activities – ISIC, Statistical Classification of Economic Activities by the European Community – NACE from the French acronym, North American Industry Classification System – NAICS). The decision tree used for the allocation of a unit of activity within ISIC classification includes five levels structured from the top to the bottom, organised in 21 sections, 99 divisions, 990 groups, 9,900 classes (UN 2008). Even though the classification systems provide datasets with methodological consistency and the possibility of comparison among them, each specific sector measures the number of the units of activities (establishments), not of firms. In addition, sometimes it can be a set of different types of production processes. For example, the financial sector is easily circumscribable because it is homogeneously included in financial and insurance activities (Section K, Divisions 64, 65, 66).[14] Instead the ICT sector includes activities of different sections: manufacturing industries (Section C, Division 26), trade industries (Section G, Division 46), and services industries (Section J, Divisions 58, 61, 62, 63 and Section S, Division 95).[15]

The evolving firm in search of power through the production chain control

The strategies implemented by the firms to improve their marker position through the organisation efficiency following from the reduction of the unit output cost produced relevant structural consequences. The first was the transformation of some fixed costs, which are invariant regardless the amount of output produced, into variable costs that are proportional to it. Such a process consists in the substitution of the expenditures held up for buying long-lasting machineries or recruiting open-ended contract workers to be used and paid for more production processes, with disbursements in line with the actual production. The purchase of component parts in place of in-house semifinished products creation, of labour service from providers bought when needed (this is the case of contract workers) or from autonomous functional service providers' piece work paid produces the reduction of the output unit cost because of the avoidance of machine and worker idleness that increases their service unit costs; also, the removal of other costs like the machines upkeep and fixing of as well as the social security and annual leave contributions for workers, contribute to such a reduction. The second consequence of the unit output cost reduction was that industrial companies gradually concentrated on the setting-up phases of the transformation process because of the ejection of the phases producing component parts or firm services; a lot of new business service companies entered the service sector of the economy, turning it into the main contributor to the GDP.

The search for a market position through organisation efficiency was successful, but it showed a big weak point in the new context of globalisation – that is, in an environment characterised by a new social technology favouring global trade through both the trade rules issued by the World Trade Organisation (WTO) and the supervision of agreements signed by the member states joining it. Despite the unit output cost reduction enabled to maintain high gross operating revenues in the short run, the vertical disintegration, offshoring and outsourcing following from them risked to be insufficient for the long-run firm survival; in fact, the 'system integrator outsourcing the production of elements to supplier firms not only transfers production, but to a large extent loose competence and control to bring about innovations in these elements' (Frenken 2006: 288) and right inside the integrator production too. The retention of the market position in a long-run dynamic environment showing a new technological phase, new institutional framework and new demanding customers solicits improved, differentiated or new products by the firm, but the companies disintegrating their production chain cannot produce them. Thus, a technological contrivance and a new recombination of production has been introduced to maintain the production chain control in a more complex, networked and globalised production system.

To succeed in the aim, a technological device named 'module' has been introduced in many new and old industrial productions. Each product is categorised by four elements: the technical components necessary to give it a specificity, the technical interface representing the connections among the components, a set of elementary functions (power function, motion function, spin dryer function and so on) implemented at different intensities that characterise its performance during the use and the allocation of each function to physical components. The last three items represent the 'product architecture' – that is, 'the scheme by which the function of a product is allocated to physical components. . . . In a modular architecture, there is a one-to-one mapping between physical components and functional elements, and the interfaces between components are de-coupled' (Brusoni and Prencipe 2001: 182). Thus, a 'module' is a separate component that can perform a function in a variety of systems (portability) and operate with the other components of a new system (interoperability) thanks to standardised technical interfaces. Sometimes a module itself is a component acting as a standardised technical interface between other components. Thus, given this product architecture a firm can 'outsource one subsystem while controlling innovative activity in the second subsystem. . . . Products (like personal computers and stereo sets) are complex whole in the sense that the subsystems are physically interconnected through interfaces. Though different elements can often be produced independently, the product functions as a single system through the use of technical interface standards that interconnect the different modules. . . . The use of standards in complex production systems thus allows a firm to render its production system modular in the sense that a mutation in one element can be implemented without negatively affecting the functioning of other elements in the system' (Frenken 2006: 297–8).

Alongside the modularisation of the production chain to maintain the market power through the outsourcing and the innovation ability, other configurations of firms have emerged.

Concluding remarks: Production as the engine of the capitalist economy

The analysis of the structure and evolution of the production process has highlighted its role as the engine of capitalist economies and its nature as an economic phenomenon based on technological and social components. The centrality in the economy is due to the convergence in the production processes of all the economic activities (execution of human effort/skill, transformation of materials and exchange of semi-finished products) to create goods and services as inputs for new production processes or as consumption items to satisfy needs as well as the purchasing power to consume; thus, the production is the base to implement all other activities in an economy. The technical and social nature of production displays along its evolutionary path the interplay between technological progress and the transformation of social habits and rules aimed at causing more welfare for the community; thus, the upgrading of the economy comes true when there is technological progress only if there is also a coevolution of social institutions.

Inside the capitalist economic system, production appears as a hyper-structure, centred on a new and dedicated form of organisation charged with the management of its processes (the firm) in autonomy with regard to the other organisational subjects of society (the family and the state). The out-and-out transformation processes carried out by the firms have been arranged and managed according to the efficiency criterion of the removal of machinery and worker idleness and of zero value added operations. This criterion, which reduces the output unit costs, has been gradually introduced in all the other departments of the firm and in its external relations, but such efficiency has not always resulted in effectiveness – that is, in the achievement of the aims of the firm (this is the case of vertical integration).

As to the role of labour in the evolution of the firm, its direct involvement has been reduced in production because of mechanisation but has increased in the provision of services and in projecting, as the introduction of new goods and new machinery has become more and more important as instruments of competition among the firms. In addition, the shifting from industry to service increases the needs of skilled workers.

Notes

1 'Despite the conceptual difference between "production" and "manufacturing," in English usage, the term "manufacturing system" addresses a complete enterprise or a group of enterprises, an individual production department (e.g., foundry, turnery), or even a single work station' (CIRP Dictionary of Production Engineering 2015). In this work 'manufacturing system' is interpreted as materials, 'equipment, people, information,

control and support functions for the economic and competitive development and production' of outputs to satisfy market and societal needs (*Journal of Manufacturing Systems*). 'This gave rise to various types of manufacturing systems ['manufacturing system configurations'] from job shops to mass production, flexible manufacturing, and potentially reconfigurable manufacturing systems' (ElMaraghy, Kuzgunkaya and Urbanic 2005: 445).

2 In fact, computer integrated manufacturing is a set of numerical control machine tools connected to each other and controlled by computers that can design a product and fulfil its production (providing all the resources needed just in time) by monitoring and controlling the oversights in real time, thanks to the database of the in-house management information system. The advantages of this productive system are both the maximum flexibility in respect to the task that must be performed and the precision/speed in executing it, all elements reducing the time of use for both the machine and the worker and thus minimising the cost of the inputs.

3 According to the definition presented in Chapter One, technology is a set of theoretical and operational knowledge, physical devices and routines coming into the possession of a society to solve its socio-economic problems.

4 A share is a title certificate representing a fixed part of the corporate stock that gives to the holder the right to take part in general meetings appointing managers, approving the financial reports and making decisions on the firm's failure and to receive the unitary issued profit. The share is traded in the stock market and, its value depends on the value attributed to the firm in relation to its performance.

5 This is true also for services. In fact, all the wards of an hospital, the terminals of an airport, the classrooms of a school, the counters of a bank and so on are the plants of many companies arranged in the best way to provide services.

6 It is necessary to distinguish biological production processes from production processes transforming biological outputs. In fact, the first ones are those characterised by the cultivation or breeding of living organisms using biological plants, while the second are the transformation of products generated by living organisms (like dairy products, jam, sugar and flower production).

7 Biological plants refer to the equipment necessary to carry out biological productions (fields, grazing lands, woodlots, woodlands and fish pools), while biological assets are living organisms like plants and animals that grow, regenerate and produce goods that can be traded as such or transformed into other products.

8 For some examples regarding agricultural production see Romagnoli (1996b); for the industry see Landesmann and Scazzieri (1996).

9 The constancy of the material coefficients of production is the consequence of the technical definition of the production technique, that thus mathematically presents limitation, linearity and discrete variation when a change in the coefficients or in the procedure determines a change in the technique of production. Given that also the coefficients of production for capital asset services are constant because they are measured in terms of time used for executing a task in a specific production organisation.

10 It must be pointed out that, given the definition of technique of production, its components are correlated among each other in a way that the introduction of a new procedure or of a new and more specialised machine determines the need for a different kind of labour, a reorganisation of the operations and, maybe, a new provisioning arrangement for the inputs. Thus, the production technique change could derive from innovations introduced in the process of production or in the variety of products.

11 The bond is a credit instrument having a nominal value and a definite yearly interest rate that gives right to the bond loan return at maturity.

12 All these objectives involve earning profit margins in the long run.

13 On the contrary in the current decade vertical integration processes emerged in ICT products and internet service provision; the online retailer Amazon, besides investments

in warehouses and parts of its distribution channel, has become a publisher of books with Kindle Direct Publishing and television and film producer and distributor with Amazon Studios; the Apple company, which downward sells hardware, software and services and has its own retail space, backwards integrated AuthenTec, which makes the touch ID fingerprint sensor for its iPhones, and Dialog Semiconductor, which produces power management circuits.

14 'Section K Financial and insurance activities This section includes financial service activities, including insurance, reinsurance and pension funding activities and activities to support financial services' (UN 2008: 216).

15 'The production (goods and services) of a candidate industry must primarily be intended to fulfil or enable the function of information processing and communication by electronic means, including transmission and display' (UN 2008: 278).

References

Brusoni, S. and Prencipe, A. (2001) 'Unpacking the Black Box of Modularity: Technologies, Products and Organizations', *Industrial and Corporate Change*, 10 (1): 179–206.

Dietrich, M. and Krafft, J. (2012) *Handbook on the Economics and Theory of the Firm*, Cheltenham: Edward Elgar Publishing Limited.

ElMaraghy, H. A., Kuzgunkaya, O. and Urbanic, R. J. (2005) 'Manufacturing Systems Configuration Complexity', *CIRP Annals*, 54 (1): 445–50. https://doi.org/10.1016/S0007-8506(07)60141-3

Frenken, K. (2006) 'A Fitness Landscape Approach to Technological Complexity, Modularity, and Vertical Disintegration', *Structural Change and Economic Dynamics*, 17: 288–306.

Georgescu-Roegen, N. (1976) *Energy and Economic Myths*, New York: Pergamon Press.

International Institution for Production Research, C.I.R.P. Office (2015) *Wörterbuch der Fertigungstechnik. Dictionary of Production Engineering. Dictionnaire des Techniques de Production Mécanique Vol. I/1*. Berlin Heidelberg: Springer-Verlag. https://doi.org/10.1007/978-3-662-43960-9

Jovanovic, J. R., Milanovic, D. D. and Djukic, R. D. (2014) 'Manufacturing Cycle Time Analysis and Scheduling to Optimize its Duration', *Journal of Mechanical Engineering*, 60 (7–8): 512–24.

Kaiser, F. and Obermaier, R. (2020) 'Vertical (Dis-)integration and Performance: A Management Paradigm Revisited', *Schmalenbach Business Review*, 72: 1–37. https://doi.org/10.1007/s41464-020-00083-1

Kapás, J. (2008) 'Industrial Revolutions and the Evolution of the Firm's Organization: An Historical Perspective', *Journal of Innovation Economics & Management*, 2 (2): 15–33.

Kusiak, A. (2018) 'Editorial: Intelligent Manufacturing: Bridging Two Centuries', *Journal of Intelligent Manufacturing*. https://doi.org/10.1007/s10845-018-1455-2

Landesmann, M. and Scazzieri, R. (1996) 'Forms of Production Organization: The Case of Manufacturing Processes', in M. A. Landesmann and R. Scazzieri (eds.) *Production and Economic Dynamics*, Cambridge: Cambridge University Press: 252–303.

Langlois, R. N. (2003) 'The Vanishing Hand: The Changing Dynamics of Industrial Capitalism', *Industrial and Corporate Change*, 12 (2): 351–86.

Langlois, R. N. (2007) *The Dynamics of Industrial Capitalism. Schumpeter, Chandler, and the New Economy*, London: Routledge.

Lazerson, M. (1995) 'A New Phoenix? Modern Putting-out in the Modena Knitwear Industry', *Science Quarterly*, 40: 34–59.

Malerba, F. (2006) 'Innovation and the Evolution of Industries', *Journal of Evolutionary Economics*, 16: 3–23.
Malerba, F., Nelson, R. R., Orsenigo, L. and Winter, S. G. (2016) *Innovation and the Evolution of Industries. History-Friendly Models*, Cambridge: Cambridge University Press.
Nelson, R. (2003) 'Physical and Social Technologies, and Their Evolution', *Laboratory of Economics and Management, Working Paper Series No. 9*. https://www.lem.sssup.it/WPLem/files/2003-09.pdf
Nelson, R. and Sampat, B. (2001) 'Making Sense of Institutions as a Factor Shaping Economic Performance', *Journal of Economic Behavior & Organization*, 44 (1): 31–54.
O'Driscoll Jr., G. P. and Rizzo, M. J. (1985) *The Economics of Time and Ignorance*, Oxford: Basil Blackwell.
OECD and Eurostat (2005) *Oslo Manual. Guidelines for Collecting and Interpreting Innovation Data*, Paris: OECD Publishing.
Potts, J. (2000) *The New Evolutionary Microeconomics*, Cheltenham: Edward Elgar.
Romagnoli, A. (ed.) (1996a) *Teoria dei processi produttivi. Uno studio dell'unità tecnica di produzione (The Production Process Theory. A Study of the Production Unit)*, Torino: Giappichelli.
Romagnoli, A. (1996b) 'Agricultural Forms of Production Organisation', in M. A. Landesmann and R. Scazzieri (eds.) *Production and Economic Dynamics*, Cambridge: Cambridge University Press: 229–51.
Teece, D., Rumelt, R., Dosi, G. and Winter, S. (1994) 'Understanding Corporate Coherence: Theory and Evidence', *Journal of Economic Behavior and Organization*, 23: 1–30.
United Nations Department of Economic and Social Affairs Statistics Division (2008) *International Standard Industrial Classification of All Economic Activities Revision 4*, New York.
Von Tunzelmann, N. (2003) 'Historical Coevolution of Governance and Technology in the Industrial Revolutions', *Structural Change and Economic Dynamics*, 14: 365–84.
Whitley, R. (2006) 'Project-Based Firms: New Organizational Form or Variations on a Theme?', *Industrial and Corporate Change*, 15: 77–99. http://doi.org/10.1093/icc/dtj003

Glossary

American system of manufacturing is a factory system production organisation introducing on the one hand machine tools for shaping wood, metals, etc. – like the lathe and the milling machine – and on the other hand the production of semi-finished interchangeable parts that are components of several products.

Assembly production line is a factory system production organisation characterised by machines, tools and workers, where the semi-finished parts of the product are assembled moving onwards thanks to conveyors, forklifts and cranes.

Coefficients of production are the amount of inputs necessary to obtain one unit of output. They are fixed and can be measured in real or in monetary value; in this case they depend both on market prices and on assets idleness.

Computer integrated manufacturing is a production process management entirely controlled by computers.

Consortium is a coalition of companies established by articles of incorporation to achieve a common productive or distributive objective.

Corporate capitalism is a manufacturing system configuration where large capital-intensive firms are characterised by labour-assisted machinery due to the adoption of assembly production lines, high fixed costs due to plant investments and lowering unit costs due to high throughput, produce according to new management methods and legal institutions. The managers are the centre of this configuration.

Firm is the economic unit of production that organises and manages the process of creation and distribution of goods and services.

Holding company is a corporation whose social object is the ownership and control of the capital stock of other companies.

Human resource management is a personnel management model that considers labour as a resource of productive organisation that must be motivated towards this role through specific policies.

Joint venture is a business arrangement to accomplish a specific task independent from the other businesses of the participants.

Just in time is a method of resources provision production designed to remove storage by having the resources available just when they must be processed.

Layout is the arrangement of machines in a working environment compliant with the technological cycle, the production arrangement and the production technique.

Labour productivity is the value of the output produced by a unit of labour in a specific productive context (economy, firm, etc.). It is measured by the ratio between the total output value (gross domestic product or gross value added) and the amount of labour (total number of hours worked by the persons employed or total employment). Although generally attributed only to such resource, it reflects the quality and the quantity of the tools and also organisational efficiency because the coefficients of production are fixed.

Manufacturing process is the set of technical steps activated by firms to transform raw materials, intermediate inputs and other resources into final manufacturing products. The expression is generally used for any industrial process.

Manufacturing system is 'the arrangement and operation of machines, tools, material, people and information to produce a value-added physical, informational or service product whose success and cost is characterised by measurable parameters' (mailto:info@sysdesign.org).

Marketing innovation 'is the implementation of a new marketing method involving significant changes in product design or packaging, product placement, product promotion or pricing' (OECD 2005: 49).

Network capitalism is a manufacturing system configuration presenting world district firms characterised by a high-throughput system and work closely and more co-ordinated than before, information-assisted automation and networking propensity. Production develops in an external integrated 'project-based firm', and the industrial system is seemingly co-ordinated through the market exchange but actually by multinationals.

Organisation of the industry is the group of institutions that govern market mechanisms and structures, public policies, legal and regulatory structures (Nelson 2003).

Organisational chart is a representation of the firm organisation where people are positioned in different departments according to the job they perform. It also puts in evidence the hierarchical position of each firm official, department or function.

Organisational and management methods are procedures showing through analytical techniques, indicators and standards, how firm's resources and processes can be efficiently managed in different fields of operation like finance, human resources, marketing, etc.

Organisational innovation 'is the implementation of a new organisational method in the firm's business practices, workplace organisation or external relations' (OECD 2005: 51).

Outsourcing is an agreement by which a company hires another company for the responsibility and risk of the realisation of some production stages previously carried out internally.

Personal capitalism is a manufacturing system configuration characterising the first phase of capitalism, where small-scale factories scattered on the territory produce their distinct products by machine-assisted labour and supply them in local markets thanks to 'all-purpose generalist merchants' who were the hub of this industrial configuration.

Physical technologies represent the technical configurations of manufacturing systems and thus the set of machineries and their technical coordination and operation according to routines.

Process innovation 'is the implementation of a new or significantly improved production or delivery method. This includes significant changes in techniques, equipment and/or software' (OECD 2005: 49).

Product innovation 'is the introduction of a good or service that is new or significantly improved with respect to its characteristics or intended uses. This includes significant improvements in technical specifications, components and materials, incorporated software, user friendliness or other functional characteristics' (OECD 2005: 46).

Production arrangement is the activation of production processes over working time, which can be 'in succession', 'in parallel' and 'on assembly line'.

Production planning is the organisation of the layout and the unit output processes on the base of the technological cycle, of the plant and production objectives, and on the idleness and downtime reduction criteria.

Production operating unit is a sub-system of the firm whose function is the execution of the technical transformation of inputs into outputs according to the single-product technological charts and to the production arrangement.

Professional division of labour is the labour organisation in an economy characterised by production processes where each worker, performing a craft or a profession, can go through all the operational procedures to produce complete goods or services.

Putting-out system was a production organisation where an entrepreneur or a merchant owning raw material hired equipment to subcontractors, who produced at home the product and were piece rate paid.

Sector is a partition of the production system of an economy where firms producing the same goods or services operate interdependently and compete to carve up sales.

Social technologies represent the configurations of business organisations, management practices, market mechanisms and structures, public policies, legal and regulatory structures, etc. consistent with the manufacturing systems; it is the institutional framework enabling the conversion of the technological output into consumer goods and services.

Technical division of labour is the labour organisation in an economy characterised by the production processes of goods or services that are split into many simple works that can be accomplished by workers provided with specific basic competences.

Technique of production is a feasibility study to produce a unit of output, based on scientific and operational knowledge including a set of qualitative and quantitative prescriptions (a sequence of interconnected tasks, a set of operating methods and of coefficients for the material inputs) judged the most technically fitting to obtain a unit of output. It becomes a production plan when the capital asset coefficients are determined.

Technological cycle represents the structure of technological transformation depending on the sequence of operations and the methods for fulfilling them on the one hand and on the origin of the semi-finished product at all the production stages on the other hand. Depending on its features the production is organised in 'in-line' or 'assembled product' processes.

Technological chart is the sequence and the arrangement of the phases characterising the technological cycle of a single output.

World class manufacturing is a set of managerial methods of production optimisation.

Workflow management systems is the coordination of productive tasks in a sequence to produce the output better and as quickly as possible.

7 Consumption

Needs satisfaction driven by production and social institutions

Consumption is the set of economic activities carried out within an economic system to satisfy the needs and wants of people's material and social life. The processes bringing it to completion, which entail the appraisal of the spending capacity, the purchase of more suitable goods or services and their fruition, are just as many moments of the execution of such function of the economy. From the point of view of the economy consumption is the counterpart of production because it complements the capitalist process through the conversion of the output into economic value; thus, it is a constituent of the economic system, whose role is essential for the existence of capitalist economies. The final markets are the interface between production and consumption that make the system work, thanks to the financial flows of the income that people get from their jobs and the payments they make for final goods and services. In such a framework consumption involves not only the spheres of wishes, values, and economic behaviours of an individual but also the goods and services technical features, the market structures, and the social values. Moreover,

> 'Consumption is a mirror of the human condition. Our understanding of how people consume has always reflected our views about how they ought to live. There are few subjects that have undergone a similarly profound shift in perspective in the last half-century. Routinely decried for most of the twentieth century as leading to alienation, waste, and selfish materialism, consumption in the 1970s and 1980s appeared in a new, positive light. It was hailed as a source of creativity and meaning central to social relations and identity formation. What had been the object of condescension – a minor, private, or mindless pursuit that at best followed, at worst distracted from work and community – now emerged as the very stuff of history. Consumption stepped out of the shadow of production. *Homo consumens* took the place of *homo faber*'.
>
> (Trentmann 2012: 1)

Consumption has been for a long time overlooked by economists because at the beginning of the capitalist evolution it was unremarkable with respect to the riotous development of production technologies, and later it has been subsumed under

DOI: 10.4324/9781315679730-10

the consumer market demand. When its relevance for the whole economy has been acknowledged, only the individual aspects of binomial choices (made between two goods or services, consumption and saving, or present and future consumption) have been considered. The study of the relation between people's needs/desires and goods and services did not go further the analysis of the good characteristics, while as to the behavioural choice only the utility and lexicographic approaches have been explored; all these theoretical explanations are confining the analysis of the phenomenon to the consumer sphere of influence (Nelson and Consoli 2010).

Yet, in a historical perspective consumption is much more. It is the result of the quantitative and qualitative evolution of goods and services production, of changes in social values and lifestyles that emerged in the communities or provoked by the evolution and the structure of international trade. It is the chased effect of governmental policies aimed at promoting commerce by tax cuts or by easier and more deferred payment methods. It is the outcome of strategic targets and marketing policies of companies working hard to customise the buyers. In search of the stylised facts of capitalist consumption systems, the chapter will go deep into all these aspects of the phenomenon.

Consumption from necessity to social exhibition

It is a current opinion that consumption emerged on the way of the capitalist evolution and that fashion is connected to its development, but this is not true. Certainly, in the pre-industrial societies personal consumption through the market was limited because the self-consumption at the subsistence level was carried out by most parts of the population; despite that the purchase of luxury goods, practised by wealthy people since the year dot, had appeared occasionally over time and had been often supported by the fashions. Furthermore, it is a hackneyed phrase to say that only in the capitalist society are people's tastes, food diets and lifestyles quickly changing, but this does not match up with the historical evidence that highlights specific moments of change of such habits in pre-industrial societies. The conventional wisdom just reported on one side shows that the idea of consumption is related to a present and individualistic Western point of view; on the other side it confers the attribute of uniformity to the phenomenon, a trait contradicted using terms like 'self-consumption', 'mass and personal consumption', and 'consumerism'. Thus, a deep inquiry from a historical perspective is necessary to define both the phenomenon and its multifaceted aspects, as well as the other elements that joined it during the capitalist evolution.

Determinants of the consumption organisation in pre-industrial societies

Consumption is the way by which an economic system arranges for the livelihood of people. It shows the goods and services at the people's disposal, the way to their fruition and the needs that are satisfied – that is, the living standard of societies. Nevertheless, it indirectly reveals the structure of both the production and commercial interchange of an economic system too. Thus, on one side, the patterns of consumption display the economic conditions of communities, but on the other side, they disclose the cultural and social organisation that characterise them; for all these reasons the consumption structure changed in history.

Since early ancient empires (China, Rome) and communities (Greek cities), the countryside and the urban agglomerations presented differentiated forms of consumption organisation. In rural areas the peasants of the farms, crofters or estates performed the 'self-consumption' – that is, they ate the food they obtained from agriculture, ship farming and livestock rearing activities they directly or indirectly performed; in addition, they used wool, skins and agricultural textile fibres to make their items of clothing or everyday things. As to the consumption in the cities, there were three different forms: the 'subsidised consumption' represented by the distribution of food to soldiers, veterans, or immigrants from the countryside at the expense of the political and/or administrative powers; the 'staple goods consumption' practised by the artisans and shopkeepers who mainly purchased commodities in the market at prices established by authorities; the 'conspicuous consumption', centred on the luxury goods bought at bargained market prices with the merchants by the wealthy families. Thus, at that time various forms of consumption coexisted that differed both in the subject disbursing the goods and services (the same working peasant, the public authority, and the consumer) and in the forms of obtaining them (broadly speaking self-production, gift, or market), as well as in the share of the total consumption they represented. Personal consumption by means of market exchanges (both in the form of fixed prices for staple and bargained ones for luxury goods) was extremely limited even though rising over time, while subsidised consumption fed a large number of citizens; anyway 80 per cent of the people practiced the self-consumption.

Only the prevalence of such a form of need satisfaction, inside the diversified structure of consumption just described, remained unchanged up to the advent of capitalism. In fact, subsidised consumption became negligible over time and changed into the ration book, while personal consumption experienced an increasing variety of goods because of the appearance of new crops and other products. These modifications were the consequence of the changes in the intensity and direction of short and long-range commerce, as well as of two other structural forces; income and the fashion modified from time to time the models of consumption of the communities. As to the local and foreign trade, although very often cut down because of wars, famines and poverty, they had always been practised for providing the communities with the essentials of the food consumption models (like spices, sugar, staple) and with luxury goods that were trendy. In days of old, for example, the Roman empire imported wheat from North Africa, oil from Spain, spices, as well as potteries and scents from India and China, and in Medieval times the European cities stocked staple and luxury goods coming from afar.

Over the centuries the expansion of trade flows between Europe and Asia, increased thanks to the Arab merchants and the Silk Road, produced important changes in the structure of personal consumption. 'By the twelfth century, dyed and block-printed cottons from India were traded in Cairo and East Africa. Venice, Florence, and Genoa acted as gateways between Europe and the Orient, pulling in oriental silks and Turkish carpets in exchange for European metals and furs' (Trentmann 2017: 23). Back then the trade flows were lopsided because the Italian imports from the Oriental markets included local products and precious luxury handcrafted goods, while their exports toward them were constituted by low-quality raw materials (like wool, timber and metals) imported in Italy from other European trading cities; thus, the Italian merchants acted as buyers and sellers between the Oriental and North European producers. Nevertheless, the merchants also imported the techniques of production of pottery, blown glass, and silk so that by the 13th and 14th centuries started to produce those goods at home. The development of production for the domestic and foreign European markets, as well as the following trade escalation, raised the income of artisans and the living standards of the Italian cities; this gave space to the home demand for personal and luxury goods. For the merchants and aristocrats:

> silver and tableware were signs of an emerging culture of domestic sociability and politeness. . . . While possessions and ideals of comfort had begun to fill the home, they remained part of a civic culture that continued to be oriented towards public display and posterity, not private pleasure or the lure of novelty. Its animating spirit was magnificence, its goal perpetuity. The spending on personal possessions was trivial compared to the outlay on monumental city palaces and public banquets. These were the main drivers of Renaissance consumption.
>
> (Trentmann 2017: 30, 32–3).

Therefore, in a context where the increase of family revenues feeds the demand for gourmet food and luxury goods, private consumption has become nothing else but 'civic virtue and pride' – that is, an aimed social model of behaviour in fashion also in other European cities.

At the beginning of the 16th century the Atlantic trade flows were added to those that the European merchant maintained with the Orient. Besides the lengthening of the trading routes, the openness of new markets and the introduction of new goods in the old ones, new traders emerged who substituted the Italians; they were British, Dutch, Spanish, French and Portuguese people who settled their commercial hubs in the ports of Northwestern Europe and from there reached by sea the Oriental markets too. World trade increased 23 times between 1500 and 1800, thanks to the silver mined in the Americas and used by the Europeans to buy goods in Asia and to mint coins up to the mid-18th century.

> Tea, porcelain and even sugar flowed from China to Europe and the Americas as well as Japan. American tobacco, maize and the sweet potato went to China; cotton textiles from Gujarat and the Coromandel coast found new customers in Europe and her Atlantic colonies, in addition to established markets in Japan and East Asia.
>
> (Trentmann 2017: 23).

The use of new crops in the European and Asian diets come out on top; in some cases the products imported from the Americas became in fashion (as coffee, tobacco, and chocolate did); in some others imported crops were cultivated because of their nourishing and high-yielding harvest (potato and maize). As to the luxury goods of such a period, they were not attractive either for their novelty or for their materials, but for their fine quality that displayed the ability of the artisans. For this reason, the linen and the silverware had an intrinsic value that could be kept over time and transferred to the next generations. In a society characterised by limited resources, luxury goods had a conservative character showing both the economic stability of the owner and his prudence; conspicuous consumption shifted its meaning from civic virtue to personal trustworthiness. Given that nature, some luxury goods could not be perishing or too much outlandish; the exhibition of luxury goods could be a socially accepted fashion, but in fashion goods could not be socially acceptable. This was the case of wearing apparel that could be wasteful if too much chichi.

But starting from mid-17th century there was another important transformation both in the kind and in the direction of the Atlantic interchange. British and Dutch vessels, transferring commodities harvested by slaves and servants in the colonial farms to the homeland and Europe, made the outward route loaded with domestic products that were sold in the colonies, where the colonisers started to also control the price of cash crops on the end markets.[1] The emergence of an Atlantic export/import stream diverted the trade from Asia to Americas and enriched the merchants who, in turn, increased the financial resources of native countries; the producers of woollen and linen cloths, hats, cutlery, and the other goods exported to the colonies got also rich, contributing to the domestic demand rise of luxury goods. Despite that, the weight of the conspicuous consumption over the total consumption of the economies changed a little bit because to collect such goods remained a trait of a minority share of the urban population. Neither has its social meaning changed.

Mass consumption: Urbanisation purchasing power and lifestyle

The previous historical overview put in evidence that trade, production, income and social conventional wisdom have been the main drivers of consumption evolution up to the dawn of capitalism. In fact, the qualitative structure of the purchased goods resulted extremely modified by the international trade increase and evolution. Moreover, the expansion of personal consumption of society was closely related to domestic production (not to the buying and selling activities) via the distribution of incomes; it was the development of the handcrafted productions of commercial cities that broadened the number of skilled salaried workers and increased their incomes, enabling them to enlarge their consumption beyond the basic goods, and the economy to potentially push the exports. Finally, the changes in social opinion were the phenomenon that legitimised the consumption of not basic goods (conspicuous consumption).

As to the changes in conventional wisdom about conspicuous consumption, starting from the 18th century a new practice emerged as an additional determinant factor for its potential diffusion. Side by side the functions of intrinsic value conservation and personal trustworthiness demonstration, the luxury goods became instruments to show and preserve a graded social hierarchy and a corresponding consumption morality. In particular, the wearing apparel served the purpose, as the promulgation of 'sumptuary laws' can prove; in fact, in that legal framework, if on one side the outlandish clothing were banned as a general principle, on the other side detailed codes of dress for the different social groups were enforced to impose a social identification. Conspicuous consumption became the exhibition of social inequality, but at the same time it was the manifestation of people's identity according to each status. Thus, if the first two qualities of luxury goods slowed down their pace of diffusion and their novelty, the last one opened to the acceptance of social exhibition.

It was a different attitude towards the goods over the 17th and 18th centuries that changed the social approval for conspicuous consumption. The exploration of new lands produced the import of raw materials and new agricultural crops, but also of new exotic plants and animals. This phenomenon spread the curiosity and the knowing desire about them, and in general about novelties. Some Dutch and British scientists and philosophers adopted a similar approach to the knowledge, overturning the traditional research methodology; the study did no more move forward from general theoretical principles to the analysis of the real word, but from the observation and cataloguing of things to the general laws. 'The empirical, material approach to knowledge made trade a virtuous partner of science and sociability. Goods and goodness advanced hand in hand' (Trentmann 2017: 96). Moreover, the idea that the research and possession of rare things or natural organisms is a natural desire of human beings made one's way through society as a new view of human nature. Thus, purchasing luxury goods and following fashion ceased to be wasteful behaviours and the old moral resulted no more in step with the times; conspicuous consumption became even a vehicle of progress.[2] But this change of attitude spread in European countries only when the urbanisation came out on top. Until then the rational behaviour of people about the spending style was based on these principles: be penny-wise, save, and plan the future.

The diversified structure of consumption of traditional societies (not considering the marginalisation of subsidised consumption) remained unchanged for centuries and evolved toward a new form of consumption organisation characterised by market transactions with the advent of capitalism. It was the emergence of industrialisation, associated with the agricultural restructuring, that triggered the process. As the industrial activities required a concentration of workers in factories greater than the population living in cities, an exodus of peasants from the countryside emerged to offset such a shortage. The inflow of migrants increased the amount of staple goods sold in the urban markets and decreased the quantity of the ones produced and consumed by the peasants in the countryside; thus, the market share of staple consumption little by little prevailed over self-consumption, which after all vanished because of the agricultural reforms. Such a structural change in the consumption organisation, and the other one connected to the luxury goods extension, represented a process characterised by different lengths of time depending on a lot of phenomena: the shrinking of agricultural employment, the degree of urbanisation, the purchasing power of city workers and the change of pattern

Table 7.1 Annual rates of urbanisation increase (in %) in different periods for selected countries

Country	*1850–1880*	*1880–1910*	*1910–1950*	*1950–1973*	*1973–1990*	*1990–2018*
UK	0.55	0.43	0.24	–0.07	0.04	0.18
USA	0.66	0.56	0.56	0.42	0.09	0.24
France	0.27	0.36	0.42	0.74	0.10	0.22
Germany	0.47	0.66	0.48	0.19	0.04	0.14
Italy	0.17	0.40	0.35	0.48	0.07	0.13
Japan	–	–	–	0.90	0.18	0.49
Russia	0.11	0.12	0.74	0.90	0.50	0.03
Brazil	–	–	–	0.98	0.82	0.47
India	–	–	–	0.16	0.28	0.30
China	–	–	–	0.23	0.54	1.13

Source: Author elaboration from: a) Bairoch and Goertz (1986) *Urban Studies*, p. 288; b) *World Bank Open Data 2019*.

of consumption. As to the urbanisation process (see Bairoch and Goertz 1986), inversely proportional to the decrease of the peasantry, the most sudden was that of the United Kingdom: people living in the cities shifted, with decreasing rates, from the 40 per cent in mid-18th to nearly the 70 per cent before WW1 (see Table 7.1). The United States, whose 95 per cent of the population lived in the countryside in 1850, arrived at the same urbanisation level of the UK only in the 1970s, recording annual rates of urbanisation increase between 0.66 per cent and 0.56 per cent in that period. France and Italy, which had nearly four-fifths of their population in the countryside at the beginning of the period, experienced a constant process of urbanisation up to the 1970s, with a high increase in urban population between 1910 and 1973. Germany, instead, passed from a level of urbanisation of 15 per cent in 1850 to nearly 70 per cent in 1950, speeding the pace between 1880 and 1910. The Russian level of urbanisation, which was under 15 per cent in 1910, reached the 65 per cent gradually in 1973, just when China started its process that in 2018 achieved nearly the 60 per cent.

Although the levels of urbanisation and their progress status rates are important to record the share of the earning living people that passed to a model of consumption based on market transactions, the change of 'real wages' (the set of goods and services that the wage can buy) must be introduced to synthetise the quantitative transformation of the personal consumption. Once arrived in the industrial cities and gained a job, the workers faced a shopping list longer than that they were used to before in the countryside, not only because the everyday routines changed but also because new needs related to urban life (like transport) were added to. In addition to the food, clothing, and transport, they had to pay for housing and charcoal for the stove and the heater, as well as running water and electricity when the houses were equipped with them at the beginning of the 1920s. At the turn of the 19th century, when the people of industrialised countries living in cities were about 40 per cent of the population (the United Kingdom excluded), the increase in wages was high (as Table 7.2 shows), but the money received was in some cases barely sufficient to pay all the items mentioned, because of the level of the money wage. In fact, the per cent increments of salaries (conventionally measured by the number of subsistence baskets that can be bought with a daily wage by building labourers) recorded for Italy and Japan, for example, corresponded to a level of salary three times lower than that of Germany, France and the United Kingdom and eight times of the United States (compare the Table 7.2 with the Table 2.6). Thus, despite the rise of average wages was high between 1880 and 1910, the expansion of personal consumption was limited to basic goods, and conspicuous consumption increased only for the wealthy families of capital and industrial European and North American cities.

It was only after WW2 that the consumption volume increased highly and spread all over the society of industrialised countries due to increased salaries. Such economic phasis, characterised by increased production and a higher purchasing power

Table 7.2 Variation in the average number of subsistence baskets that can be bought with a daily wage by building labourers (% points)

Country	*1820s*[a]	*1820–1870*	*1870–1910*	*1910–1950*	*1950–1970*	*1970–2000*
UK	16	31	9	57	72	169
USA	–	–	73[a]	45	68	173
France	17	–6	48	–55	158	21
Germany	10	30	108	–15	213	72[b]
Italy	4	0	125	44	231	94
Japan	4	0	75	0	286	67
India	–	3[a]	33	75	-57	133
China	3	0	0	25	260	22[b]

Source: Author's elaboration from Table 2.6

[a] The value is calculated in the opening decade.

[b] The period considered is 1970–1990.

Table 7.3 USA consumer expenditure shares

Categories	*1901*	*1934–1936*	*1950*	*1972–1973*	*2002–2003*
Food	42.5	33.6	29.7	19.3	13.1
Alcoholic bev. & tobacco	3.0	–	3.5	2.9	1.6
Apparel and services	14.0	10.6	11.5	7.8	4.2
Housing	23.3	32.0	27.2	30.8	32.8
Transportation	–	8.3	13.4	19.3	19.1
Healthcare	5.2	3.9	5.2	6.4	5.9
Personal care	–	2.0	2.2	2.0	1.3
Entertainment	1.6	5.4	4.4	8.6	5.1
Education and reading	1.1	0.5	1.5	1.9	2.1
Miscellaneous	9.3	3.7	1.4	1.0	14.8[a]

Source: Author's elaboration of data from US Department of Labor and US Bureau of Labor Statistics (2006)

Notes: [a]includes also personal insurance and pensions.

of the middle and lower classes of industrialised economies, opened to the so-called 'mass consumption society', a generalised condition of the economy where most part of the population made high average levels of consumption by purchasing a large amount of goods and services. In this framework not only the spending for discretionary goods approached the basic ones, but the individual desires and tastes could also be satisfied by a production more and more client compliant. The display of such preferences, on the one hand increased the variety of goods and services produced and changed the qualitative structure of consumption, but on the other hand it made personal consumption increasingly connected to fashions and to 'lifestyles'. 'A lifestyle can be defined as a more or less integrated set of practices which an individual embraces, not only because such practices fulfil utilitarian needs, but because they give material form to a particular narrative of self-identity' (Giddens 1991: 81). The individual self-adaptation to lifestyles drives the patterns of consumption towards shared models of consumption, created and spread by producers, distributers and promoters that strengthen social belonging, self-esteem and self-actualisation. Such socioeconomic processes contributed not only to the expansion and the spread of personal consumption but also to a structural change of individual patterns of consumption.

The evolution of patterns of consumption in the last century

Behind the historical evolution of consumption there has always been an individual process of choice, purchase and use of goods and services to satisfy the needs emerging from his living conditions and aspirations. Such needs can be of primordial kind when they are basic subsistence requirements (to eat, get dressed and accommodate) or social ones if they are connected to the other conditions and activities of human life. Thus, from a historical perspective, when the shift from a rural society to an urban one made everyday life different and more complex, new needs emerged that pushed the people to adapt the structure of their consumption to them. This phenomenon has been documented through the accounting entries of the goods and services categories appearing in the household budgets, whose study started with the statistical analyses by Ernst Engel (Engel 1857 and 1895). He reported that in 1850 a worker family in Saxony spent between 85 per cent to 95 per cent of his salary on nutrition, garment, shelter and fuel, which is just what happened in the other developing countries of Europe. A half century later the urbanised people, whose wage was higher than that of rural workers, found themselves in the same situation because they were forced to face new essential needs at home and outside; to have running water, heating service and home lighting and to move away from home for going to work became necessities whose charge joined the expenditure for food, clothing and housing. Thus, the 'bound' outlay for 'basic' needs remained nearly at 80 per cent up to the beginning of the 20th century.

This result has been confirmed by the analysis of the 'household consumption patterns', showing the set of weighted categories of goods and services purchased with the salary. Figure 7.1, which presents the evolution of the consumption patterns of a family in the United States during the last century, accounts for Engel's outcome by showing in the left pie chart that in 1901 the share of necessities (the first four items) inside the total expenditure was 82.8 per cent. By 2002–2003 their share reduced to 51.7 per cent of the total expenditure, but as the transportation costs (a big part of which was essential for everyday life) reached 19.1 per cent, the necessities accounted for about 70 per cent of the total. Despite that, it cannot be overlooked the quantitative and qualitative increase of discretionary consumption that rose from 18.2 per cent to more than 30 per cent of total expenditure. The comparison of the two pie charts also enables us to put in evidence the dynamics of the patterns of consumption – that is, the change in the good shares along the development path of the US economy. In this respect it must be highlighted that if the decrease of share of necessities lowered by 37 per cent, the component of food expenditure dropped by about 70 per cent while housing increased by 40 per cent (from 23.3 per cent to 32.8 per cent of the total, aided by the fact that the home ownership shifted from 19 per cent in 1901 to 67 per cent of US families from 2002 to 2003 and utility costs increased; US Department of Labor and US Bureau of Labor Statistics 2006: 66).

Side by side with the evolution of the necessities and discretionary shares of the household consumption patterns, Figure 7.1 accounts for the dynamics of their qualitative changes too:

> In the 1970s 'the average US family allocated 72.4 per cent of food expenditures for food eaten at home and 26.4 per cent for food eaten away from home. . . . By the 21st century, however, the average US family allocated just 58.1 per cent of food spending for food eaten at home and 41.9 per cent for food eaten away from home. . . . Changes in diets also occurred over the 100-year period. In 1901, New York City families allocated 40.4 per cent of their grocery expenditures for meat, poultry, fish, and eggs; 16.3 per cent for dairy products; 14.5 per cent for fruits and vegetables; and 11.0 per cent for cereals and bakery products. . . . By 2002–03, grocery expenditure shares for meat, poultry, fish, and eggs had decreased to 28.3 per cent in New York City. . . . Shares for dairy products had decreased to 10.4 per cent . . .; shares for fruits and vegetables had increased to 19.2 per cent in . . .; and shares for cereals and bakery products had increased to 15.0 per cent. . . . In the clothing category, in 1901 New York City families allocated 6.3 per cent of total spending for children's clothing, 3.8 per cent for men's clothes, and 3.9 per cent for women's apparel . . . By 2002–03, women's clothing had become the single largest component of the clothing budget. . . . The ability to buy more discretionary goods and services also improved the US standard of living. The emergence of the family car was one example. In 1934–36, 44.4 per cent of US households owned an automobile, . . . By the 21st century, there was at least one vehicle in 88 per cent of US households, with the average family owning 2.0.'
>
> (US Dep. of Labour 2006: 66, 68, 69).

The evolution of household consumption patterns following the joint effect of urbanisation and wage improvement can be resumed by the Chinese experience. In

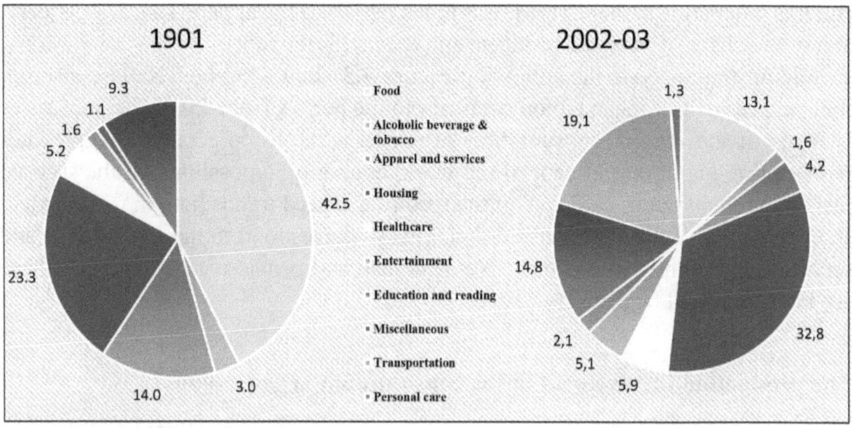

Figure 7.1 USA consumer expenditure shares (% values)

Source: Author elaboration of data from US Department of Labor and US Bureau of Labor Statistics (2006)

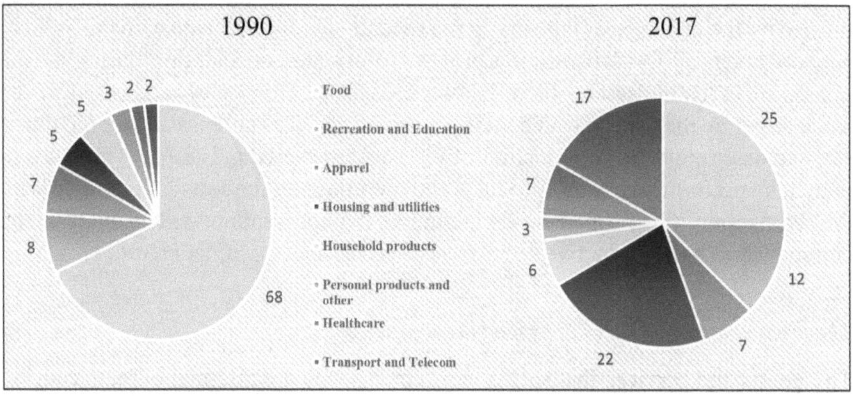

Figure 7.2 Annual expenditure distribution of urban households in China in 1990 and 2018, by type of goods or services

Source: Author's elaboration from https://www.statista.com/statistics/1038069/china-urban-household-spending-share-by-product-type/

Figure 7.2, that presents the annual expenditure distribution of urban households in China in 1990 and 2017 by type of goods or services, the stylised facts about consumption are evident; the prevalence of the necessities share (82 per cent) over the discretionary consumption one (18 per cent) at the beginning of the period, when the urbanised people were the 26.4 per cent of the population; the 60 per cent decrease of the food consumption share (from 68 to 25 per cent) in the period, the fourfold increase of the housing and utilities share (from 5 to 22 per cent), and the eightfold rise of the transport and communication expenditures (from 2 to 17 per cent).

But it is interesting also the steadiness in the period of the apparel share (7 per cent) and of the share of personal products and others (3 per cent).

Joining the analysis the following Figure 7.3 shows the household consumption patterns of European Union countries in the period 1996–2018, a comparative analysis of the current consumption structure in the three economic aggregates representing about 60 per cent of the world economy is possible. All the stylised facts previously put in evidence of the resulting shared trends both in the long and short run, even if the aggregates do not always correspond to the same goods and service baskets and some entries like insurance and pension are absent. But these are items that will be discussed later.

The production involvement in the consumption organisation

The previous historical review put in evidence the role played both in the traditional economies and in the capitalism by the production system in the consumption organisation and in its evolution. In fact, it has been shown how the prevalence of forms of communal agriculture in the countryside and of trading and artisan activities in cities limited the expansion of personal consumption to a small part of society in the first case and how the expansion of market transactions has been pushed by the presence of industry in the second one. Side by side with the indirect support given by the urbanisation process to private consumption during all the phases of industrialisation, there is also a constant direct push addressed to the same target by the firms through their goods and services policies and by the financial sector through the introduction of the consumer credit. The firm strategies to match the performance of the products and the fitness of the services provided with the satisfaction of consumer needs facilitated the consumption extension, like the emergence of new productive sectors: advertising and consumer credit.

The product quality strategy to expand the firm sales

The goods and services that satisfy consumer needs are the final outputs causing relief and wellness to the people. Some final goods/services (like, for example, the car and legal advice) don't display as such, because they can be required both for personal and corporate needs; thus, it is their use that defines if they are consumer products/services or inputs of production. Anyway, the firms design their output in a way that the destination emerges as obvious (due to the dimension of a good, for example, like a home washing machine and a launderette) because in general output is produced to target the needs of a specific buyer. On the other hand, when consumers buy something to satisfy a need they expect that the good or service acquired fit the purpose – i.e. that its performance or fitness matches as much as possible their necessity.

The performance of a good is the result of the set of tasks it can execute, thanks to the technical functions it is endowed; for example, the performance of a robot vacuum cleaner includes the capacities of sweeping, washing and drying the floor by moving around it because the technical components of this appliance enable

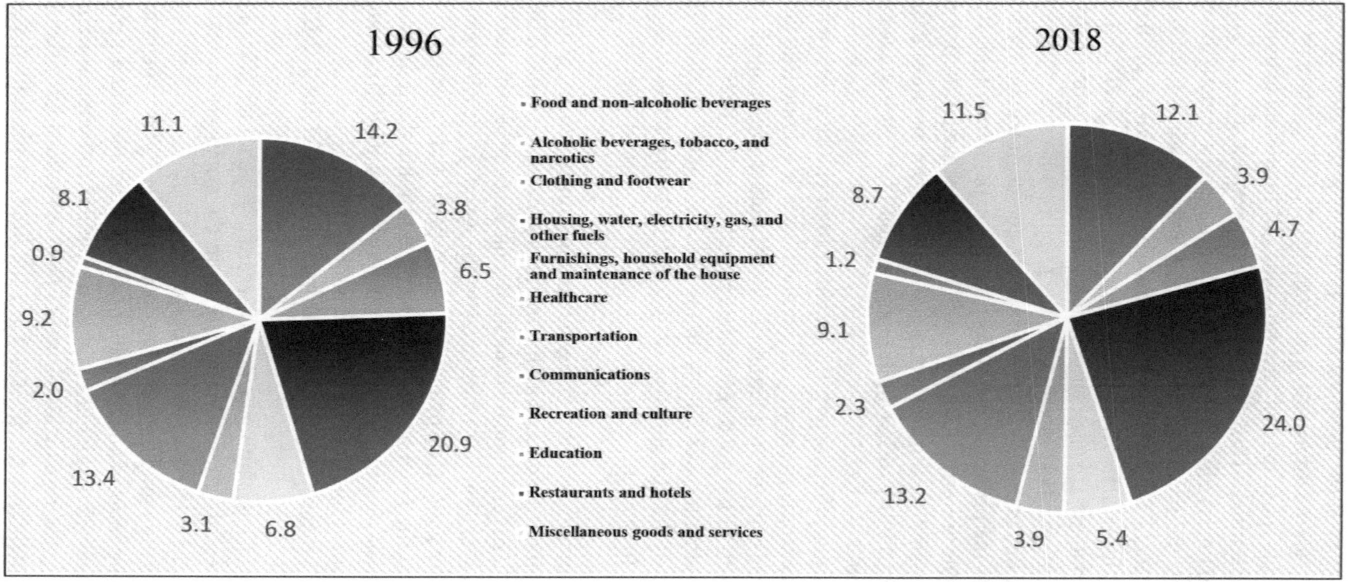

Figure 7.3 Household consumption patterns of European Union countries (% values)

Source: Author elaboration of data from *Eurostat online data*

the implementation of such functions. The fitness of a dry cleaner service consists of these tasks: garment inspection, selection and tagging, stain pre-treatment, machine dry cleaning, post spotting and finishing, all functional activities fulfilled by workers and machines. Thus, all the customers expect that the good performance and service fitness align with the technical functions underlying them, feature guaranteed by the producer, and that good and service innovations contain improved or additional functions. The number and the intensity of the technical features (the functions) active in a device, or the functions preferred inside the ranking of those contained in each unit of the good/service category, is for the consumer those enabling the best matching of the good performance with the need to be satisfied. Thus, this is the criterion used for the choice of a good (or service), in concomitance with the price and the budget for this expenditure item. In choosing a vacuum cleaner the preferred function could be the intake capacity or the wireless power source accessibility, and when booking a hotel room, the most desired facility could be the possibility of having free airport shuttle or an in-house restaurant or a swimming pool.

In the mass consumption society, the mechanism of choice implemented by the consumer for every single good/service purchased was less knowledgeable of that just presented because of the standardisation of the output, which meant a reduced technical complexity of the goods and simplicity of services. Thus, the customisation put pressure, among other things, on the psychological nature characterising the ownership/use of the consumption item – that is, on the chances of subjective and exclusive use. In fact:

> Psychological ownership has value-enhancing consequences, which stem from an association of a good with the self and/or categorisation of the good as MINE. Due to psychological ownership, traits associated with the self and positive self-association are transferred to the good, increasing emotional attachment to the good and enhancing its perception and value. . . . Explicit categorisation of the good as MINE appears to reframe the reference point from which it is viewed, changing the evaluation of the good from something that could be gained to something that could be lost.
>
> (Morewedge, Monga, Palmatier, Shu and Small 2021: 197)

Given the good/service performance/fitness, a certain psychological ownership/use feeling and a degree of self-exhibition, the more the good/service matched up a specific necessity, the wider was its consumption.

Such a customisation model functioned only up to the 1970s, when the consumers turned out to be more demanding high-spending people and a general modernisation of the ways by which the customers choose and consume emerged. In addition, since then the production structure transformations have required more output-dedicated strategies. On the one hand the firms inside fully fledged industries, solicited by the increasing competition to undertake a continuous innovation or substitution of products and services, set them before a change in consumption patterns and lifestyles. On the other hand, the new products/services connected to the technological revolution (electronic goods, communication and entertainment services, and applications to enjoy them) had to gain ground into optional consumption. Both the restructuring of production, sided by the emergence of new industries and market difficulties, required a new product quality management.

Technological innovation came to the rescue of the firms by suggesting strategies aiming at shifting the consumption nature from solid material goods to liquid experiential ones and the availability model of goods/services from legal ownership to the access right. Thanks to 'capitalist platforms' (Uber, Airbnb, Baidu), programs and applications, or to suitable payment methods for durable goods, consumers started to substitute the ownership of the goods (car, flat) with the rent of their service as they wish. Likewise, digitalisation shifts the property of books, DVD, games or shows, concerts and technical quick response to fee-paying services provided by specialised platforms (Amazon, Netflix).

> Whereas property rights are typically bundled in private ownership . . . fractional ownership models unbundle property rights, allowing consumers to acquire a right to temporarily use goods and services that are often shared with tens, hundreds, of thousands of consumers (e.g., by paying for or sharing personal data). . . . In access-based models, the goal is typically to provide financial or efficiency gains for consumers and firms.
>
> (Morewedge, Monga, Palmatier, Shu and Small 2021: 199–200)

As to the marketed output the managers started to pursue the maximum customer satisfaction within the decisions and practises intended to produce and develop an output with respect to the aims of the company (survival, growth, flexibility and scalability). Total quality management was introduced as an instrument by which 'all of the company's people are involved in constantly improving the quality of products, services, and business processes' (Kotler and Armstrong 2018: 249) in order to make customer-driven quality a way of doing business. The improvement of output performance and fitness, the adoption of international standards, the products and services innovation and the introduction of new ones capable of satisfying new needs are activities matching up the consumer's current and attractive needs and pushing consumption.

The emergence of advertising industries to enhance the consumption

The customisation is not sufficient to strengthen the market position along the product/service lifecycle; the quality and the features of the output must also be communicated and disseminated to the customers. For these reasons, the companies introduced the advertisement. Although advertisements appeared in written documents (Egyptian papyruses), Roman mosaics, paintings and printed books of the 16th/18th centuries, advertising emerged as an entrepreneurial activity only in the mid-18th century. In truth, until then the advertisements were mere personal information, as shown in the case of Théophraste Renaudot. He was a French doctor who, having established a recruitment office and notice board for the jobless, founded in 1631 the first newspaper of the country to disseminate these notices widely and to give to 'those seeking and offering works, buying, and selling goods, and making public announcements of all kinds' (Tungate 2007: 11) the chance of publishing their personal information. Thus, advertising emerged as information conveyed by paper records about something or someone.

Information is an output of human thought that can be communicated to other people orally, through supports (stone, paper, magnetic strip, celluloid and digital file) or through electromagnetic waves. Information, if it is recorded, can be repeated and as such can be an input of production processes (a speech to teach a lesson, a tale to produce a book, a lyric for giving a concert and a script to shoot a film). It is generally considered as an 'experienced good' because its usefulness emerges after the consumption (becoming knowledge) and as 'public good' because there is no rivalry in the consumption (one person's consumption doesn't reduce the satisfaction of other people). From the point of view of production, if the costs to produce information are high, the copy costs are low or even zero; in addition, the scale returns of production are increasing and in some sectors forms of monopoly or oligopoly can appear.

Since their emergence, advertising agencies used all the disposable media at the time to inform people and expand the market of publicised goods for the firms that turned to them. Initially they purchased advertising spaces in newspapers where inserted sentences or/and drawings, then they installed billboards. In the 19th century:

> In Britain one of the most prominent clients was A&F Pears, maker of Pears' Soap. The company's success was assured by prototype adman Thomas J. Barrett, who joined the firm in 1862. As well as securing one of the first celebrity endorsements – from Lillie Langtry, actress, courtesan, and mistress of the Prince of Wales – Barrett convinced the popular artist Sir John Everett Millais to sell him a painting of a young boy gazing at rising soap bubbles. Not only that, but he persuaded Millais to add a bar of Pears' soap to the scene'. . . . In 1870s Paris the Printing house Chaix and the artist Jules Chéret were taking advantage of the development of lithography . . . to produce ground-breaking posters for the Folie-Bergère cabaret' (that) 'were complemented by Henry de Toulouse Lautrec's equally vibrant work for the rival Moulin Rouge nightspot.
>
> (Tungate 2007: 12–13)

When film performance and radio and television programmes appeared, the agencies also purchased advertising times to broadcast video clips, which with the advent of the internet spread in all the online sites and applications.

The expansion of the advertising industry has given rise to filières composed of firms working at the different levels of the activities necessary to produce advertisement – that is, in the phases of planning, creating, producing and placing the output. Some agencies provide all the services included in the filière (full-service agencies), some others focus on a specific phase of the production (specialised agencies); there are also

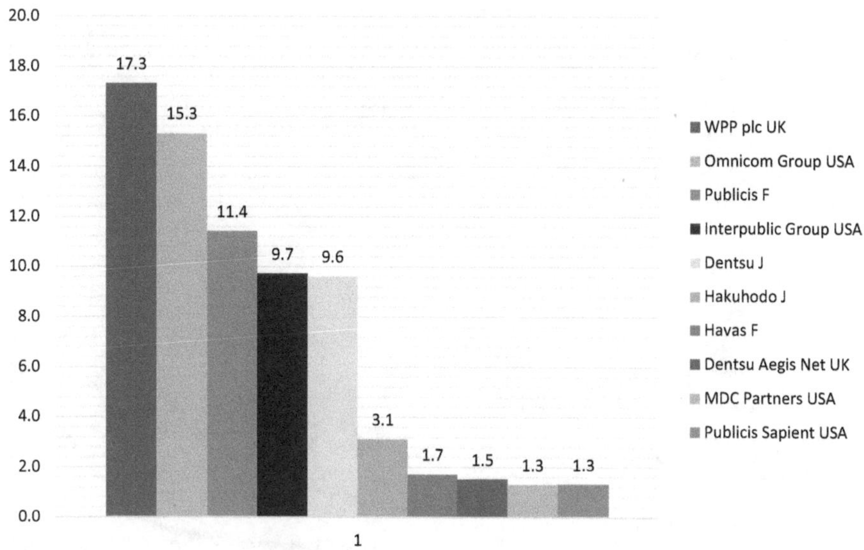

Figure 7.4 Largest AD agencies worldwide by revenue 2020 ($ billions)

Source: Author's elaboration from https://www.bizvibe.com/sign-up accessed the 29th of March 2021

advertisers that are firm divisions producing advertising independently (in-house agency) to control the placing.[3] Today the advertising agencies and marketing companies are controlled by few international holding companies (WPP Group PLC, Omnicom, Publicis Groupe, Interpublic and Dentsu) so that they constitute a thick web of interconnected firms operating worldwide (Figure 7.4).

The rising revenue of the world's advertising industry during the last 40 years has been as formidable as the structural change of its output. In fact, the annual global expenditure on advertisement has endlessly grown about eight times in the period, but the destinations of the industrial output (representing the media preferred by the advertisers) have recorded turning points in 2000, 2008 and 2014. At the turn of the century newspaper advertisement expenditure, even if growing, stopped being the media leader because it was overtaken by television. Eight years later all the print media (newspapers and magazines) finished the rising trend of advertisement expenditure and started a fast downturn that will take them back in 2020 to the 1980 values. Meanwhile, in 2002 the global advertisement expenditure on internet search emerged, followed by that on social media (2010), on e-commerce and online video (2012); their rising trend, carried out at the expense of television since 2014, was so fast that they reached in 2020 nearly the 60 per cent of the annual global expenditure on advertisement (Figure 7.5).

Figure 7.5 represents the evolution of the advertisement destination following the technological advancement of the media (or channels by which this kind of information can be communicated). Such a long-term trend, which changed the structure of the advertisement market, transferred in all the advanced economies,

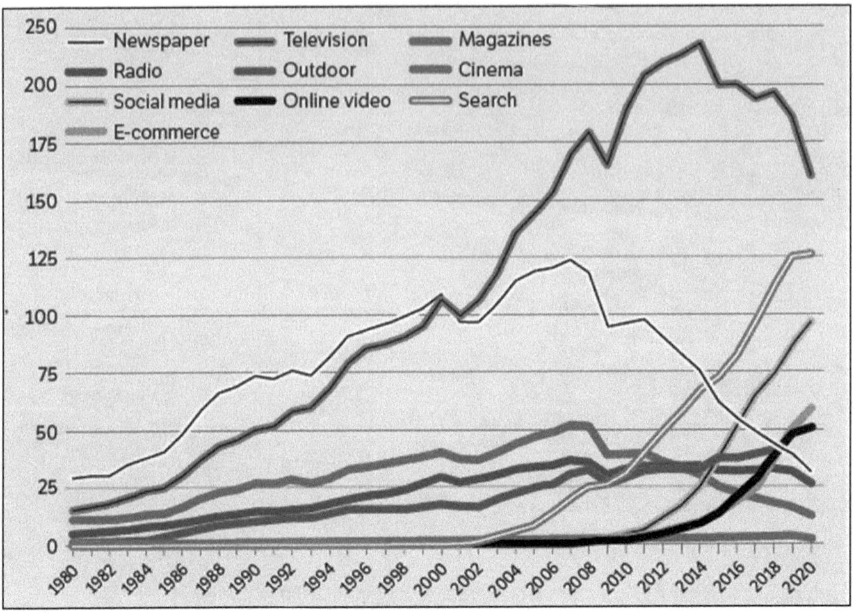

Figure 7.5 Advertisement annual global expenditure on the different media for the period 1980–2020 in billion dollars (current prices)

Source: RACONTEUR eMarketer/Linkedin 2020

even if with some local variation. The European Union's average distribution of advertisement spending based on different channels in 2014 showed that print media received 26 per cent of the total expenditure, the radio and television 37 per cent, internet 30 per cent, outdoors 6 per cent and 1 per cent the cinema. At the national level 'internet accounts for 43 per cent of advertising spend in the UK but only 20 per cent in Japan; Television accounts for 42 per cent of advertising spend in Hungary, but only 25 per cent in Germany; and Press (Newspapers and Magazines) accounts for 39 per cent of advertising spend in Germany but only 19 per cent in the UK' (Deloitte 2017: 10). The situation in the USA in 2018 recorded 16 per cent of the total advertisement spending was in newspaper and magazines, 35 per cent in television and 9 per cent in radio, 34 per cent in the internet, 4 per cent in outdoors and 1 per cent in cinema (STATISTA 2021).

The deviations that the national shares of media advertisement present with respect to the EU average generally depend on the country codes that place restrictions in the interest of competition in the media sector. In fact, if on one side, the advertisement expenditure of the firms supports the expansion of their market by informing the consumers about the characteristic of goods and services, on the other side, it represents a channel for financing the activities of the media. The corporate revenues of the print media stem from the sale of newspapers and magazines but for the most part from the sale of the advertising spaces. Only the last ones are the source of revenues for the commercial broadcasting companies (radio and TV)[4] and for the internet. As the pervasiveness ability is increasing from the first kind of media to the last one, in some countries where the print media are considered a form of public information the authorities put advertisement ceilings to the different forms of outputs to help the weaker competitors.

The importance of the advertising industry for the economy is not restricted to the expansion of the firm markets through a dedicated industrial sector and to the creation of advertising space demand for the information media. There is a wider effect on the economy calculated by the multiplier of the advertisement expenditure: in 2014 its effect on the GDP was between six and eight times in higher-income economies (Deloitte 2017: 7).

The financial support to the consumption: The consumer credit industry

Lifestyle, product quality strategy and advertisement are undoubtedly environmental components capable of fostering potential consumption, but only the current and/or prospective income will realise it. Since the early 20th century, American companies looking for new consumers became aware of the fact that, despite the increase in wages, the workers couldn't save in a short period the amount of money necessary to buy durable goods such as cars, or sign promissory notes entailing to binding clauses. On the other hand, the companies couldn't any more directly sell their output by instalments because in the long run their consumer credits would burden the balance sheet. Therefore, the company's high throughput that could be technically feasible was lacking the corresponding demand. The mismatch of the purchasing power of people with the higher sale of durable goods could prevent the expansion of consumption (and of production) if the consumer credit companies didn't emerge.

At the beginning of the twentieth century, the system of deferred payments granted by the producers had already been applied in some sectors up to the financial critical threshold that couldn't be overstepped; in fact, 'in America as in England the furniture trade and sellers of musical instruments have used the system for some time' (Rodd 1926: 204), It was the car industry that in the twenties went beyond by launching the first consumer credit company as affiliate of a parent manufacturing one. After 'two or three years the system has been introduced into almost every branch of retail business, with the consequence that sales have been actively stimulated' (Rodd 1926: 204). Such financial agencies worked in this way: first they provided the dealers with money enabling them to stockpile products by giving a down payment to the producers, then they lent money to the costumers to pay for the product to the dealer who, in turn, settled the manufacturing company. At the time of the purchase the customer paid in cash 20 per cent–30 per cent of the good price, returning the loan and the interests by instalments to the consumer credit company in the following 12–18 months. The deferred payment system, besides the increase in sales, gave rise to other effects on the production system. On one side, it relieved the producer of the insolvency risk enabling him to cash in at the product sale and of the market risk because it was downloaded on the dealer. On the other side, it caused the emergence and strengthening of the consumer credit sector, whose financing agencies assumed all the creditor rights and duties.

Such a payment system, which increases the consumption by extending the payment process to the medium term, spread in all the higher income economies as a facilitator for the purchase of specific durable goods (the car, the home, and the appliances) as well as other spending like tuition fees, medical treatments, wedding expenditures or holidays. The financial instruments created by the consumption credit companies to face specific purchases were the auto loan, the mortgage, and the student loan, all generally granted by giving as collateral the salary slip, a movable property, and a home. Instead, to provide the consumer with a general line of credit, the home equity and the credit card have been introduced in the last quarter of the 20th century. Due to the introduction of these instruments and to favourable rates of interest the household's consumption increased intensely, starting from the 1990s. Figure 7.6 shows that between 1990 and 2019 the household spending value increased 16.4 times in China, 4.6 in Russia, 3.8 in the USA 3.1 in France, 2.8 in Germany, 2.7 in U.K, 2.6 in Italy, 2.4 in Japan, and 2.0 in Brazil. Despite this escalation the share of household consumption expenditure in the percentage of the GDP presented, between 1990 and 2018 fluctuations lower than 5 per cent (China excluded); in fact the values went in China from 49.9 per cent to 38.5 per cent, in Russia from 48.7 per cent to 49.5 per cent, in the USA from 63.9 per cent to 68.2 per cent, in France from 55.2 per cent to 53.9 per cent, in Germany from 56.3 per cent to 52.1 per cent, in UK from 66.7 per cent to 65.5 per cent, in Italy from 58.7 per cent to 60.3 per cent, in Japan from 51.2 per cent to 55.6 per cent, and in Brazil from 59.3 per cent to 64.7 per cent (OECD 2021).

Simultaneously, also the household indebtedness increased in some countries during the period, going beyond the value of the net disposable income; nevertheless, the growing trend arrived at the top for Germany and Japan in 2000 and for

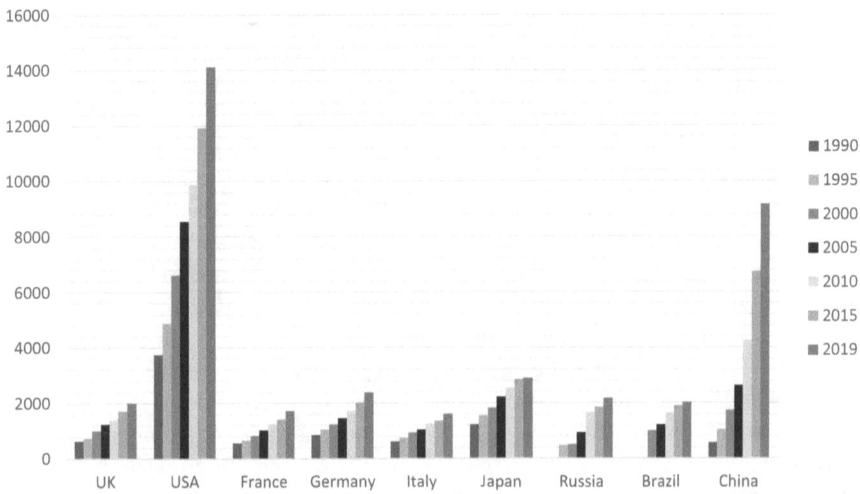

Figure 7.6 Evolution of household spending value of selected countries between 1990 and 2019 (billion US dollars)

Source: Author's elaboration from OECD (2021), Household spending https://doi.org/10.1888/b5f46048-en (accessed on 08 April 2021)

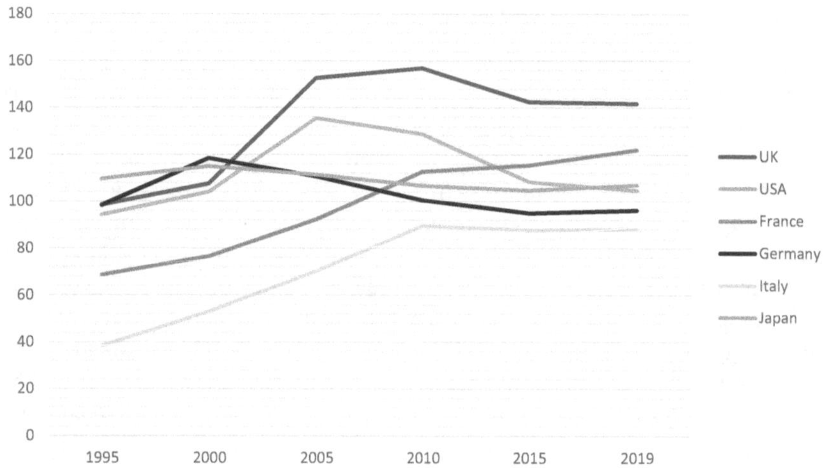

Figure 7.7 Household total debt for selected countries between 1995 and 2019 (% of net disposable income)

Source: Author's elaboration from OECD (2021), Household debt https://doi.org/10.1888/f03b6469-en (Accessed on 03 April 2021)

the UK and Italy in 2010, declining then for all the countries, France excluded (see Figure 7.7). The same evolution is presented by the household debt as a share of GDP: it was nearly 60 per cent for the USA, the UK and Germany in 1990, it increased up to the 71 per cent in the case of Germany in 2000, to 98.5 per cent for the USA and 96.5 for the UK in the period 2006–2008, and it declined to 61.1 per cent, 75.3 and 79.8 respectively in 2019. France and Italy presented an ever-growing path from 32.7 and 16.8 in 1990 up to 61.1 and 41.2 respectively in 2019, while Japan, after ten years' fluctuation around 70 per cent, reached in 2019 the value of 62.8. (www.imf.org 2021). Finally, it is interesting to notice that in the new century the structure of US household debt has changed: although mortgages have never pulled such a debt, representing the most part of it (68 per cent in 2003 as in 2020 after a jump to 72 per cent in 2006), the student loans shifted in the period from 3 per cent to 11 per cent, the auto loans remained at nearly 9 per cent, the credit card passed from 9 per cent to 6 per cent, and home equity from 11 per cent to 6 per cent (New York Fed Consumer Credit Panel/Equifax 2021). Considered in value:

> Student loan debt is at an all-time high in the US, growing at an unprecedented rate over the past two decades. New data shows just how student debt has outpaced other household debt like home, auto and credit card. In data from the New York Fed Consumer Credit Panel compiled by the Wall Street Journal, student loan debt in the US has surged by 350 per cent in the last 17 years. That's nearly 10 times higher than the 40 per cent increases in auto loans and mortgage debt. The one bright spot of good news shows how credit card debt has scaled back slightly by 15 per cent since 2003.
>
> (STATISTA, Sept. 21, 2020).

Consumption organisation and social priorities

That in modern economies consumption rests on exchange contracts carried out by the consumers in conformity with social institutions, habits and lifestyles to satisfy the constantly growing and mutating needs is the main stylised fact emerging from the analysis now made. But the consumer is not the unique player inside the working of this function of the economic system because the trade of goods and services is made through the intervention of the dealers and service providers, following the best match of need details-good performance (or service fitness) arranged by the activities of the firms and of the state, as well as to the relations among the three players: thus, the consumption function presents a systemic structure. The participation of the state in the consumption operating method is two-pronged: it directly substitutes for the consumers as the payer of some services they consume in specific situations, and it is the organiser of the consumption organisation through its role of institutional source (lawmaker issuing trade or loan contracts, administrative authority supervising commercial activities, etc.).

The systemic nature of consumption and its organisation

The historical and structural survey on consumption, just brought to completion, reveals both the complexity of the phenomenon and of its fulfilment as well as the features of the organisation of such function of the economic system. At the centre of this arrangement there is the consumer who implements three processes coming in succession, in which a lot of participants take part. The starting moment of the consumption activity is the choice of good/service by matching the performance/fitness of the items sighted as suitable with the needs to be satisfied. Such comparison, driven by a technical assessment once roughly decided the dedicated budget, is heavily affected by social habits and lifestyles or by advertisement; thus, next to the consumer, the producers of goods/services, the society and the advertising industry intervene (see the black arrows in Figure 7.8). The relations among these participants to the process are different in nature: the bidirectional contacts between the consumer and the producer are technical feedbacks on the performance/fitness of the product/service and the consumer expectations/requirements to satisfy his needs (remember the product quality strategy); the influences exercised by the advertisement and/or by the social habits on the consumer choice are instead psychological unidirectional relations. In this process there is also a lateral bidirectional economic relation represented by the assignment of creating the advertisement given to the advertising agent by the producer of the good/service.

The second step of the consumption process is the purchase of the good/service believed to be the more appropriate to gratify the consumer's wants. This acquisition, mediated by the retailer according to the payment rules established in accordance with the law (sometimes called 'market rules'), presents a third potential key player if the consumer needs a loan to pay for the item: the consumer credit agency. In fact, the exchange includes two different kinds of relation: the real flow that is

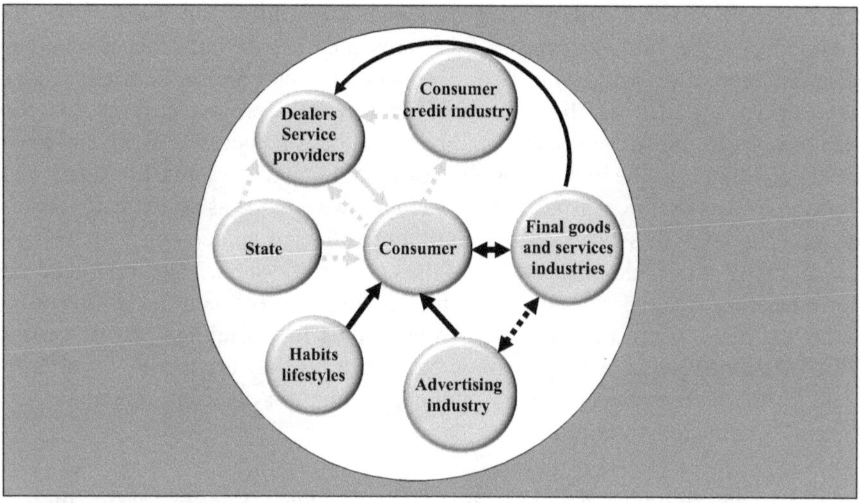

Figure 7.8 Elements and connections of the consumption system

Source: Author's elaboration

the transfer of the good from the dealer (or of the service from the service provider) to the consumer and the monetary flow from the second player to the first one. The payment is direct if the consumer pays the price to the dealer/service provider, but if he needs a loan the consumer credit agency assumes the disbursement by implementing a lateral financial process of credit with a refund in instalments (see the grey dotted lines in Figure 7.8). The third step of the consumption process is fruition, but this activity is run by the consumer without any intervention of other economic subjects.

In Figure 7.8 the state also appears as a component of the consumption system: admittedly, the government and local administrations carrying out their institutional functions (defence, justice, and police) purchase goods and services to persecute the activities entrusted to them. But such expenditures are borne for a productive reason; thus, no consumption relation connects the retailers and service providers with the state in these cases. The dotted grey arrows going from the last component to the first ones are in fact payment for goods and services enjoyed by the consumers but paid by the state. Such an intervention of the state in the consumer activity as a player deserves a digression.

The evolution of consumption in the capitalist advancement meant not only an increase in the amount of purchased goods and services but also a structural change in consumer spending. This restructuring was due both to the appearance of new goods and services suitable for the old need satisfaction and to the emergence of new devices capable of gratifying the requirements caused by everyday life modification. The big part of the last category of needs emerged over time and turned out to be ultimately basic requirements whose satisfaction increased the expenditure for the necessities. The case for utilities and transport at the beginning of the 20th century has been presented above, but other necessities also emerged after World War Two. The education and the services needed by the workers and their families in case of unexpected or enforced events (like the healthcare system, social security and pension) became necessities whose items of expenditure must be included in the household financial report. Moreover, the fruition of these services is also acknowledged worldwide as an indicator representing the level of social and economic upgrading of an economy, to such an extent that it is considered a priority of the economic system. Thus, the spending for education, healthcare system, social security, workers' compensation insurance and pension can be considered expenditures for social and private necessities. Accordingly, in some economic organisations they are totally or partially paid by the state and recorded as public consumption or disbursement for the 'social benefits to household'.

> In national accounts social benefits to households are broken down into two distinct categories: social benefits other than social transfers in kind; and social transfers in kind. The former transfers are typically in cash and so allow households to use the cash indistinguishably from other income, whereas transfers in kind are always related to the provision of certain goods or services (predominantly health care and education), and so households have no discretion over their use. Social benefits other than social transfers in kind may be further broken down into two key components: pensions benefits and non-pensions benefits. The latter consists of cash transfers made by government or by non-profit institutions serving households (NPISHs) to households to meet their financial needs in case of unexpected events, such as sickness, unemployment, housing, education, or family circumstances.
>
> (OECD accessed on 07 April 2021)

If household consumption increased sharply in the past 30 years, the social benefits to the household, represented in Figure 7.8 by a real flow from retailers and service providers to consumers (grey continuous line) and by a monetary flow from the state to the sellers as corresponding payment (grey dotted line), presented in the new century diversified trends. The share of such services values in percentage of the GDP declined after an initial increase in the UK, the USA and Germany, stopping in 2019 between 12 per cent and 16 per cent. In the case of Italy, France and Japan the trend has been a rising one, stopping between 12 per cent and 20 per cent (Figure 7.9). The values and the trends of the shares in the different countries vary according to the role plaid by the state, given that such services are totally or partially provided by public organisations depending on the state legal system. Considering the public support to household consumption and the legislative strategy in matters regarding this activity, the state results both a component of the consumption process and the planner of the consumption organisation.

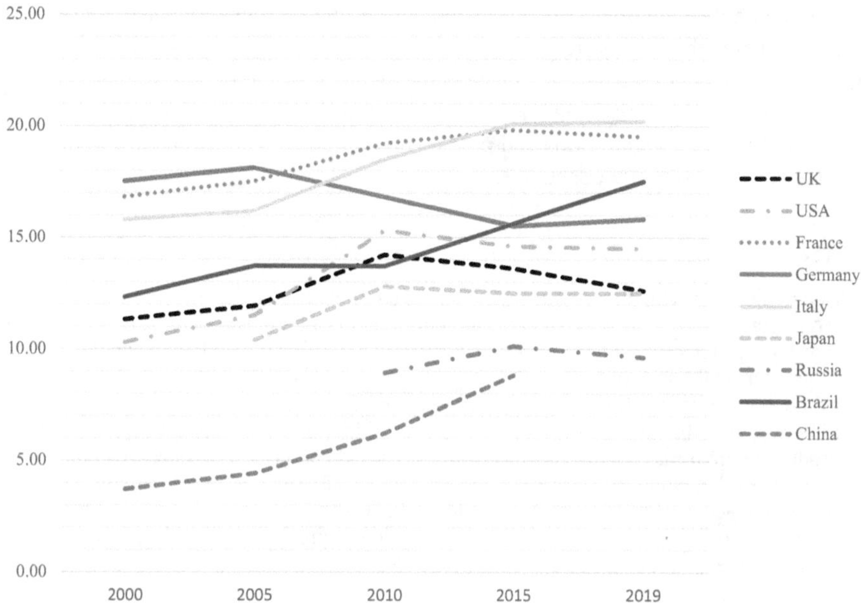

Figure 7.9 Social benefits to household in selected countries between 2000 to 2019 (% of GDP)

Source: OECD (2021). Social benefits to households Doi: 10.1888/423105c6-en (Accessed on 18 April 2021)

Concluding remarks: The consumer as an economic other-directed subject

Consumption is the realisation of production, in the sense that production shows an economic meaning only in the presence of needs that must be satisfied by goods and services; this is the reason why the production sphere tried to encourage in some ways the consumption. This constitutive necessity originated some stylised facts during the consumption evolution. The first has been a pushing role plaid by trade and new goods/services creation in widening the variety of instruments at consumers' disposal to satisfy their needs and in promoting new lifestyles that changed the consumer tastes. The second has been the improvement of consumer satisfaction, carried out by the firm strategy of product innovation and/or quality upgrading aimed at matching the performance/fitness of the product/service and the consumer expectations/requirements. The third stylised fact has been the persuasion and fashion strengthening carried out by the firms through advertising to reinforce their sales. The fourth is that all these consumption enhancers have been ineffective without an increase in the purchasing power of the consumers: this is the reason why the consumer credit industry has developed.

All these stylised facts highlight some features of the consumer and of its behaviour. Although he is at the centre of the consumption system, he cannot be considered either the organiser or the manager of the organisation carrying on this function inside the economic system; in fact, the productive sectors, the social habits, and the dealers manage the consumption activity of the people in many ways. But the state is the entity that shapes the consumption organisation by legislating trade contracts, financial loans and cases when it substitutes the consumer in paying for some services he consumes.

Notes

1 In colonies 'peasants reverted from selling sugar, pepper and cloves on the market and buying cloth and other goods in exchange to a hand-to-mouth existence of subsistence farming. . . . This was the most extreme form of commodification' (Trentmann 2017: 27).
2 In that period the idea of progress became clearer, mainly thanks to the authors who contributed to the French Encyclopaedia (Voltaire and Turgot).
3 Side by side with advertising, the firms carry out price policy to introduce a new gifted product or invite a customer to buy another one whose price is reduced (promotion). Sometimes they support sporting events or teams, solidarity and other initiatives (sponsorship) to acquaint the customers or promote the brand.
4 In the case of cable or satellite receiver TV or in the presence of a public broadcasting company, the revenues also stem from licence fees.

References

Bairoch, P. and Goertz, G. (1986) 'Factors of Urbanisation in the Nineteenth Century Developed Countries: A Descriptive and Econometric Analysis', *Urban Studies*, 23: 285–305.

Deloitte LLP (2017) *The Economic Contribution of Advertising in Europe. A Report for the World Federation of Advertisers*, London: Deloitte LLP.

Engel, E. (1857) *Die Productions- und Konsumtionsverhältnisse des Königreichs Sachsen (Production and Consumption Conditions in Saxony Kingdom)*, Statistischen Büreaus des Königlich Sächsischen Ministeriums des Innern.

Engel, E. (1895) *Die Lebenskosten belgischer Arbeiter-Familien früher und jetzt* (*The Cost of Living of Belgian Worker Families in the Past and Actually*), Dresden: C. Heinrich.

Giddens, A. (1991) *Modernity and Self-Identity. Self and Society in the Late Modern Age*, London: Polity Press.

Kotler, P. and Armstrong, G. (2018) *Principles of Marketing*, Harlow: Pearson Educational Limited.

Morewedge, C. K., Monga, A., Palmatier, R. V., Shu, S. B. and Small, D. A. (2021) 'Evolution of Consumption: A Psychological Ownership Framework', *Journal of Marketing*, 85 (1): 196–218.

Nelson, R. R. and Consoli, D. (2010) 'An Evolutionary Theory of Household Consumption Behavior', *Journal of Evolutionary Economics*, 20 (5): 665–88. https://doi.org/10.1007/s00191-010-0171-7

OECD. (2021) *Household Spending*. Accessed 08 March 2021 https://doi.org/10.1888/b5f46048-en

Rodd, F. (1926) 'The Deferred Payments System in the United States', *The Economic Journal*, 36 (142): 204–14.

STATISTA. Accessed 1 April 2021 https://www.statista.com/statistics/387655/advertising-expenditures-share-by-medium-usa/

Trentmann, F. (ed.) (2012) *The Oxford Handbook of the History of Consumption*, Oxford: Oxford University Press.

Trentmann, F. (2017) *Empire of Things. How We Became a World of Consumers, From the Fifteenth Century to the Twenty-First*, London: Penguin Books.
Tungate, M. (2007) *Ad Land: A Global History of Advertisement*, London: Kogan Page Limited.
US Department of Labor and US Bureau of Labor Statistics (2006) *100 Years of US Consumer Spending. Data for the Nation, New York City, and Boston*, Report 991. https://www.bls.gov/opub/100-years-of-u-s-consumer-spending.pdf

Glossary

Conspicuous consumption is personal need satisfaction by purchasing luxury goods.
Discretionary consumption is spending for non-basic goods and services.
Household consumption pattern is the structure of household consumption presenting the weight of each category of goods and services over the total expenditure.
Lifestyle is a set of combined habits characterising the way of life of people, on one side by reflecting his values and self-image and on the other side by affecting his behaviour (consumption model included).
Mass consumption society is a particular phase of capitalist evolution where the production conditions and the consumer purchasing power enable assorted and plentiful patterns of consumption for a large part of the population.
Purchasing power is the measure of the amount of goods and services that the wages can buy.
Self-consumption is personal need satisfaction by using foodstuff, clothing or everyday things obtained on one's own from agricultural activities, ship farming and livestock rearing.
Staple consumption is personal need satisfaction by purchasing foodstuff and clothing.
Subsidised consumption is personal need satisfaction by using foodstuff and clothing given by a public administration or charities.
Utilities are service supplies of electricity, water, waste disposal, heating and sewage whose costs is paid by end users (households, companies, associations).

8 The market

Regulated exchanges allowing capitalist economies' operation

The term 'market' is commonly used to define a lot of concepts: the space where goods and services are exchanged, the meeting place where the forces of the demand and supply determine the quantity of goods and services exchanged and the unit price, the meeting place where the consumers' desires and the producers' self-interests are fulfilled through the exchange of goods and services, the environment where the companies implement their strategies against the competitors.[1] Apart from the last definition that is misleading because it has to do with the sector, the other ones don't explain what a market is; they identify an abstract place where the unit price at which a definite amount of exchanged good or service emerges or focus on the assumed consequences that the exchange has on the contracting parties. In agreement with such opinion was also Coase, who wrote that:

> Although economists claim to study the working of the market, in modern economic theory the market itself has an even more shadowy role than the firm. . . . In the modern textbook, the analysis deals with the determination of market prices, but discussion of the market itself has entirely disappeared. This is less strange than it seems. Markets are institutions that exist to facilitate exchange, that is, they exist in order to reduce the cost of carrying out the exchange transactions. In an economic theory which assumes that transaction costs are non-existent, markets have no function to perform, and it seems perfectly reasonable to develop the theory of exchange by an elaborate analysis of individual exchanging nuts for apples on the edge of the forest or some similar fanciful example.
>
> (Coase 1988: 7–8)

And Hodgson specified that:

> Markets dominate modern life, and economists have for long been concerned about market prices, but, despite this ongoing preoccupation, until recently there has been little discussion of the nature and operation of markets themselves' . . . While market outcomes such as prices are always central to the

DOI: 10.4324/9781315679730-11

> discussion, there is generally little consideration of the detailed rules and mechanisms through which prices are formed, and the concept of the market itself often goes undefined.
>
> (Hodgson 2008)

To clarify the concept, it is worthwhile to start with the role performed by the market in the economic system. The market connects the production units among themselves and with the consumption units' demand and manages the distribution of resources and outputs within the economic system; thus, it is a mechanism enabling the operation of the capitalist economy. Such connections emerge in the form of exchanges, regulated by the purchase agreements for goods, labour or financial services, whose integral components are the buyer, the seller, the traded item, the price and the secondary liabilities of the contracting parties. To close the contract sometimes it is also required the intervention of a mediator or of an agent[2] who offers their services upon specific contracts. Although the market activities are usually implemented in specific organised spaces giving permanency and regularity to them (such as indoor or open air-markets, stock exchanges, fairs, shops, agencies, notary, or accountant offices), nevertheless they occur irrespective of these organised places too: everywhere a legitimate economic transaction takes place there is a market activity because that exchange ultimately establishes also legal obligations. Thus, the market activities are something more than simple exchanges; they are organised operating routines that implement social institutions; as such they have functions and organisation forms (See Chapter Three).

Being the market a sort of gear train, only assessments related to its technical nature can be befitting, like the judgement about its effectiveness and efficiency; within this context it can be said that more exchanges are implemented, the more effective is the market that, nevertheless, is more efficient when smaller are the costs connected to the transaction. Therefore, it isn't acceptable, the frequently maintained claim according to which only transactions free from whatever procedural or legal regulation, the so-called 'free market', can promote the advancement of the economy. Despite this matter of fact, the market is always associated with positive moral values: it is considered as the metaphor of democracy because, by definition, all the contracting parties are considered equivalent competitors; it is also claimed as the only means enabling the efficient allocation of resources because its working is believed compliant with the perfect competition. The market has also been elevated to a paradigm for the representation and explanation of the capitalist economy, forgetting that capitalism isn't a plain trading system like mercantilism.

The market emerges to fulfil the exchanges necessary to carry out production and satisfy social needs. To accomplish such function easily and safely, the buying and selling of goods and services require the execution of a set of procedures and the observation of rules; hence, the market changes when the needs of the socioeconomic system and such rules and procedures change. In light of this feature the exchange of goods, labour and financial services is not a peculiar trait of a capitalist economy; in fact, as the historical documents prove, they date back to ancient societies where they have been the expression of different economic needs and systems. Just for this reason, it would be erroneous to consider them equivalent to modern markets.

All this food for thought will be historically proved in the chapter beside an in-depth analysis of the characteristics of the sale contracts, of the kinds of market process and of the mechanisms of price determination to inspect the nature, structures, and workings of the capitalist markets.

The creation of markets

After the collapse of the Soviet Union and of the national economies that joined the *Council for Mutual Economic Assistance* (whose acronym was COMECON), a new interest in the creation and evolution of the markets emerged among historians, sociologists and economists involved in the discussion about the transition of Eastern European countries toward the market economy (Coase 1991). Such interest strengthened then in connection with the comparison of the economic performance of China and of the other former planned economies (Nee 2000), as well as in relation to the recent globalisation of all the markets. Even though the debates focused on the role of market building in restructuring the economies, sometimes the study has been steered to investigate if the market is a typical capitalist entity or an unhistorical natural one or to trace the origin of markets. Although the debates didn't face the problem of the nature and working of the market, they have been important for the identification of some features characterising it and for the emphasis attributed to the role of the economic and political players in its historical building and modification. The following historical overview will deepen such insights, searching for the stylised facts that can explain the market building, evolution, and current working.

The market of goods: A long historical building process

At the beginning of human civilisation, when farming was the only form of economic activity, self-consumption did not make way for the market; just occasional exchanges of goods in the form of barter occurred to redistribute the resources that were necessary for the life and the working of the economy. Only when the cities emerged and a part of the population became engaged in commercial and artisan activities did the city market of goods extend, supported by the city currency and by agreements legally or conventionally differentiated according to the economic activities. In this phase the institutional framework supporting commerce was generally that of the private law governing the civil relations among the citizens; only when the cities started to trade outside their territories, especially across the seas, specific public regulations were introduced to manage these exchanges and regulate imports, exports, and customs.

An example of goods and financial services markets in ancient societies is given by the Rome experience between 242 BC and 235 A C (Sirks 2018: 54). In that period the legal experts updated the first written code of Rome (the *Twelve tables* issued in 451 B C) and expanded it to new social phenomena. Commercial activities were not considered in such a legal framework, but the use of some dispositions of civil law for commercial transactions became possible. The Romans used a variety of contracts whose stipulations could be verbal or written. The contracts of sale (*emptio venditio*), hire (*locatio conductio*), mandate (*mandatum*) and partnership (*societas*) as well as loan for consumption (*mutuum*, particularly used for money loans) represented the most used legal devices to manage the Roman economic activities. The barter was considered the specimen of the sale contracts for it contained in a nutshell the typical form of negotiation process, as well as all the elements that are pertinent to a legal transaction: the similarity of the obligations of the parts and their simultaneous performance (consisting in the transfer of money in exchange for a transfer of good, and conversely), and the consensus about the exchanged thing and its price emerging from the deal. For its simplicity this contract was used in the sale of generic consumer goods, while for the sale of specific goods (land, slaves, animals) this specimen was conveniently specified in some parts. For example, in the sale contract named *emptio vendition,* whose purpose was the actual control of a corporeal asset, explicit consent was required to transfer the possession and the intrinsic risk of the good from the seller to the buyer, also before the fulfilment of the exchange; this endowed the buyer with an unconstrained possession and with the possibility to open hiring and leasing contracts[3] (Sirks 2018: 66–70). Even though at that time property right was not full as it is in capitalism, because it was not guaranteed in some cases in contracts among the Romans and towards the non-Romans, nevertheless, the trade flourished.

Besides the market process by negotiation, based on the barter, there was another well-organised form of market among Romans: the auction. Because of insolvency

> a volume of forced sales made this type of industry – since we see people professionally occupied with auctions – worthwhile. Bankers were also involved in this industry since they could provide advances. The fisc [the public treasury] always sold by way of auction the assets of its defaulting debtors. The difference from a normal sale is that the first bidder has not yet concluded a contract: the auctioneer concludes a contract with the highest bidder and only at the moment when the time open for bidding is over.
>
> (Sirks 2018: 71)

The Romans also used contracts as objects for ware management (deposit, pledge) or financing, but to organise production and commercial activities they relied on mandate and partnership contracts besides those of sale. The mandate was a very important contract for long-distance trade: it consisted of an obligation accepted by one part of the undertaking to do a service on behalf of the first part (for example, to buy wares in a distant place). To carry out a business in all the admitted economic activities (commerce, production, properties management) they used a form of organisation constituted by a contract of partnership: more partners committed their properties to a *societas* and shared in equal parts losses and gains. 'The most prominent partnerships were the *societates publicanorum*, the companies that farmed the collection of taxes, or undertook public works or transport for the armies. Here too managers could take care of the daily business' (Sirks 2018: 74). Also, the banking activities were conducted under the form of *societas*, but contrary to what happens today, they took care of the interest of the banker instead of the depositors; they made deposit and loans without interests unless in the case of high commercial risk. In addition, financial activities were limited to interpersonal economic relations so that, contrary to the good markets, the financial markets were underdeveloped in Roman society. Nonetheless, both kinds of markets, although also oriented to preserve the value of the asset exchanged, were effective mechanisms to support the economy and, in particular, long-distance trade.

That historically there has been conformity between social customs and the regulations managing the economic activities of a community is probably more evident in the Muslim commercial rules than in the Roman ones. An example was the qualities that the merchant could have and the contracts that could be stipulated in those societies. In the Quran commerce was considered the way by which the welfare was distributed to all the community, so the merchant must be an honest Muslim people pursuing such aim and implementing religious and commercial principles in doing his professional activity. He had to act in 'good faith', a quality already required among the Romans, and to be a 'good Muslim'; in addition, he couldn't practise usury *(riba)* or gambling *(maysir)* nor conclude contracts involving wine, pigs, water, blood, idols, crosses and statues *(haram)* or whose object wasn't known upon agreeing *(maysir;* Saleem 2013: Introduction). Moreover, the merchant had to follow the principles on which the Muslim social life had been organised: he enjoyed the freedom of action of everyone who, acting as an integral part of the whole, was free from public concession to follow their own path in social and economic activities, and he pursued his personal interest being responsible for chasing the social interest.

If the Romans, who were interested in the effectiveness of the exchanges, tried to bend the private law to create wider domestic and international markets, the Muslims instead were interested in the efficiency of the exchanges; thus, they tried to make them more certain, safe, and equitable between the 8th and the 14th centuries. Such features of the market resulted from the implementation of the general principles of the commercial contracts that were: the compliance of the obligations, which made the market activities indisputable, was guaranteed by the binding strength of the contract towards both the contracting parties (contractual constraint); the validity of the exchange made under the freedom of contract was provided by analogy with the typical sale contract, on condition that the exchange was not forbidden; and the equity of the contract was ensured in the absence of fraud, violence, error, market power mistreatment, and imbalance of the obligation of one part. As to the typology of exchange contracts, the sale *(salam)* was the model that could take different forms: the sale of goods in exchange for other goods, the sale of goods in exchange for cash compensation, and cash in exchange for cash. By analogy with the sale, other contracts could be stipulated: the barter, the exchange of precious metals, and the manufacture (where one part buys an object that the second part takes it upon himself to produce – service agreement). The long-distance trade was managed by a special contract named *mudarabah*, in which an investor provided financial capital to a manager borrowing them to undertake a business, in compliance with the general principles of merchant's activity. According to the contractual conditions the manager, who was not responsible for any losses of the venture commercial activity, received a fee for his work deducted from the profits and a share of profit according to a pre-agreed ratio; instead, the investor, who supported any risk of the undertaken business, received his own profit share. Such a contract was used in the Middle Ages European trade under the name of *commenda*.

After the downfall of the feudal society and the upswing of the European cities, commerce came back, supported by new economic conditions and by the empowerment of merchants. The concentration of people in the cities, due to the bad economic conditions in the countryside, pushed the emergence of artisan production and encouraged the trade towards the other cities by the only social group that had the financial capital to find new export and import markets. Thus, the artisans became workers for commission of merchants, who exported their output and imported the raw materials they needed. This gave the merchants a dominant position in the economy and enabled them to shape the goods and finance markets in accordance with their own interests. Established evidence of such a trend was the commercial code (the *lex mercatoria*), an exclusive collection of regulations issued by the merchants and effective only for them, that sprang from the municipal merchant charters, from the merchant guild charter, and from the best commercial practices. In addition, a further strengthening of the merchant's position derived from the favour of the seller in the contract structure and from the increase of the trade through the broadening of the markets. As a result, if in the Roman world the markets were oriented to the protection of the owner of real or financial assets and in the Muslim society to the protection of community welfare, in the late medieval Europe they were built to strengthen the economic, social and sometimes also political position of merchants.

As to the legal innovations, some new contracts were introduced to protect the capital involved in the commercial business, like an insurance contract on the economic undertaking, as well as loan and exchange rate contracts for the maritime missions. Some rules were also introduced to regulate the competition and bankruptcy for the accounting entries and for the participants in the activity (the agents managing the transport, the deposit, and the sale of merchandise). To carry out the commercial activities two new legal associations were created: the *company,* that was similar to the general partnership, and the *commenda*, similar to the limited partnership company. Also, a new financial operator appeared to support long-distance trade: the bank. In truth bankers drawing up the deposit service and loan contracts existed already in ancient societies, but the usury prohibition in Christian and Muslim societies slowed down the money market. However, the increase in long-distance trade, the need for the merchants to pay wares away from their residence cities and the risk of taking along money addressed the banks to specialise in the money changing activity and in the bill of exchange issue.[4] In the 13th century in Florence, Genoa and Venice a lot of such financial operators emerged and made prosperous their cities.

From domestic markets to the international trade regulation

The evolution of the markets in the time of the emergence and advancement of capitalism can be analysed from three different points of view: the expansion of the markets in terms of new marketable goods and opportunities of exchange, the expansion of the exchanges inside and outside of the states, and the building of the financial and labour markets. As to the first matter the creation of the land market has been one of the first institutional commitments of the state in the 19th century, necessary not only to develop agriculture through the trade of its main productive resource among new entrepreneurs but also to codify the right and the use of the private property also for business activities. Although the introduction of private ownership and the protection of the holder have represented an important step to create the bases for industrialisation, the impact on the circulation of the asset was sometimes unsatisfactory for agriculture; in fact, land taxation and the delayed implementation of the cadastre have slackened the land transfer and circulation. As to the increase of the opportunities of exchange, some innovations facilitating access to the market emerged over the course of time both on the supply and on the demand inside the sale contract. Such innovations increased the efficiency and thus the reliability of the market, making the circulation of goods and services more certain and safe; in fact, they triggered the virtuous process according to which the market is considered more endowed with such features by the contracting parties, more will be the number of exchanges. Probably the most important innovation in the obligations of the parties has been the change in the terms and conditions of the purchase agreement; it is a matter of a deferred payments system sponsored by the producers at the beginning of the 20th century and then implemented by specific consumption credit companies. Such a system, extended to the purchase of a lot of durable goods or services by coupling the sale contract with a loan contract whose payment is by instalments. In this way the buyer is endowed with extra purchasing power; this buying on credit has enlarged the market just like a credit card at the disposal of a consumer does. Another phenomenon leading to the same consequence is the substitution of the property with leasing when some durable and swift obsolescent goods (the car, copy machine, vending machine, etc.) or some machine tools are needed. In these cases, the cost for the instrumental good use isn't that of its purchase but that of its service acquisition; over a certain stretch of time this gives the customer the availability of the good upon payment of a monthly rent and higher financial resources for additional purchases. The same situation emerges when the sale of computer programmes has been substituted with the disposal of a service in exchange for a yearly rent.

The international exchanges of goods, as documented throughout the book, have been already implemented by the ancient civilisations and have evolved in space and time, switching between expansions and restrictions of the flows. Their creation and enlargement have been the consequence of a volume of domestic production exceeding domestic consumption or of the need to import essential non-available resources and goods required for sustaining the internal production and luxury consumption. International trade has always represented a source of financial entries for the community/state budgets because the entrance, the leaving, or the passage of wares on their territories was allowed subject to the payment of customs duties by the merchants. The rising and falling of such fiscal fees on export as well as on import, due to the community/state financial needs, have been very often at the base of the trends in international trade because they reduced or increased the exchanges. The innovation that emerged in 19th century capitalism on the subject has been the reduction of customs duties in-house and on the outside up to their removal to create a 'market' extending beyond the state borders. Such change was in the interest of goods producers seeking foreign buyers but to the detriment of the state, unless there was compensation by the domestic taxes paid to produce the goods that would be exported (excises) or by the introduction of new taxes. This is the reason why the policies of customs reduction created some conflicts of interest between the governments and the entrepreneurs disadvantaged by these measures, and their adoption occurred only when the government supported the interest of the exporters. As things stand, the enlargement of the international trade of goods was due, besides economic reasons, to the direct intervention of the state that implemented customs duty policies and signed bilateral or multilateral trade agreements (Graff, Kenwood and Lougheed 2014).

The situation of Great Britain after the Napoleonic Wars is emblematic of these dynamics. In fact, the reduction of the customs duties on both the exports and imports could favour the industrial exporters but disadvantage both the public budget and the agriculture producers, who were protected by the Corn Law against the foreign competitors and by complaisant governments defending the food self-sufficiency. Only in the 1840s was this stalemate overtaken by income tax and a new governmental elite, so that firstly the export duties on manufactured goods were abolished, followed by those on raw materials, and then at the end of the decade also a big part of the import duties was unilaterally abolished, agriculture goods included. Such policies increased the number of exchanges, and so expanded British international trade, but it was only by the Cobden-Chevalier Act of 1860 that a further step forward for the expansion of international trade occurred. In fact, such a trade agreement between Great Britain and France established a common territory where the goods of both countries could be traded by the merchants of both nationalities on equal terms – that is, without paying duties or with the lowest level of customs duties for the goods considered typical for the respective economies. This trading system, which was established by a bilateral agreement between states, is usually considered the first 'multinational market', but on closer view it can't be considered as such because it missed some market features that had been elaborated during its historical building process (see Chapter Nine); for this reason, it would be better to say that the Cobden-Chevalier Act opened to the creation of a 'trade area' by an important economic prerogative of the states on the subject of international economic relations that thenceforth will be intensely practised (see Chapter Nine).

Creation and evolution of the financial markets

Although the historical overview shows that some modern financial instruments supporting commercial activities date back to the Middle Ages (see Munro 2003), this isn't sufficient to maintain that there were financial markets at that time. The bond, for example, that is a financial instrument of indebtedness that can be issued by a state or by a company was casually issued first by the Venice Government in the twelfth century to finance its wars and then by the Dutch East India Company in 1623 to finance its commercial activities. These occasional events don't show the existence of financial markets because a series of continuous exchanges of such kind, the definition of rules, operators, and established procedures, and a clear distinction of the traded financial instruments are necessary to certify them. As far as the last requirement is concerned, it is the object of the exchange, the element enabling the distinction among the financial markets in the following types: money market, debt market, capital market, derivatives market and foreign exchange market (FOREX). This classification will be used for the analysis of the creation and evolution of financial markets (Caprara 1940).

Based on the previous premise the origin of the financial markets can be traced back to 1602 when the Dutch East India Company, a commercial organisation established in the form of a join-stock,[5] was granted by a royal charter with the monopoly on the trade with East India. When in 1611 the Amsterdam Stock Exchange (the first in the world) was established, such a company, keen on supporting its trading activities, joined it to sell first its stocks and then in 1623 to issue its bonds. Another financial institution, the *Wisselbank,* was founded in 1609 by the Dutch Republic to convert deposits in foreign coins into domestic payments through the issuing of a bank receipt denominated in equivalent bank money (*Banco shillengen*), and to provide the customers with the currency exchange service. A few years later the deposits were guaranteed by the city of Amsterdam against the potential creditors and declared no longer reimbursable, *Banco shillengen* actually became a currency, also used for exchanges; thus, the *Wisselbank* (also called Bank of Amsterdam) became the first central bank in the world (Quinn and Roberds 2006). 'By the seventeenth, and especially the eighteenth, centuries, Amsterdam increasingly financed the defence of the Dutch state by issuing general obligation bonds that were more readily transferable. . . . These new debt instruments, together with equity issued by joint-stock companies, most notably the Dutch East India Company, gradually supplanted real estate holdings in the portfolio of wealthy institutional investors such as orphanages, hospitals, and the poor house' (Atack 2009: 12–13). The creation of the stock exchange and a central bank that performed the financial functions really implemented the monetary, debt, capital, and FOREX markets.

Differently from the Dutch situation, the introduction of financial institutions in Great Britain occurred first through a private initiative, followed later by the state organisational intervention. So, the London Stock Exchange was formally established in 1773, although the sharebrokers were trading equities of joint-stock companies like the British East India Company for more than one century and a half in the coffee houses of the city of London. On the contrary the Bank of England (1694) was created just as the government needed to finance the war against France, so its assignment was to issue state bonds and to provide deposit services giving notes in return for them. As public debt increased later, the bonds were eventually converted into perpetuities that gave forever annual payments; when the interests were abolished, they became paper money.

As well in France the creation of the financial markets was the result of the private initiative creating joint-stock companies certified by the state and banks sponsored by the government to sell its debt to the investors. Such initiatives, sometimes characterised by 'sophisticated financial engineering', resulted in crises and bubbles that affected the financial markets, and only public reforms led to their stability; this is the case of the Napoleon reform that created in 1800 the Bank of France. A successful reform was also that made by Hamilton in the United States at the end of the 18th century that established a US mint, adopted the bimetallic standard, created a joint-stock independent central bank (1791), consolidated the federal sovereign debt, and regulated the payments of interest on the public debt; in 1790 the Board of Brokers of Philadelphia was established, followed in 1792 by The New York Stock Exchange.

The trial-and-error process of financial markets creation, carried out during the 17th and 18th centuries, provided the industrialising economies with structured financial systems characterised by banking systems with central banks exclusively or not issuing notes in national currencies, stock exchanges trading both company stocks and private and public bonds and financial institutions offering currency exchange services. All the financial markets expanded in the period: for example, during the Napoleon wars the stock market capitalisation (the value of the total companies listed on the stock exchange) in Britain was fluctuating around 50 per cent of the GDP and in the USA near 25 per cent, while the public debt of Britain reached a value equal to two and a half times that of the GDP. Despite a long-run upward trend, also in the last two centuries there have been expansions and restrictions of the financial markets, frequently created by crises that emerged inside them. Some international agreements and institutions have tried to find a solution to such recurring problems by institutional arrangements aiming at creating a balanced coevolution of the real and financial international markets and at managing the 'trilemma' that such a process entails (James 2014: 296). In fact, the enlargement of the goods market beyond the national borders needs a) an international monetary market characterised by steady exchange rates among the currencies to enable the export programmes of the firms; b) free movement of capital among the economies to grant the best firms with investment funds; and c) an autonomous national monetary regulation to tune the national economy with the international monetary and capital markets. A satisfactory arrangement of two among these conditions inhibits a satisfactory arrangement of the third one, but to succeed in doing an agreed international economic order the states have created over time the Gold Standard, the Bretton Woods System, and the liberalisation of the capital movements.

The building process of labour institutions

To make a historical review of the labour market evolution, aiming at highlighting the stylised facts characterising it, some premisses are necessary. Human labour is considered a productive resource consisting in the practice of human energy, knowledge and skills applied to obtain a result that can be an object, a performance or an execution. When the labour is practised by the worker to obtain an object or to perform an activity through a production organisation and execution that she/he makes independently, the energy, knowledge, and skills employed result in the output (a good or service) exchanged on the market. In such a case the worker acts both as an entrepreneur and as an executor of the production process as well as a seller on the corresponding final markets; thus, the labour employed is remunerated, as one among the production costs, through the 'service contract'[6] price that pays for all the result. When the worker service is applied to execute a job or a part of a production process, that can also entail the intervention of a group of interconnected workers and is organised and supervised by an entrepreneur; her/his human energy, knowledge and skills are hired by a specific agreement called employment contract. The previous distinctions about the nature of the labour served as a resource in the production was also adopted by Roman law, which distinguished between 'locatio conductio operis' and 'locatio conductio operarum', respectively the forms of labour used for productive activities. Such a distinction is at the base of the current difference between the self-employment work and the employment contract; by virtue of this distinction it is possible to concentrate the interest on the second one because it is the true kind of labour characterising the production in capitalist economies.

Considering the nature of the labour in both the working performance, it emerges that the employment contract doesn't shape up an exchange because there isn't a transfer of ownership but an agreement for subordinate work. Thus, as it is an agreement between two contracting parties, an effective and efficient market must anyway provide the binding strength of the contract towards both the contracting parties, protect the weakest one from the market power mistreatment, and from the imbalances of the obligation of one part. Therefore we expected a long process of institution building on the matter. This doesn't feel like as 'the contract of employment is a more recent innovation than is widely thought, and . . . its essential features owe as much to legislation as they do to the . . . law of contract' (Deakin 2001: 3). As a matter of fact the evolution of the legal framework underlying the employment went beyond the employment contractual terms to consider the social aspects of the working people: in fact, the topics that have been developed on the subject are the kinds of employment contracts, the employment relationships, the work conditions, the remuneration, the bargaining, the collective representation, the worker social protection, and the provision of special conditions for particular occupational groups. This is the reason why today the argument is framed in the building and evolution of the labour institutions in the context of industrial relations.

As confirmation of the feature of the labour laws in the Anglo-Saxon tradition (UK and USA) the first problems that emerged about labour were pertinent to the amelioration of working conditions; in this context the potential enforcement of guilds regulations to the new industrial activities and the use of child labour were discussed. The protection of young workers was adopted in Europe in the fourth decade of the 19th century, the legal working hours were introduced in Switzerland in 1848 and worker compensation and sickness insurance were introduced in Germany in the 1880s. Starting from the 1930s all the developed economies were equipped with labour protection in the field of health, safety, welfare and social security, as well as labour codes.

As to the evolution of the labour market regulation in Great Britain, the path passed through some different models:

> The 'guild employment which characterized parts of the urban trades as late as the early nineteenth century, and . . . the settlement model which prevailed in agriculture until roughly the same period. The focus then shifts to the master-servant relationship as the pivotal concept through which employment relations were conceptualized in the nineteenth century. The . . . influence of the master servant model, reached beyond the legislation from which it initially sprang, . . . persisted after the last of the Master and Servant Acts was repealed'. Finally, there was 'the emergence of the modern contract of employment from its beginnings in the classification of managerial and professional workers in the nineteenth century, and . . . its later development to the growth of social legislation, and in particular to the conceptions of employment generated by workmen's compensation and social insurance legislation'.
>
> (Deakin 2001: 8)

After a forty-year period of increasing institution building on the labour market, in the 1980s the approach to employment was reduced to a problem concerning a factor of production instead of a teammate of the production process. The internationalisation of industrialised countries introduced the competition between national workers and employees of the countries where the companies outsourced part of their production. Employment has increasingly become temporary and contracts have approached forms of self-employment. Thus, a reduction of the labour contribution to the GDP followed.

The nature, structure and operation of the markets

From the previous historical overview, it emerges that the creation and evolution of markets were generally pushed by urbanisation and international trade. The first phenomenon enabled the development of artisan/industrial and services clusters in the cities and the chance to exchange its production on site, while the second one facilitated the creation of foreign exchanges where the surplus produced in the city could be sold and some insufficient inputs or missing consumer goods and services could be bought. While international trade gradually progressed and became more sizable and complex, production even followed the same path creating intermediate markets for the provision of human and financial resources as well as materials and services. As a result of these evolutions in the matter of commercial activities a lot of financial instruments and contracts were introduced to keep intact the values of the wares beyond the borders, to protect the commercial interests in the case of fluctuating good prices and exchange rates, and to increase the commerce. As for production activities, on the one hand, the financial instruments and contracts enabled the financing and splitting the costs of business ventures and creating and trading shares, bonds and credits; on the other hand, the establishment of the job market made possible the provision of labour through a lot of contracts. In addition, the segmentation of the production filières and the emergence of new services pushed the development of new intermediate and final markets for the provision of production resources. Thus, the quantitative and qualitative expansion of the markets was due, after the creation of cities and the development of international trade, to the growth of production, to its sectoral differentiation, and to the fragmentation of its production filières.

Side by side with these economic variables, the evolution of the markets has been favoured by the role of the political authorities that created the legal framework supporting and easing the exchanges by issuing sale contract laws for the transfer of both material, financial and service resources and outputs. This cooperation between the state and the economy also in the working of the markets proves both their systemic structure and their nature of institutional organisations implementing socioeconomic exchange rules. All these arguments will be analysed in this part of the chapter besides the development trends of the distribution channel, the workings of retail, wholesale and financial markets, and the ways by which the prices are determined.

The market as a system: Its institutional nature and its function

The previous historical review is important because it clarifies the nature of the market, in addition to the ways by which its creation and evolution occurred. Based upon that analysis it is possible to define the 'market' as a set of exchanges of a saleable item, specified regarding quantity, price, and contract terms and conditions between two agreed contracting parties. The 'market process'[7] through which the transaction comes true consists in the working of the 'market organisation', that is, in the operating procedures implemented through the sequence of the steps necessary to arrange the bargaining and to allow the contracting parties to accomplish the due performances according to the ways and times established by the terms of the deal. Thus, as a first step, the market can be represented as a system whose components are the buyer, the seller, and the saleable item, while the connections are the performances that the parties committed to do by common consent. This simple representation can be more or less complex, depending on the different

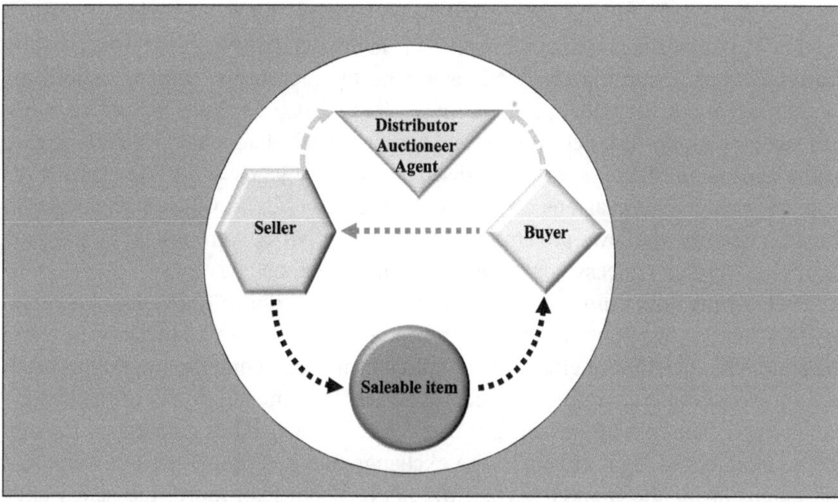

Figure 8.1 The market system

Source: Author's elaboration

'kinds of market process'; it is well-structured when the market organisation calls for an additional participant who runs the exchange, as the auctioneer in the sale at auction, the distributor, or an agent (see Figure 8.1).

Given the definition and the representation of the market, the in-depth analysis of its nature follows from the stylised facts presented by the previous historical review. The fact that the commercial and financial markets have always operated in accordance with habitual or legal rules resulting from long building processes shows the institutional nature of the market; both the contract and the market organisation provide behavioural rules that have been created and have evolved to find a solution to the problems emerging in the actual exchange activities. Such rules are nothing but operating routines implementing 'social institutions' (Swedberg 1994) that, as such, are characterised by 'mental representation', 'temporal dimension' and 'learning-by-doing acquisition' (Antonelli and Teubal 2012: 549). As they are co-ordinated to create a logical, consistent, and aimed set, they constitute an organisation that sometimes takes the shape of a dedicated corporation, as in the case of the stock exchange or of auction houses or other centralised facilities.

That the markets are historical institutions created and evolved through dialectics between the businesspersons and the political authorities to support the expansion of trade and production is confirmed by historical analyses. Sometimes the commercial rules were different from the civil ones because of the empowerment of merchants, sometimes they must be extracted from the civil code, and sometimes they were created by the states for their political aims. In fact, when the market managed by the domestic merchants corresponded to the territory of the political/administrative authority it was ruled by the regulations governing the relations among the citizens (Roman civil law, Muslim regulations[8]) and the international ones by the agreements signed among the political/administrative authorities. When the exchanges managed by the domestic merchants overshot the national territories, they were ruled by the regulations governing the relations among the merchants, sometimes fostered by political authorities (the *lex mercatoria*, *World Trade Organisation Agreement*). Instead, when long-distance commercial activity was a state matter, like in the case of the expansion of Rome, or of the discovery of new lands in the Mercantilist era or of the colonialist invasions carried out by the newly industrialised economies in the 19th century, the laws governing the trading activities were issued by the state through sovereign concessions or national commercial codes.

That the incompatibility between state and market doesn't have any historical bedrock, and on the contrary the coevolution processes between the economy and the state have been more effective and efficient for the economic upgrading when both powers cooperate rather than compete, are fundamental points of the historical analysis. The role of the state has been basic because it has guaranteed for sure the economic and legal effects of the exchange and has promoted and supported the extension of the market beyond the national borders; more, the states have favoured the whistle-stop route leading to a supranational economic entity (like the 'globalised exchanges') to which they have delegated their typical prerogatives like the redistribution of income. In light of this insight into the nature of the market, an updated and wider definition can be proposed:

> 'the market' is a landless entity expanding itself in a virtual space limited by the domain of the exchange rules agreed by contracting parties. National security and welfare are warranted on the market (thus also on the territory of other nation states) when the international market power is held by domestic suppliers or buyers. So, the market, extending itself irrespective of the state borders, on one hand is more powerful than territory occupation in promoting the interests of a national economy, and on the other is more influential in endorsing the expansion of international trade agreements. This change in the strategy of powers, enabling them to govern the world scenarios and to gain security and welfare without occupying territories, marks the shift from geo-politics to geo-economics, that is to 'the interaction of economics and finance with global political and security considerations'.
>
> (Romagnoli and Mengoni 2014: 30)

As a consequence of this definition the market presents an additional function to those enabling the working of the economic system through the exchange and of achieving the material aims of the society: the pursuit of the national economic interests beyond the state borders.

The distribution channel and the market process

To better understand how the markets enable the economic system to work, and in particular how they connect production with consumption, it is necessary to analyse the 'distribution channel' – that is, the chain of intermediate markets managed by professional traders through which a good or service passes, once let out from the production firm, until it reaches the end consumer. Although getting increasingly complex, such a chain generally presents key players having specific roles and expertise: the producer, the distributor, the wholesaler, and the retailer. The commercial brokering between the producer and the wholesaler is made by a 'distributor', who is an independent agent whose mandate is to make known the represented output to the seeking merchants and to put on the producer to the wholesaler. The distributor couldn't have in its portfolio competing outputs of different producers, and sometimes he has the exclusivity of a specific brand, or he is required to have the wares stocked in store; as he is a broker, his reward for the working activity is a fee. The 'wholesaler' is a businessperson who buys, through the brokerage of a distributor, a large amount of goods or services from a producer at a discount price to stockpile and sell them in smaller quantities to the wholesalers of lower levels or to retailers at a higher price. He can be specialised in specific goods and services or trade several of them, and sometimes he wraps them to get them ready for retail. Retail is the last step of the distribution channel connecting the 'retailer' to the customer through the sale contract. The markets constituting the distribution channel represent the path from the business to the consumer made by the goods and services, but there is another chain of markets to provide the producers with the materials and semi-finished products, the business-to-business way; in this case the transactions are made by producers and represent the interfirm relations resulting from the strategies of production (see Chapter Six).

The structural function of the distribution channel in the economic system is to ensure the delivery of outputs from the producers to the end users and of payments for them conversely. From the operational point of view the distribution channel represents the logistics of consumption that is the way by which the provision of goods and services for the consumption markets works. Thus, the wholesale markets must allot these flows in an effective manner, avoiding the imbalances between the goods and services demanded and those supplied at any transfer of the wares; otherwise, such imbalances create sudden changes in the prices. The establishment and the management of the slop chests by the wholesaler at any level of transfer compensate for these imbalances and prevent short-medium term distresses to the economy, but they also increase the storage costs and then the price of the consumer goods. However, in a phase of world economic growth and structural transformations, like that experienced during the first two decades of the 21st century, the excess demand for goods and services couldn't be satisfied by the supply at the different levels of the distribution channel: only a generalised increase in the prices could complete the transactions.

The structural dynamics of the distribution channel depend on the balance of power among the businesspersons who manage it, and in particular between the producers and the wholesalers and the wholesalers and the retailers. The producers must sell their products in the shortest possible time to avoid unsold stock just as the retailers do; thus, they respectively apply a discount or the minimum selling price. The wholesalers have the market power in all the levels of transaction given that the markup system (a pricing strategy consisting in adding a percentage of value to the cost paid to obtain the selling price) is generally used along the distribution channel for the determination of the selling price. Moreover, as each intermediate market of the chain presents few sellers than buyers, such players enjoy further market power in determining their selling prices. Such structure of the distribution channel is a cause of potential conflicts between the wholesalers and the producers on the one hand and between the wholesalers and the retailers on the other hand; such a conflict can result in a structural change of the balance of power in favour of one of the extremes of the distribution channel. Some retailers, like the department stores, convenience stores, supermarkets or outlets, to face their structural position that reduces the prospective market and squeezes their market surplus, have tried to shorten the distribution channel by buying directly from the producers through a distributor. Similarly, sometimes producers have tried to reduce the chain to seize more market surplus by selling to the consumers if the productive sector made this system feasible.

With the introduction of the internet, a lot of e-commerce providers have emerged, sometimes as distributors mediating directly between the producers and the consumers, some as dealers. Such retailing system (including business to business, B2B; business to customer, B2C; and customer to customer, C2C) has rapidly developed in the last decade, recording an increase in global e-commerce sales between the 2015 to 2020, equal to 140 per cent, that is estimated in 2025 equal to 550 per cent, and a share of total retail sales worldwide from 20 per cent to 25 per cent in the period (Statista accessed the 30 of May 2022). This strategy caused the emergence of big world e-commerce B2C companies (see Figure 8.2) that, aiming at reducing the retailing prices and increasing their profits, squeeze the gross operating revenues of producers forcing them to fail; this is because they are fewer than the producers, and this gives them additional market power.

The wholesale and retail markets are different with respect to the way by which they work. The taxonomy that puts in evidence such a feature and enables distinguishing different 'forms of market' is based on the 'market process' – that is, on the

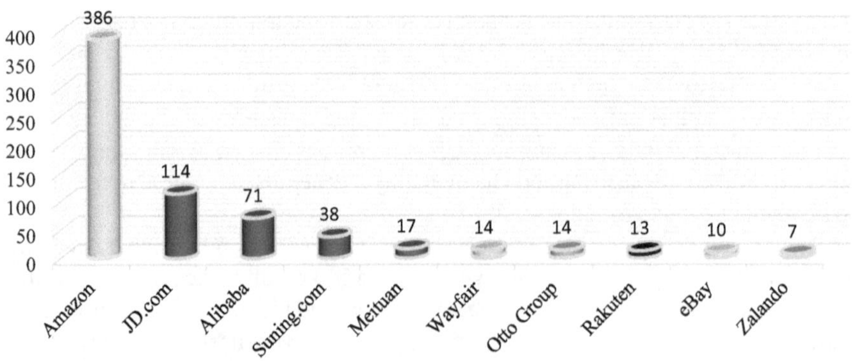

Figure 8.2 Top 10 world e-commerce B2C companies by revenue USA $

Source: Author's elaboration from *Statista* accessed the 13 June 2022.

ways by which the operations of negotiation, deal and execution of the contractual obligations necessary to complete a transaction are performed. The market process starts when the buyer, once deciding on the kind of good or service satisfying its requirement and the kind of vendor that can provide it, enters the marketplace (a shop, an open market, an agency, a bank, an online market or a centralised facility, wholesale store, etc.). The organisation and operation of a market processes (the forms of market) depend first on the amount of traded goods and services, then on the number of players carrying out the process, on their roles in it, and on the clauses of the contract. Concerning the first element, it's important to distinguish the wholesale from the retail market because in the first case both the buyer and the seller are businessmen engaged in exchanging lots of wares to resell (stockist, trader, storekeeper), while in the second case one of them is a customer and the other is a retailer trading in units of a consumer good. In addition, wholesale is an economic activity consisting of a sequence of markets whose processes sometimes need the intervention of other kinds of markets (namely financial ones) to conclude the transactions, while retail is an economic activity consisting of only one exchange (the selling by instalments excluded). Inside each category of exchange different kinds of market processes are implemented that diversify the other features intervening in its organisation and operation.

Forms of market and pricing in retailing and wholesale

There are different ways to exchange goods and services in retailing that amount to as much as kinds of market process. The 'bilateral trade' represents the specimen of the business deal because the market process is jointly carried out by both parties. Its organisation consists of two players (buyer and seller) who on their own look for the counterpart and carry out all the operations of the process. The central step of the market process is the negotiation between the parties, which include the respective examination of the item under transaction and the haggling over it; once agreed on the price and on the other terms of the exchange (delivery of the good or fulfilment of the service and terms of payment) the consent of the parties is reached, and the transaction takes place. Such a transaction can be carried out everywhere without any formality, but it must respect the regulations about the marketable items and the purchase agreement law. Bilateral trade has been practised widely in traditional societies for both wholesale and retail transactions, and it is still diffused in Asian and African countries; its exemplary representation for retail is the bazaar or the Suk of Muslim societies. However, it stays alive in some open markets or local fairs in advanced countries and in the transactions between private citizens regarding flats, second-hand cars, jewellery, antiquities and vintage objects. Such a kind of market, displaying the free will of the contracting parties, results in an economic advantage for both in the case of a deal; in fact, being the seller aware of the price under which he will lose and the buyer of the maximum price he is willing to pay, the agreed price will be in this range if the transaction will take place. At the market price, in addition to 'seller surplus', also 'buyer surplus' can emerge if the market price is lower than what the buyer is willing to pay.

A second consequence of the bilateral trade market is that the same good or service is paid different prices by the customers; this is the result of the practice of a bilateral monopolist market power by the trading parties, and of differences in willingness to pay among buyers in view of a constant minimum price of the seller.

The process characterising the 'posted price market' is the most practised in retail trade (e-commerce included) in medium-higher income economies. It is like that of the bilateral trade market regarding the players, but it doesn't either include the negotiation or allow the change of the general terms of the contract; in fact, the single price of the for sale item ('posted price') is decided and exhibited by the seller, as if to say 'Take it or leave it', and the transaction takes place upon the request of the item with the system 'immediate delivery upon payment'. Since such kind of market doesn't allow to defer the payment, the sale agreement for durable consumer goods (appliances, furniture, cars) is connected to a loan contract with payment by instalments. In the case of purchase agreements for real estates from a company or of services from financial or insurance enterprises, the contract will be promoted by the intervention of an agent paid by a fee. The economic literature has for a long compared the bilateral trade market and the posted price market debating the consequences on the division of the so called 'market surplus'[9] deriving from the different degrees of negotiation freedom allowed to the buyer in those markets (Cason, Friedman and Milam 2003). Beyond the different conclusions of the scholars, when the transaction is made in the second kind of market, all the customers pay the same price. Although the transaction occurs in a situation of monopolistic market power of the seller that establishes the unit 'market surplus', a buyer surplus can emerge if the market price (or posted price) is lower than the buyer is willing to pay.

The 'auction', implemented both in the end and intermediate markets, is a market process presenting different kinds of negotiation that enable different behaviours to the three players taking part in the process. In the general form the market at auction presents a seller who is the owner of the item put up for sale (generally having a 'reservation price' below which he is unwilling to sell), an auctioneer who is a broker managing the transaction through the competitive bidding process (by posting asks and receiving bids) and the execution of the trade, and the buyer who is the bidder having a 'buy reservation price' (that is the price above which he is unwilling to pay). This is the typical kind of market used to trade real estate, antiquities and artwork and to carry the judicial sales and tender bidding for public works. As the opening bid generally represents a selling reservation price, the seller gains a 'market surplus', but the buyer can also enjoy a buyer surplus if the auction price is lower than the buyer is willing to pay. In wholesale such a kind of market is used both to sell wares batches of different producers or of the auctioneer who, in this case, acts as a dealer.

Considering the three kinds of markets just examined some shared characteristics emerge: each transaction is always a singular independent event that cannot influence the performance of the market (quantity and price), the market power is always exercised by the seller, and the buyer enjoys a surplus in the exchange only when the market price is lower than his willing to pay. The last feature has grabbed

Table 8.1 Forms of market

Forms of markets		*Participants*	*Types of markets*
Wholesale markets	Auction market	Auctioneer, wholesalers	Goods
	Exchange market	Brokers	Goods, fin. serv.
	Over the counter market	Traders	Goods, fin. serv.
	Bilateral trade market	Brokers, dealers	Goods, services
Retailer markets	Auction market	Buyer, seller, auctioneer	Goods
	Bilateral trade market	Buyer, seller	Goods, services
	Over the counter market	Dealers, clients	Financial services
	Posted price market	Retailer, consumer	Goods, services

Source: Author's elaboration

the eye of the sellers trying to take over the maximum share of the buyer surplus by determining a selling price closer to what the buyer is willing to pay. Sometimes this strategy has been applied using the product advertisement that, giving information on the qualities of the object, connects the one willing to pay to the posted price. But the most used trading technique is price discrimination.

Price discrimination is a strategy for selling price fixing, consisting in the positioning of the customers in groups based on certain attributes and in posting the price of a particular good or service near the alleged customers of each group who are willing to pay. The result is a different price paid by the customers for the same good or service and a seller market surplus that also includes the buyer surplus. There are three different ways of applying this strategy:

i. First-degree price discrimination is a seller strategy aiming at price personalisation that consists in posting a price just equal to what the buyer is willing to pay. Although it is a theoretical situation leading to perfect price discrimination, it is applied in the internet search engines or advertisement positioning that, requiring higher prices for better exposures, convinces the customer to buy the position corresponding to what the customer is willing to pay.
ii. Second-degree price discrimination occurs when the consumers choose to consume a good or enjoy a service in the way or in the condition for which the posted price corresponds to what the customer is willing to pay. It is the case of the 'multiple prices of train and flight tickets, hotel rooms, or of the 'nonlinear prices and pay as you go rates' for internet providers or telephone companies. Other cases are the 'versioning' or the goods and services having small differentiations to validate different prices (like hardback and paperback books and movie or theatre tickets).
iii. Third-degree price discrimination consists in posting different prices depending on socio-economic categories of consumers (old and young people, students, and conscription soldiers).

In the wholesale marketplace the more frequent market processes are those implemented by traders 'over the counter' (OTC) and in 'exchange markets'. The over the counter is a decentralised market without a physical location and formalities where the market process is carried out by the dealers who trade not listed stocks (securities, merchandise and real estates) directly through computer networks and phones; it is used to avoid the fees, the transaction control and the cost of regulatory requirements. The 'exchange market' presents instead a centralise and regulated trading process, organised in specific stock exchanges, wherein listed stocks (securities, merchandise and real estate) are traded between buyers and sellers who, by purchasing and vending them, determine their price, supported by a clearing-house that settles the transactions trying to prevent speculations.

The exchanges in the wholesale markets are more complex than the retailing ones because the delivery of the good can occur after a while since the contract drafting due to the time needed for its production and/or transport. If this span lasts a few days, the payment is immediate (spot transaction); if it goes on for months or even years the payment is deferred (forward or future transactions). Thus, in the second case the businesspersons need to establish in advance the sale terms and conditions to hedge the value of the wares from the price changes[10]; this is generally made by establishing a selling price on delivery and committing to pay the difference between it and the spot price on that date, from the buyer to the seller if the sport price will be lower than the established one, and from the seller to the buyer if the spot price will be higher.

The recent globalisation of the markets increased the trading risks in the wholesale and made the hedging more complex; in addition, the risk offsetting ended up affecting the spot prices of goods and services because of the financial contracts connected to the transaction of specific wares like commodities. The 'commodities' are basic goods and raw materials that are exchanged as qualitative interchangeable items in each category (fungible goods); thus, they are not distinguishable with respect to the producer. They are grouped into three major categories: agriculture (including sugar, cocoa, coffee, live cattle and pork, cotton and lumber), energy (crude oil, gasoline, natural gas, heating oil and electricity), and metals (gold, copper, silver and platinum). As the production of such goods depends on the climate conditions in some cases (as the agricultural goods), or on the political conditions in some others (like the energetic and the mineral materials), and as sea shipping is sometimes subject to glitches due to the global health and climate, shortages and excesses in the inventories are frequent, although the wholesaler stockpile them at the end of the harvest or gradually along the year to be ready at the moment of the consumption climax. In addition, not all commodities can be stored because of their perishability, so in these wholesale markets the imbalances between the demand and the supply are recurrent. These events cause fluctuations in the prices that join the exchange rate fluctuations and freight rates too. To offset such price volatility some accessory financial contracts have been introduced that actually free the wholesale market prices from the production conditions (then from the supply and the excess demand conditions) and expose them to speculation, as we will see later.

The financial markets

The financial markets are sets of regulated or informal exchanges of saleable financial services – that is, of tradable securities by which the economic subjects can manage their deposited savings, invest their savings for a short or long time, lend money, borrow money, hedge or speculate. Such transactions are carried out by centralised licenced organisations (generally companies like the stock exchange) or decentralised ones (like banks), but also by informal web networks. The market processes carrying out such businesses are the 'over the counter' and the 'exchange market'. The traded financial instrument identifies the specific financial market; thus, the money deposit account is managed in the 'money market', the currencies are exchanged in the 'foreign exchange market – FOREX', the certificates of title in the 'stock market', the certificates of loan in the 'bond market', the certificates that manage financial risks in the 'derivatives market' (Table 8.2).

The 'money market' is constituted by a set of decentralised exchanges of short-term securities carried out by dealers (banks or businessmen) who buy and sell 'over the counter' to provide themselves, people, governments, and companies with low-cost financing for a short time. All the traded securities (more than 10 different types) are safe and highly liquid; thus, they are easily interchangeable for money. To raise financial capital for their lending activity the banks provide people and companies with saving accounts ('money market accounts') at low interest rates, but when they need short-term cash (with redemption at 6 to 12 months) they issue the 'certificates of deposit' having a higher interest rate and lower liquidity. The lending activity is generally concentrated in trading 'money market funds' – that is, in purchasing short-term instruments issued by corporations to finance payroll and inventories ('commercial papers') or short-term securities issued by the state to

Table 8.2 Types and features of financial markets

Types of financial markets	*Market process*	*Financial services or instruments*
Money market	Over the counter	Money market accounts Certificate of deposit Money market funds
Foreign exchange market	Over the counter	Currencies
Stock market	Stock exchange Regulated over the counter	Equities (stocks, shares)
Bond market	Stock exchange Over the counter	Private and treasury bonds Mortgage-backed bonds Pension fund bonds Insurance fund bonds
Derivatives market	Stock exchange Over the counter	Futures Forwards Swaps Options

Source: Author's elaboration

finance public debt ('treasury bills') or in pledging short-term debts of corporations and institutions ('bankers' acceptance').

The 'foreign exchange market' is the set of the world transactions of currency pairs carried out by currency brokers in decentralised marketplaces (currency trading platforms[11]) through the over-the-counter-market process. The participants in the market, who are dealers selling a currency to buy another needed currency, can be differently motivated: the commercial and investment banks act on behalf of their clients involved in international trade and business and the national central banks try to control their currency value, the companies want to hedge the value of their activities in foreign countries, and the individual traders speculate from the different prices of a currency. The price of one currency in terms of another one (the exchange rate) can be fixed when one country pegs its currency to an anchor currency or floating when it is the result of the total amount of demanded and supplied currency.[12] Starting from the end of the gold standard in 1971, all the countries chose one between the two systems: the developing countries generally chose the fixed exchange rate to have exchange rates more stationary, while the developed ones the floating exchange rates to use the monetary policy to develop the economies. As for the 10 countries under consideration in this book, all of them present floating exchange rates except the Chinese Renminbi, which is pegged to the value of a basket of other currencies. Starting from the 1970s the foreign exchange market increased the number of transactions, so much so that today it is the largest financial market in the world. Table 8.3 presents the top eight most traded currencies.

The 'stock market' is a centralised and organised set of exchanges, carried out formally by professional licenced stockbrokers selling and buying listed equities of public companies through the market process modalities of the stock exchanges and the regulated over the counter. The stockbrokers having access to the transactions in person and electronically are the market makers – that is, the subjects that

Table 8.3 The top 8 most traded currencies measured by the daily turnover in 2019

Currency	*Code*	*Symbol*	*Share*
United States dollar	USD	US$	88.3
Euro	EUR	€	32.3
Japanese yen	JPY	円/¥	16.8
Pound sterling	GBP	£	12.8
Australian dollar	AUD	A$	6.8
Canadian dollar	CAD	C$	5.0
Swiss franc	CHF	CHF	5.0
Renminbi	CNY	元/¥	4.3
Other pairs			28.7
Total			200.0*

Source: Author's elaboration from https://www.bis.org/statistics/rpfx19_fx.pdf

* As each currency is traded in pairs because to exchange currency α for β, α must be sold to buy β, each currency share also includes all the other currencies sold to obtain it; thus, the total sum is 200 per cent.

provide the 'bids' and 'asks' for a particular security. These authorised broker-dealers, whose business is trading securities for their own accounts or on behalf of their customers, can be a person, a company and a business unit of commercial and investment banks. The traded equities are shares of the capital stock of a company endowing the owner with the pro-quota full property right, with the participation of the management through the shareholders' meeting and the profit distribution. The equity quotation is the result of the buying requests and selling supplies for each security at quoted prices. The participants in the stock market are individual investors, banks, insurance companies, pension funds and hedge funds that want to invest their savings, increase the value of the funds they manage, hedge their investments, and speculate.

The 'bond market' is a centralised and organised set of exchanges carried out formally by professional stockbrokers selling and buying debt securities through the market process modalities of the stock exchanges and of a regulated over the counter. The market is like the stock exchange except for the security issued and traded – that is, a debt instrument of a borrower (seller) that commits to a lender (buyer) to pay an 'annual interest rate' in percentage of the 'face value' that will be refunded at the 'maturity date'. The issuers of a bond are the companies that want to finance current operations or new investments and the governments that had to finance the budget deficits: they issue private bonds or Treasury bonds in the primary market. The traders of bonds, besides the transaction of these financial instruments, can also exchange those issued in the secondary market by the mutual funds pooling the homebuyer debts (mortgage-backed bonds), by the pension funds collecting the workers' retirement accounts (pension fund bonds), and by insurance companies managing the life insurance policies.

The 'derivatives market' is a set of exchanges, carried out through the market process modalities of the stock exchanges and of the over the counter, between two parties trading financial instruments based on one or more underlying assets or benchmarks. The underlying assets can be stocks, bonds, commodities, currencies, interest rates, and market indexes. They are traded by the holders to hedge a position (for protection against risks), to give leverage to holdings (to strengthen financial operations), or to speculate on the trend of the underlying asset. The futures, the forward, the swap, and the options are the most common types of derivatives. The futures are standardised sale contracts involving the purchase and delivery of an asset at a future date at a fixed price.[13] The forward is an unregulated sale contract traded in the over the counter; thus, it is riskier. The swap is a derivative connected to a benchmark (for example, to an interest rate) that is traded to change a cash flow connected to a loan in another (for example, a variable interest rate in a fixed one). The option is a derivative similar to the future, but the buyer isn't obliged to buy or sell: it is used to affect the price of the underlying asset. As the buying and selling of derivatives depend on the expectations of the changes in the price of the underlying asset, they end up affecting the price of the asset itself; in fact, the derivatives are traded every day and in some wholesale markets as those of commodities their expected prices are used as the current price of the transactions.

Concluding remarks: The market as the transmission belt of capitalist economies

The stylised facts recorded by the historical investigation on the markets and the in-depth analysis of the ways by which they are carried out show on one the hand that the concept of market prevailing nowadays completely distorts the truth and on the other hand that its current functioning is largely unknown. Thus, some diffused beliefs about it must be challenged, starting from its placement in the capitalist economy. The market isn't the core of the capitalist economy, but rather the transmission belt channelling the resources to the production and allowing the meeting of the outputs with the people needs: as such the market is a gear train of the economic system. The market doesn't consist of instantaneous acts but in process activities managed by routines that, being institutions, reflect the historical features of the societies. The institutional nature of the market sets something straight about the antinomy market-state; in fact, given this feature and the subset position held by the market in the economic system, such a contrast doesn't exist. Instead, there is evidence of a proactive role of the state in the market building and upgrading as the economic conditions changed.

As to the transactions occurring on the market some common ideas must be disputed. A market transaction isn't a simple economic exchange because it involves a legal transfer and two commitments for the contracting parts; thus, it is a complex process carried out in different ways that implement changes in the distribution of resources in the economy. The transaction is an individual economic action where contracting parties come face to face; the buyer entering the market doesn't interplay with the other people who have bought or will buy other units of the same sealable item.[14] Therefore, the number of players in both contracting parties (buyers and sellers) that defines the so-called 'forms of market' (perfect competition, monopoly, etc.) doesn't matter, also because the market power is mainly in the hands of the seller. The market demand in retailing loses importance too, as all the goods and services are exchanged using the posted price form of the market, and the producers/sellers try to identify the consumers willing to pay to apply the price discrimination strategy.

The capitalist economy is not able to leave the market out of consideration, but the market effectiveness and efficiency depend, likewise what happens for whatever mechanism, on the fine-tuning of the builder and of the manager; in that case it is a matter of the state's legislative power jointly with economic powers.

Notes

1 There are other concepts of market in the handbooks: a) the market is an 'abstract and natural' notion emerging from the fact that if transactions are present in everyday life, some underlying markets must exist; b) the market is a homogeneous and undifferentiated entity, constituted by a multiplicity of consenting buyers and sellers contractually committed and by the exchanges among them, aiming at transferring the ownership or property rights over a good or a service in return for money; c) the markets are the devices to reduce the transaction costs and thus to facilitate exchanges (Coase 1988); d) the market is the device favouring division of labour, innovation the learning process,

and economic growth (Smith 1776). The first is a tautological statement while the other ones identify some features and consequences of the market instead of its nature.

2 A mediator is a person independent from the parts who tries to fulfil the exchange; an agent is a person who acts on the seller's behalf to fulfil the exchange.

3 'This contract was first and foremost used in agriculture and formed part of the husbandry of the great landowners and the public bodies that let out land, and where also land labourers were hired. . . . The Roman state farmed out public works and provisioning of the armies and public distributions. Because of the size of these contracts, their commercial interest must have been great. Further, cargo and passenger space on ships was let or rented and was also the object of commercial activity; and all kinds of artisanal production were done by way of this contract' (Sirk 2018: 71).

4 Initially the Lombard merchants in the 9th century in North Italy advanced to farmers the value of the crop yield reduced by a fee for the risk, thus lending to sustain production costs.

5 Before 1600 when commercial ventures were organised the financial investment was accumulated through the sale of parts of the needed capital. The merchants, by investing in several ships, could reduce their economic risk. Starting from the creation of the Dutch and British East India Companies the investors bought shares of the company and not of individual voyages.

6 The 'service contract' is an agreement between a client and the executor of a service or a producer. The outcome of the activity of the executor is specified in the terms and conditions of the contract that includes the outline of the service or work, its timeline, the compensation terms, the insurance, the indemnification, the warranty and default terms, and the dispute resolution.

7 The term 'market process' is used to identify the procedure performed to complete the sale contract. It has nothing to do with the concept of the market process used by the Austrian School to represent the behaviour of the individual agent (in particular the entrepreneur) working in a market economy whose attitude can be favourably inclined to the 'discovery' or the 'creation' (see Sandye Gloria-Palermo 1999).

8 The Muslim commercial regulations represented a special case because, complying with the *Quran* and *Shariya* principles accepted by all the Muslim societies/states, they were at the same time private and public rules. Similarly, they were applied both inside and outside the Muslim territories for a long period because they were more favourable to the commercial activities than the Christian and Jewish regulations.

9 The 'market surplus' (or seller surplus) is the difference between the price paid by the buyer for a good or service and the price paid to stock them by the seller in the wholesale market – that is, the difference between the market price and the seller reservation price. If the market price is lower than the buyer reservation price, in addition to a market surplus for the seller a buyer surplus can emerge in the bilateral trade market because of the haggle, but also in the posted price and at auction markets.

10 In the medium and long term, the price changes can derive from the cost of raw materials, energy resources, insurance and freights as well as from the change of the exchange rates.

11 'A currency trading platform is a software interface provided by currency brokers to their customers to give them access as traders in the FOREX markets. This may be an online, web-based portal, mobile app, a standalone downloadable program, or any combination of the three'. https://www.investopedia.com/terms/forex/c/currency-trading-platforms.asp

12 Notice that a certain amount of the currency α is demanded by offering a corresponding amount of the currency β, and a certain amount of the supplied currency α corresponds to a request of a certain number of other currencies (β, γ, etc.).

13 'For example, say that on Nov. 6, 2021, Company A buys a futures contract for oil at a price of $62.22 per barrel that expires Dec. 19, 2021. The company does this because it needs oil in December and is concerned that the price will rise before the company needs to buy. Buying an oil futures contract hedges the company's risk because the seller is obligated to deliver oil to Company A for $62.22 per barrel once the contract expires.

Assume oil prices rise to $80 per barrel by Dec. 19, 2021. Company A can accept delivery of the oil from the seller of the futures contract, but if it no longer needs the oil, it can also sell the contract before expiration and keep the profits' (Investopedia accessed the 1st July 2022).

14 This is also true in the selling action because only one saleable item is sold and only one will be the buyer; the competition among the prospective buyers is to make the highest price they are willing to pay required by the seller.

References

Antonelli, C. and Teubal, M. (2012) 'From the Corporation to Venture Capitalism: New Surrogate Markets for Knowledge and Innovation-led Economic Growth', in M. Dietrich and J. Krafft (eds.) *Handbook on the Economics and Theory of the Firm*, Cheltenham: Edward Elgar: 545–60.

Atack, J. (2009) 'Financial Innovations and Crises: The View Backwards from Northern Rock', in J. Atack and L. Neal (eds.) *The Origin and Development of Financial Markets and Institutions. From the Seventeenth Century to the Present*, Cambridge: Cambridge University Press: 1–31.

Caprara, U. (1940) 'L'evoluzione storica del commercio bancario: dal commercio di cambio al commercio di credito' ('The Historical Evolution of the Banking: From the Currency Exchange to the Credit Market'), in A. M. Galli (ed.) *La formazione e lo sviluppo del sistema bancario in Europa e in Italia (The Establishment and the Development of the Banking System in Europe and Italy)*, Milan: Vita e Pensiero, 1992: 26–62.

Cason, N. T., Friedman, D. and Milam, G. H. (2003) 'Bargaining Versus Posted Price Competition in Customer Markets', *International Journal of Industrial Organization*, 21: 223–51.

Coase, R. H. (1988) *The Firm, the Market, and the Law*, Chicago: The University of Chicago Press.

Coase, R. H. (1991) *The Institutional Structure of Production*, Nobel Prize Lecture, Stockholm: The Nobel Foundation.

Deakin, S. (2001) 'The Contract of Employment: A Study in Legal Evolution', *ESRC Centre for Business Research, Working Paper, No. 203*. https://www.cbr.cam.ac.uk/wp-content/uploads/2020/08/wp203.pdf

Graff, M., Kenwood, A. G. and Lougheed, A. L. (2014) *Growth of the International Economy, 1820–2015*, London: Routledge.

Hodgson, G. M. (2008) 'Markets', in M. Vernengo, E. P. Caldentey and B. J. Rosser Jr (eds.) *The New Palgrave Dictionary of Economics*, London: Palgrave Macmillan. https://doi.org/10.1057/978-1-349-95121-5_2113-1

James, H. (2014) 'International Capital Movements and the Global Order', in L. Neal and J. G. Williamson (eds.) *Capitalism. Volume II. The Spread of Capitalism: From 1848 to the Present'*, Cambridge: Cambridge University Press: 264–300.

Munro, J. H. (2003) 'The Medieval Origins of the Financial Revolution: Usury, Rents, and Negotiability', *The International History Review*, 25 (3): 505–62.

Nee, V. (2000) 'The Role of the State in Making a Market Economy', *Journal of Institutional and Theoretical Economics*, 156: 64–88.

Quinn, S. and Roberds, W. (2006) 'An Economic Explanation of the Early Bank of Amsterdam, Debasement, Bills of Exchange, and the Emergence of the First Central Bank', *Federal Reserve Bank of Atlanta Working Paper, No. 2006–13*. https://www.atlantafed.org/-/media/documents/research/publications/wp/2006/wp0613.pdf

Romagnoli, A. and Mengoni, L. (2014) *The Economic Development Process in The Middle East and North Africa*, Abingdon: Routledge.
Saleem, M. Y. (2013) *Islamic Commercial Law*, Singapore: John Wiley & Sons.
Sandye, G. (1999) 'Discovery Versus Creation: Implications of the Austrian View of the Market Process', in J. Groenewegen and J. Vromen (eds.) *Institutions and the Evolution of Capitalism: Implications and Evolutionary Economics*, Cheltenham: Edward Elgar: 78–91.
Sirks, B. (2018) 'Law, Commerce, and Finance in the Roman Empire', in A. Wilson and A. Bowman (eds.) *Trade, Commerce and the State in the Roman World*, Oxford: Oxford University Press: 53–116 (Kindle edition).
Smith, A. (1776) *Inquiry Into the Nature and Causes of the Wealth of Nations*, London: W. Strahan and T. Cadell.
Swedberg, M. (1994) 'Markets as Social Structures', in N. Smelser and M. Swedberg (eds.) *The Handbook of Economic Sociology*, Princeton: Princeton University Press: 255–82.

Glossary

Auction is a kind of market in which the transaction is carried out by a person (auctioneer) who manages the sale in the interest of the seller by announcing the lots, controlling the buyers' bidding and ending the contract with the highest bidder if the price is in line with the seller's expectation.

Broker is an agent who buys or sells for another.

Bilateral trade is a kind of market where two players (buyer and seller) on their own look for the counterpart and carry out all the operations of the process by respecting the legal rules established for the buying and selling.

Bilateralism is a form of coordination through an agreement between two trading countries that is designed to mutually grant preferential conditions about customs duties, quotas and no-tariff barriers. It may be asymmetrical because of the countries' bargaining power and endowment of the good exchanged.

Bond is a debt security issued in the bond market in the form of a promise (IOU, I Owe You) by a borrower (company, state) that commits to a lender (buyer) to pay an 'annual interest rate' in percentage of the 'face value' that will be refunded at the 'maturity date'.

Bond market (or debt market, credit market of fixed-income market) is a centralised and organised set of exchanges carried out formally by professional stockbrokers selling and buying debt securities through the market process modalities of stock exchanges. It can also be a decentralised and deregulated one when the exchanges are over the counter.

Buyer surplus is the difference between the market price paid by a buyer for a good or a service and the amount of money he would spend for it.

Capital market is the exchange of long-term securities issued by corporations (equities and bonds) and governments (bonds).

Commodities are basic goods and raw materials that are traded as qualitative interchangeable items (fungible goods) in each category (agriculture, energy and metals) and thus not distinguishable with respect to the producer.

Derivatives market is a set of exchanges between two parties of financial instruments based on one or more underlying assets or benchmarks, whose values depend on the changes in the price of the underlying asset.

Distribution channel is the chain of intermediate markets managed by professional traders through which a good or service passes once let out from the production firm until it reaches the end consumer.

Distributor is an independent agent of the distribution channel whose mandate is to make known the represented output to the seeking merchants and to put on the producer to the wholesaler. He couldn't have in its portfolio competing outputs.

Equity (or share, or stock) is an ownership security, issued in the capital market and representing a portion of a corporation stock, enabling the holder to participate in the management of the company through the shareholders' meeting and the profit's distribution.

Exchange is a kind of market process characterised by a centralised and regulated trading path, organised in specific stock exchanges wherein listed stocks (securities, merchandise and real estates) are traded between buyers and sellers determining their price supported by a clearinghouse that settles the transactions.

Foreign exchange market (FOREX or currencies market) is the set of world transactions of currency pairs carried out by currency brokers in decentralised marketplaces (currency trading platforms) through the over-the-counter market process.

Markup pricing is a strategy to determine the selling price that consists in adding a percentage of cost value to the expenses paid in inputs to obtain the price of a unit of output.

Market is a system of exchange activities for goods and services authorised and organised according to certain terms and conditions. It is the mechanism that makes the economic system work. It consists in sets of exchanges of a saleable item, specified regarding the quantity, the price and the secondary liabilities of the contracting parties that are carried out between two agreed subjects (the buyer, the seller) according to different market processes. The taxonomy of the markets can be made by species of saleable item (types of goods and services: commodities, financial products, etc.) or by the kind of market process.

Market cap (or capitalisation) is the total value of all outstanding shares of the companies listed on the stock exchange.

Market process is the ways by which the operations of the negotiation, deal and execution of the contractual obligations necessary to complete a transaction are performed. The different market processes give rise to markets as well: the bilateral trade, the posted price, the auction, the over the counter and the exchange market.

Market surplus (or seller surplus) is the difference between the market price and the seller reservation price (the price paid by the seller in the wholesale market).

Money market is constituted by a set of decentralised exchanges of short-term securities carried out by dealers (banks or businessmen) who trade 'over the counter' money market accounts, certificate of deposit and money market funds to provide themselves, people, governments and companies with low-cost financing for a short time.

Multilateralism is a form of coordination through an agreement collectively drafted by a group of trading countries, which is designed to establish the general rules ruling international trade in the collective interest. It is generally symmetrical unless one or more members can write the rules or have a veto power.

Over the counter is a kind of decentralised unregulated exchange process, without a physical location and formalities, carried out by the dealers who trade not listed stocks (securities, merchandise, and real estate) directly with the buyers through computer networks and phones.

Posted price is a kind of market process carried out by the seller, who posts the single price of the for-sale item with reservations 'take-it-or-leave-it' and brings into being the transaction on request with the system 'immediate delivery upon payment'.

Price discrimination is a strategy for selling price fixing, consisting in the positioning of the customers in groups based on certain attributes and in posting the price of a particular good or service near to the alleged price the customers of each group are willing to pay.

Securities are financial instruments holding monetary value exchanged in different financial markets according to their nature: the equities in the stock exchange, the bonds in the bond market and the options in the derivatives market.

Stock market is a centralised and organised set of exchanges, carried out formally by professional stockbrokers selling and buying listed equities of public companies through the market process modalities of the stock exchanges and the regulated over the counter.

Wholesaler is a businessperson who buys a mass of goods or services from a producer at a discount price and sells them at a higher price in smaller quantities to the wholesalers of lower levels or to retailers.

Willing to pay is the amount of money that a buyer can pay for a good or service.

Part III

The coordination of the economic relations among the states

The world economy

9 The world economy and the coordination of international exchanges

To study the spread of capitalism inside the evolution of the 'world economy' entails to clarifying the meaning of both expressions (Gereffi 2005). The 'world economy' is often defined as 'the system of industry and trade around the world that has developed as the result of globalisation (= the way in which economies have been developing to operate together as one system' – Cambridge Dictionary). Instead, the 'spread of capitalism' is considered as the result of the adoption of specific institutions in a context of open economies; in fact, 'the emergence of world capitalism as an *international economic system* required not only that the institutions of capitalism be introduced in the economies of all world participants, but also that those participants allowed a wide range of economic interactions to take place between them' (O'Rourke and Williamson 2014: 1). Both the definitions share the assumptions that the world economy is an economic organisation similar to the economic system and that its existence is due only to the adoption of capitalist institutions that, in turn, bring into being the globalisation. Differently from the economic system of a country, it's impossible to replicate at the international level the same relation existing between the national state and its economy (see Chapter Five), provided that it could be possible and desirable. In fact, the 'world economy' isn't a co-ordinated group of organisations and working procedures arranged and supported by a political/administrative authority to provide society with welfare by means of the economic process (see Chapter four). Neither the 'world economy' can be considered as an economic unit; in fact, the production activities are managed following the national institutions and the advantage of the national companies, even though the rules of international trade are, in the abstract, conceived as compliant with a higher common interest. Thus, the world economy is nothing but the result of the international agreements signed by the states to manage their international economic exchanges. As to the assumption that only when the capitalist institutional homogeneity has been achieved inside all the participants in the international trade the flows of goods and services have thrived, the historical stylised facts show that the implementation of commerce has required state agreements, not capitalist institutions. Only the progression of the capitalist economies and the drafting of international agreements to manage interstate economic relations can help to understand what the world economy is and the advancement it experienced in the time of capitalist evolution.

DOI: 10.4324/9781315679730-13

The international exchanges are therefore the driver of both the spread of capitalism and the evolution of the world economy. They supported the capitalist upgrading of both the advancing economies and a staggered sequence of countries that successfully introduced capitalist production processes. But they also made at the newcomer's disposal the physical, human, and financial resources, conveniently endowed with technological and institutional knowledge, to economically progress; thanks to international exchange some missing productive resources necessary to promote the adoption of capitalist production processes could be imported by the transition countries, and a possible financial capital accumulation could be brought about by traditional economies. Thus, international trade has been, at the same time, the cause both of the long-established capitalist countries growth' and of transient economies' development.

The spread of capitalism took advantage of the process that ferried international trade towards the trade areas. In this process the most decisive driving force has been the institution building and change. Such economic prerogative of the state has been implemented to sign agreements favouring the different forms of internationalisation of the exchanges (the trade regimes). The international agreements aimed at promoting the exchange of goods and financial services have been signed by the states also to protect the national economic interests; in this context such prerogative has been applied in association with other political ones, like the infliction of the receivership to the balance of the in arrears states, or the imposition of trade conditionalities or the trade sanctions to trade partners, and even the declaration of war. In any case the historical stylised facts show that the institution building and change processes, promoted by the economic powers to manage the international exchanges, have addressed the economic upgrading of both developed and developing countries towards specific 'international economic orders.' The emergence of such configurations of the 'world economy' followed one another from the introduction of capitalism throughout its evolution. Thus, the upgrading and the spread of capitalism and the configuration of the world economy must be analysed considering the agreements supporting the development of international trade and the resulting 'international economic order'.

The evolution of the world economy in the time of capitalism

If it is wrong to consider the world economy as like a national economic system, it can be correct to represent it as a system whose elements are the national economies and whose connections are the flows of goods, workers and financial services co-ordinated according to international institutions arranged by agreements among states. In this context the configuration of the world economy represents a specific 'state of the system', with specific conditions of the national economies and of their international economic relations; thus, the 'spread of capitalism' results from the transition from one state of the world economy system to the other (see Chapter Three). Such a process can be represented by the increase of the number of countries that have changed the structure of their economies, by the economic evolution of such economic players of the world economy and by the increase of international exchanges among them. Keeping in mind that such an upgrade of the economies is a gradual path chasing after a phenomenon advancing over and over again (that is, the evolution of capitalism), the new entries present degrees of capitalism increasing over time. Thus, the spread of capitalism generates at any one time a world economy characterised by a different intensity of 'capitalisation', because it includes both 'developed economies' and 'developing ones' having irreversible traits of capitalism. As to a first assessment of capitalism's spread and of the world economy's evolution, the development of countries and of international trade can show some trends.

The spread of capitalism in the world economy

If to look at the spread of capitalism within the evolution of the world economy it is necessary to consider the countries that have changed the structure of their economies, the group of countries put under consideration all throughout the book fits the purpose. In fact, it is representative of both the time sequence characterising the adoption of capitalism and the top ten economy rankings from the beginning of the period up to recently.[1] All the big economies adopting capitalism during the three waves that came in succession during the capitalist evolution are part of this group: the 'first comers' (UK, USA and France), the 'latecomers' (Italy, Germany and Japan), and the 'new entries' (BRIC – Russia,[2] Brazil, India and China). In addition, as these countries have been also the most populated ones for a long period between 1820 and 2021, the number of their inhabitants can provide, as a rough approximation, an indicator to measure the diffusion of capitalism in the world. So, the first step for an appraisal of the spread of capitalism is the analysis of the evolution of world population.

The demographic transition that occurred in the world during the last two centuries has produced a continuous increase of the world population and some staggered movements abroad of single migrants in search of better economic conditions. Both phenomena have influenced the world economic environment's weather for the countries introducing capitalism (as shown in the first part of the book) and for those approaching it, as well as for the traditional economies. Among the demographic powers bringing into being the growth of the world population there were, right from the beginning, the Asian countries China and India, as well as Russia, followed since 1913 by the United States and Japan and later by Brazil. According to historical statistics, between 1820 and 1990 the world population increase was a little bit more than five times, while between 1820 and 2021 it has been 7.5 times; the intensity of such a trend showed a doubling between 1913 and 1950 and a 50 per cent increment in the last 30 years. In this context the group of 10 countries under consideration represented the three-fourths of the world population (75.3 per cent) in 1820; the share declined as time went by up to 57.6 per cent in 1990 and 49.7 per cent in 2021 (see Tables 9.1 and 9.2).

Table 9.1 Population for a group of selected countries at the end of the periods (millions) between 1820 and 1990

	1820	*1870*	*1913*	*1950*	*1973*	*1990*
UK	21 226	31 393	45 649	50 363	56 223	57 561
USA	9 981	40 241	97 606	152 271	211 909	249 984
France	31 246	38 440	41 463	41 836	52 118	56 735
Germany	24 905	39 231	65 058	68 371	78 956	79 364
Italy	20 176	27 888	37 248	47 105	54 751	56 719
Japan	31 000	34 437	51 672	83 563	108 660	123 540
Russia	54 765	88 672	156 192	180 050	249 748	289 350
Brazil	4 507	9 797	23 660	53 443	103 463	151 040
India	209 000	253 000	303 700	359 000	580 000	839 000
China	381 000	358 000	437 140	546 815	881 940	1 135 185
World	1 041 834	1 271 915	1 791 091	3 524 324	3 916 489	5 280 000

Source: Author elaboration from Maddison (2003) *The World Economy. Historical statistics*, Paris: *OECD, Table A1-a, A2-a, A3-a, 8a.*

Table 9.2 Population for a group of selected countries at the end of the periods (millions) between 1990 and 2021

	1990	*2007*	*2021*
UK	57 248	61 322	67 327
USA	249 623	301 231	331 894
France	58 236	64 016	67 499
Germany	79 433	82 266	83 129
Italy	56 719	58 438	59 066
Japan	123 478	128 001	125 682
Russia	147 969	142 805	143 446
Brazil	149 003	190 130	213 993
India	873 278	1 183 209	1 393 409
China	1 135 185	1 317 885	1 412 360
World	5 280 063	6 674 182	7 836 631

Source: Author's elaboration from *World Bank, World development indicator database*, accessed August 25, 2022

Considering the share of the world population that each subgroup of capitalist countries showed in the three years chosen as the lookout, the 'first comers' represented, in 1820, 1990, and 2021 respectively, 6.0 per cent, 6.7 per cent, and 6.9 per cent of the world population. The values for the 'late comers' were 7.3 per cent, 4.9 per cent, and 3.4 per cent, and for the 'newcomers' 62.4 per cent, 45.8 per cent, and 40.4 per cent (see Figures 9.1 and 9.2). As the three groups of countries adopted the capitalist economy in different periods of the capitalist evolution, the resulting spread of capitalism measured on the bases of the world population shows this trend: in 1820, 6.0 per cent of the world population lived in 'capitalist' countries; in 1870, with the entry of the latecomers countries, the share increased

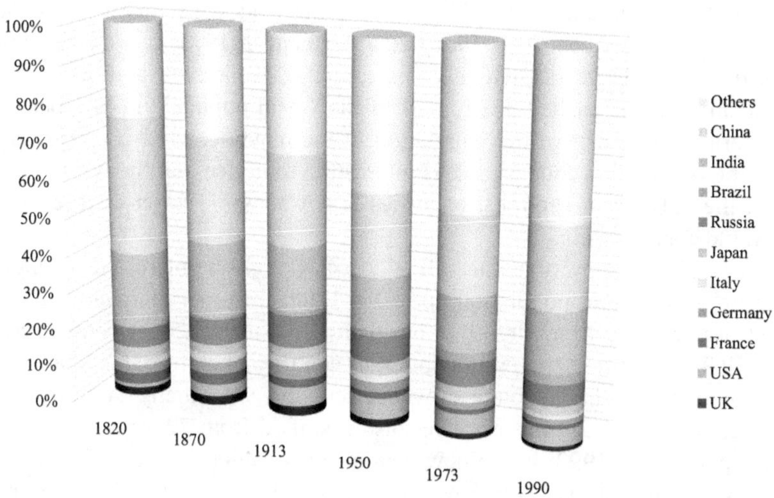

Figure 9.1 Shares of world population for a group of selected countries between 1820 and 1990

Source: Author elaboration from Maddison (2003) *The World Economy. Historical statistics*, Paris: OECD, Table A1-a, A2-a, A3-a, 8a

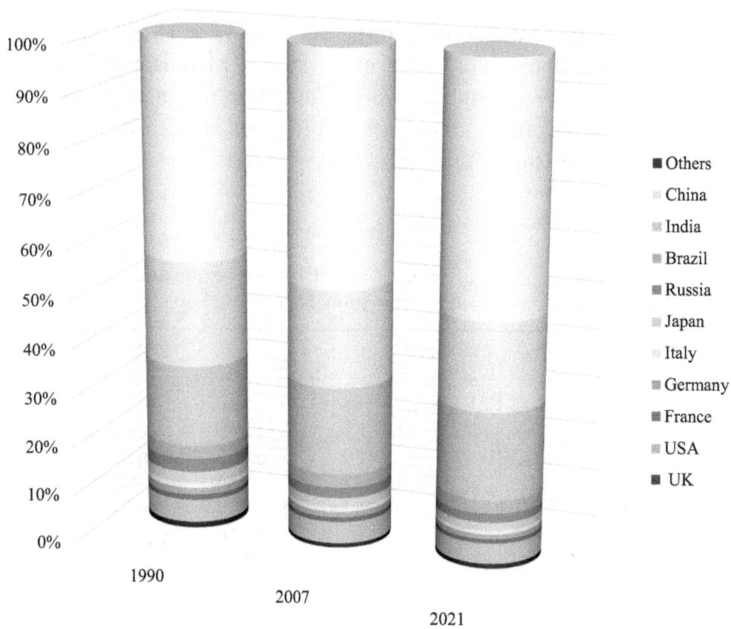

Figure 9.2 Shares of world population for a group of selected countries between 1990 and 2021

Source: Author's elaboration from *World Bank, World development indicator database*, accessed the 25th of August 2022

up to 16.7 per cent and later in 1913 to 27.5 per cent; after this peak the value declined to 24.7 per cent in 1950, to 20.7 per cent in 1973, to 17.3 per cent in 1990. In the last 30 years BRIC became capitalist economies, and the spread of capitalism in 2021 reached nearly half of the world population (49.7 per cent). Considering that a part of the population of the newly entered countries is still practising traditional economies, it is interesting to notice that the world population of the 'advanced' capitalist countries is nowadays 11.2 per cent, excluding China, India and Brazil.

Such statistics show that the diffusion of capitalism interested an increasing share of the world population up to 1913, but then this share slowed down; in fact, it decreased from slightly more than a quarter (27.5 per cent) to near a sixth (17.3 per cent) at the end of the 19th century. Therefore, the share of the world population living in countries whose economy was chiefly a traditional one increased during the 20th century because it shifted from 72.5 per cent in 1913 to 82.7 per cent in 1990; in the new century the development of BRIC reduced to nearly half of such share (50.3 per cent), but as 38.5 per cent of the population living in the group of capitalist countries is partially practising traditional economies, the spread of capitalism roughly reached just barely one-third of the world population (see Tables 9.1 and 9.2).

To appraise the contribution of capitalist economies to the world's economic evolution it is necessary to measure the growth of the GDP produced by such countries with respect to the world economy's GDP. There isn't a comprehensive historical series for all of the period, so the trend between 1820 and 1990 will be described using the country's GDP level elaborated by Maddison (Maddison 2003) and that of the last 30 years by the World Bank data. From the data it emerges that the world GDP has grown 48.6 times in 170 years and 3.6 in the last 30 years according to the World Bank[3] (see Tables 9.3 and 9.4).

Table 9.3 GDP level for a group of selected countries during the advent and evolution of capitalism (millions of 1990 international $)

	1820	*1870*	*1913*	*1950*	*1973*	*1990*
UK	36,232	100,179	224,618	347,850	675,941	944,610
USA	12,548	98,374	517,383	1,455,916	3,536,622	5,803,200
France	38,434	72,100	144,489	220,492	683,965	1,026,491
Germany	26,349	71,429	237,332	265,354	944,755	1,264,438
Italy	22,535	41,814	95,487	164,957	582,713	925,654
Japan	20,739	25,393	71,653	160,966	1,242,932	2,321,153
Russia	37,710	83,646	232,351	510,243	1,513,870	1,987,995
Brazil	2,912	6,985	19,188	89,342	401,643	743,765
India	111,417	134,882	204,241	222,222	494,832	1,098,100
China	228,600	189,740	241,344	239,903	740,048	2,109,400
World	694,442	1,101,369	2,704,782	5,336,101	16,059,180	33,725,635

Source: Author elaboration from Maddison (2003) *The World Economy. Historical statistics*, Paris: OECD, Table 8b

Table 9.4 PPP GDP level for a group of selected countries between 1990 and 2021 (billions of 2017 international $)

	1990	*2007*	*2021*
UK	1,787	2,712	3,087
USA	10,097	16,834	20,932
France	1,964	2,760	3,050
Germany	2,915	3,874	4,400
Italy	2,075	2,650	2,477
Japan	4,056	5,028	5,124
Russia	3,179	3,377	4,080
Brazil	1,567	2,579	3,127
India	1,583	4,332	9,301
China	1,616	8,955	24,861
World	51,241	90,205	133,857

Source: Author's elaboration from *World Bank, World development indicator database*, accessed July 29, 2022

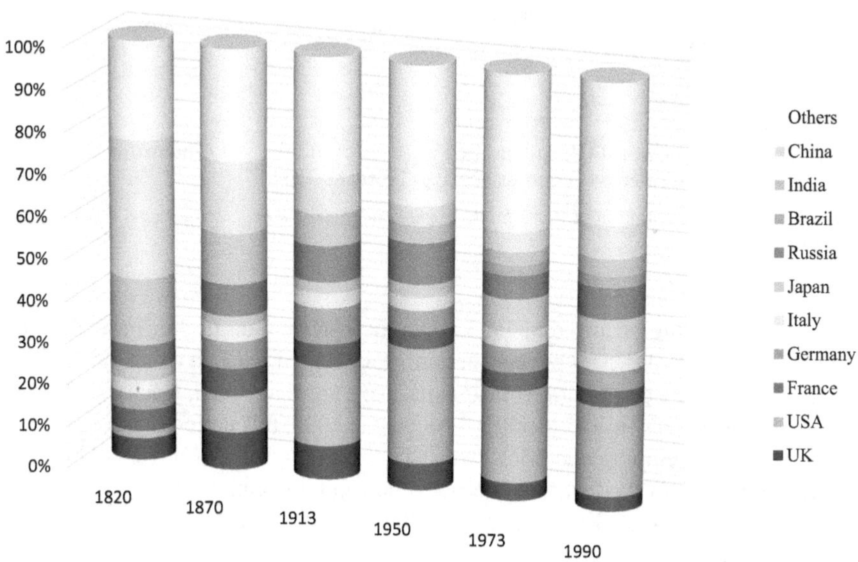

Figure 9.3 Shares of world GDP for a group of selected countries between 1820 and 1990

Source: Author's elaboration from Maddison (2001) *The World Economy. A millennial perspective*, Paris: OECD, Tables A-c, A1-b, A2-b, A3-b

At first glance, along the 19th century the contribution of the capitalist countries to the world GDP has been low, although growing, because it was 12.1 per cent in 1820 and 36.9 per cent in 1870 in view of that of traditional economies' (headed by the economic powers of the time, China, India and Russia), which was respectively 87.9 per cent and 63.1 per cent (see Figures 9.3 and 9.4). In the 19th century the

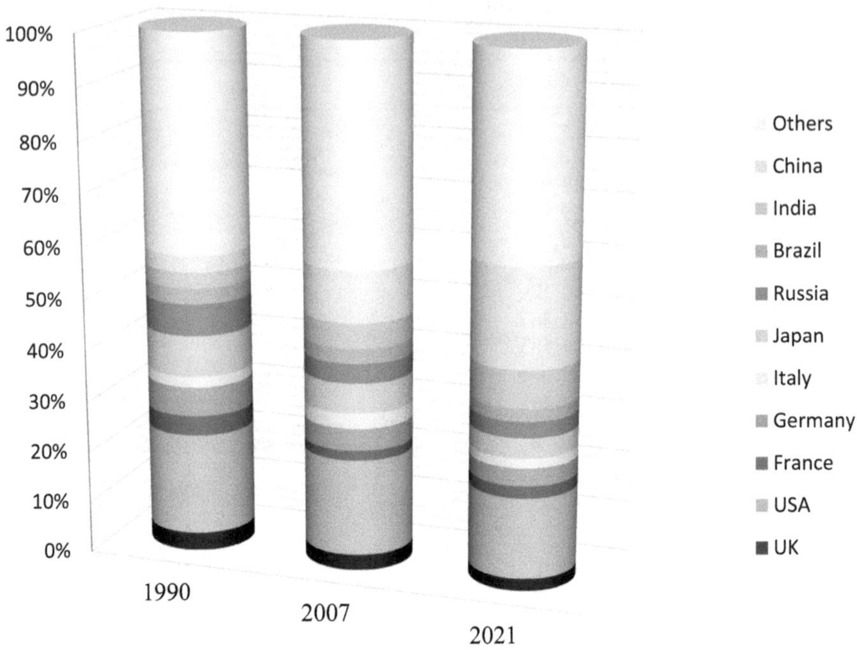

Figure 9.4 Shares of world GDP (measured in terms of PPP by 2017 international $) for a group of selected countries between 1990 and 2021

Source: Author's elaboration from *World Bank, World development indicators database*, accessed July 25, 2021

capitalist overtaking occurred in 1913 when the contribution to the world GDP of capitalist countries was 55.7 per cent and in 1950 when it reached a pick of 58.6 per cent. After 1950 the contribution of capitalist economies declined, reaching 53.3 per cent of the world GDP in 1973 and 49.5 per cent in 1990; this period registered came out on top of developing countries, whose contribution to the world GDP became more than a half. In the last three decades the capitalist contribution to the world GDP went back up to 61.3 per cent in 2021, thanks to the success of China, India and Brazil (whose shares are 19.1 per cent, 7.1 per cent and 2.4 per cent respectively).

In comparing the population levels and the GDP performance of the capitalist countries and of the world some conclusions emerge. The world economy has grown more than the population along the period under consideration, specifically 10 times up to 1990 and 1.4 times in the last 30 years. Between 1820 and 1913 the share of the capitalist population contributed to the world GDP for a double percentage compared to its size; this ratio increased to 2.4 times in 1950 and 2.7 times in 1973 and 1990, but it was 1.2 times in 2021 (2.9 times considering only the 'first comer' and 'latecomer' countries). This concentration of the economic power in developed countries, measured in terms of world GDP share compared to the share of world population, didn't prevent the overtaking by developing countries with regard to their contribution to the GDP of the world economy along the last quarter of the 20th century; the trend has become evident in the new century, when BRIC (that are only in part capitalist economies) brought back the GDP share of capitalist countries over 50 per cent of the world GDP. This trend posed the problem of the economic development of traditional countries along the second half of the last century, a problem that, although mitigated by the development of BRIC in the new century, remains topical because the recent spread of capitalism is due only to three countries came from that group of economies.

The evolution of capitalist countries inside the world economy

Another step to assess other aspects of the spread of capitalism in the world economy is to trace the evolution of the capitalist countries between 1820 and 2021. Getting a glance of countries' placement up to 1913 in terms of GDP (See Figure 9.5a), there emerges the relevance of China and India as real economic powers for the large part of the 19th century; even when at the beginnings of the 20th century USA, Germany, Russia, and UK, in order of importance, established themselves at the top of the ranking, China maintained the first place and India the sixth. The second phenomenon characterising this phase of intense spread of capitalism is the leap ahead of the USA in terms of GDP increase in the last 40 years of the period (5.3 times), obtained also by an increment of the population equal to 2.4 times. It is interesting to notice that the first four economic powers in 1913 were also highly populated countries.

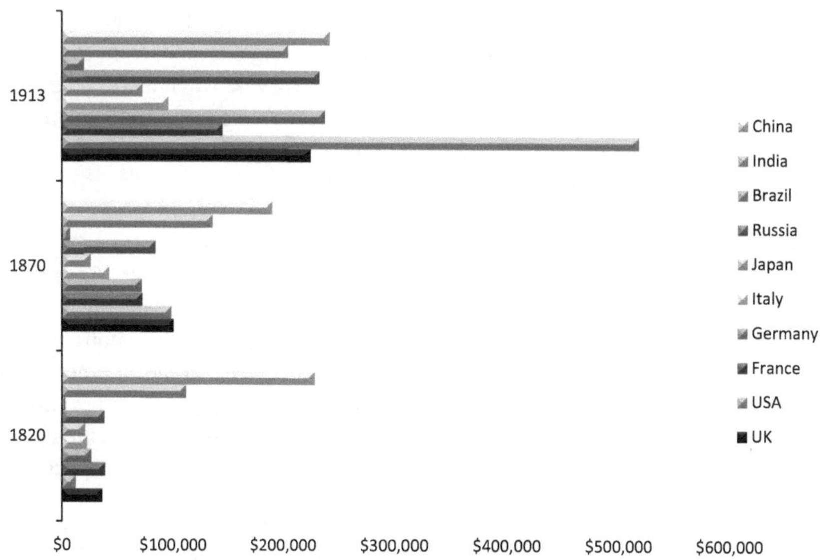

Figure 9.5a GDP of a group of selected countries between 1820 and 1913

Source: Author's elaboration from Maddison (2003) *The World Economy. Historical statistics*, Paris: OECD, Table 8b

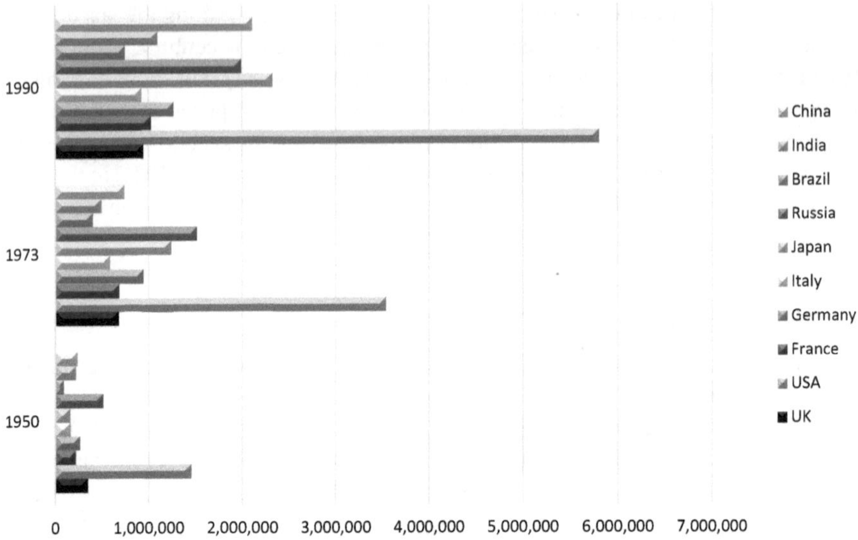

Figure 9.5b GDP of a group of selected countries between 1913 and 1990

Source: Author elaboration from Maddison (2003) *The World Economy. Historical statistics*, Paris: OECD, Table 8b

The main feature of the 20th century world economy is the undisputed championship of the USA, a phenomenon that confirms the concentration of capitalism rather than its spread. To the second place of the ranking climbed, from the fourth position obtained in 1913, the Russian economy up to 1990, when it was overtaken by Japan and China. Germany, France, UK and Italy had good performance in the second part of the century (See Figure 9.5b), but their relevance in the world economy emerged when they constituted a common market.

The countries that present the highest GDP increase between 1820 and 1990 are those that had the highest increase in population; in fact, the comparison between Tables 9.1 and 9.3 shows that the USA and Brazil, which improved their GDP 462 and 255 times, respectively, increased their population 25 and 33 times. But considering the ratio between the two variables, the economies that grew more than their population are Japan (28 times), USA (18 times), Germany, Italy and France (between 16 and 14 times); Russia, the UK and Brazil (between 10 and 8 times); and India and China (3 and 2.5 times).

The world economy of the last 30 years is characterised by the impetuous leap forward of China and India, whose GDP increased 15 and 6 times respectively, while that of USA increased only 2 times. If at the beginning of the period the top five economies were USA, Japan, Russia, Germany and Italy at the end they became China, USA, India, Japan and Germany, followed by Russia, UK, France, Brazil and Italy (See Figure 9.5c).

The spread of capitalism from the USA and Europe towards Asiatic economies occurred at the beginning of the 21st century representing thus one of the

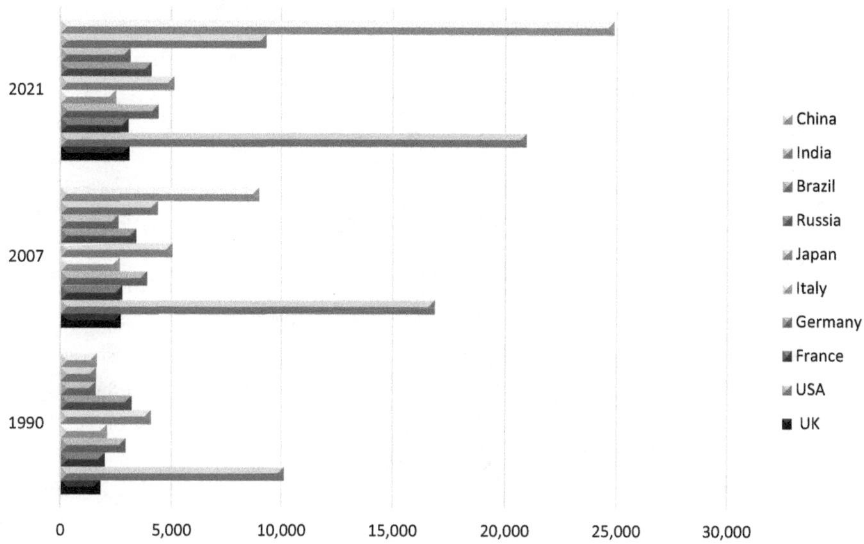

Figure 9.5c PPP GDP of a group of selected countries between 1990 and 2021

Source: Author's elaboration from *World Bank, World development indicator database*, accessed July 29, 2022

main features in the present, the second being the creation of the European Union. Although from the institutional point of view such a 'multi-state' entity couldn't be considered a subject of international politics because it lacks a unitary foreign policy and a common army, from the economic point of view its common market and a currency shared by the European Monetary Union countries (a wide group of European Union states) transform it into an economic power. Its contribution to the World GDP in terms of PPP is the highest in all the 30-year period up to 2020, when Brexit downgraded the EU to the third position in the world placement. Nevertheless, its share shrunk from 23.40 per cent in 1990 to 14.70 per cent in 2021, more than that of the US, which passed from 19.69 per cent to 15.64 per cent. Due to the constitution of this multi-state entity, the present structure of the world economy shows three poles contributing to the world GDP by different shares: North America (17 per cent USA and Canada), Europe (17 per cent Eu and UK), and Southeast and East Asia (33 per cent India, China, Japan, South Korea and Indonesia).

The evolution of the world economy in the time of the capitalism resulting from these statistics shows that the key players have been the same for nearly two centuries, but they have changed their placement in the power ranking. However, in the new century the situation has changed because one-third of the world GDP is produced by developed and developing Asian countries (India, China, Japan, South Korea and Indonesia), one-third by the first comers and latecomers (the UK, the USA, the EU), and one-third by the remaining economies, mainly developing ones.

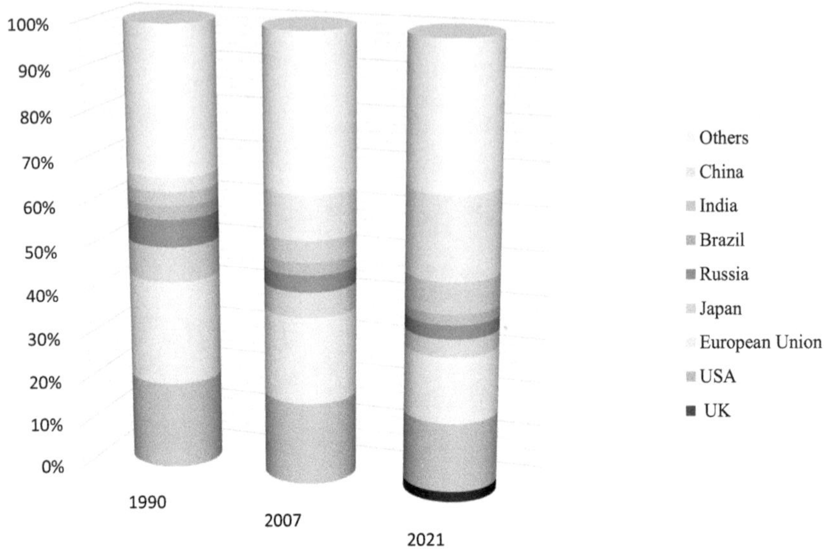

Figure 9.6 Shares of world PPP GDP for economic blocks and powers between 1990 and 2021

Source: Author's elaboration from *World Bank, World development indicators database*, accessed July 25, 2021

The evolution of the international trade

Side by side with the dynamics of the capitalist economies that describe the geographical diffusion of capitalism, the dynamics of international trade reveal the structure of the world economy. The world export has sharply increased in the last two centuries; in fact, its volume index referred to 1913 as a base year equal to 100 presented in 1820 a value of 3.35 and that reached in 2014 the value of 4,428 (Figure 9.7). This upward trend presents two hollows of about 25–30 points in the periods 1913–1924 and 1929–1938 and four periods of increase having different intensities that are, starting from the greatest, between 1950 and 1973, between 1983 and 2008, between 1820 and 1870, and between 1870 and 1913. Considering the phases of the capitalist development, the export increased about 7 times between 1820 and 1870, 4 times between 1870 and 1913, 1.5 times between 1913 and 1950, 6.2 times between 1950 and 1973, 1.9 times between 1973 and 1990 and 2.8 times between 1990 and 2008 (Trade and Globalization – Our World in Data, accessed September 27, 2022).

At first sight the growth of the aggregate exports in nominal terms has been on average every year equal to 3.9 per cent from 1827 and 1913 and 11.4 per cent between 1945 and 2014, with scarce swinging between 1913 and 1945. Inside both growth paths the deviation of the real values from the mean show as much as subperiods characterised by different intensities of export growth: between 1840 and 1885 such intensity was higher than the mean, while between 1885 and 1913 it was

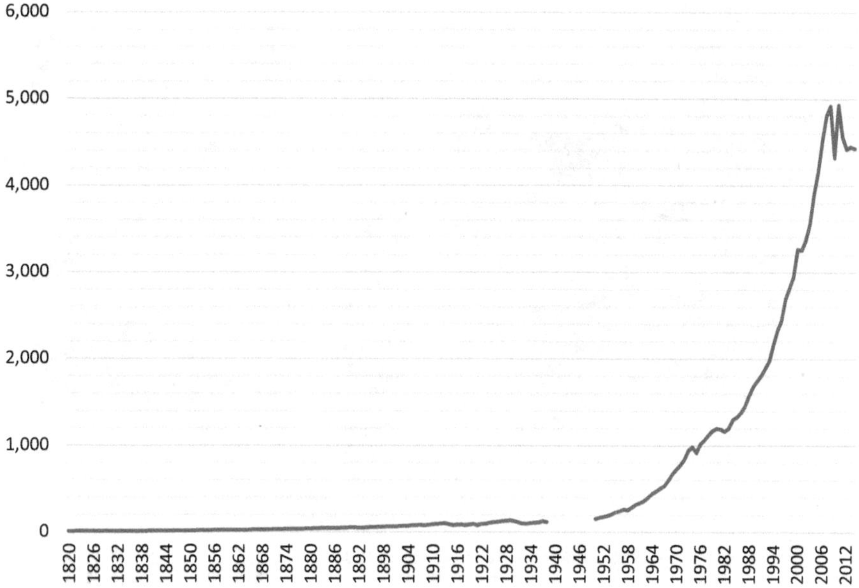

Figure 9.7 Global export between 1820 and 2014 (volume index, 1913=100)

Source: Author's elaboration from https://ourworldindata.org/trade-and-globalization, accessed September 27, 2022

lower; between 1945 and 2014 the years after the war and the 1970s were the more dynamic times within the period. Moreover, the growth trend of exports in both growth paths presents a point of change, respectively, in 1870, in 1950 and in 1985 (Fouquin and Hugot 2016: 12–13).

The analysis of the cumulative flows of export across the continents (see Figure 9.8) shows that in the 19th century nearly 40 per cent–50 per cent of the yearly trade was intra-European countries, 20 per cent between Europe and America, 10 per cent–12 per cent between Europe and Asia, and 5 per cent–8 per cent intra-American countries and intra-Asian countries as well. Once again, 1870 represented the watershed between a first period where the Europe–America trade reduced nearly in half and the intra-Europe flow fluctuated between 35 per cent and 45 per cent, and a second period where the intra-Europe trade decreased at 40 per cent and the constancy of other shares left space for the increase of other countries' trade up to 8 per cent–10 per cent (Fouquin and Hugot 2016: 24). In the 20th century the interwar period represents a transition moment towards a new configuration of the world structure of international exports. The intra-Europe share of world export increased from 25 to 35 per cent in 1930, coming back to 30 per cent when the Second World War started, and the Europe–America portion decreased by nearly 8 points over 25; these trends resulted in the shrinking of Europe's contribution to world trade, which shifted from nearly two-thirds to less than a half. After the Second World War the main trends have been a slight recovery of intra-Europe

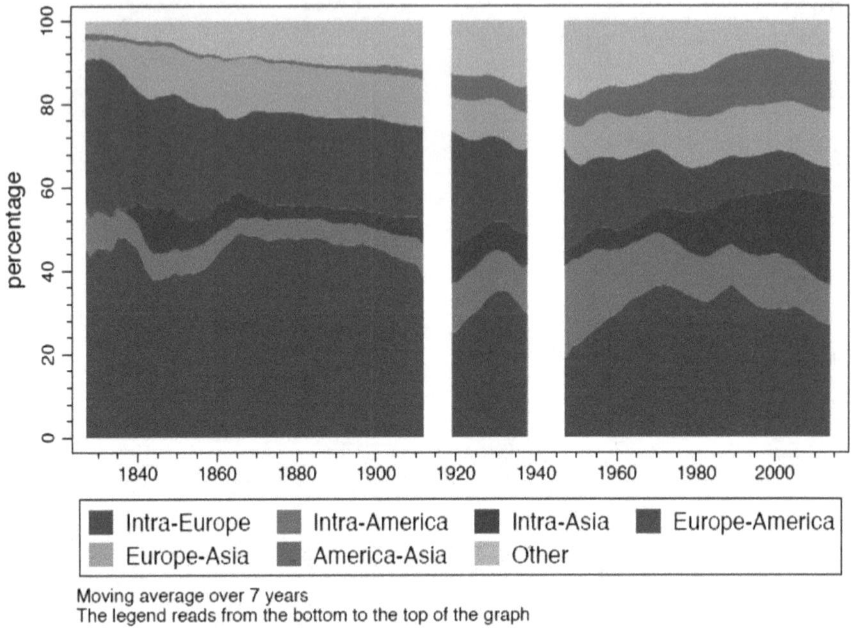

Figure 9.8 Shares of cumulative world export across the continents from 1827 to 2014 (seven-year average % values)

Source: Fouquin and Hugot (2016: 24).

trade, a decrease of Europe–America, intra-America, and other continents' trade, and an increase of intra-Asia and America–Asia trade. The changing moments of the European contribution to the world export have been the mid-seventies and 1990; the intra-Europe trade increased from 20 per cent to 35 per cent in the 30 years after the end of the war and after a short decrease came back to this value in 1990 but retreated to 30 per cent at the end of the period. The Europe–America trade shrunk from 20 per cent to 12 per cent in 1975 and to 5 per cent in 2014; thus, Europe contributed about a third of the world export in the new century. The intra-America trade decreased from a share of 20 per cent to 10 per cent in 2014, like the other continents, while the America–Asia contribution shifted from 5 per cent to 15 per cent. The intra-Asia contribution increased sharply from 3 per cent–4 per cent at the end of the war to 20 per cent in 2014.

The analysis of the shares of world exports by income level of the trade partners confirms that the world trade has for a long time supported the strengthening of capitalist economies. Figure 9.9 shows that up to 1880 the export between rich countries counted on average up to 75 per cent of the world trade and that towards the non-rich ones nearly 15 per cent. On the eve of the First World War the intra-rich countries' trade fell to 60 per cent because the interchange (exports and imports) with non-rich ones rose nearly to 15 per cent–18 per cent. The interwar

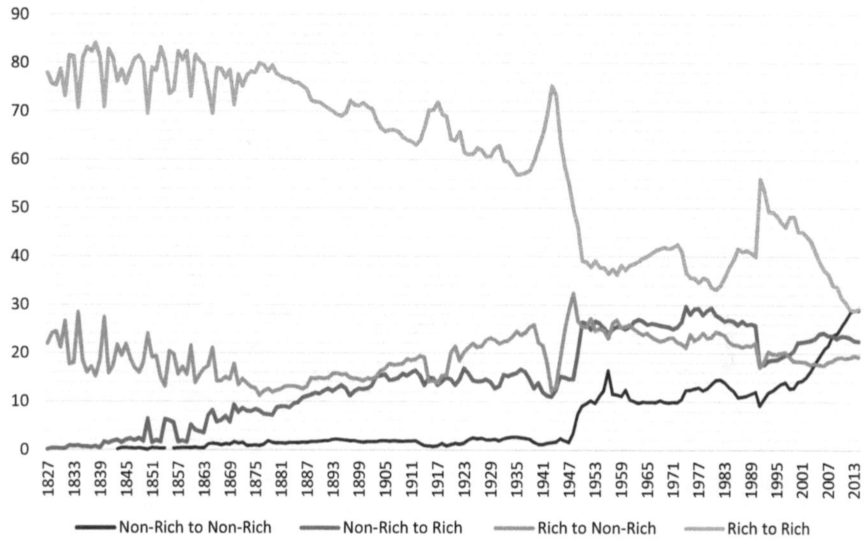

Figure 9.9 Share of global exports from 1827 to 2013 by income level of the trade partners (% values)

Source: Author's elaboration from https://ourworldindata.org/trade-and-globalization, accessed September 27, 2022

period changed completely the trade flows so that starting from the late forties only 40 per cent of the world trade was between rich countries, and their interchange with non-rich countries lined up to 25 per cent; it is interesting to notice that in this period emerged the interchange between non-rich countries with a share of 10 per cent of the world trade. These trends lasted up to the 1990s when a sharp increase of trade between non-rich countries and a sharp decrease of trade between the rich ones led to a share of nearly 30 per cent for both flows in 2014. Instead, the post-war flows of trade between rich and non-rich countries have declined slightly their shares to a value near 20 per cent, with a surplus of 3–4 points along the period in favour of non-rich to rich countries' flow.

As the world export increased during all of the period about 74 times and the world income about 52 times (see later Tables 9.3 and 9.4), the value of exported goods as share of the GDP increased. Despite such a general trend the openness of the world economies has been discontinuous in all of the period under consideration, and every year it was jumping up and down. Between 1827 and 1870 the exported share of the GDP shifted from 7.15 to 9.12 with a fall to 3.91, from 1870 to 1913 the value rose to 13.96, and from 1913 to 1945 it collapsed to 4.16; after World War II the internationalisation of the world economies got back up slowly to 1970, when the index became 9.07, and then more quickly to the point that it reached the value of 16.61 in 1980. Subsequently, after a new fall up to 13.42 in 1986 a jump started that pushed the index to 26.23 in 2008 (Figure 9.10).

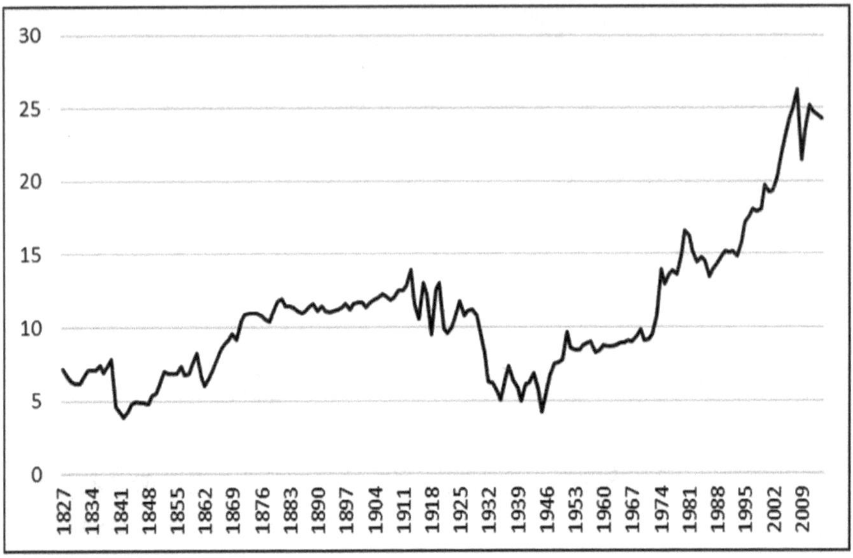

Figure 9.10 Value of the world exported goods as a share of world GDP between 1827 and 2014

Source: Author's elaboration from https://ourworldindata.org/trade-and-globalization, accessed September 27, 2022

Capitalism beyond the nation borders: The international exchanges

Throughout the course of capitalist advance the export of goods and the import of raw materials and foodstuff by the first comers allowed them to strengthen their economies; nevertheless, the movement of resources (machinery, financial instruments, and people) toward and out of the latecomers transferred in some cases technologies and knowledge that enabled them to undertake the capitalist economy. Thus, the international trade of materials and goods, the migration and the financial flows can be considered the 'driving forces' behind both the continuous reinforcement of national capitalisms and the capitalist propagation worldwide. These flows emerged not only on impulse of the exporters and importers of the economies, but also by the intervention of the respective states that transformed the international exchanges in the 'trade areas'. In fact, the enlargement of trade beyond the national borders have entailed the drafting of international trade agreements by the states. Such intervention has given rise to 'trade regimes' (trading rules and organisation procedures), but also to international flows of personal chattels and knowledge (management practise), so that another driver of the expansion of the capitalist economies beyond the national borders are the institutions. All these institutions shaped the trading activities and the other economic undertakings connected to them (infrastructures building, transformation, and shipping of the wares, and so on), finalising them to the interest of the promoter of the trade agreement: thus, an international economic order compliant with the economic powers emerged.

From the international trade to the trade areas

The extraordinary development of international trade in specific periods of the capitalist evolution was certainly caused by the need for the national production systems to expand beyond the state borders to take advantage of the technical and economic progress, but it was even the result of the institutional activity of the states. In fact, international trade was strongly practised before the advent of capitalism, and administrative/state interventions in support of or keeping it under control authorised goods in and out of a country upon payment. However, except for occasional events, the outbound and inbound custom duties have never been managed as instruments to narrow or wide the domestic markets: they have been generally implemented to have public revenues. The situation changed when the technical development of industry pushed the level of production beyond the domestic absorption capacity and/or when the domestic endowments of raw materials were exhausted; these situations made it necessary to find new end/or raw material markets – in short, to increase sales beyond domestic markets and to stock mineral inputs. To trade in other countries required the consensus of the authorities ruling them, thus the implementation by the involved states of an institution-building process to agree trade rules and conditions for carrying out those exchanges.

During the Mercantilist period the international trade of goods, aiming at increasing the prosperity of the European Monarchies (Great Britain, France, Holland, and Spain) by encouraging exports and dissuading imports, thrived between the states and their colonised territories protected by the domestic naval forces and armies. To maintain the comparative advantage of the national productions against the foreign countries the exports of tools, capital equipment, and skilled workers were banned or subject to high export duties, while to protect the domestic markets from the foreign competitors some import duties were established. The British Navigation Act of 1651, aware of such a situation and of the British sea dominance, turned the system of privileged trading blocs into a world institutional setting, dictating that the export from Europe towards the other continents must be carried out by British ships or by ships registered in the countries where the goods were produced.

The disregard of this Act by a lot of international traders, the USA Independence Declaration of 1776 also aimed at freeing the colonies from it, and the recognition of the monarchic states as international legal subjects by the Vienna Congress in 1815, favoured the issue of the Reciprocity of Duties Act by the British Parliament in 1823. By this act the reciprocal lowering or removal of import duties, creating a 'preferential trade system', could be allowed to the British government under bilateral trade agreements signed with other states. Its implementation between Great Britain and its colonies made the emergence of a trade area 'with British goods receiving preferential treatment in the colonies, and colonial produce gaining tariff preference in the British market' (Graff, Kenwood and Lougheed 2014: 70). This was the first step in the process of ferrying the international trade flows of goods toward a trade area. Besides the import, the export duties were also reduced in Great Britain, and a similar process of unilateral lowering customs was adopted by other European countries.

To explain how international trade was channelled through international agreements into trade areas devoid of whatever kind of import and export barrier, an inspection is necessary to show the economic differences concerning that point presented by the trade areas. The removal of import barriers and the export easing give rise to various kinds of 'trade areas' – that is, of state territories where a specific 'trade regime' is effective, pursuant to interstate agreements. The Hungarian economist Bela Belassa, who ordered the matter as a sequence of steps to integrate more economies in a single economic unit (Belassa 1961), identified the following kinds of trade areas distinguished according to the degree of protection of the inner productions vs the outer ones, and to the parity of production conditions of the producers belonging to the different countries of the trade area:

i. The '*preferential trade area*', which is constituted by the territory of both states signing a bilateral trade agreement, is an area where the reciprocal lowering or removal of import duties and/or limitations to trade due to the level of tariffs, quotas and the kind of traded goods are allowed.
ii. The '*free trade area*', which is constituted by the territory of the contracting states through a bilateral or multilateral trade agreement, is the space where the imports and exports of goods are carried out without customs duties and limits to the origin of the traded wares by the traders of the contracting states.
iii. The '*custom union*' is a free trade area characterised by a single discriminatory trade policy towards third parties (common customs tariffs and rules of products origin) to prevent the members to act as an intermediary for a third discriminated country.
iv. The '*common market*' is a custom union more economically designed, where the economies involved also abrogate the non-tariff barriers and adopt the same institutional forms and common technical standards. In a common market the circulation of financial assets and workers is also allowed.
v. An '*economic and monetary union*' is a common market sharing the same economic institutions and a single currency.

The comparison between the trade areas just presented and a domestic market shows some analogies and some differences. First, both trade organisations are the result of state activity because the first is issued by the domestic legislative organisms and the second originates from an international agreement signed by governments. As to the retention of an appropriate degree of equality of the contracting parties, which is an aim in building domestic markets, the first trade area discriminates against the sellers of imported goods because of the presence of trade barriers; thus, it cannot be considered a market. In a certain sense this discrimination also remains when there are non-tariff barriers for some goods or services and when in an economic and monetary union the exchanged ones come from producers enjoying favourable conditions of production due to different institutions or fiscal systems of a state member. That said, the trade areas could have a 'deepness of market' only in an economic and monetary union homogeneous from the point of view of the fiscal system and institutions, and this is a situation that neither in the EMU occurs. Thus, the trade areas are always 'quasi markets' because when they present all the features of a national market they represent a unified territory under one state (see the case of Zollverein and the German state).

The creation of 'preferential trade areas' carried out in the first decades of the 19th century spiked in 1860 with Great Britain as the first free-trade country for export and most imports and presented other ongoing processes that boosted international trade flows: the creation of 'custom unions' and the establishment of 'free-trade areas'. Both experiences, representing different steps in the process of an economic union formation corresponded to different historical events – that is, to the creation of nation states and the formation of an entity operating beyond the states. To the first phenomenon the creation of a national markets in Germany and Italy can be attributed, and to the second the Cobden-Chevalier Act. The merger of the Bavarian Custom Union created in 1827 with the Prussian Custom Union founded in the 1831 gave rise to the Zollverein in 1833, a treaty building a common market of goods collecting the most part of the states that would form the German Empire in 1871; the process of a domestic market formation also occurred in Italy in 1861, when the unification of some former independent states under the Kingdom of Sardinia gave rise to the Kingdom of Italy.

The trend towards a demolition of customs barriers instead led Great Britain and France to create a 'free trade area' by signing in 1860 the Cobden-Chevalier Treaty. The agreement, which freed from the customs duties the interchange of most goods, enabled the traders of both countries to work at unified conditions in a 'quasi-market' extended beyond the borders of their own states. Moreover, it introduced the 'most-favoured nation clause', according to which the reduction of a customs duty sanctioned towards each other by France and Great Britain against specific goods, was extended to any third country that exported those goods in the free trade area. Thanks to this clause and the bilateral trade agreements in force between some European and Asian countries on the one side and France and Great Britain on the other side, a wide international 'free trade area' came through. The adoption of such an international trading regime, sponsored by exporters, importers, bankers and investors of the developed and developing European countries, helped the industrial economies because it highly increased the trade among the European countries and between them and the countries of the other continents. However, the traditional economies based on mining activities and plantations didn't take advantage of the participation in the free trade area, as the primary outputs they produced were financed and managed by foreign companies belonging to the higher income countries, the revenues coming from the exports returned to developed economies instead to be invested in the economies producing them. Moreover, some emerging economies also didn't find it advantageous to join the free trade area: the USA and Canada remained protectionists because their economies weren't ready to face the competition of foreign companies. As far as that is concerned, the acceptance of the 'free trade area' for a large part of the 19th century was the reflection 'of the unique and highly profitable positions of the world's supplier of manufactured goods in exchange for food and raw material that Britain occupied in the world economy' (Graff, Kenwood and Lougheed 2014: 72) together with the joint participation of the other European emerging economic powers.

Such an enlarged trade area, based on bilateral agreements sponsored by industrialised countries and on the 'most-favoured nation clause', also created a false multilateralism; in fact, this clause deprived single countries of their right to determine the tariff policy.

> A particular revolting episode in this context were the so-called Opium Wars (1839–42 and 1856–60), in the course of which British East India Company (EIC) facing the old trade deficit of the West with the East had the way for British opium export into China forcefully opened. The US and France free rode and joined the British in the profitable business in 1844; and in China this is today remembered as the beginning of the 'century of humiliation'.
>
> (Graff, Kenwood and Lougheed 2014: 70)

Although the process of customs duties decreasing resulted in a quadrupled international trade between 1830 and 1880, since 1890 in the United States 'high duties were placed on textiles, iron, steel, glass, and to appease the farmers, who were facing increasing competition from Canadian imports, tariffs were imposed on a number of agricultural products' (Graff, Kenwood and Lougheed 2014: 73). The same happened in Europe when in the 1880s a deep crisis occurred and the competition among the industrialised European countries arose; the protectionist policies caused the dismantling of the free trade area but despite that, up to the First World War, the international exchanges increased. But it was between 1925 and 1932 that a collapse of the international exchanges among the economies occurred, shifting the values of the world exported goods as a share of world GDP from 12 per cent to 5 per cent, value around which it waved up to 1946. After this year another phase of increasing internationalisation of the economies followed, pushed by new institutions built for the purpose: the General Agreement on Tariff and Trade (GATT) and the World Trade Organisation (WTO), that will be analysed in Chapter Ten.

The international system of payments

If the certainty of the legal effects of the exchange, of the merchandise safety, and of the parity of the contracting parties have encouraged the increase of the exchanges in the national good markets, the certainty of the value of the good exchanged in the international trade made likewise. Such certainty, obtained by the equivalence of the price across the different currencies, was first the result of the unilateral adoption of the 'bimetallic system' by the states. This procedure establishing the 'par value' of a currency unit consisted in pegging it to the 'mint price' (the cost of the fixed amount of gold or silver contained in it). The gradual implementation of such a procedure by the countries resulted in an 'international monetary system' characterised by fixed exchange rates and the convertibility of coins in bullion at home and abroad, both features to the advantage of the international trade. After the international monetary congress held in Paris in 1867, the countries abandoned the bimetallic system[4] and joined the 'gold standard system' one after the other up to the end of the century. At the centre of the system there was the British Pound, as the only currency used in the international trade of goods; this position was due to the fact that Great Britain was the first world importer and exporter, and that some services connected to the transport of goods (insurance, freight) or to commercial activities (bank bills, bills of exchange, international securities) were issued or traded in London.

The First World War and the following sequence of events caused the gold standard distress for some reasons: the government control of the exchange rates, the gold shortage and redistribution among the countries, and the inability of Great Britain to maintain the Pound convertibility due to the reduction of its gold reserves. All these problems made unworkable the old international monetary system after the WW1, despite the attempts to restore it; in addition, New York substituted London as financial centre and only the US Dollar could comply with the rules of the gold standard system. As a consequence of this distress during the 1920s the old international monetary system was substituted by the 'gold-exchange standard system', that enabled the countries lacking gold to issue banknotes only if they held an equivalent quantity of convertible currencies as reserves.

Such arrangement of the international system of payments wasn't a currency market because the convertibility among the currencies wasn't automatic, despite some activities implemented by the Central Banks to sustain the system. A new arrangement designed to promote the stability in the international payments system was promoted in 1944 in the Conference of Bretton Woods as a part of a set of institution built to promote the openness of the economies (see Chapter Ten).

Migration flows for the capitalist development and growth

Another international flow connecting the economies of the countries and thus revealing the structure of the world economy is migration. Migration is a social phenomenon connected to the capitalism. It has nothing to do with the occupation of third-party territories made by invader or conquering populations, because it is an individual movement that takes place to seek a job away from the dwelling place or home. The 'domestic migration' has been first experienced by the countries at the beginning of their capitalist development as a process of urbanisation; this intense phenomenon, that can be deduced from the Table 2.4, emerged when the peasants leaved the countryside in search for a job in the industrial cities, pushed by the agricultural unemployment in the countryside. Even the 'international migration' has emerged in the same conditions, but the transfer has been from the home country to another country. Thus, as in both cases the cause of the movement of the people is the lack of a job or the preference for another one better paid, the migration isn't a phenomenon of exclusive social relevance; it is of noteworthy economic relevance too (Taylor 1999; Constant and Zimmermann 2013). That the importance of the phenomenon be due to the provision of labour force to the factories of the cities lacking workers, or to the supply of people for the already capitalist economies having capitals and technologies but being short of workers, or to the financial inflow that the transient economies obtain from their emigrated citizens in the form of remittance, the migration received inadequate attention by the economics up to the 1990s. The phenomenon has been for long consigned to the demographers and the sociologists who are generally interested in its social and political aspects. Besides that, the migrants represent important players in the labour market of the receiving country and undeniable resources for the development of the origin country whose flows circulated across the countries since the beginnings of capitalism.

Generally speaking the international migrant is 'a person who moves away from his or her place of usual residence across an international border, temporarily or permanently' (International Organisation for Migration – IOM). It was for this reason that the statistics about the outbound and inbound transit in the ports or at the borders constituted for a long time the way by which the outflows and the inflows of migrants were measured. Despite their importance for pointing out the extent and the trend of the phenomenon, these records were inaccurate because they didn't consider the people coming back home. Starting from the mid-twentieth century a more accurate measurement of the phenomenon has been obtained by adopting a new definition of migrant. The international migrant is a person who leaves its country of origin to establish himself/herself either permanently or temporarily in another country, where it is registered as a foreign-born people. Although this definition enables to calculate to a certain date the number (the stock) of the migrants living in the country avoiding the miscalculation connected to the flow's measurement, however it includes all the categories of displaced people: the 'migrant workers', the 'forced migrants' and the 'asylum-seekers', the 'EU internal migrants', and the 'irregular migrants'. To measure the size of each group of displaced people the different legal standings must be considered (Romagnoli 2019: 246–9).

It was first around the thirties and forties of the 19th century the moment when the high rate of growth of the rural population, the famine and the starvation in the countryside pushed a lot of people living in the Northwest Europe[5] to migrate abroad. Between 1821 and 1850 nearly three forth of these migrants leaved the British Isles and one forth the German territories toward the Americas, numbering 3.4 million people (Graff, Kenwood and Lougheed 2014: 54). The migrants became nearly 8 million in the following 30 years, thanks to a sub-flow of people coming from the Southeast Europe[6]; British Isles and Germany represented still the main countries of origin, but their share on the total flow became 57 per cent and 26 per cent respectively. It was between 1881 and 1913 that the Atlantic migration system recorded the highest flow of people: about 32 million people moved between European and American countries coming from British Isle (28 per cent), Germany (7 per cent), Italy (24 per cent), Spain and Portugal (more than 13 per cent), and Austro-Hungarian territories (13 per cent). In this period Southeast European share increased to 57 per cent of the total European migration vs 43 per cent of Northwest European share. Between 1820 and 1913 the countries contributing to the Atlantic migration flows were in this order (see Figure 9.11): British Isles (37 per cent of the total), Italy (18 per cent), Germany (more than 11 per cent), Spain and Portugal (11 per cent each one), and Austro-Hungarian territories (10 per cent).

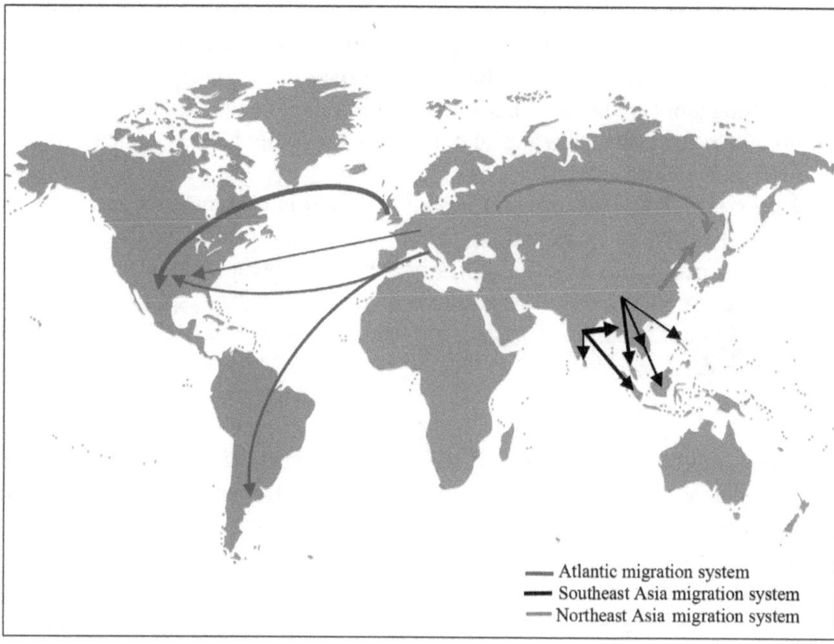

Figure 9.11 International migration flows operating from 1830 to 1940

Sources: Author's elaboration

Side by side the migration flows crossing the Atlantic Ocean, other two migration movements (the Southeast and Northeast Asian ones) evolved in the 19th century, starting after the issue of the Slavery Abolition Act of 1833 by the British Parliament, which was also extended to the colonies and the emancipation of serfs in Russia that occurred in 1861.

> Migration to Southeast Asia and lands around the Indian Ocean and South Pacific consisted of over 29 million Indians and over 19 million Chinese. Most migration from India was to colonies throughout the British empire. Less than 10 percent of this migration was indentured,[7] although much of it was undertaken with assistance from colonial authorities, or under some form of debt obligation under *kangani*[8] labor recruitment systems. . . . Migration expanded with the increasing restriction of indenture contracts after 1908 and the abolishment of indenture in 1920. Nearly 4 million Indians travelled to Malaysia, over 8 million to Ceylon, over 15 million to Burma, and about 1 million to Africa, other parts of Southeast Asia, and islands throughout the Indian and Pacific Oceans. . . . Chinese worked for Chinese employers under various forms of contract and debt obligation, wage labor, and profit sharing. Up to 11 million Chinese travelled from China to the Straits Settlements, although more than a third of these transhipped to the Dutch Indies,

> Borneo, Burma, and places farther west. Nearly 4 million travelled directly from China to Thailand, between 2 and 3 million to French Indochina, over 1 million to the Dutch Indies (for a total of over 4 million if transhipments from Singapore are included), less than 1 million to the Philippines, and over 500,000 to Australia, New Zealand, Hawai'i, and other islands in the Pacific and Indian Oceans. . . .
>
> Between 28 and 33 million Chinese migrated into Manchuria and Siberia (most of whom embarked on a short sea voyage from Shandong to the Liaodong peninsula), along with nearly 2 million Koreans and over 500,000 Japanese. Another 2.5 million Koreans migrated to Japan, especially in the 1930s. At least 13 million Russians moved into central Asia and Siberia over this period.
>
> (McKeown 2004: 157–8, 9)

The three migration movements of the period between 1830 and 1940 present common characteristics. All three stabilised in the sixties and hit the wall astride the new century, and all three displaced a similar amount of people. Considering the wakes of the period between the World Wars, the Atlantic migration system totalled 55–58 million workers between 1840 and 1940, the Southeast Asian flow 48–52 million people, and the North and Central Asia one 46–51 million (McKeown 2004: 156). In addition, all the migration flows were related to the capitalist development of European countries because they were indispensable to manage the colonial economic activities (plantations and mines) or the development of US economy. The difference among the three migration movements is due to the recruiting and managing methods: while the European migrants coming to the Americas were people moving on purpose to become contractual workers, the Russian and Chinese people going towards North and Central Asia were pushed by the governmental homesteading policies aimed at colonising those territories, and the Indian and Chinese people constituting the Southeast Asian migration system were recruited by European merchants or local foremen to work in the economic activities of the colonisers under numerous forms of contract like debt obligation, wage labour and profit sharing.

Differently from the long-distance migration that occurred between the mid-19th and mid-20th centuries, after the Second World War the flows concentrated mainly in three world areas (North Central Americas, Euro-Mediterranean and Arab Gulf spaces, and Southeast Asia), creating just as many 'migration systems'. A migration system is a set of networks based on continuous, intense and constant flows of migrants connecting different countries for a period. In fact, such flows of labour services generally give rise to feedback and adjustment streams between the related countries, like flows of knowledge and information, flows of financial capitals (remittance and foreign direct investments), and cultural flows. Each migration system, by nature, changes and evolves, and this is the reason why the post–Second World War migration systems have intensified their dimension due to the huge decrease of transport costs and the advancement of transport systems and have evolved pursuant to the economic evolution of the countries (Figure 9.12).

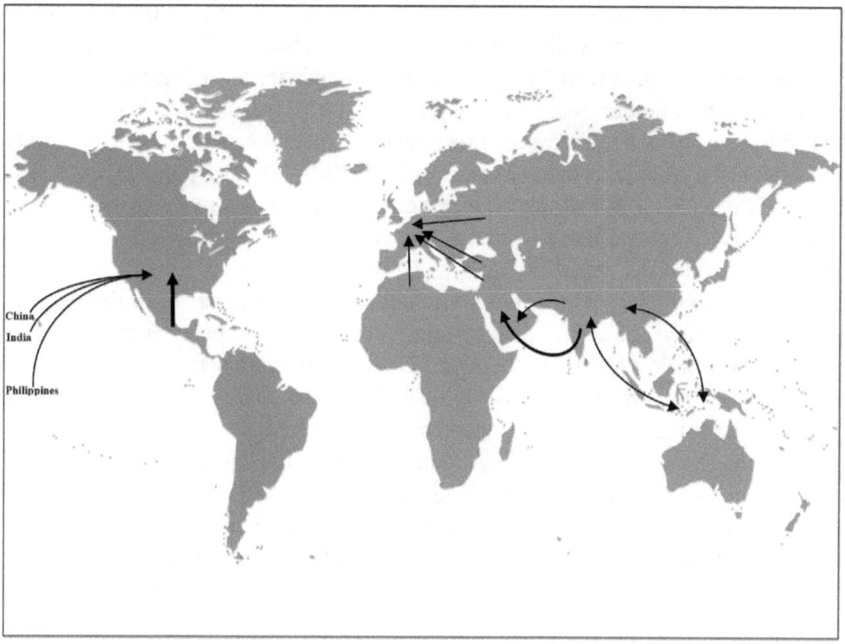

Figure 9.12 International migration systems operating in recent decades

Sources: Author's elaboration

As to the flows, after the Second World War they continued and intensified but changed features. Starting from 1960 the stock of international migrants increased slowly up to 1985 (from 71,884 million people to 104,614 million ones) and had a jump of 50 per cent in the following five years and of 80 per cent in the last 30 ones so that it reached 280 million people in 2020.[9] Such an upward trend presents a decrease of the rate of international migrants over the world population up to 1980 (from 2.6 per cent to 2.3 per cent), a sharp increase up to 2.9 per cent in the following decade, and a further jump in the new century from 2.8 per cent to 3.6 per cent (Zupi 2021: 36). The highest share of world migrants in 2020 moved towards and across Europe (30.9 per cent), followed by Asia (30.5 per cent), North America (20.9 per cent), Africa (9.0 per cent), Latin America (5.3 per cent), and Oceania (3.4 per cent), considering that in the hosting country the USA live 18.0 per cent of world migrants followed by Germany with 5.6 per cent, Saudi Arabia with 4.8 per cent, Russia with 4.1 per cent, and United Kingdom with 3.3 per cent. The highest share of migrants with respect to the native population is in Oceania (21.98 per cent), followed by North America (15.92 per cent), Europe (15.60 per cent), Latin America (2.26 per cent), Africa (1.89 per cent) and Asia (1.84 per cent). Considering the countries, a high share of migrants emerges over the nationals for those economies that have an insufficient population to exploit the productive capacity they have implemented (like the United Arab Emirates having a share of 88.1 per cent, Kuwait with 72.8 per cent, Saudi Arabia with 38.6, Canada with 31.6 per cent, Australia with 20.4 per cent and Kazakhstan with 19.9) and for those that host a high number of refugees as in the case of Jordan and Lebanon (33 per cent–34 per cent). As to the other developed countries the share of migrants over the nationals is 18.8 per cent in Germany, 15.3 in the USA, 13.8 per cent in the UK, 13.1 in France, 10.6 in Italy and 8.0 per cent in Russia. There are also countries characterised by high emigration that also have a high share of foreign-born people like Ukraine (11.4 per cent) and Turkey (7.2 per cent).

The trend of the international migration presented above puts in evidence other features. The first is the fact that sending countries in the postwar period, once in better economic conditions, became receiving ones: this is the case of Italy and Spain but also of Turkey and Morocco. This has enlarged the area attracting migrants that in the case of the European migration system now expands beyond the Mediterranean and outside the EU. Another feature is that developed countries also present new outflows of people seeking better jobs in other developed countries: this is the case of the people living in the European Communities that can move in all the economic spaces thanks their legal status of citizens. A further stylised fact emerging from the historical review of international migration in capitalism highlights another difference between the two historical periods under consideration. Between mid-19th and mid-20th centuries the countries experiencing emigration were those that had already realised the transition to capitalism and maybe were even recording a high rate of income increase. The presence of a strong international emigration in such an economic environment could appear to be a contradiction, but it isn't so because its emergence happened when the industry achieved the level of workforce necessary to exploit its maximum production capacity, and thus, it couldn't absorb all the people outgoing from agriculture. In the postwar period emigration also emerges in transient economies without industrial development and in developed economies just for a lack of jobs. This proves that emigration is an economic activity of investment in seeking out jobs that involve money to travel and living expenses during the unemployment period; the 'migration project' can't be carried out in very poor societies where it is impossible to fundraise, maybe by borrowing from the relatives, but it is implemented in all economies in transition and development if there is a lack of jobs.[10] Despite international migration being an economic activity that is important for both the receiving countries and the sending ones, the international initiatives of the states to manage it by agreements are absent. The developed countries hamper it while the developing ones encourage it, yet it isn't connected only to the problem of development of transient economies; it also relates to the growth of advanced economies experiencing birth rate and labour force reduction.

International exchange coordination: The international economic order

The previous historical review of the development of economic powers, international trade, the monetary system and migration processes during the evolution of capitalism put in evidence, from the point of view of the international economic relations, three phases that represent as much as 'states of the system' (see Chapter Three) – that is, three configurations of the world economy. Up to the eve of the Second World War the exchange of goods was a capitalist economy matter because the largest part of the world trade was among them (about 65 per cent at that time – see Figure 9.9) and the non-rich countries were involved mainly to support the advanced economies. Such a trend is revealed by the surplus of the trade balance between rich and non-rich countries, which was nearly equal to 10 points in favour of the first group (22 per cent–23 per cent of exports versus 12 per cent–13 per cent of imports). In the second period, between 1950 and 1990, the situation changed because the trade among developing countries lined up to 10 per cent of the world trade, just when one among the rich economies swung around 40 per cent and the trade surplus between rich and non-rich countries reversed by 7–8 points (29 per cent versus 22 per cent of the world trade between 1960 and 1990). After the 1990s, in the third phase, the trade among the rich countries and that among the non-rich ones presented an inverse trend until they converged to about 30 per cent of the world trade, while the trade surplus between the non-rich and rich countries reduced to 3–4 points (23 per cent vs 19 per cent). Even migration supported the development of capitalist economies up to the Second World War, both reducing their unemployed people in the phases of introducing and upgrading capitalism and providing with workers the countries rich of capitals and technologies but poor of people. After the Second World War the migration flow from developing countries came up besides that of the latecomers' capitalist economies to help the Central European economies that had a reduced native population. Such a double role of support to developed and developing economies carried out by migrants is continuing in the third phase, although for different reasons.[11] Thus, the three configurations of the world economy emerging from these stylised facts are characterised by the concentration of capitalism in a limited group of developed countries in the first period, a prominent position challenged in the second phase by the competition of the capitalist latecomers and developing countries, and an empowerment of the last group of economies that has conquered some places in the new configuration of the world economy in the third phase (see Figures 9.3, 9.4, 9.6).

While waiting for a deep inspection of the second and third phases of international economic relations during the evolution of capitalism, which will be the argument of the next chapter, the concept of a world economy configuration deserves reflection. The trends of the world economy in the 19th century and in the first decades of the 20th occurred because of the strengthening of first comers' and latecomers' economies and the process of institution building carried out by the states to govern international economic exchanges. The rules that have been elaborated reinforced the balance of power existing in the world economy. The coevolution between states and economies to obtain such balance has been analysed in a famous book by Polanyi, whose inception is:

> Nineteenth century civilization rested on four institutions. The first was the balance-of-power system which for a century prevented the occurrence of

> any long and devastating war between the Great Powers. The second was the international gold standard which symbolized a unique organization of world economy. The third was the self-regulating market which produced an unheard-of material welfare. The fourth was the liberal state. Classified in one way, two of these institutions were economic, two political. Classified in another way, two of them were national, two international.
>
> (Polanyi 1944: 3)

This well-known sentence of 'The Great Transformation' can usefully recap the features of international economic relations governing capitalism up to the First World War. In fact, on the one hand it clarifies the political role of the state in creating an international environment suitable for trade development by maintaining an accepted or agreed-on balance of power; on the other hand, it shows the economic role of the states in building institutions to regulate international economic exchanges. However, it also shows that the international economic relations were compliant with the economic power of the century, because the bilateral and free trade agreements signed at that time were compliant with the policies of Great Britain, and the introduction of the gold standard system was a unilateral decision taken first by the Bank of England. Nevertheless, the historical review has shown that such measures weren't in the interest of all countries involved in international trade; in fact, the missed acceptance of free trade by important players like the United States or the return to protectionism of most European countries at the end of the century confirm that such a trade regime wasn't convenient for all the economies, at whatever level of development they were.

Those stylised facts haven't been singular events that emerged in the first configuration of the world economy since they will be brought back up in the following ones (see Chapter Ten) to the point that each historical coordination of international exchanges among the economies can be considered a real 'international economic order'. Every phase of the world economy is thus the result of a configuration of international relations among the states resulting from the power relations accepted by the states or agreed through an institutional building process aiming at organising them; whatever are the criteria used in this organisation, the state will be the responsible for the resulting institutional setting ruling the economic activities beyond the nation borders.

After the crystal-clear analysis of the international economic relations in the capitalist evolution up to the first decades of the 20th century made by Polanyi, its innovative study had a follow-up in the 1970s by some researchers studying the international political relations among the states through the approach of the 'international regimes theory' (Gilpin 2001: Chapter Four). But also the UN General Assembly of May 1974 adopted a 'Declaration on the Establishment of a New International Economic Order' that proclaimed the need for 'interdependence, along with common interest and cooperation among all States, sovereign equality, and equity, as its underlying objectives' (McFarland 2015: 219). This declaration, which was the result of political interventions of the developing countries inside the United Nations to question the international economic order, arrived in a critical moment. In this respect (as will be explained in the Chapter Ten) the economist W. A. Lewis wrote a disciplinary essay to discuss the argument (Lewis 1978). The topic acquired new fame recently in the debate about globalisation as among the most important problems of capitalism in these decades, showing again the relevance of the argument to understand the evolution of capitalism beyond nations' borders.

Following these streams of thought and the historical review of the evolution of world economy in the capitalist era made in the chapter, it is possible to propose a definition of the 'international economic order'. The 'international economic order', which summarises the features of the world economy's configuration in force for a certain period, is the tendency of the structural arrangement of international economic exchanges towards the interests of one or more participants to the agreements signed to promote trade; such propensity results from the way of coordinating economic activities, the way of ruling the international organisms and the structure of the international payments system.

Concluding remarks: The world economy as the playing field of national capitalisms

If the concept of economic system is a missed one in economics and in mass culture, the world economy is a misleading one because it has taken on different meanings depending on the historical period. Up to the Second World War the idea of the world economy was nothing but a group of states whose international importance was due to the amount of their merchant navies and to the military presence in foreign countries (colonialism). In this framework the expansion of national economies beyond the nation border in search for foreign resources and products markets was as one with the extension of the nation's sovereignty; thus, the competitive advantage of an economy was coupled to that of the state, and the problem of the coordination of international economic activities was solved by such a balance of powers. Therefore, the development of the international trade has been the result of a unilateral adoption of an instrument useful for the interchanges that all partners will share to participate in international activity (the Gold Standard system), or the consequence of an agreement signed by the major powers (the free trade regime) and extended as such to all the other partners.

When some emerging political/economic powers found improper to participate to the international exchanges or thought disadvantaged their role, they implemented some policies (like the competitive devaluation) to counterbalance their position in the world economy, considered by the participants to that system 'beggar-thy-neighbour' policies. As these measures increased, the international institutions set up crashed opening to political disorder or wars and to an economic protectionism. Such a sequence of events, that represents the evolution of capitalism up to the Second World War, shows how the world economy was an international economic order based on the balance of power among the participants to the trade regime and on international institutions established by agreements. In fact, 'Much of what happens in the world economy is determined by the rich countries, without even trying. . . . This means that their national policies can strongly influence the world economy. But more important that their sheer weight is the rich countries' willingness to throw that very weight about in shaping the rules of the world economies' (Chang 2008: 31).

Notes

1 Recently Canada entered in the top ten ranking because Russia left for the decrease of the level of the GDP.
2 Although Russia is considered an economy introducing capitalism at the same time as the other BRICS countries (where 'S' represents South Africa), its industrial revolution started between the 19th and 20th centuries and the importance of its economy dates back that period.
3 While in Table 9.3 the variable is the GDP measured in constant 1990 international $, in Table 9.4 it is the PPP GDP measured in constant 2017 international $. The last variable, considering the prices of a fixed basket of goods and services in domestic currencies and in USA dollars, enables the derivation of an exchange value that can be applied to the GDP in national currencies to transform it in dollars purchasing power parity. Thus, the value of the yearly domestic product of all the countries (GDP) measured in dollar PPP reflects the real value of goods and services produced in them.
4 Great Britain took this step in the 1820s.
5 Northwest Europe includes Great Britain, Ireland, Norway, Sweden, Finland, Denmark, the Netherlands, Belgium, France, Switzerland and Germany.
6 Portugal, Spain, Italy, Austro-Hungarian and Russian territories belong to Southeastern Europe.
7 'Indentured work' is a medieval form of voluntary unpaid work used for five years to train apprentices that was applied by European traders providing colonisers with workers to be employed in the plantations. It was a contract of service due by Indian people as a payment of the travel cost to expatriate in the other British colonies.
8 It is a form of recruitment of Indian workers employed in a plantation similar to the indenture service practised and managed by foremen.
9 The number of refugees and asylum seekers is nearly 34 million people (12 per cent of all world migrants).
10 Historically, in a sending country the relation between the rate of migration of the population and the GDP presents a 'bell shape'. When the country achieves a certain level of income the outflow of workers starts, increasing at a rising rate first and at a decreasing one then up to a maximum value; after the top the increasing GDP reduces the rate of growth of migration first quickly then slowly up to zero; thus, emigration stops and the country becomes a receiving one because it needs workers for demographic reasons.
11 'Economic migrants support the hosting economies through: the provision of a supplementary labour force to maintain the level of activity of the economy, the supply of workers in industry and services where the number of nationals is insufficient, the contribution to the sustainability of retirement funds, the increasing engagement in entrepreneurial activities, in consumption of goods and services. The income received by migrants saved and remitted to the original countries enable: 'to buy goods thereby increasing the standard of living, or to buy accommodation thereby raising the aggregate domestic demand, to support with investments existing entrepreneurial activities of families (agriculture, commerce), to improve the education of the members of the family and, possibly, to finance their departure' (Romagnoli 2019: 247).

References

Belassa, B. (1961) *The Theory of Economic Integration*, Homewood, IL: R. D. Irwin (reprinted by Routledge, 2012).

Chang, H.-J. (2008) *Bad Samaritans. The Myth of Free Trade and the Secret History of Capitalism*, New York: Bloomsbury Publishing.

Constant, A. F. and Zimmermann, K. F. (eds.) (2013) *International Handbook on the Economics of Migration*, Cheltenham: Edward Elgar.

Fouquin, M. and Hugot, J. (2016) *Two Centuries of Bilateral Trade and Gravity Data: 1827–2014*, Paris: CEPLII Working Papers.
Gereffi, G. (2005) 'The Global Economy: Organization, Governance, and Development', in N. J. Smelser and R. Swedberg (eds.) *The Handbook of Economic Sociology*, Princeton: Princeton University Press, Ch. 8: 160–182. https://doi.org/10.1515/9781400835584.160
Gilpin, R. (2001) *Global Political Economy. Understanding the International Economic Order*, Princeton: Princeton University Press.
Graff, M., Kenwood, A. G. and Lougheed, A. L. (2014) *Growth of the International Economy, 1820–2015*, London: Routledge.
Lewis, W. A. (1978) *The Evolution of the International Economic Order*, Princeton: Princeton University Press (Reprinted in 2016).
Maddison, A. (2001) *The World Economy. A Millennial Perspective*, Paris: OECD.
Maddison, A. (2003) *The World Economy. Historical Statistics*, Paris: OECD.
McFarland, V. (2015) 'The New International Economic Order, Interdependence, and Globalization', *Humanity: An International Journal of Human Rights, Humanitarianism, and Development*, 6 (1): 217–33.
Mckeown, A. (2004) 'World Migration, 1846–1940', *Journal of World History*, 15 (2): 155–89.
O'Rourke, K. H. and Williamson, J. G. (2014) 'Introduction: The Spread of and Resistance to World Capitalism', in L. Neal and J. G. Williamson (eds.) *Capitalism Volume II. The Spread of Capitalism: From the 1848 to the Present*, Cambridge: Cambridge University Press: 1–21.
Polanyi, K. (1944) *The Great Transformation*, Boston: Beacon Press.
Romagnoli, A. (2019) 'Bound to Share Aims and Instruments: The Future of Euro-Mediterranean Migration Policy', in S. Capasso and E. Ferragina (eds.) *Mediterranean Migration and the Labour Markets. Policies for Growth and Social Development in the Mediterranean Area*, Abingdon: Routledge: 238–58.
Taylor, J. E. (1999) 'The New Economics of Labour Migration and the Role of Remittances in the Migration Process', *International Migration*, 37: 65–87.
Trade and Globalization – Our World in Data. https://ourworldindata.org/
Zupi, M. (2021) *Flussi migratori (Migration Flows)*, Osservatorio di politica internazioale (International Policy Observatory), n. 40, Rome: CeSPI. www.parlamento.it/osservatoriointernazionale

Glossary

Common market is a custom union where there aren't non-tariff barriers, and the same institutional forms and common technical standards are adopted.

Custom union is a free trade area characterised by a single discriminatory trade policy towards third parties.

Economic and monetary union is a common market sharing the same economic institutions and a single currency.

Free trade area is a territory across two or more countries where the goods circulate and are exchanged without restrictions by virtue of an international agreement.

General Agreement on Tariff and Trade (GATT) is a multilateral treaty in force between 1948 and 1995 aimed to pursue the maximum drop of customs duties, the elimination of quotas as well as tariffs and subsidies to the exports, and to apply to all the participants the most-favoured-nation principle.

Gold-exchange standard is an arrangement of the international monetary system where the banknotes can be issued only if the central bank issuing them held an equivalent quantity of convertible currencies or gold as reserves.

Gold standard is an arrangement of the international monetary system where the 'par value' of a currency unit is equal to the value of the fixed amount of gold contained in it. Pegging the currencies of the countries participating to the international trade to the 'mint price' results in both their convertibility into gold and fixed exchange rates.

International economic order is the configuration of the world economy in force for a certain period, representing the tendency of the structural arrangement of the trade regime and institutions as well as the organisations managing it towards the interests of one or more participants in the system.

International monetary system is a set of international rules (agreed by the states or unilaterally adopted) and institutions arranging the ways by which the comparative value of the different currencies is established to provide internationally acceptable means of payments having convertibility. It must provide a mechanism for the pegging of currencies (gold, basket of currencies) and for their exchange (fixed or floating exchange rates).

International trade is constituted by the flows of goods and services incoming and outgoing in the national markets according to the procedures and restrictions established by the trading countries.

Migrant is a person living permanently for a long period in a place (internal migrant) or in a country (international migrant) where he wasn't born. He can have the legal status of migrant worker, forced migrant, asylum seeker, EU internal migrant or irregular migrant.

Migration system is a continuous, intense and constant flow of migrants connecting different countries for a period that enables the emergence of financial, technical, professional and cultural networks.

Most-favoured nation clause is the customs reduction or removal on goods and services, granted reciprocally unilaterally to an international trade partner, that can be the extended to third states trading with them.

Preferential trade system is a bilateral trade system established by an international agreement in an area corresponding to the territories of both states, entailing the reciprocal lowering or removal of import duties.

Spread of capitalism consists in the diffusion of capitalist production technologies across world economies through international trade and investments.

Trade area is a geographic space in which the exchange of goods is managed according to homogeneous conditions or trade systems. Different trade systems, established by state agreements, give rise to different kinds of trade areas.

Trade regime is the set of trading rules and organisation procedures characterising a kind of trade area established by international agreements.

World economy is the set of the national economies of the world characterised by their structural features and welfare conditions and of the international agreements signed by the states to manage the international economic exchanges.

World Trade Organisation (WTO) is an intergovernmental organisation that came into force in 1995 to establish, revise and enforce the rules governing the international trade.

10 The international economic order toward one-dimensional world economy

The evolution of the world economy after the Second World War appears to be very complex and multifaceted because of the economic changes that followed one another, the different perspectives from which they should have been managed and the international political events that have interfered with them. Since the aim of the chapter is to examine the driving forces coordinating the international relations among the economies in the period, the focus of the analysis will be on the institutions building process that has characterised the 'world economic architecture' (least biased phrase to express the international economic order) and on the technological advances that made it possible. The agreements among the states to improve and safeguard the international exchanges economically have probably shaped the world economy more than ever; in fact, the Bretton Woods conference planned the rules that would co-ordinate the economic relations among the countries even before the end of the war, and the institution of the World Trade Organisation – WTO, in synergy with the technological advances of the last quarter of the century, sponsored the advent of the so-called 'globalisation'.

The world economy devised at Bretton Woods conference enjoyed success for more than two decades, so much so the period was labelled the 'Golden age'. However, the international economic order issued from that convention had to cope with some unexpected economic events, like the failure of 'Fordism' and the oil and financial crises but also with some consequences of its working like the competition emerging between the developing and the developed countries as well as within the capitalist economies. After a period of 20 years characterised by economic instability and contrasts, another kind of institutional set fulfilling the General Agreement on Trade and Tariffs – GATT was introduced to provide against the changing world economy: the 'liberism'. It was an interpretation of the working of the capitalist economies associated with a group of co-ordinated recommendations for the policymakers to comply with in arranging a well-formed and well-functioning economy. The adoption of these 'Liberist' recipes concentrated capitalism on developed countries up to the 1990s, strengthened their power in the international exchanges, homogenised the economic policies in developing and developed countries and paved the way for a one-dimensional world economy.

Meanwhile, technological advances gave rise to a new epochal change, the Digital Revolution, based on the establishment of the electronic industry, the adoption

DOI: 10.4324/9781315679730-14

of automation and on the use of computers, all processes that changed the operational routines of production and consumption and introduced new devices and final goods. The application of such a technology in the communication systems enabled it to reduce the time and the costs of the services and to push the implementation of new information systems like the internet. These improvements, together with the agreements to fulfil the international movements of capital and financial securities and those to introduce a new trade regime (the WTO), allowed the increase of the international economic exchanges and the implementation of the so-called 'globalisation'. The resulting world economy was thus characterised by flows of final goods and services, but also of semifinished products and intermediate services resulting from the technological process of production fragmentation. All these trade flows, that by mistake are thought to have emerged from 'international markets', frequently get away from the national or international laws because they are sometimes managed by agreements 'over the counter' rather than by official contracts on the markets, and are monitored by private international organisations; this is the case of the exchange of raw materials and financial derivatives by international operators and multinationals. These unofficial exchanges, associated with the other trends in the configuration of the international economic relations among the states, have caused the commitment of the economic prerogatives of the state to international 'self-ruled private authorities' and mechanisms.

The building of a new economic order

The postwar period opened up an urgent need for international appeasement and cooperation in order to leave behind three decades of economic and political disasters. This meant not only a request for new institutions ruling the international economic and political relations but also for widely shared decisions, more participated organisations and more equal membership for the states taking part to them (multilateralism). To this end it was crucial to engage in the project the United States, which previously kept away from the international organisations fearing that the membership will bound their capacity to protect the national interests[1] (Jeffry 2012: 12–17). On these premises not only the United Nations, the General Agreement on Trade and Tariffs (GATT), the International Monetary Fund, the Organisation for Economic Co-operation and Development (OECD), etc. have been created to manage the economic and political relations among the states, but also a new procedure to build the international institutions was introduced. In fact, until then the coordination of the international exchanges had been a deal of a group of Western countries, so the international economic order mainly implemented the European rule of the world economy. When international relations went beyond the European countries this configuration of the international economic order fell apart, even if it was kept alive up to the 1930s by the support of the US dollar to the Gold Exchange standard and of the New York Stock Exchange to the financial system. The institutional setup issued from the building process implemented in the aftermath of the Second World War was more consistent than the previous one because it combined the physical technologies of production of the industrial economies with the trade regime and the system of international payments that enhanced their potentialities. Leveraging these strong points, it succeeded in recovering the Western countries to such extent that their development processes up to 1973 were due mainly to the implementation of 'export led' policies.

The Fordism as a new production technology

Just before the First World War, Henry Ford completely changed the structure of the automobile production process from the technological and managerial points of view. The main innovations introduced were the assembly line and the customised machine tools moving no more through steam power but through electricity, and the new working tasks and division of labour complying with the new plant and its operating procedures. Even 'the new buildings were designed specifically to house assembly line production. Design and layout went hand in hand with materials handling and internal flow, so when drafting new buildings for these systems Ford's engineers thought about the factories as a whole seeing them as great master machines' (Halpern 2022).[2] Such a oneness wasn't only limited to the 'physical technologies' (mechanisation, technical division of labour and customised factory building) but included also the 'social technologies' pertaining to the firm (higher wages, new forms of business organisation and of managerial methods to develop strategies upgrading the market position of firms (see Chapter Six). More, these innovations spread inside and beyond the industrial sector so much so that, because of the transformations they brought about in the economic and sociopolitical organisations, a phase of the capitalist evolution was named after the pioneer 'Fordism'.[3]

After the Second World War this industrial production technology had the opportunity of spreading in the other Western capitalist countries thanks to the 'European Recovery Plan' (ERP), usually known as the 'Marshall Plan'. The ERP represented, between April 1948 and June 1951, a transfer from the USA to European countries of Dollar grants, grants in kind, and loans, counting to 13.3 billion dollars (equivalent to about 115 billion Dollar in 2021).[4] 'The American role in promoting Europe's recovery during these years extended far beyond the disbursement of aid.' . . . In fact, it provided for entrepreneurial internships by sending 'businessmen from across Europe to the United States to study American production techniques. The ECA [Economic Cooperation Administration, an agency of the USA Government organising the ERP and reporting both to the Department of State and to the Department of Commerce] also had a small-business division which distributed information and held counselling sessions' (Kunz 1997: 168). In parallel to the ECA in Europe the Organisation for European Economic Cooperation (OEEC) was created in 1948, an intergovernmental administration to allocate and distribute the Marshall Plan.

Pushed by these circumstances and treasuring similar industrial experiences that emerged in Europe in the interwar period (Settis 2016), Fordism became between 1950 and 1973 not only a consistent managerial philosophy capable of increasing the production and lowering the costs, but also a social philosophy creating a rising welfare in Western capitalist countries. In fact, from the business point of view the technological innovations opened to the mass production of standardised affordable goods that, being bought by a large part of people, gave rise to mass consumption. However, these outcomes were achieved associating the adoption of such 'physical technologies' with the implementation of some 'social technologies' at the level of both the company and the economy. The managers provided workers with higher wages in return for the acceptance of the technical division of labour, and the states drafted legislation protecting workers and favouring the wage bargaining between the trade unions and the associations of entrepreneurs. In addition to the monitoring of the 'labour market', the state social philosophy of the Fordist period accepted the state-owned companies, a limited competition among oligopolistic ones and even monopolistic companies, facilitated the advertising and the emergence of the consumer credit industry, secured the full employment, established a welfare state, and supported the participation to the GATT requiring policies for the control of financial capitals and public finance (see Watson 2019).

The Bretton Woods conference and the new trade regime

It was not yet finished the Second World War when, in July 1944, the delegates of 44 states[5] gathered in Bretton Woods (New Hampshire, USA) to talk about the conditions under which international economic relations could be developed after the war. In particular they had to decide about the creation of a new international monetary system that could be stable, safe and able to prevent the 'beggar-thy-neighbour' policies of the countries engaged in the international exchanges; they had also to draft the basic rules for the development of the international trade and of the economic growth promotion. Despite two different points of view on the future configuration of the monetary system,[6] a deal was made on some institutions. The promotion of international monetary co-operation and exchange rate stability, as well as the connected balanced growth and expansion of international trade were attributed to the International Monetary Fund – IMF (Orastean 2014), an agency of the United Nations that became operating in 1945. The international payments system elaborated by the IMF was a new version of the Gold-exchange standard system. In fact, the agency established that the 'anchor currency' used in international trade must still be a national one (the US Dollar) instead a supranational one (the Bancor proposed by Keynes) issued by a specific Global Central Bank working as a Clearing Union. Such a choice was justified by the fact that the United States, holding most of the world's gold reserves, could comply with the principle of the gold convertibility for the bills. The dollar/gold parity was established at 1/35 ounces, and all the other currencies of the states joining the IMF were pegged to it; in such a way a system of currencies characterised by fixed exchange rates was created, having the convertibility into US dollars and then into gold. The promotion of balanced international trade growth was guaranteed by the permission granted to the IMF to loan short-term funds to the member countries having a temporary balance of payments needs due to a shortage of foreign currencies; to manage this activity the IMF used the fund subscription quotas of the state members. The second institution established at Bretton Woods Conference was the International Bank for Reconstruction and Development (IBRD), which was entrusted with the promotion of the long-term growth of member countries by providing loans to finance the reconstruction of European economies destroyed by the Second World War. The funds used to achieve such an aim were constituted both by the member states contributions and by the bonds issued by the bank on the capital markets to create its functional fund.

The certainty of the international prices, given by the international payments system coming out from Bretton Woods, favoured international trade. Such positive effect was further enhanced by the GATT, a multilateral treaty in force between 1948 and 1995 aimed to pursue the maximum drop of custom duties, the elimination of quotas as well as tariffs hampering the imports and subsidies to the exports altering the comparative advantage, and to apply automatically to all the participants the most-favoured-nation principle. A lot of trade agreements emerged worldwide in the second half of the 19th century following the GATT that established a free trade area; someone remained at the stage of the free trade area, some others became a common market or an economic union using a common currency. The complete path toward the integration of the markets was made by the European Economic Community (EEC)[7], which was established in 1957 and transformed in 1993 into the European Union (EU). The first January of 2002 the European Monetary Union (EMU) and the euro notes and coins were introduced in the first group of European Union countries, giving rise to an 'optimal currency region'.

> As many as 17 trading blocs were established in other parts of the world in the 1960s – regional arrangements of varying degrees of integration covering more than 80 contracting parties. These included the Latin America Free Trade Area (LAFTA) of seven countries, set up in 1961, and the Central American Common Market (CACM), which was to become full integrated by 1967. In Africa, the seven former French West African colonies formed a new trading bloc, and Chad, Gabon, and the Central African Republic formed the Equatorial Customs Union. The successful Associations of Southeast Asian Nations (ASEAN), covering Brunei, Indonesia, Malaysia, Philippine, Singapore, and Thailand was set up in 1967. In 1992, ASEAN established the ASEAN Free Trade Area (AFTA), accepting Vietnam as a member in 1995, and Burma (Myanmar), Laos, and Cambodia in 1997. The Australia-New Zealand Closer Economic Relation (CER) agreement commenced in 1965. Other preferential arrangements were established elsewhere, but they were important only within their own region, and many of them did not last for more than a decade.
>
> (Graff, Kenwood and Lougheed 2014: 267)

Besides the European Economic Community another international organisation was established in Europe between 1949 and 1991: the Council for Mutual Economic Assistance (whose English acronymous was COMECON). It was an organisation whose members were Bulgaria, Cuba, Czechoslovakia, East Germany, Hungary,

Mongolia, Poland, Romania, Soviet Union and Vietnam. It was established to promote the coordination of the economic activities of the members and to develop multilateral economic, scientific and technical co-operation among them. Thus, its aims were not mainly addressed to the promotion of international trade among the participants to the organisation.

The configuration of the world economy came to light at the end of the Second World War and presented some differences with respect to that of the 19th century. First of all, the international monetary system planned in the conference of Bretton Woods wasn't the result of a series of unilateral deeds of the states as it happened in the adoption of the Gold Standard system, but the result of a multilateral agreement. This multilateralism, reflected also in the GATT, was the inner meaning at the base of the United Nations (UN) organisation and in the operation of all the agencies carrying out their activities. Despite that, the multilateralism resulted in being fictitious because the anchor currency was once again that of the economic and commercial power, and the working of the international economic organisations wasn't balanced. The fact that the US dollar was put as an anchor currency gave the country a lot of economic advantages. The first is the fact that the price of exported goods and services from the US was lower than that of the other countries that had to pay to change their currencies in Dollars. In addition, the loans required by the US worldwide are at a lower rate because the dollars are reserves of all the world banks. Finally, the risk of the reduction of the purchasing power of the dollar is unloaded on the foreigners holding or borrowing it.[8] As to the unbalanced power of the members of the international financial institutions, the decision mechanism of their working was based on the contribution share to the institution fund, which in turn was consistent with their economic power: this unbalanced the management towards the interests of the economic powers and of the Dollar. The same situation emerged regarding the function of the International Bank for Reconstruction and Development in the case of the European Recovery Plan. The distribution of this aid was directly managed by the government of the USA instead of the International Bank for Reconstruction and Development (IBRD). Considering these and other features of the 'global economic architecture' in force after the Bretton Wood Conference, the international economic order appeared biased towards the USA and on other powers' interests.

Success and failure of the new economic order

In the second half of the 19th century the structure of the world economy changed not only because of the success of the new institutions in recovering the economies destroyed by the war but also because unexpected political events extended the number of key players in the world economy. While during the Golden Age the industrial economies were taking advantage of the new economic order, the world was changing because the dismantling of colonialism and the empowerment of oil producers were causing the entrance of the developing countries in the international arena. As the international economic order couldn't in and of itself consider or cope with the change in the structure of the world economy, the competition among the industrial economies resulted in monetary and financial crises. In addition, the model of industrialisation promoting development came to an end due to pressure from new customer desires and the fall apart of the 'social technologies' supporting the Fordism. Thus, the collapse of the 'institutional technologies' associated with those of 'physical technologies' and 'social technologies' created a perfect storm for the economies in 1980s.

The evolution of the world economy up to the 1990s

The evolution of the world economy after the Second World War has been vertiginous, so much so that the world GDP grew nearly more than nine times starting from 1950 to 2020 and eight times from 1960, passing from a value of 11.3 trillion in 1960 to 86.8 trillion in 2021 (see Figure 10.1). Despite such a rising trend, two setbacks, in 1973–175 and in 1980–1982, and also two downturns, in 2009 and 2020, occurred in the period. In addition, three different phases that can be identified considering the evolution of the world GDP and of the world export followed one another. Between 1950 and 1973 the world economy increased nearly three times (see Table 9.3), and the yearly rate of growth of the per-capita GDP was the highest in the evolution of capitalist economies (Table 2.2). In the same period a big increment of the international trade occurred, so that the index number of the world export, which was equal to 164 in 1951, jumped to 931 in 1973 with a boost of 5.7 times (see Figure 9.7). The extraordinary growth of the capitalist economies and the big leap ahead of developing countries during the Golden Age were due to the spread of industrialisation following the adoption of Fordist production methods and to the increase of the internationalisation of all the economies due to the restructuring of the rules governing the international economic relations. The following two decades are considered a 'transition period' because not only the institutional framework favouring the exceptional outcome of the previous period fell apart, but also the technological model did, upsetting the policymakers, academics and opinion makers. In the period the value of the world GDP just doubled, and the per capita yearly rate of growth of income in capitalist economies was lower than that of the Golden Age (see Table 2.2 and Table 9.3); the export had a lesser performance than the income, as the index number of the world export in 1990 reached only a value of 1744 starting from a value of 931 in 1973 (see Figure 9.7). The last 30 years represent for capitalism a new technological phase and another institutional setup favouring the diffusion of a new international economic order and the utmost 'globalisation phase'; the index number of the world export jumped to 4,914 in 2008 (see Figure 9.7), and such an increase of 2.8 times has been more than the increase of the world GDP that grew 2.2 times between 1990 and 2015 (OurWorldInData). Despite these results the annual average rates of growth of the per capita GDP of capitalist economies in the sub-period swung between 0.42 per cent recorded by Italy and 1.50 per cent of the UK (except India and China, whose values were 4.7 and 8.8 per cent, respectively – see Table 2.2).

Behind the long and virtuous process of economic growth, although characterised by discontinuous performance in GDP growth and in international trade expansion

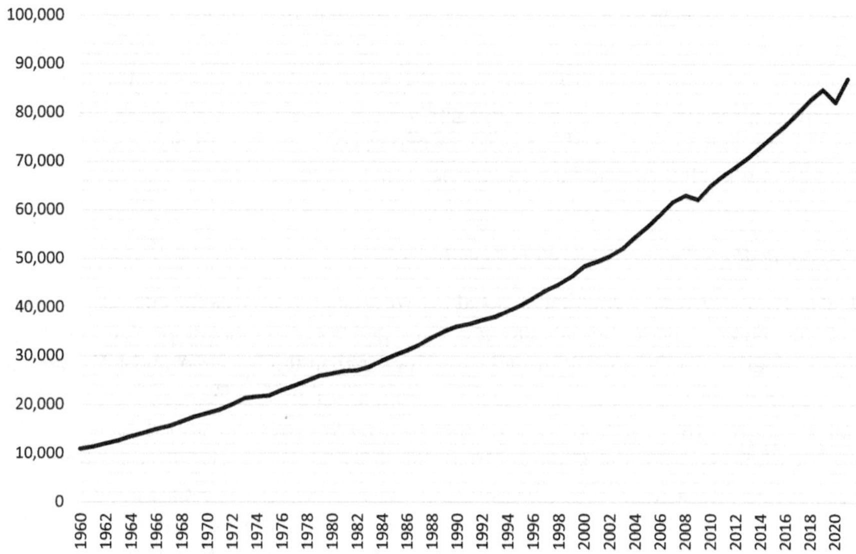

Figure 10.1 World GDP growth between 1960 and 2021 (constant 2015 billion $)

Source: Author's elaboration from https://ourworldindata.org/economic-growth accessed the 28th of January 2023

and by discordant trends of the variables in each sub-period, a lot of structural transformations occurred in the world economy due to the processes of change of both developed and developing countries. Two among them, the economic empowerment of the developing countries and the counterbalance of the economic power among the developed nations, emerged during the Golden Age and continued for all of the post-war period, even if in different forms due to the intersections with other political and economic events. The first one, already highlighted in Chapter Nine, reveals itself in the reduction of the share of world GDP produced by the capitalist countries (see Figure 9.3). Despite the impressive economic growth that characterised the Golden Age the capitalist countries' contribution to the world GDP shifted from 58.60 per cent in 1950, the best value of the capitalist era, to 53.20 per cent in 1973 and 52.8 per cent in 1990. This trend turned to developing countries' advantage (Brazil, India and China included), which increased from 41.40 per cent to 46.80 per cent and 47.3 per cent their contribution to the world GDP up to 1990. This result was obtained by a generalised process of development implemented in the countries characterised by traditional economies and by the good performance of some developing economies. The yearly average rate of growth that Brazil and China's GDP presented in the period 1950–1973 (8.30 per cent and 5.02 per cent, respectively) was consistent with those obtained in other developing areas such as Latin America and the Caribbean, where the variable was 4.22 per cent between 1960 and 1973, and Middle East and North Africa where it was 11.0 per cent in the period 1969–1973. This leap forward stopped in the following sub-period characterised by the crisis that affected the developing areas more than the developed ones. Another element favouring the economies of developing countries was the increased participation in international trade; in fact, the share of exports among the non-rich countries grew from 2 per cent of the global export in 1947 to 10 per cent in 1973 and 12 per cent in 1990, and the share of exports of non-rich countries toward rich ones swung in all the period around 26 per cent (see Figure 9.9).

The competition among the developed economies

The second structural trend that affected the world economy was the economic counterbalance in favour of the latecomers and France inside the developed countries up to the nineties, due to a GDP growth pace higher than that of USA and UK. Such a phenomenon, just having emerged in the beginnings of the Golden Age, is represented in Figure 10.2, where the number of times the GDP of each developed economy has grown with respect to the value of 1960 put equal to 100 can be detected from the value of the index number on the vertical axis. The yearly value of the variable for France, Germany, Italy and Japan up to 2000 is higher with respect to those of USA and UK, but in the new century US economic advancement overtook European countries in terms of growth pace. Japan didn't suffer such overtaking because its GDP index value in 2020 was 7.5 times that of 1960. The UK, which for all of the period presented the lowest GDP growth, reached in 2020 the index value of 369 as Italy did, even if its behaviour was in line with Germany and France 20 years before.

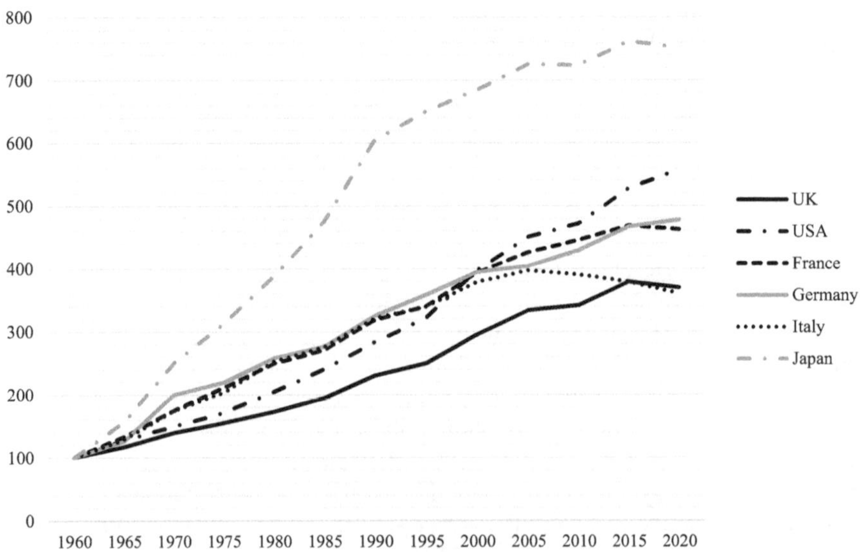

Figure 10.2 GDP growth for selected countries between 1960 and 2021 (index number 1960 = 100)

Source: Author's elaboration from World Bank *World Development Indicators* and *Federal Reserve Bank of St. Louis*; https://fred.stlouisfed.org/series/DEURGDPR, February 16, 2023

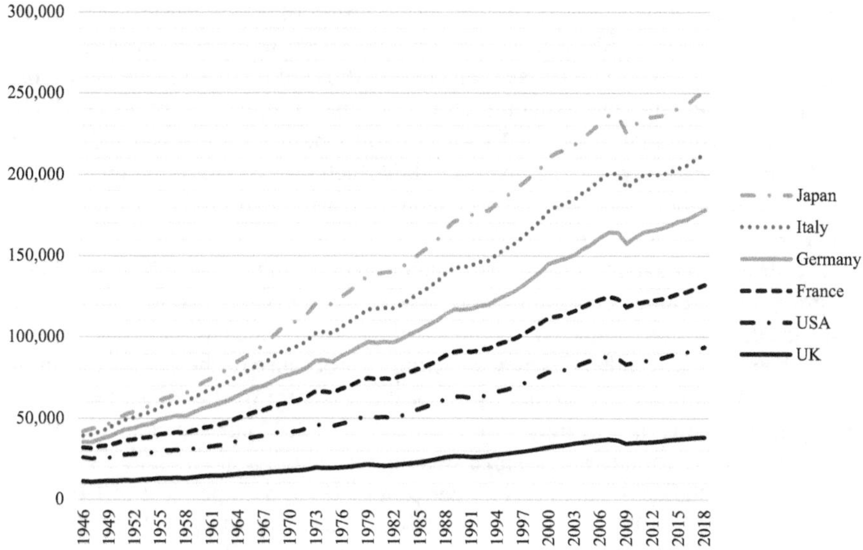

Figure 10.3 A stacked line chart for the per capita GDP of higher-income countries between 1946 and 2018 (constant 2015 US$)

Source: Author's elaboration from https://ourworldindata.org/economic-growth, accessed January 28, 2023

Such best performances of the latecomers also meant a reduction of the distance from the US in terms of living standards; in fact, as the US per capita GDP grew 3.7 times between 1946 and 2018, in the same period the increment of the variable was 6.3 for France, 13.2 times for Germany and 13.8 for Japan. Such values can be detected in Figure 10.3, where the grade of the lines representing the evolution of per capita GDP of each country in the period measures the yearly pace of growth. The lines are piled in descending order so that the top belongs to the country having recorded the highest increase (Japan), and the yearly values of the variable for a country is measured by the difference between its lines and that below; thus, the lowest line is that of the UK, whose per capita GDP increased in the period only 3.5 times.

The increased importance of the European developed economies was reinforced by the creation of the European Economic Community (EEC), a regional trade area that entered into force in 1958 and transformed into the European Union in 1993. In 1968 the EEC removed the customs duties among the member countries and introduced common customs tariffs and rules of products origin towards third parties, thus becoming a Custom Union acting as a common market. In 1993 the EEC was transformed into the European Union, a supranational political and economic union of European member states, having from 1994 a single market based on the same rules enabling the free movement of persons, goods, services, and capital. Starting from 2002 a group of increasing member states over time adopted the EU new currency – that is, the euro (€). The creation of this new economic entity changed the world economy because a group of Western European countries emerged in the 1970s as a single economic player in the world economy. Its contribution to the world GDP has been close to those of the USA since the 1970s; in fact, the GDP value in constant 2015 US$ of the European Union in 1970 was 5.131 billion while that of the USA was 5.186 billion; in 1978 it was 6.725 against 6.881, and in 1980 it was 7.131 against 7.080. Such overtaking lasted up to 2012, but such a run after between the two economic powers in 2016–2017 China overtook both (see Figure 10.4).

The structural change in the world economy, due to the counterbalance inside the group of developed economies, wasn't restricted only to a higher growth pace of the latecomers and France with respect to the USA and the UK and to the shrinking of the number of industrial players acting in it because of the establishment of the European Economic Community; also, the structure of the industrial economies was becoming increasingly differentiated (Aoki 2013). In the Golden Age the openness of EEC countries and Japan was higher than that of USA, as their trade was a share of the GDP equal to 41.9 per cent in 1973, 51.6 per cent in 1980 and to 53.1 per cent in 1990, while the respective values of USA were 13.1 per cent, 20.1 per cent and 19.8 per cent. Likewise Japan behaved like EEC economies up to 1980, as its trade share on the GDP was 19.3 per cent, 27.2 per cent, and 19.7 per cent in the three years taken as landmarks. Another difference between the two big economic zones was that the EEC countries were more 'mixed economies' with respect to the USA. The presence of state-owned enterprises in these economies,

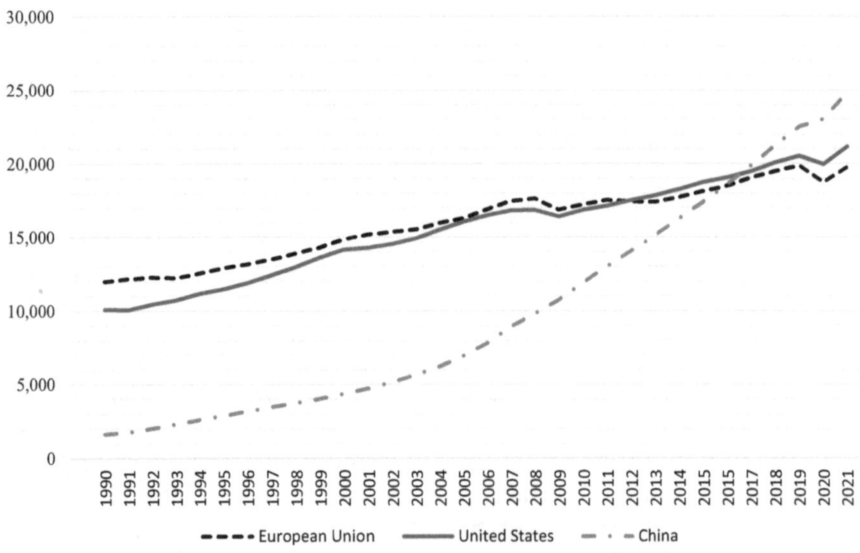

Figure 10.4 GDP level, in terms of PPP, for the world economic powers between 1990 and 2021 (billions of constant 2017 international $)

Source: Author's elaboration from World Bank *World Development Indicators*

whose pick was achieved in the 1970s, resulted from a stated tendency of governments to strengthen the reconstruction and growth policies, and to provide citizens with a universal system of welfare. As to the dimension of the state intervention in the industrial production in Europe 'some scholar argued that during the early 1980s, 10–25 per cent of manufacturing output was accounted for by public enterprise in industrial countries like Italy' (Toninelli 2008: 680). In the other countries of EEC this share fluctuated between 7 and 15 per cent of the GDP, while the share of total investments varied between 11 and 23 per cent (see Chapter Five). Also, in public service productions like transport, gas, water and electricity distribution, healthcare, education, pension systems, and social protection, the state intervened. Such involvement was due to the fact that in Europe the governments wanted to ensure that the economic development went well together with the social upgrading, and thus provided welfare systems based on a redistributive model with an ex-ante allocation of resources and a universal criterion for the provision, or on a work-related model with resources allocation through the salary as well as the intervention of the state and a job criterion for the provision. Instead in the USA the welfare state system was based on a residual model, in the sense that it intervened ex-post when the personal resources couldn't provide basic services like healthcare and education; all the other social services were up to the market.

The structure of the world economy in the lead-up to the 1970s was totally different from what the Bretton Woods Conference expected and for which it had provided a new international economic order (see endnote 1). Even though some structural features were side effects of the economic recovery and of the growth of international trade, their presence created problems in the workings of the institutional framework planned at Bretton Woods, all the more because in those days, the driving force of the economy, Fordism, was also running out of energy. When Fordism was introduced in industrial production it triggered a lot of capital investments, whose returns were guaranteed by the high throughput allowed by the economies of scale and by the limited competition on the domestic markets. As full employment and plant exploitation progressed, the wages rose and the maintenance services increased the costs of production; thus, the product prices increased more than the salaries and the sales reduced. In addition, the obsolescence of machinery on one side required replacements and on the other side made its financing more expensive because of their depreciation; in such a situation the investments fell down, the production capacity reduced and unemployment increased. 'The growth of multinational firms in Europe and the generalisation of Fordist methods in Europe and Japan qualitatively and radically modified the international configuration from 1967 onwards: the level of productivity in Japan and Europe (particularly West Germany and France) converged on that of the USA to the point where wage cost per unit produced became higher in the USA. From this point onward, the US trade balance was in deficit' (Lipietz 1985: 8). The maturity of industrial products, the obsolescence of the plants, and the increased costs of labour and money put the physical technology of Fordism in a quandary. Moreover, the social technologies could no longer sustain this production philosophy because the public debt of industrialised countries was increasing due to the previous indebtedness made to implement these policies. On this situation fell the oil crisis of 1973 that imposed not only higher prices for the energetic resources but also the need to restructure the production processes to save such energetic resources.

The empowerment of developing countries

At the same time as the developed countries and some of their partners were framing the new trade regime and building the international monetary system, another unforeseen process introduced new countries to the group of players acting in the world economy. In fact, the end of the Second World War marked the beginning of the process of decolonisation that, having started since 1946, interested the colonies of the powers worldwide for more than two decades. The process caused the emergence of newly independent states that, aiming to implement their path towards industrialisation and economic development, on the one hand expanded the group of developing countries and their contribution to the world economy and on the other hand claimed an active role in the management of the international economic relations. The acceptance of the phenomenon was only in appearance since it was officially sustained by the United Nations only in 1960 by Resolution n. 1514-XV of the 14th of December. Although these countries didn't have a voice among international organisations up to the 1960s, dissatisfaction with the management of the GATT had already emerged in the second half of the 1950s; the primary product exporter complained (and the Haberler Report commissioned by the GATT confirmed) that 'the agricultural protectionism in the industrial countries had minimised the benefits that the traditional food-exporting countries could have expected to receive from their membership of GATT, and that many of the developing countries had also been disadvantaged by the commercial and other policies of the industrial nations' (Graff, Kenwood and Lougheed 2014: 265).

The accession of the new states to the United Nations changed the equilibrium of the assembly because the ratio between developed and developing members overturned; in fact, the new states grew from 23 members in 1955 to 46 in 1960 and to 70 (more than a half of the total members) in 1971. Moreover, it has been on the initiative of the developing countries that the United Nations established a lot of agencies supporting their development. In 1964 the first United Nations Conference on Trade and Development (UNCTAD) was created to integrate developing countries into the world economy, help them in overtaking their vulnerabilities and improve their competitiveness; in 1965 the United Nations Development Programme (UNDP) was established, an agency whose fund is constituted by voluntary contributions from UN member states to eliminate poverty, and to promote growth and human development; then in 1966 another agency to promote the industrialisation of developing countries was created, the United Nations for the Industrial Development Organization (UNIDO). In addition, in 1964 inside the group of UN members participating in the Non-Aligned Movement[9] the '77 Group' was created, a coalition of countries aiming at enhancing a joint capacity of negotiation to sustain their collective economic interests inside the United Nations.

Beside the empowerment of the developing countries inside the UN and their agencies devoted to development support, there was another important event that revealed other key players of the world economy: the setting up of the Organisation of the Petroleum Exporting Countries. The OPEC is a permanent intergovernmental institution established in 1960 by Iran, Iraq, Kuwait, Saudi Arabia and Venezuela, joined over time by other oil producers, to unify petroleum policies among Member Countries, secure stable prices for petroleum producers, provide regular supply of petroleum to consuming nations as well as return on capital to the investors in the industry. It wasn't a simple association of states but a cartel of the main world oil producers that, after the nationalisation of the oil production that put an end to the monopoly of the big British, French and US oil companies, controlled the world oil exchanges. It was the first time that countries rich in a crucial resource for the functioning of modern economies posed themselves as key players in the world economy.

The emergence of developing countries in the international arena put in the limelight the problem of economic development and of co-operation and financial and technical assistance that the developed countries donated for the success of the process. Bilateral programmes of official development assistance (ODA) were implemented in the 1950s by donor economies (the developed ones, USSR and China) but unevenly and clumsily; in addition, sometimes the donors' countries considered in this category the loans or the financing conditioned for the purchase of weapons and industrial products. Moreover, as to the aid loans the grace period (the span from the credit concession and the first repayment), their date of maturity and their interest rate were at the discretion of the donors. In the sixties the United Nations and the Organisation for Economic Co-operation and Development (OECD) got involved to work on the ODA definition, on the harmonisation of the concession procedures, and on the creation of a code of conduct for the donor countries; this work had to regulate, in a multilateral framework, the financial funding for the integration of developing economies in the world trade and for the fulfilment of their infrastructural investments. The UNCTAD and the DAC (Development Assistance Committee) were appointed by the UN and OECD to solve the political and applied problems.

> Institutionally, the decade-long process of setting objectives for aid volume and terms was both a collaboration and a tug-of-war between the DAC (representing the donors) and the UN (dominated by aid recipients). The first UNCTAD in 1964 and its recommendation on Growth and Aid gave impetus to existing DAC work to agree a Terms Recommendation. . . . The pressure there for an aid target and for further softening of terms led directly to a revised Recommendation, which introduced the ODA concept almost by the back door. Yet only 18 months later ODA became the subject of an iconic UN target. The 1971 'defection' of a DAC official to UNCTAD then spurred the creation of the new LDC [Least Developed Countries] category, for which the DAC agreed special favourable terms in 1972.
>
> (Scott 2015: 21).

The definition of ODA and the setting of conditions and practises to be accomplished by the developed countries to manage it marked a success for the developing countries. In fact, it was established that the ODA were concessional, that 84 per cent of the value of the ODA should be a grant, that the official financing should contain a grant of 25 per cent of the value in case of a loan and that all the developed countries should devote the 0.7 per cent of their national income to the development aid. But the most relevant success was due to the fact that the agreement was reached by a multilateral political negotiation, that it was recognised de facto by both developing and developed countries that 'the political will of higher-income countries was necessary for the economic upgrading of developing ones, . . . that the financial aid from the advanced economies was a necessary condition to trigger the process in the third world, (and that) economic development was vital for both groups of economies. As to the advancement of development economics, the ODA validated the theoretical need for an initial capital and for infrastructures to sustain the "big push"' (Romagnoli 2022: 716). Once again, the states have been key players in this institution-building process through DAC and UNCTAD, showing their role not only in organising the international flows of financial capitals but also in leading the process of national economies' development. Despite that, this outcome turned out to be ephemeral and irrelevant for the international economic order in force. After 1973 the DAC donors, that in the sixties spent in ODA a share of their national incomes decreasing from nearly 0.5 to 0.3 per cent, maintained this quota up to the nineties, when it dropped and come back to this value ten years later. Meanwhile, the ODA turned into an economic activity no more managed by the states rather than by private credit institutions; as such it was affected heavily by the financial crisis.

The failure of the international monetary system and the financial crisis

Price certainty due to the system of fixed currencies pegged to the US Dollar and the trading rules introduced by the GATT boosted world trade. Since the US dollar was used as an exchange currency, as time went by the amount of dollars circulating in the world became greater than the quantity necessary to the USA economy, and also more than the gold reserves necessary to convert them at the conditions established. This event, which was 'widely perceived as a structural core deficiency' (Murau, Rini and Haas 2020: 772) of the international monetary system because it wasn't considered by the Bretton Woods agreements, reduced the dollar's reliability. This untrustworthiness increased especially when the US trade balance deficit and the public debt worsened with the occurrence of the Vietnam War jointly with the inflation. The US Treasury couldn't either devaluate the dollar or issue additional money without the golden collateral. The need for additional collateral to finance the increasing international trade was already fulfilled in 1969 by the IMF with the creation of 'Special Drawing Rights' certificates, additional reserves addressed on request to each member to expand the amount of its mintage.[10] This measure wasn't sufficient to restore the international payments system, so in 1971 the convertibility of the Dollar into gold stopped. This event caused a shock in the international trade system because it trickled away the certainty of the international prices of the merchandises, but it wasn't the only distress because USA imposed a duty of 10 per cent on imports too. At the end of the year a new parity among the currencies of the industrial countries was established to restore a fixed exchange rate system (Smithsonian Agreement), but when in 1973 the dollar was again devaluated by a 10 per cent, a floating exchange rate system emerged.

Just before the end of the convertibility of the US dollar with gold the country members of the EEC decided to establish an economic and monetary union, both for political reasons and to guard against the dollar crisis. Thus, in 1972 to create monetary stability they introduced a system of currencies pegged to one another and adjustable in the amount of +/– 2.5 around their parity value, called a 'snake in the tunnel'; this mechanism was replaced in 1979 by the European monetary system that also introduced the monetary policy cooperation. In 1999 the Economic and Monetary Union (EMU) adopted a system of fixed exchange rates among the national currencies that paved the way in 2002 for a common European currency unit: the Euro. Such structural change in the international system of payments caused over time a reduction of the dollar used as currency in international trade and an increasing share for the euro; in 2017 39.9 per cent of international trade used the US$ (10 per cent more than the US trade share) and 35.7 per cent used € (in line with EU trade). Despite the relative reduction of the use of the US dollar in international exchanges, its central position in the international monetary system has been strengthened, thanks to the financial crises of the nineteenth seventies.

The financial crisis has been, in a certain sense, another side effect of the increased international trade during the Golden Age. As the volume of international trade progressed, the demand for dollars outside the issuing country increased, and the Central banks of the developed countries had to hold them to satisfy the needs of domestic traders. Also, US multinational companies held dollars outside the USA as well as the exporters of all the countries, but they could neither deposit nor transfer them in the banks of the hosting countries because the financial operations in foreign currency were banned by the regulations of the international payments system. Some London bankers, supported by the Bank of England, in 1956 cracked those rules by creating deposits in US Dollar at interest rates higher than those authorised in the USA. In this way the trade in Eurodollars was created by non-official banks offshore[11] – that is, by financial institutions that offered both saving and loan services without respecting the financial rules of the country issuing the currency or those of the hosting country, which accepted offshore money creation. In the 1960s some banks of New York started to make financial transactions with the foreign non-official banks to bypass US regulations:

> the 'roundtrip transactions from the US via London back to the US became the dominant feature, turning the EuroDollar market into . . . an extension of the US onshore interbank market, the Fed Funds market, into the offshore segment. . . . Non-bank financial institutions based in the US invented new instruments that, just as the instruments on the Eurodollar market, competed with the highly regulated onshore USD bank deposits. A key prerequisite

> was to find ways to establish par between those 'shadow money forms' and onshore deposits. This was achieved through a combination of private guarantees, creative accounting techniques and exploiting the balkanized US regulatory system. . . . From 1974, after the first oil crisis, the G-10 central banks decided to actively use the Eurodollar market to tackle the policy challenges they were facing and began to organize 'petrodollar recycling' through the Eurodollar market. This turned offshore USD creation into a truly world phenomenon and filled the gap that the collapse of the Bretton Woods System had left.
>
> (Murau, Rini and Haas 2020: 774).

Such unofficial banks not only created speculation on the currencies that already were floating but also destabilised the domestic monetary systems of the European countries. In fact, they attracted Eurodollars by offering short-term deposit accounts at high interest rates and by giving loans at medium-long term maturity to the commercial banks at the highest interest rates. In this way they risked defaulting because they used short-term current assets for long-term credits, thus having to give back on request the deposits before the maturity of their loans; by 1973 some German and British banks failed in this way. In the following years the offshore US dollars increased even more because of the oil crisis, pushing up the price of the resource, on the one hand fostered the demand for dollars to the purchases and on the other hand issued plenty of petrodollars in search of profit-making businesses coming from the oil exporter countries. This huge amount of current assets implemented competition among the banks and tried to attract them to issue medium-term loans in dollars at floating rates of interest. Although such terms and conditions for the loans transferred the risk on the borrower, the insolvency due to the different maturity times of deposits and credits wasn't avoided.

This vulnerability was also transferred to the European banking system because, in the meantime, the national banks were authorised to trade in eurodollars to sustain the domestic importers. The alarm bell about the risk of crises emerged, and the problem was debated in 1972–1973 at the conferences of the G-10 central banks; at the Bank for International Settlements (BIS) a negotiation also started on whether the eurodollar market could and should be regulated, but without results. The problem was discussed also in USA, and 'from the outset, the main banks involved . . . envisaged lending these funds to the developing countries, whose [liquidity requirements were growing because] public and trade deficit increased sharply following the oil price hike, with at least the tacit approval and at most the overt encouragement of western monetary authorities, the International Monetary Fund, the World Bank, and the Federal Reserve. Henceforth up to the early 1980s international capital investments were dominated by commercial banks credit to Third World Countries' (Cassis 2011: 38). The huge amount of current assets held by the Western banks went thus to finance the developing countries that, being short of ODA for the developed countries crisis and of money to buy food and industrial goods and oil because the reduced exports, get into debt at variable interest rates and short maturity. When at the end of the seventies the central banks of developed countries raised the interest rates to solve the problem of inflation, their banks also did it to put in order their financial statements. In this way the debt service of developing countries amounted to a high percentage of the public budget, giving rise to the 'souverain debt crisis'; thus, the financial crisis created in developed countries was dumped on developing ones (Romagnoli 2022: 715).

Towards a one-dimensional world economy

The 1970s and 1980s were years of crisis but also of deep transformations of both economic structure and institutions. The failure of Fordism and the oil crisis implemented transformations of the production structure leading to another industrial revolution that, as such, influenced both consumption and lifestyle. The failure of the Bretton Woods institutional framework, instead, triggered on the one hand a new rewording of the international economic order and on the other hand a new interpretation of the working of the economic system consistent to it. In the meantime, the structural trends of the world economy have deepened some contrasts (the divide between the developed and the developing countries, the competition among the industrialised countries, the segmentation of the production processes and globalisation) and have highlighted new trends like the increasing power of the multinational companies over the state's economies and rising inequalities inside the economies between the asset owners and the working people.

From the power of the economies to the economics of the powers

Despite the expectations of a multilateral approach in line with the times for international economic relations, the Bretton Woods institutional building process created a framework looking to the past. In fact, it brought back up a nineteenth-century set of organisations managed by a narrow group of separated economies (someone having still colonies or protectorates) and coordinated by a leading player (USA) whose dominant position was due to its economic (and military) power and to the use of its currency as a monetary unit in the international payments system. In such a framework the antagonism between developed and developing countries and the competition among developed economies couldn't find room; either the development process of newly independent states or the state intervention in industrial countries were in principle out of the school of thought prevailing at Bretton Woods. Despite the emergence of such intrinsic shortages of the international economic institutions, the crisis of the financial and monetary system spiked in 1970s and the *Declaration on the Establishment of a New International Economic Order* made by the UN General Assembly in 1974 couldn't be sufficient to find a remedy. Quite the opposite, the lacking management of the crises by the states wasn't considered as their failure but a way by which the international payments system, the crisis of the financial sector and the balance of payments of both developed and developing economies could be restored. But it was the industrialised states' waiver of carrying out the management of the international economic relations in a multilateral context that resulted in the rewording of the Bretton Woods philosophy about the international economic order, that in turn was paid by the disentanglement of the financial activities from whatever supervision.[12] Nevertheless, for such a rewording,

> hegemons need followers and must make concessions to obtain agreements. The liberal trade regimes that emerged in both the 19th and the 20th centuries were founded on asymmetric bargains that permitted discrimination, especially against the hegemon. The agreements that lowered tariff barriers led to freer trade not free trade; resulted in subsystemic rather than global orders; and legitimated mercantilistic and protectionist practices of exclusion and discrimination, and thus did not provide a collective good. Moreover, these trade agreements (and trade disputes as well) had inherently international political underpinnings and did not reflect economic interests alone. Trade liberalization also required a certain internal strength on the part of the government. Furthermore, only a complete political rupturing of relations, such as occurs in wartime, can destroy such a regime.
>
> (Stein 1984: 355)

In the crises of the 1970s and 1980s there were all the elements that Stein lists as necessary to maintain the hegemony of the Bretton Woods international economic order, despite its ruinous results. The stagnation of domestic production in the developed economies, associated with the energetic crisis, the deficit of the trade balance, and the public debt constituted an economic framework that was difficult to be managed by economic policies. Even the disequilibrium of the balance of payments and the public debts in the developing countries represented long- and short-run insuperable problems because it made difficult the completion of investments started in the recent past and the food provisions. On the spur of the moment, the presence of financial institutions having a huge amount of offshore dollars at their disposal seemed to match with the need for credits of the distressed developed and developing economies. The banks of industrialised countries had the possibility to expand the loans beyond the domestic borders at good profit margins and to free their business from the ties of national financial markets, thus taking the chance to manage their problems and the domestic and foreign crises according to their interests. The developing countries, on their part, could have the current assets necessary to face, among other needs, the budget deficit and food imports. This seemed to the policymakers the best solution for all the crises because it wasn't a 'political' stretch dictated to the economy, but a normal function of the 'market rules'. Once the financial operators were authorised to expand the credit in those directions, they were entrusted with the state privilege of self-organisation and self-management of the rules of their working activity.

The policies of financial liberalisation didn't solve the problems of the economies (Department of Economic and Social Affairs 2017); rather, they added to the stagnation of the economy inflation that, in turn, convinced the central banks to increase the rates of interest at the end of the 1970s. While this measure started a phase of 'austerity' in developed economies characterised also by unemployment, in the developing ones it caused a debt crisis. The upset of citizens, public opinion, and a part of economists that followed was appeased by the political advent of two champions of these policies in the USA and the UK: Ronald Regan and Margaret Thatcher. These chiefs of states turned out to be important because their support to the management of the crises through such financial policies validated a new set of institutions to manage the economy promoted by a school of economic thought.

Throughout the book it has been put in evidence the importance of institutions for the functioning of the economy. Besides the institutions that structure the economic routines made by the legislative power of a state or even by international agreements, there are other economic institutions built jointly by the society and the state. They are the analytical frameworks explaining the functioning of the economy theorised by the economists that are transformed into routines by the economic policies addressing the economic activities on those bases to the desired aims. Such routines are based on a 'politico-economic paradigm' (Hall 1993). A 'politico-economic paradigm' includes 'political/economic goals, analytical/theoretical frameworks for understanding the functioning of economies and societies, narratives which describe and justify the goals and analytical framework, as well as economic and social policies, based on the analytical framework, that seek to achieve specific goals.' (Jacobs and Laybourn-Langton 2018: 113). Such a frame of mind constituted by economic models, a social narrative and a political implementation represents a consistent and prevalent instrument enabling the economic operators and the government to manage the economy as long as there is a cooperative interaction and a certain degree of consistency among the three components. A prevailing politico-economic paradigm is weak when one among the components is ineffective in coping with economic events not considered by the paradigm but manageable by another approach. When such a new component is reinforced by another one of the three, the new approach is going to become a new politico-economic paradigm that establishes itself whenever also the remaining components are accepted. 'The concept just presented explains properly the alternation of "neoliberalism" to the Keynesian economic doctrine just expounded (see Stirling and Laybourn-Langton 2017), because its logical structure fits well the sequence of the events historically following one another and the behaviours of all the subjects engaged in the three social fields promoting the change (academia, public opinion, and political sphere)' (Romagnoli 2022: 718).

Such a new politico-economic paradigm, nicknamed 'Washington Consensus' because it was promoted by some economic institutions based in Washington DC (IMF, WB and US Department of Treasury), is a set of prescriptions considered a 'standard' reform package to develop economic policy measures suitable for restoring the economies having disequilibria in the fundamental accounts. Such measures, suggested to the developing countries asking for loans to restore their deficit in the public budget and balance of payments and then considered the foundation of the 'neoliberal paradigm', prescribed the opening of the economies to trade and foreign investments and the removing of tariffs and restrictions; the deregulation of all the markets from controls and bureaucratic procedures; the privatisation of state enterprises and reduction of public expenditure for the welfare state; the adoption of moderate marginal tax rates and exchange rates free from domestic policies to control them; and the implementation of such policies both to developed and developing economies. The fall of the Berlin Wall and the disintegration of the centralised planned economies at the beginning of 1990s were other events that strengthened the neoliberal paradigm, which was further supported by the creation of the World Trade Organisation (WTO) in 1995, an intergovernmental organisation to regulate and facilitate the international trade. The new paradigm, adopted by all the economies from 1990 onwards, not only reinvigorated in a new form the old international economic order, but provided it with a theoretical support; thus, such 'economics of the powers' established itself as the only economic theory suitable for the 'economies of 21st century' too.

The world economy beyond the globalisation

Starting from the last decade of the 20th century the world economy has shown some new trends that have changed its structure. In Chapter Nine and in the previous paragraphs some of them have been already explored:

i. An increase of the world GDP by 2.4 times in the period while the world global exports increased by 2.8 times up to 2008.
ii. An increasing contribution to the world GDP from the developing countries between 1990 and 2008 and a very small decrease thenceforth balanced out from Brazil, India and China, whose contribution shifted from 17.5 per cent to 29 per cent in 2021 (see Figure 9.4).
iii. An increasing concentration of capitalism in the first-comer and latecomer economies, whose share of the world GDP equals 2.9 times their share of the world population.
iv. The worst annual average rates of growth of the per capita GDP in the capitalist economies from 1870 (interwar period excluded).

Another important trend characterising the world economy in the last 30 years has been the relocation of the gravity centre of the world economy. Such a process began just at the end of the 1940s, when the fast-growing Japanese economy emerged, and was followed a few decades later by the development of South Korea and at the end of the century by the extraordinary growth of China. These economic improvements led the East Asia and Pacific economies to reach the GDP value of North America, Europe and Central Asia, and then to overstep them by a third of their value in 2021 (see Figure 10.5). In addition, the interregional trade also grew in the period between both Europe and Asia (from 10 per cent to 16 per cent) and North America and Asia (from 10 per cent to 23 per cent) and contemporarily decreased in the Atlantic Ocean between Europe and North America (from 18 per cent to 11 per cent) and conversely (from 41 per cent to 13 per cent – OurWorldInData).

The other developing regions maintained their position in the ranking for all the period, except the South Asian economies that thanks to the performance of India reached the Middle East countries. The European and Central Asian region (that

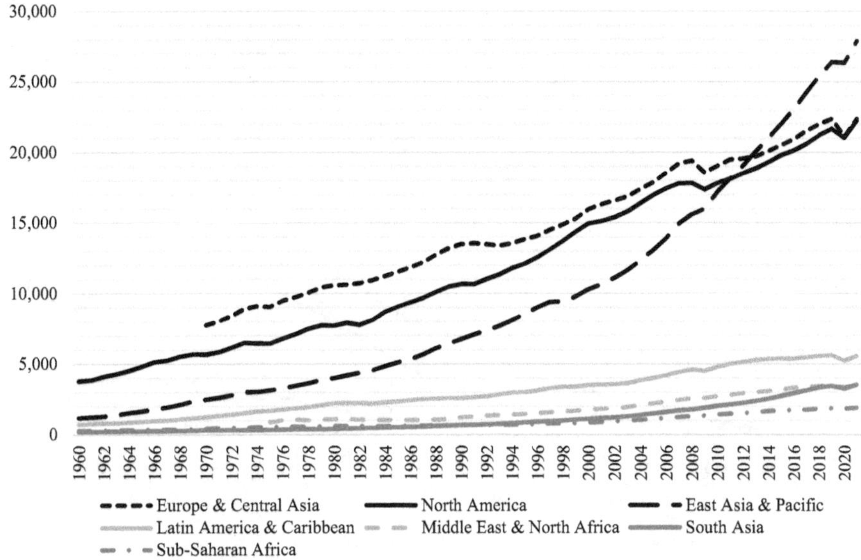

Figure 10.5 GDP value for different world regions from 1960 to 2020 (billions of constant 2015 US$)

Source: Author's elaboration from World Bank *World Development Indicators*.

is the European economies and USSR/Russian one), after the upgrading of the Golden Age, maintained the first position in the ranking until 2013, when it was replaced by East Asia and Pacific economies; however, starting from the 1990s its performance was affected by the worst economic conditions of Russia.

Despite the economic improvement of East Asia and Pacific countries, and to a lesser degree of South Asia, the economic divide among the world regions with regard to the standard of living remains, as it appears from the growth pace of the world regions in Figure 10.5. The proof of this trend is clearer in Figure 10.6, which shows the per capita GDP values recorded in the world areas in the evolution of capitalism; although in some regions the variety of economic conditions is wide because of the presence of advanced economies side by side very poor ones, the divergent path between Western Offshoots (North America, Australia and South Africa) and Western Europe on one side and all the other world regions on the other side is evident. In particular it is interesting to notice that between the end of the Second World War and the 1970s Eastern Europe, the Middle East and East Asia experienced increasing per capita GDP, but in the subsequent three decades the reduced pace of growth again increased the divergence up to three times the value of 1970; this gap has been reduced to 2–2.5 times in 2000, an upswing point that, anyway, didn't change the disparity up to now. From the 1970s also Latin America and South and Southeast Asia started to grow their per capita GDP, but despite their progress only Latin America moved close to the previous regions.

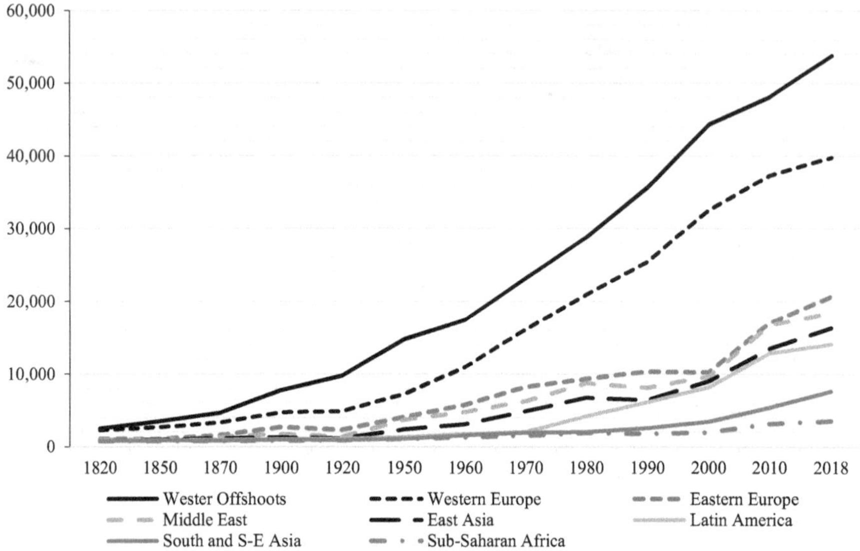

Figure 10.6 Per-capita GDP for different world regions between 1820 and 2018 (international-$ in 2011 prices)

Source: Author's elaboration from https://ourworldindata.org/economic-growth, accessed January 28, 2023.

Despite the upgrading trends of the economies of Brazil, India and China, the divide with the developed ones in terms of per-capita GDP value have increased after the 1970s, as it is shown in Figure 10.7. However, the growing path of their per-capita GDP has been discontinuous in the time, as it is shown in Figure 10.8, where each line represents the value of a country in a specific year but stacked to avoid intersections and to highlight the more dynamic country; thus, after an increase of the value up to the seventies, a swinging path around the reached value has been recorded for two decades before a jump in the new century.

The geographical rearrangement of world production and of the international exchanges of goods and services, the increased movement of people in search of jobs that are lacking in their motherland, the international outsourcing of production processes in search of cheap labour costs and high profits, the cross-border movement of people, and financial assets, legal head offices and factories of companies enabled by the sharp reduction of transport costs and by deregulations are other events characterising the world economy of the 21st century. However, they are not considered important features of the world economy that is generally characterised by 'globalisation', a phenomenon whose nature is commonly perceived as modernity and progress. After all its meaning, generically connected to the technological progress in transport and in information technologies to the advantages of international trade and of people's movement, has broadened to include cultural, political and also environmental dimensions

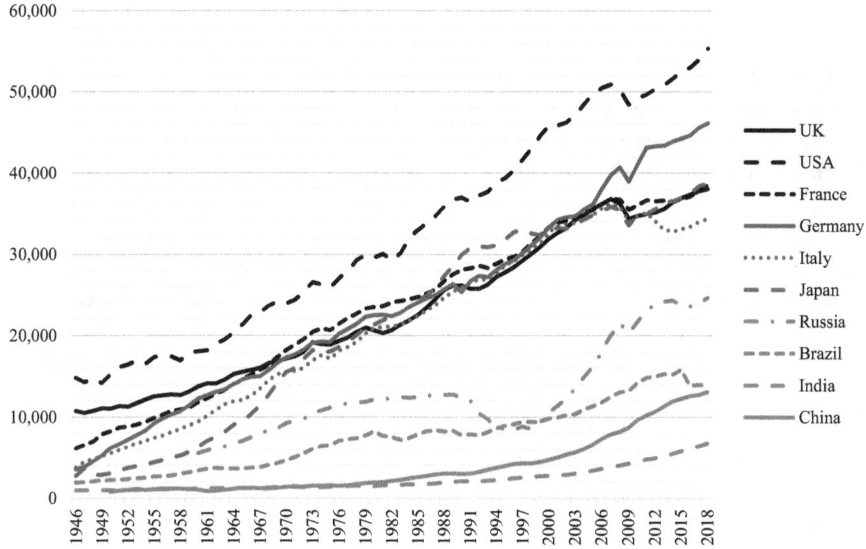

Figure 10.7 Per-capita GDP of selected countries between 1946 and 2018 (constant 2015 US$)

Source: Author's elaboration from https://ourworldindata.org/economic-growth, accessed January 28, 2023.

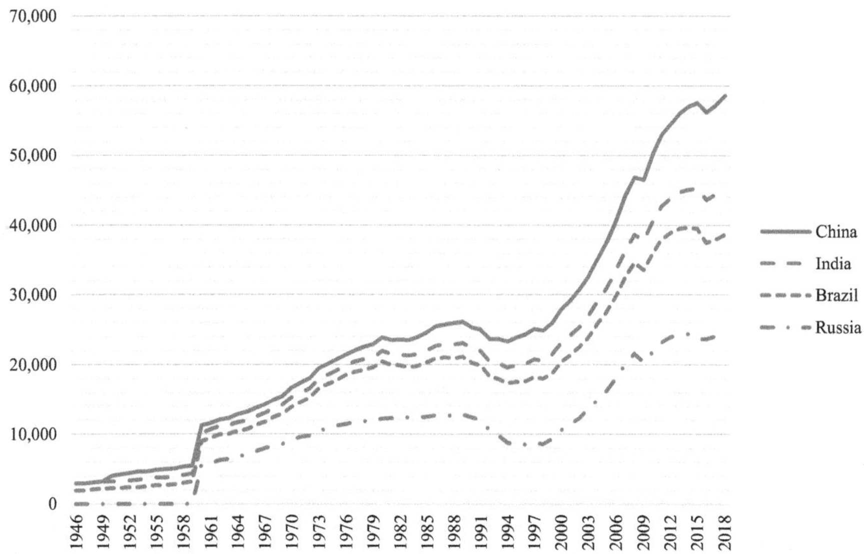

Figure 10.8 A stacked line chart for the per-capita GDP of BRIC countries between 1946 and 2018 (constant 2015 US$)

Source: Author's elaboration from https://ourworldindata.org/economic-growth, accessed January 28, 2023

and all the new phenomena belonging to the social life, especially if connected to the internet.

In fact, in a generic and simple definition globalisation is the speed-up of movements of human beings and of exchanges of goods, services, capital, technologies or cultural practices all over the planet. The Committee for Development Policy of the United Nations, defining from an economic point of view the globalisation, highlights three features characterising it: increasing international trade, increased 'marketisation' and the spread of information technologies to all economic activities. According to the website of the Internationally Monetary Fund the 'term globalization began to be used more commonly in the 1980s, reflecting technological advances that made it easier and quicker to complete international transactions both trade and financial flows. It refers to an extension beyond national borders of the same market forces that have operated for centuries at all levels of human economic activity village markets, urban industries, or financial centers'. No reference is made to the role of the WTO in its establishment, no hint to the role of international agreements signed to co-ordinate the international economic relations of the states. Globalisation only supports the extension of the 'natural market' forces that from far villages of past times today go to rule the world economy.

Concluding remarks: The world economy as a 'self-ruled mechanism'

The manner in which globalisation is treated by public opinion and by most experts reveals the insufficient knowledge about the nature of the world economy and of the forces that produced its present configuration. It is also the proof of the prevalence of the politico-economic paradigm established since the 1980s, according to which the economy is a self-ruled mechanism that works efficiently only if it follows the 'market forces'. In this context the private institutions and the international organisation monitoring the economies in view of the observation of the models that describe a well-performing theoretical economy can give suggestions to restore the economies in crisis. This is believed a scientific neutral approach to the economic policy because it suggests an impartial procedure that must be adopted by economies in crisis because of their failed application of the 'economic rules'.

The idea of a self-ruled economy and its extension to the global system indicates, in light of the stylised facts presented in the chapter, an insufficient knowledge of the structure and functions of the economic system, associated with a misunderstanding of the role that the state has carried out during the evolution of capitalism. From the analysis carried out emerges stylised facts at the base of the coordination of international economic relations in the last 30 years, and thus, the configuration of the world economy calls on the political and economic interests of the economic powers that have been considered in building the international economic order. As a result, the international economic order established by the economic powers through their politico-economic actions and the politico-economic paradigm result in a one-dimensional world economy governed by a self-ruled mechanism.

> Since the East Asia crisis in 1997, there has been an enormous number of discussions on the reform of the world economic architecture, but almost

nothing has happened. For those who have been participating in that process, this does not come as a surprise: the very parties that played a central role in the failures associated with the crisis have played a pivotal role in the reform discussions. To be sure, changes in international institutions will, under the best of circumstances, be difficult. But given the seeming momentum behind change, the fact that so little seems to have emerged is, to say the least, disappointing. But, in retrospect at least, it should now be clear why nothing has happened, and why little should have been expected to happen. To put it perhaps a little too bluntly and oversimplified: it was because of the role of special interest groups, particularly in what I call the G1 (the United States). (Stiglitz 2003: 4)

Notes

1 'After World War One, despite the attempts of the administration of Woodrow Wilson to rebuild the international order, the United States had quickly retreated into non-involvement in world affairs. In the 1920 elections, a Republican Party dominated by its "isolationist" wing swept into power. As a result, the United States did not ratify the Versailles Treaty, did not join the League of Nations, and refused to participate in most of the international economic consultations that were attempting to restore an open world economy. American isolationism ruled the nation until 1934, when it began to be undone by New Deal Democrats; but this reversal was made largely irrelevant by depression and war. . . . As World War Two came to an end, Americans and Europeans who wanted to avoid another collapse into conflict feared that the United States might repeat its previous trajectory'. But 'the new world economic order built after 1945 was largely designed by Americans and implemented under the leadership of the U. S. government'. In addition, 'there were two principal reasons for the American commitment to economic openness in the aftermath of World War Two, one economic and the other political. . . . After the second war, most of the country's potential competitors were in shambles, while the U. S. economy was booming. The world's thirst for American goods seemed endless, and no other country's industries seemed capable of contending with American industry for global markets. American manufacturers who had previously worried about imports, and had little concern for markets abroad, were now increasingly interested in exports and little troubled by foreign competitors. . . . There was an intellectual consistency to the argument that an inclusive pro-American, anti-Soviet alliance in the military and diplomatic spheres also needed to be inclusive in the economic sphere; that the United States could not go about building an integrated Western political bloc without also building an integrated economic bloc' (Jeffry 2012: 12, 13, 15).

2 Such a new image of industrial production was celebrated by industrial designers also outside the United States in the 1920s, as shown by the Fiat automobile factory of Lingotto built in Turin (Italy) between 12916 and 1923, by Renault's Île Seguin factory near Paris and by the tobacco factory in Linz (Austria) both built in the 1920s (see Halpern 2022).

3 The word 'Fordism' was used first by Antonio Gramsci (1978), an Italian intellectual and politician who in 1934 titled as 'Americanismo e Fordismo' (*'Americanism and Fordism')* the *'22nd notebook'* of his political writings published later with the title of *'The prison notebooks'*.

4 'Overall, around one-third of ERP imports were agricultural, but imports of capital goods also proved crucial. Many of the aid Dollars remained in the United States, as the secretary of agriculture had declared that surplus American agricultural products had to be purchased in the country; moreover, 25 percent of the total wheat or wheat products sent to Europe under the first ERP legislation had to be in the form of flour milled in the United States' (Kunz 1997: 168).

The shares of the ERP value received by the countries were 23.99 per cent to the UK; 20.41 per cent to France; 11.35 per cent to Italy; 10.46 per cent to West Germany; 8.15 per cent to the Netherlands; 5.32 per cent to Greece; 5.10 per cent to Austria; 4.20 per cent to Belgium and Luxemburg; 2.05 per cent to Denmark; 1.69 per cent to Turkey; 1.69 per cent to Norway; 1.11 per cent to Ireland (Statista, *Distribution of aid from the European Recovery Program (Marshall Plan) per country from 1948 to 1952*).

5 The delegates participating to the Bretton Woods Conference represented the following states: United Kingdom, France, Belgium, Netherlands, Luxemburg, Norway, Iceland, Poland, Soviet Union, Czechoslovakia, Yugoslavia, Greece, Egypt, Ethiopia, South Africa, Liberia, Iran, Iraq, China, British India, Philippine, New Zealand, Australia, Canada, United States, Mexico, Cuba, Costa Rica, Haiti, El Salvador, Panama, Dominican Republic, Nicaragua, Guatemala, Honduras, Colombia, Ecuador, Venezuela, Peru, Brazil, Bolivia, Chile, Paraguay, Uruguay.

6 There were two proposals for the new monetary system to prevent the troubles of the Gold-exchange standard system (that penalised the economies lacking gold reserves) and the devaluation of the national currency to cancel the deficits in the balance of payments (that penalised the credit economies). The economist John Maynard Keynes, who at the time was an adviser to the British Treasury, proposed the creation of a Global Central Bank (the Clearing Union) issuing a new currency (the Bancor) whose amount would be held in shares by the states that would use it to pay their trade imbalances. The second proposal, put forward by the chief international economist of the US Treasury Department Harry Dexter White, suggested the creation of a Stabilisation Funds associated to a new version of the Gold-exchange standard system, plan in some way like that adopted. https://www.federalreservehistory.org/essays/bretton-woods-created

7 The European Economic Community was established by six European Countries (Belgium, France, West Germany, Italy, Luxemburg, and the Netherlands) that in 1957 signed the Treaty of Rome. It was joined by Denmark, Ireland, and United Kingdom in 1973, by Greece in 1981, by Portugal and Spain in 1986. Since 1993 the EEC was transformed into the European Union (EU) after the drafting of the Maastricht Treaty; Austria, Finland, and Sweden joined it in1995, followed in 2004 by Slovenia, Estonia, Latvia, Lithuania, Poland, the Czech Republic, Slovakia, Hungary, Cyprus and Malta, and in 2007 by Romania and Bulgaria, and by Croatia in 2013. In 2020 the United Kingdom left the European Union.

8 For a more balanced mechanism for the international system of payments see the proposal by J. K. Keynes at the Bretton Woods Conference (see note n. 6)

9 Non-Aligned Movement is a forum of 120 countries, representing 55 per cent of the world population. It was established in 1961 by a group of 25 countries not formally joining any power block to promote peace and cooperation among the developing states and counterbalance the blocks engaged in the Cold War.

10 The SDR unit value, quoted in US Dollars, is calculated from a weighted basket of major currencies (that from 2015 are the Japanese yen, the US Dollar, the Chinese Yuan, the Pound sterling, and the Euro), and is re-evaluated every five years. The amount of SDR obtained by each member depends on its subscription that, in turn, is determined by its development level; thus, the more advanced countries receive more SDRs.

11 'Offshore' money is the amount of money created outside of a state's monetary jurisdiction, but within the monetary area of that state's unit of account' (Murau, Rini and Haas 2020: 769) by the debt certificates denominated in a certain currency that the banks issue to certify the solvency of the bearer.

12 The proof of this restoration in favour of a tight group of industrialised countries is the creation of G7 between 1973 and 1975. It is an intergovernmental political forum of the most contributors of the IMF that have great economic power and political, diplomatic and military relations. As a political forum G7 introduces itself in this way: 'The seven members (UK, USA, Canada, Japan, Germany, France, and Italy, plus the EU)

are all bound by shared values as open, democratic and outward-looking societies'. In respect to its activities, 'This year, the UK has taken on the Presidency of the G7, the only forum where the world's most influential and open societies and advanced economies are brought together for close-knit discussions'. https://web.archive.org/web/20220122144337/https://www.g7uk.org/what-is-the-g7/

References

Aoki, M. (2013) *Comparative Institutional Analysis: Theory, Corporations and East Asia, Selected Papers of Masahiko Aoki*, Cheltenham: Edward Elgar.

Cassis, Y. (2011) *Crises and Opportunities. The Shaping of Modern Finance*, Oxford: Oxford University Press.

Department of Economic and Social Affairs (2017) *World Economic and Social Survey 2017. Reflecting on Seventy Years of Development Policy Analysis*, New York: United Nations. https://www.un.org/development/desa/dpad/wp-content/uploads/sites/45/publication/WESS_2017-FullReport.pdf

Graff, M., Kenwood, A. G. and Lougheed, A. L. (2014) *Growth of the International Economy, 1820–2015*, London: Routledge.

Gramsci, A. (1978) 'Quaderno 22. Americanismo e Fordismo', Torino: Einaudi, Engl. trans. 'Americanism and Fordism', in Q. Hoare and G. N. Smith (eds.) *(1999) Selections from the Prison Notebooks*, London: ElecBook: 561–3.

Hall, P. A. (1993) 'Policy Paradigms, Social Learning, and the State: The Case of Economic Policymaking in Britain', *Comparative Politics*, 25: 275–96.

Halpern, R. (2022) *The Rational Factory, Labour, and the Fordist Visual Imaginary*, Berlin: Forum Transregionale Studien. Accessed 29 November 2022 https://trafo.hypotheses.org/38784

Jacobs, M. and Laybourn-Langton, L. (2018) 'Paradigm Shifts in Economic Theory and Policy', *Review of European Economic Policy*, 53 (3): 113–18. http://doi.org/10.1007/s10272-018-0737-4

Jeffry, F. (2012) 'America in the World Economy: From the American Century to Globalization', in A. Bacevich (ed.) *The Short American Century – A Postmortem*, Cambridge, MA: Harvard University Press.

Kunz, D. B. (1997) 'The Marshall Plan Reconsidered. A Complex of Motives', *Foreign Affairs*, May/June: 168.

Lipietz, A. (1985) 'The World Crisis: The Globalisation of the General Crisis of Fordism', *IDS Bulletin*, 16 (2), Brighton: Institute of Development Studies: 6–11.

Murau, S., Rini, J. and Haas, A. (2020) 'The Evolution of the Offshore US-Dollar System: Past, Present and Four Possible Futures', *Journal of Institutional Economics*, 16: 767–83. http://doi.org/10.1017/S1744137420000168

Orastean, R. (2014) 'The IMF Lending Activity – A Survey', *Procedia Economics and Finance*, 16: 410–16.

Romagnoli, A. (2022) 'The Emergence of the "Sovereign Debt Crisis" in 1970s MENA Economies', *Middle Eastern Studies*, 58 (5): 712–27. http://doi.org/10.1080/00263206.2022.2081555

Scott, S. (2015) 'The Accidental Birth of "Official Development Assistance"', *OECD Development Co-operation Working Paper*, 24: 21.

Settis, B. (2016) *Fordismi. Storia politica della produzione di massa* (*Fordisms. Political History of Mass Production)*, Bologna: Il Mulino.

Stein, A. (1984) 'The Hegemon's Dilemma: Great Britain, the United States, and the International Economic Order', *International Organization*, 38 (Spring): 355–86.
Stiglitz, J. (2003) 'Globalization and the Economic Role of the State in the New Millennium', *Industrial and Corporate Change*, 12 (1): 3–26.
Stirling, A. and Laybourn-Langton, L. (2017) 'Time for a New Paradigm? Past and Present Transitions in Economic Policy', *The Political Quarterly* 88: 558–69.
Toninelli, P. A. (2008) 'From Private to Public to Private Again: A Long-Term Perspective on Nationalisation', *Anàlise Social*, 43 (189): 675–92.
Watson, D. (2019) 'Fordism: A Review Essay', *Labor History*, 60 (2): 144–59. https://doi.org/10.1080/0023656X.2019.1537031

Glossary

Development Assistance Committee (DAC) is an international forum established in 1961 by the OECD, constituted of countries providing and managing the ODA to a list of admitted countries considered by the UN as Less Developed Countries.

European Economic Community (EEC) was a regional trade area established in 1957 by six European countries and entered into force in 1958 up to 1993, when it was transformed into the European Union.

European Union (EU) is a supranational political and economic union of 27 European member states established in 1993 and endowed with a legal personality starting in 2009. It is a common market inside which 20 countries constitute an economic and monetary union whose currency is the Euro.

Fordism is a set of technological innovations aiming at obtaining the maximum production at a minimum cost through high volumes of a limited number of standardised products. The exploitation of such technological potentiality required a careful balance between mass production and mass consumption, thus increasing wages and social provisions for workers.

General Agreement on Tariff and Trade (GATT) is a multilateral treaty in force between 1948 and 1995 aimed at pursuing the maximum drop of custom duties, the elimination of quotas as well as tariffs and subsidies to exports, and apply to all the participants the most-favoured-nation principle.

International Bank for Reconstruction and Development (IBRD) is a financial institution created at the Bretton Woods Conference and entrusted with the promotion of the long-term growth of member countries by providing loans to finance the reconstruction of European economies.

International Monetary Fund (IMF) is a financial agency of the United Nations whose aims are to foster world monetary cooperation securing financial stability, facilitate international trade and economic growth, and promote high employment and poverty reduction.

Least-developed countries (LDC) are lower-income countries whose economy presents structural conditions insufficient to sustain the population and promote the process of development.

Organisation of the Petroleum Exporting Countries (OPEC) is a permanent intergovernmental institution established in 1960 that collect oil-producing countries to unify petroleum policies, secure stable prices and provide regular supply of petroleum to consuming nations.

Organisation for Economic Co-operation and Development (OECD) is an intergovernmental organisation established in 1961 transforming the Organisation for European Economic Co-operation (OEEC), 'in which governments work together to find solutions to common challenges, develop global standards, share experiences, and identify best practices to promote better policies for better lives' (OECD).

Organisation for European Economic Cooperation (OEEC) was an intergovernmental administration created to allocate and distribute the Marshall Plan.

Politico-economic paradigm is a frame of mind constituted by economic models, social narratives and political implementations that, when consistent in the three components, can result in economic institutions through its implementation in the economic policies.

Special Drawing Rights are certificates issued by the IMF as additional reserves addressed on request to the members of the organisation. The SDR unit value is quoted in US Dollars and is calculated from a weighted basket of major currencies.

United Nations Conference on Trade and Development (UNCTAD) is a permanent intergovernmental body established by the United Nations General Assembly in 1964 to integrate developing countries into the world economy, help them in overtaking their vulnerabilities and improve their competitiveness.

United Nations Development Programme (UNDP) is a UN agency established in 1965 to eliminate poverty and to promote growth and human development through a fund constituted by voluntary contributions from UN member states.

United Nations for the Industrial Development Organization (UNIDO) is a UN agency established in 1966 to promote the industrialisation of developing countries.

World Trade Organisation (WTO) is an intergovernmental organisation established in 1995 to regulate and facilitate the international trade of goods, services, and financial instruments.

Conclusion

It is difficult to draw some conclusions at the end of a volume that on the one hand could seem a theme essay on economic history and on the other hand recalls a handbook of microeconomics. Perhaps this book is both things, and just for this reason such feature highlights the first result that it proposes: the economic activities developed in modern economic systems have a historical dimension that changes their ways of management and organisation over time. Therefore, the economic activities examined (production, consumption, the market, etc.) have been analysed according to their organisational features and to their processes putting the attention on the changes experienced during the evolution of capitalism – thus in a perspective unknown in the books of microeconomics. Such a viewpoint is in the author's opinion necessary to explain economic phenomena because it shows how the economy has supported the needs of the societies through time. When such an 'historical essence' is omitted, the economic explanation risks resulting as 'mind behaviours.'

As a second result of the book, the 'material essence' of economic activities emerges as the object of the scientific analysis of the economic phenomena. Such a dimension enables to identify their qualities and quantities; this is important not only because, if the economy must provide citizens with material welfare this feature cannot be neglected, but also because such features are fundamental to understand the production processes that is the essence of capitalism. Material essence is also important to understand the nature and features of the economic system that today, when it isn't considered as an abstract mathematical configuration resulting from the equilibrium of variables, is understood only as a set of institutions ruling economic activities. Even in this case to consider only the institutional features to explain the structural organisation and the workings of the economic system without considering its material essence is ineffective.

The representation of the economic system as an entity coordinating and resuming the economic activities and subjects is central in this book not only because a specific chapter has been devoted to its analysis but also because such a pivotal role emerges throughout the dissertation. More, as the economic system represents the so-called economic sphere of society, it is charged with managing the relations with the other social counterpart: the political sphere and the private one. This is a

DOI: 10.4324/9781315679730-15

basic aspect to understand modern economies that has been brought to light in the books, thanks to the methodology adopted.

The historical perspective that has been adopted anables also to show that the economy and the state haven't been rivals but almost always partners, if nothing else, because the state is both a political and an economic subject. The role of the state in the economic sphere has been analysed in light of its historical and inborn prerogatives. The first one is that of the builder of the economic system through the legislative power and of the international agreements to manage the economic relations among the states; the second is that of the tuner of the working of the economy with the social rights that the state must protect. It is due to such a central position with respect to the economy that the analysis of the state as an economic subject comes before that of the other economic functions/subjects (production, consumption). The inspection has shown that historically the states have supported the economic activity in countercyclical situations and not, even outside the domestic borders. The economic function of the state consisting in taxing and managing economic activities directed to the interest of all the society has been carried out, highlighting its historical modulation. Even though the matter has triggered controversial debates within the political sphere, the historical analysis has shown the need for a coevolving path for both spheres because when the coevolution occurred, the economic and political outcomes were positive, and when one of the powers overcame the other there were always negative results.

The fifth novelty of the book is its last part, devoted to the analysis of the expansion of the economies outside the national borders; in this case, the argument is treated in a way different from the traditional approach to international trade. This has meant not only retracing the evolution of the international exchanges in view of the agreements signed by the states to guarantee the expansion of their economies but also inspecting the political meaning of the coordination of the international exchanges. In these lights the international exchanges don't shape up to be either a set of markets or a global economic system, but only as an international economic order.

All the results presented in the book aren't certainly either new or unknown, as they have been deepened in the specialistic literature; what is interesting in the author's opinion is the fact that they have been integrated into the workings of the modern economies and presented as basic contents of an introductory book to economics. As a consequence of this approach economic activities don't consist only of economic behaviours but also of organisation structures and routines that are the result of the economic subjects (and thus of the state too), of economic agreements and of the cumulated effects created by their interactions.

Index

Note: **Bold** page numbers refer to figures and tables, 'n' after number denotes note number.

Kolibri 360 GmbH
Ferdinand-Jühlke-Straße 7
99095 Erfurt, Deutschland
produktsicherheit@kolibri360.de